Joseph C. Sweeney

THE SHEPHERD
OF THE OCEAN

THE
SHEPHERD
OF THE OCEAN

An Account of
Sir Walter Ralegh
And his Times by
J. H. Adamson and
H. F. Folland

Let us now praise famous men
Ecclesiasticus

Nothing extenuate, nor set down
ought in malice
Othello

Gambit
INCORPORATED
Boston
1969

For Peggy and Helen
We send you all the thanks
our hearts can conceive

First Printing

Copyright © 1969 by J. H. Adamson and H. F. Folland
All rights reserved including the right to reproduce
this book or parts thereof in any form
Library of Congress Catalog Card Number: 69-17747
Printed in the United States of America

CONTENTS

List of Illustrations, 7

Foreword, 9

Acknowledgments, 11

1 The Land and the People, 13

2 Ralegh and the French Wars of Religion, 26

3 Interlude in England, 45

4 Ralegh in Ireland, 55

5 Utopia in the New World, 77

6 The Queen's Lover, 85

7 Ralegh and the English Navy, 107

8 The Land of the Virgin Queen, 117

9 Ralegh and the Armada, 144

10 American and Irish Colonies, 166

11 The Lovers' Quarrel, 178

12 Disgrace and the Tower, 189

13 The Golden Empire, 217

14 The Fights at Cadiz and Fayal, 250

15 Ralegh as Parliamentarian, 282

16 The End of an Age, 300

17 The Justice of the Realm, 331

18 The King's Prisoner, 367

19 The Final Voyage, 402

20 The Death of Sir Walter Ralegh, 437

Select Bibliography, 454

Index, 457

ILLUSTRATIONS

Sir Walter Ralegh as a young man, *Frontispiece*
(*Radio Times Hulton Picture Library*)

Queen Elizabeth I, 128
(*by permission of Francis Tyrwhitt-Drake*)

The Earl of Essex, 129
(*The National Portrait Gallery, London*)

Sir Walter Ralegh landing in St. Joseph, Trinidad, from
Theodor De Bry, 144
(*Radio Times Hulton Picture Library*)

The Ark Royal: Howard's flagship against the Spanish
Armada, 1588, originally built for Ralegh, 144
(*Radio Times Hulton Picture Library*)

Indians fishing in Virginia, a painting by John White who
accompanied the Ralegh expedition to Virginia in 1585, 145
(*Radio Times Hulton Picture Library*)

Lady Elizabeth Throckmorton, Ralegh's wife, 320
(*Courtesy of the National Gallery of Ireland*)

Edmund Spenser, engraved by J. Thomson, 321
(*Radio Times Hulton Picture Library*)

Robert Cecil, 321
(*The National Portrait Gallery, London*)

King James I by Paul Van Somers (*Uffizi*), 336
(*Radio Times Hulton Picture Library*)

Sir Edward Coke, 337
(*Radio Times Hulton Picture Library*)

MAPS

The New World as seen by Sebastian Cabot, 49

Voyages to America 1585, 1595, 127

Cadiz Harbour, 253
(*from* Sir Walter Raleigh *by Philip Magnus, by courtesy of
the publisher Wm. Collins Sons & Co. Ltd.*)

The Affair at San Thomé, 423

FOREWORD

The Elizabethans are not easy people to understand; their lives call for the exercise of the imagination as well as the intellect. Not one of them can be uncritically admired. Complex, sophisticated, almost excessively gifted, they are probably the most fascinating people who ever lived.

Almost every act of Ralegh's life and some of his writings are subject to dispute and involve contradictory evidence. Generally we have not presented the biographical complexities but have, rather, offered our own judgments, some of which may be wrong. However, they are not arbitrary; we examined all the possibilities and selected those we thought most convincing. We have generally standardized the spelling and punctuation of our Elizabethan sources and occasionally have speculated, in the absence of evidence, on what someone may have thought or felt.

Salt Lake City, Utah   J. H. Adamson
December 20, 1968   H. F. Folland

ACKNOWLEDGMENTS

We have acknowledged sources and scholarly debts in the Select Bibliography. However, some obligations are so large as to require a more personal expression of appreciation.

We are grateful for the support the University of Utah has given us over many years; we are also indebted to Harvard University for generously allowing us access to its splendid library collections.

For our understanding of Westcountry, its Elizabethan heroes and their relation to the New World, we are especially indebted to the brilliant works of Mr. A. L. Rowse. Our chapter on Ralegh and Queen Elizabeth owes much to Miss Elizabeth Jenkins as does the account of the Spanish Armada to Mr. Garrett Mattingly. One cannot think of Ralegh in Guiana without gratitude for the researches of Mr. V. T. Harlow, nor of the trial scene without acknowledging the superb account by Miss Catherine Drinker Bowen.

We owe much to previous biographers of Ralegh, especially to Edward Edwards, whose second volume of Ralegh's life contains the letters on which we have so frequently drawn. All scholars are indebted to Miss Agnes Latham's edition of Ralegh's poems. We also appreciate the penetrating studies of Elizabethan military life by our colleague, Dr. Henry J. Webb; they proved continually helpful.

We wish to thank Mr. Sherman Martin for producing two maps, and finally we wish to thank Dr. W. R. Slager and Dr. Kenneth E. Eble, who read the manuscript and whose suggestions improved it.

I

The Land and the People

Walter Ralegh grew up in a harsh, restless and isolated land, sharing the qualities of the stubborn and imaginative people whose ways were shaped by that land. 'Westcountry' was composed of the shires of Devon and Cornwall, a narrow peninsula that thrusts like a pointing finger from the south-west corner of England, out into the ocean towards the unknown worlds beyond a demi-island in an island.

The ocean is one of the twin spirits that dominate the landscape and the lives of the people. Cold winds blow across Iceland and the Hebrides, pushing up curled waves that crash on the northern coast. Even in quiet weather every wave is a hammer, and when the Atlantic is aroused the force is doubled and redoubled. Any softness in the land would long ago have been cut off and swallowed by the sea. But the northern headlands are solid stone, the very spirit of resistance. The crash and roar of the sea, the cries of the wheeling seabirds create the mood of the Westcountry, a mood of tension and restless movement.

The second dominating feature of the Westcountry landscape is that wild and forbidding waste called Dartmoor, which with its mysterious brooding presence has dictated the life and even the appearance of the towns around it. The Moor is a giganitc tableland of granite unadorned except for the great stone blocks called tors which thrust up from its surface. Some of them look like cairns hastily piled by an angry giant; others from afar look like the giants themselves. And from Dartmoor are fed all of Devon's wild and urgent streams; three of them rise on the Moor itself. When the rain sheets off the granite slabs the river Dart can rise ten feet in a single day. As the rivers tear and leap through beds of boulders and twist down steep gorges, they too help create the perpetual restlessness of the landscape and the animistic feeling that it has a life of its own.

To invaders of the isle of England, access to the Westcountry was from the east. But that access was not easy. The peninsula narrows to a neck that is blocked with hills through which there are only two feasible routes, both potential ambushes for an invading army. Consequently the ancient Celts who inhabited the land before history began have survived in their living descendants. When the Romans came to England, they were content to make the edge of the Moor their western boundary; they looked upon Dartmoor, but withdrew in the fifth century without having tested its spirit. Not so the Saxons. They spread across England, driving many of the natives toward Wales and the Westcountry, mingling with those that remained, buying land, creating a frontier, settling behind it, and then pushing on.

At last they plunged across what had been the Roman frontier and came to Dartmoor.

On that stone mountain they found stone monuments everywhere, as if the mountain had built monuments out of itself to itself; or else a race of giants had torn out those granite slabs and set them up for some dim and frightening purpose. There had been giants on the earth; on the lonely Moor were the lonely remnants of their vanished lives.

On the southern and western slopes were signs of human life: hut circles, the remains of what were once dwellings, animal pounds and granaries. But the people who had built them now lay in the barrows, heaps of earth or rocks that marked their burial places. And there were kistvaens, stone coffins made of granite slabs, narrow beds in which to sleep so long. There were granite stones in single, double, or multiple rows, some in circles, some in straight lines which extended for miles. Even more mysterious were the cairns and menhirs, huge standing stones and occasionally a cromlech, upright stones with a horizontal one laid across the top. These were the funerary monuments of a bronze-age people who had lived there long ago, although the Saxons thought them the remains of a city of giants.

What the Saxons had found was a city of the dead built on a dead land, over which the unexplained past brooded. When the mists swirled over it, one might hear voices and see strange visions, but when the mists cleared nothing was there but those monuments of the dead, as though from an entire people Death had taken flattery, homage, and abounding energies – and then had taken them. But the fear of death did not deter the Saxons. For them, Wyrd goeth as he will; destiny is stronger than man. What will be, will be, although sometimes human courage can alter the balance. And so they pushed around the Moor and went on into Cornwall as far as the river Ottery, where they stopped for a time. West of the Ottery was the little that was left of old Dumnonia, the Celtic name for Devon; today the place names there are still mainly Celtic.

But even Dumnonia was doomed. Over more than a century the Saxons gradually vanquished the stubbornly fighting Celts, and after 838 there remained only the sullen bitterness of the defeated. But the Saxons could not conquer one thing: the Celtic imagination. The Celts had made successful raids and forays against the Saxons and had won one memorable victory in the losing war. Soon the Celtic minstrels were glorifying in song that fleeting triumph at the tip of Cornwall under a king named Arthur. And so flowered the great legends of the British kings and knights, in which the wars were all fought again in the poet's imagination, where defeat was transmuted into triumph. And the king who had brought them victory would return; he was the once and future king. Gradually the legends of his life became attached to actual places. An old, abandoned abbey with crenellated towers standing on an island crag cut off from the mainland by the hammering surf, was said to be Arthur's birthplace. When the time would come for Arthur to return from Avalon, he would come to the place of his childhood, to Cornwall, where men could still speak his tongue and still ride with him against the Saxon.

Meanwhile the Saxon conquest proved to be short-lived; the

Saxons were overcome by the Danes in wars so fierce that it came to be said that the redness of the sandy soil in southern Devon came from the blood spilled by the cruelty of the Danes. And after the Danes came the Norman conqueror. By 1350 almost every town in Devon and Cornwall had been founded and named; every line had been drawn on the map. Granite slabs cut from Dartmoor had been carted off to build churches, bridges, houses and streets; the cities and towns were Dartmoor incarnated. By 1552 these Westcountry people – mingled Celt, Saxon and Norman – had lived on the edges of Dartmoor for 400 years when a Champernowne and a Ralegh mated to produce a dark, swarthy child who looked more Cornish than Devonian, more Iberian than Cornish, an emergence of old blood in a land of long memories. They named him Walter after his father.

Both of Ralegh's parents had been previously married, his mother to Otho Gilbert by whom she had three remarkable sons, John, Humphrey and Adrian. To Squire Ralegh she bore Carew, Walter and Margaret. Her brother, Arthur, was Vice-Admiral of Devon; the Raleghs were related to most of the seafaring families of the Westcountry.

Since the time of Edward III, from 1303 until a few years before Sir Walter was born, the Ralegh family had lived at Fardell Hall on the edge of the Moor, surrounded by barrows, crosses and tors, a land of legend and treasure trove. There was an ancient folk jingle,

> Twixt Potsan's Bridge and Fardell Hall,
> Lies more gold than the Devil can haul.

During his boyhood, young Walter's mind was saturated with the ancient lore of this moody land, kept alive by a people with a strong sense of their glorious and grievous past.

Some of the lore seems to have been an attempt to compensate in imagination for the dreariness of their lives, lived marginally on a poor land. So they imagined that a rich life had flourished in those cities of the dead, and conceived of their peninsula as a chest of hidden treasure. The kistvaens and barrows, they said, were filled with money and jewels: they called them money pits and crocks of gold. The stone circles and rows had been built to mark the site of buried treasure which lay in shining heaps under ground. When occasionally someone dared to break open a kistvaen, to find only bones and dust, he would fall sick and perhaps die. There was a curse on the treasure, but the treasure was surely there.

The folk lore and customs were a rich ore for poetry, which was minted by later poets like William Browne of Tavistock and Robert Herrick. From them we take our memories of May Day in the Westcountry when the milkmaids would decorate their pails with flowers and ribbons, when young people would dance all night and then, on May morning, deck the houses with green boughs and white blossoms. From them we know of how the Christmas mummers would enact St. George's slaying of the Saracen or a dragon, and the revival of his fallen foe with a magic liquor. And how, in blossom time, the folk would wassail the apple trees, and on Christmas Eve would hope to hear the bees singing in their hives or see the oxen kneeling in worship. And there were the 'little folk', the pixies who danced in circles, turned the milk sour, pinched slovenly milkmaids, or played will-o-the-wisp, as much at home in the Westcountry as dogs and cats and mice.

The lore had a darker side too. There were hags and night-tripping fairies who plagued the neighbourhood and stole away children while they slept, replacing them with a wizened and sour-natured changeling. Around Cranmere Bog, source of the river Dart, prints of evil cloven hoofs could be seen; on dark nights the river whispered and sang, luring the stranger down to its banks where he was never seen again. When pixies turned evil they were banished to Dartmoor, that dead land whose legends are all evil and gloomy. There when the thunder rolled over Crockern Tor, the black hunter with his raging pack would pursue the souls of the dead, those of the giants who had buried the gold or sailors who had died on the reefs; or, as some said, his hounds were ravening after the souls of unbaptized infants.

17

The Moor fought the living, took the dead to its grey bosom, and served as an ante-room for hell.

Devon is a Moor encircled by a sea. In between those two impersonal forces is a thin girdle of land which will grow wheat, apples, pasture grass and plums. It is a country without a heartland. There are many rivers, but if one follows them inland, he soon comes to that stone city of the dead. And if he follows them downstream he is soon in an estuary, a fine harbour for ships, where current and wind urge him outward. No wonder the Devon men were restless to seek treasure on the high seas or in the New World whose wonders they were inclined to believe.

An old Devon sailor named Martin Cockram, who had been to Brazil, might very well have talked about that wondrous land to the boy Ralegh, his imagination already aroused by the legends he lived among. Millais later imagined it in his painting, *The Boyhood of Ralegh*, where the boy's eyes, following the pointing hand to far-off distances, are full of wonder and belief and desire. Cockram could have told him of rivers that ran for thousands of miles into the heart of a rich land no man had ever seen, a land not barren and bony like Dartmoor. There in the bright forests were orange and tawny wings; deer fed along the streams; and lithe panthers, dappled like sunlight on leaves, screamed in the deep jungle. In that heartland was Manoa, a golden city, where an enlightened tribe of Indians lived by just laws. There once a year the king anointed his body with balsam and then had fine gold dust blown over him until he shone like the sun he worshipped. Then El Dorado, the gilded one, his hands filled with emeralds and amethysts, would dive into the sacred lake, itself as blue and pure as a sapphire. This was the dream that haunted Ralegh's life and finally drew him across the western seas to heartbreak and death.

It was Ralegh's destiny to be born in this country of grief and fable at about the time when the Westcountry men were turning from a fruitless past in a barren land towards London and the vigorous life of an increasingly assured and expanding nation. They ceased, some of them, to make a career of being persecuted and with astonishing energy set out to find fortunes and make themselves felt in the nation. Not that they forgot either that long backlog of grievances or that they were a peculiar people with a strong identity. But in Ralegh's time they were proudly Englishmen as well as Westcountrymen.

The turning point came at about the middle of the 16th century with the Prayer Book Rebellion, the climax of a series of conflicts between the Westcountry and the central government. These proud remnants of the ancient Celts, children of the Moor, were always easily stirred to revolt as they constantly resisted change which proved, however, to be more irresistible than the Moor itself.

For under the Tudors the Westcountry did change, often painfully. Much of the disruption was economic. Their traditional economy was based on agriculture and tin mining, but with the inflation caused by the flow of gold from the New World into Spain, a whole new economy emerged, based on fishing, wool-growing and privateering. The fine harbours at the mouths of the rivers opened the way for fleets to the fishing banks and the imposition from London of more and more compulsory fish-eating days increased the demand for fish. A thriving industry was built as the fishing boats sailed westward to the Grand Banks for cod; and at the same time England developed fine sailors who were capable of manning her warships. The same harbours provided a home base for privateering vessels which, under license from France, the Low Countries or even Elizabeth herself were empowered to raid the cargo and treasure ships of Spain. Even after a good share was paid to the licensing power, these raids often brought huge profits, and daring Westcountry families such as those of Hawkins, Drake, Ralegh, Grenville and others became rich engaging in this legalized piracy. They also learned to sail and to fight.

The inflation which began before Elizabeth's reign and continued during it was disastrous to men like the tin miners with fixed incomes, but land increased in value and landowners became wealthy. On the land, sheep-raising developed into a source of England's greatest industry, the wool and cloth trade.

Henry VIII's dissolution of the monasteries made available for purchase or lease great tracts of valuable land, and a rich and powerful landed gentry, the Raleghs among them, grew into increasing power and prestige.

But although the spoliation of the monasteries enriched the nobility and the landed gentry, it simultaneously worked hardship on the poorer people and generated a growing bitterness and resentment among them. Economic disruption was severe, for the many lay workers connected with monasteries were abruptly thrown out of work. At the same time, traditional sources of charity and 'relief' were wiped out, and a horde of destitute monks and nuns were left unemployed. The economic bitterness was intensified by the sense of outrage and lonely fear that ensued when the king began to obliterate Catholic rites and ceremonies which had for generations provided comfort and assurance of grace among a deprived people. The labourers cherished their holy days, not only because they were relieved from work, but also because they loved their saints who protected them in the mines and on the seas. They loved to take into their homes the holy bread and water. The heart of their faith, for centuries, had been the Latin Mass. In the dim religious light of the churches, the priest, vested in sacred garments, transformed bread, by means of a stately chant, all the richer for not being understood, into the body and blood of their Savior. God was born among them.

When both economic and spiritual security were threatened, rebellion began to simmer in the Westcountry. When Henry VIII began these changes, even his efficiency and fearful power could not prevent an uprising in the North, called the Pilgrimage of Grace; in the Westcountry there were murmurings but no revolt. But later, when the boy king Edward VI, under the persuasions of an uncompromising and militant Protestant Protector, tried to enforce even greater religious changes, resistance became real.

In 1547, William Body, a zealous dogmatist, tactless and humourless, came officially to Cornwall to call Israel to repentance. His language was filled with Puritan cant about Dagon and Bel, about idolatry and the Canaanite. And underneath his jargon lay a set of injunctions so sweeping as to be almost beyond the comprehension of the Catholic worshipper. Henry VIII had allowed only two candles to be used in the Mass; these were now denied. There would be no more sepulchre on Easter; no holy water and no washings, no ashes on Ash Wednesday, no palms on Palm Sunday; no shiftings or blessings during the Mass. At the communion of the sick and the burial of the dead there would be no crucifixes, bells or candles. All images would be removed from the churches. These Celts were suddenly torn from their past and, for the moment, all they knew was dread.

Trouble began in the town of St. Keverne in Cornwall. Offshore is a vicious reef that had brought down more ships than any other on the coast. As a result, the town was full of 'wreckers', men who made their living by salvaging the torn ships and floating cargo. There is even a persistent, unverifiable rumour that they would set up lights which lured ships to their destruction. One legend gives a terrifying picture of a wrecked sailor floating to shore clinging to a piece of wreckage. A wrecker saw him; there were two swift slashes with the sword; the hands still clung with desperate resolution, but the body floated free and the agonized face sank into the dark sea. Perhaps it was the presence of a community of wreckers, lawless by trade and disposition, who started it. Anyway they seized swords, staves, halberds and bows and arrows and soon William Body was only a body in fact as well as name. There were riots and unlawful assemblages in other parts of Cornwall and the customary Celtic robberies, rapes and aimless violence.

The rebellion was put down with much leniency and commonsense. From a general pardon that was issued, only twenty-eight men were excluded. A grand jury, headed by Sir Richard Grenville (the grandfather of Sir Walter Ralegh's famous cousin of the same name), convicted only seven of them. The terrible execution for treason was carried out in full, and the quarters of the bodies and the heads were set up in various towns to serve as warning and example.

But a far more severe breaking point came two years later, in 1549, when the Prayer Book was forced on all worshippers. This meant an end to the Mass as Catholics knew it and the substitution of the prose of Cranmer, brilliant, gem-like prose, but an alien tongue all the same; few of the Western men could hear its cadences or appreciate its beauty. To them it sounded like a mummers' play at Christmas time.

Whitsunday had been selected for the universal adoption of the new Divine Service in England. On Monday of Whitsun week the uprisings began. Large crowds assembled and became disorderly. Humphry Arundel, one of the principal leaders, held a council of war at St. Michael's Mount where the decision was made to march on London. The army marched under an emblem of the Five Wounds of Christ, and carried a pyx or consecrated host under a canopy, with crosses, banners, candlesticks, holy bread and water – all the forbidden talismans of the old faith.

Old Sir Richard Grenville tried to stop the rebels but was chased into Trematon castle; he went out for a parley under terms of safe conduct but they 'laid hold of his aged, unwieldy body, and threatened to leave it lifeless' if the castle continued to resist.

It soon became apparent that revenge on the gentry, on the rising class, was a strong underlying motive of the rebellion. Gentlewomen had their dresses torn off, and jewels and rings were seized with such violence that delicate fingers were broken.

The first death of the Rebellion occurred at Sampford Courtenay on the north edge of Dartmoor. William Hellyons of Devon tried to reprove the rebels for their treason and they slew him. Another reproof had nearly the same result. About June 22, 1549, Walter Ralegh (whose gifted son was still three years hidden in the seeds of time) saw an old woman walking along to church mumbling over her beads. He stopped, lectured her on obedience to law and avoidance of superstition, then proceeded on his way. But he had done more than he knew; she was a wild, tongue-wagging old bitch, not in the least in awe of reproof from a country squire. She ran to the church, broke in upon the service and began a hysterical tirade against the 'gentlemen'. A gentleman had threatened her; if poor people didn't throw away their beads gentlemen would burn their houses. The worshippers poured out of the church 'like a sort of wasps', and Squire Ralegh had to take refuge in a chapel; had he not been rescued by sailors from Exmouth he too might have been murdered.

Another family of the rising gentry felt the fury of the Celtic mobs. The Drakes were driven out of their home at Plymouth, and with their son Francis, then seven years old, they fled to Kent where they overhauled the beached hull of an old vessel and made their new home in it, an appropriate dwelling for the boy who was to become England's greatest sailor. Ultimately the Celtic army again reached Exeter, defended by Sir Peter Carew. But it was not until the stern Puritan, Lord Grey de Wilton, arrived with foreign mercenaries that the uprising was put down with great (and perhaps unnecessary) cruelty.

After this 'commotion' of 1549, which was the pivotal event of the century in the Westcountry, the children of the Moor were less inclined to keep alive by rebellion a past they only dimly understood. Some began to look towards London and to a future in which the names of Drake, Ralegh, Carew and Grenville would be bright. They approached this future by several routes. Some went first to France. When Sir Peter Courtenay and Gawen Carew tried to rouse the Westcountry to join a rebellion aimed at preventing the marriage of Mary Tudor to Philip of Spain, they failed and would have forfeited their heads if Squire Ralegh, who then had a two-year-old son bearing his name, had not carried the conspirators in his own ship to France. There they met some of the oppressed French Huguenots, a rising party with whose destiny young Walter Ralegh would, for a time, become involved.

And when Mary died and Elizabeth came to the throne, she brought with her a Westcountry woman who had been her stubborn and courageous guardian during her dangerous years, a woman named Katherine Champernowne Ashley who bore the same name as Ralegh's mother and was probably her aunt.

Elizabeth was grateful for the affectionate bullying and courageous protective care and showed it; several of Kat Ashley's young relatives soon turned up in London in the Queen's service. There were Humphrey Gilbert, Ralegh's half-brother; young Richard Grenville, his cousin; his brother Carew; and finally young Ralegh himself. These were representatives of the new Devonians, men of England, restless, hungry for glory, virile and desperately courageous. They had the incalculable release of energy that comes when nostalgia and romantic fictions and sour envy are put aside, along with enervating attempts to make the glories of the past compensate for the mediocrity of the present. It was the hearts of Devon oak, some said, that made England famous.

Yet the past has a strange tenacity in the lives of even the most forward-looking men. How much of Walter Ralegh's character was owing to his boyhood spent in that compelling landscape, among the folkways, legends, and moods of his people? All his life Ralegh was proudly Devonian; even under ridicule he spoke in the harsh Westcountry dialect. (His name, pronounced Watar, invited from Elizabeth a pun – he was her Shepherd of the Ocean.) Even more Celtic was Ralegh's lifelong sense of grievance, of injured merit. He could scarcely write a letter or a report without making someone aware that he was suffering injustice. And from the beginning he had a haunting sense of a personal Destiny that a man could not control. Some of this he acquired from reading the Stoics; but did that reading convince and persuade because he had lived in the presence of the Spirit of Dartmoor and knew the lingering Saxon belief in the Weird? And his bright visions of hidden gold, the restless search for a heartland in Ireland, in Virginia, in Guiana – did not that owe something to boyhood tales of buried treasure? To traditional Westcountry restlessness? Who can say?

'There are more wonders in the world,' he would later write, 'than a man can see while travelling from London to Staines.' That was the voice of a Devonian. Francis Bacon would have been sceptical of such a statement; so would the more kindly William Cecil. And with all the trust she gave Ralegh, Elizabeth was right not to entrust affairs of state to a man who thought like that, for management of money and kingdoms requires men who believe that things are pretty much the same anytime, anywhere. They are realists and make fewer mistakes. But they do not create the legends that touch the heart with pride and wonder. Dreams and facts are old enemies, but Elizabeth the Queen found room in her world for both, and made a place for Walter Ralegh, the imaginative and ambitious young visionary.

2

Ralegh and the
French Wars of Religion

Nothing is known of the first fifteen years of Ralegh's life. In his sixteenth year he went to Oxford University where, apparently, he did not have the time of his life. It may have been the tedious subtleties of Aristotelian logic that depressed the restless Celt; or it may have been the endless rules by which undergraduates at Oxford were then bound. They were forbidden to enter taverns, or, as the discreet phrasing had it, 'other dishonest places'. They were allowed no dogs, no hawks, no play with dice or cards except at Christmas and then 'in moderation' as Aristotle would have counselled. Students could not sleep outside their rooms, be 'nocturnal ramblers' or even go into town without a tutor who held a Master of Arts degree.

Whatever the reason, Ralegh left Oxford after one year and never returned. Although he later became brilliantly educated, it was entirely at his own expense, in his own way, and in a manner that universities are not inclined to recognize.

Of his year at Oxford one revealing anecdote survives. A student who was a fine archer but a little apprehensive of cold steel had been affronted by a classmate. He anxiously sought advice from Ralegh who replied that it was an easy matter: he must challenge his rival immediately – to a shooting match. To settle a solemn affair of honour in such a ludicrous way brought a smile even to the cold face of Francis Bacon.

Already Ralegh was a tall man, a little over six feet in an age when the average height was nine inches less, and he was regally slim. He was handsome, too, in a dark Iberian way, with deep brown curly hair and a trim, pointed beard which lengthened his already elegantly narrow face. His features were sharp, his nose long, his lips firm but sensuous. And there was something strange about his eyes, 'pig-eyed' he had once been called, a pejorative way of describing his narrow eyes with their somnolent, brooding look, the look of an introspective man but one whose controlled passions might break forth suddenly like fire in blown embers. He was a man to be noticed even had he not dressed in flamboyant elegance, sometimes, many thought, on the far side of excess. Fine fabrics, bold colours, high fashion marked him as a man of aggressive style as did the bright jewels flashing from his fingers, his ears and his clothes. He had a suave and polished manner contrasting strangely, when he spoke, with the rustic burr, the Westcountry rasp which he proudly retained and even cultivated all his life. He was a Westcountryman ready to out-court the courtiers, but always and stubbornly a Westcountryman.

While Ralegh was at Oxford, the Huguenots were badly defeated at the Battle of Jarnac and one of their principal leaders, the Prince of Condé, had been killed. Desperately the Huguenots appealed to Elizabeth of England, the only monarch in Europe who both sympathized with them and could provide help. As a result of that appeal, Elizabeth was again forced to review her foreign policy. She turned for counsel to William Cecil, her secretary, a man unmatched as a counsellor in all of Europe, she said, stable, patient, unwarlike, devoutly Protestant. Neither Elizabeth nor Cecil ever encouraged a Protestant crusade, but both believed that the future of Elizabeth's government was closely linked to the survival of the Protestant cause, whether in Scotland, in the Low Countries or in France.

In France, Elizabeth's Protestant allies were the Huguenots, who had been led by the recently slain Prince of Condé and by Gaspard de Coligny, Admiral of France. Elizabeth and Cecil wished to further the Protestant cause wherever possible; the problem was how they could best do it. Both realized that English policy had to be realistically adjusted to the meagre English revenue. France had great resources; Spain controlled the rich industries of the Low Countries and even richer mines in Peru, where a mountain of silver was being shovelled into

Spanish ships for the support of Philip's policies. Against this, Elizabeth had an ordinary revenue of 200,000 pounds sterling a year, a figure depressing to contemplate. In a relatively small campaign in Scotland she had spent 241,000 pounds. This, added to the debt Mary Tudor had left her, amounted to a deficit of some 600,000 pounds. Philip of Spain and Henry of France, whose passionate aims could not be hindered by such trifles as money, had borrowed heavily from the money lenders; for risky borrowers the interest was seldom less than fourteen per cent; usually it was higher and once, after Philip had defaulted, it went up to fifty per cent. If Elizabeth had tried to finance wars by such borrowing she would have ruined England. So her men of action, especially Ralegh, called her stingy, penurious, half-hearted and calculating, a niggling woman. It was England's good fortune that she was.

Elizabeth's trifling revenues made it impossible for her to build armies. To send across the channel one company of infantry consisting of 200 men would have cost her 3,240 pounds. To send the thousands of men it needed to meet the highly efficient Spanish armies was impossible. But she could and did build a navy, and she could encourage dissensions against the Spanish and French monarchs, occasionally doling out aid, but only when things were going badly and then with a parsimonious hand.

After the Battle of Jarnac, it was clear that the Huguenots must be helped. Elizabeth therefore sent them 20,000 livres on condition that the jewels of Condé and Albret be returned as security, and she privately encouraged English gentlemen to equip 'volunteers' at their own expense and sail to La Rochelle to join the French forces and thus win glory for England and for themselves their Queen's approbation. All the time, without the flicker of an eyelid, she protested to the French ambassador that she was outraged by those volunteers who had gone to France against her wishes. The ambassador nodded understandingly; he would take her at her word. Consequently, whenever the French Royalists captured Englishmen they promptly hanged them with a placard pinned to their chests which explained why they had been executed: they had come to serve the Huguenots against the wishes of their Queen. The French have always been deft with bitter courtesies. But Elizabeth said nothing; she was content 'to throw the stone and hide the arm'.

Since the time of Wyatt's rebellion the ties of Westcountry Protestants with the Huguenots had continued to grow. One of Ralegh's Champernowne cousins had married Gabrielle de Montgomery, daughter of the formidable Count Montgomery who, in 1559, had accidentally slain the king of France in a jousting duel. Count Montgomery's emblem was a grisly representation of a severed head beneath which was the motto, *Det mihi virtus finem,* 'Let valour end my life,' which implied that a valorous man, in his heroic pursuit of glory, was prepared to accept violent death.

Another of the Champernowne cousins, at Elizabeth's silent signal, raised a hundred horse in Devon. Young Ralegh left Aristotle and Oxford to join him under the black banner which had been borrowed from Count Montgomery. Under that banner, young Walter, just seventeen years of age, sailed off to France to serve his Queen and find his destiny. Shortly after the first of October, 1569, the little band disembarked at La Rochelle. There they learned that some two or three days' ride to the north the Huguenot army under Coligny was facing a much larger Royalist force. Hurriedly the troop mounted and rode toward the little town of Moncontour. But they were too late. The battle had already been fought and the Huguenots had been overwhelmed.

On October 5, at the town of Niort, some thirty-five miles northeast of La Rochelle, Ralegh and the English troop encountered the remnants of the beaten army. They saw first, perhaps, a troop of 150 lancers who had not entered the combat and who were escorting to safety the two young princes, both about Ralegh's age, Henry, Prince of Navarre, and the young Prince of Condé who had succeeded to the title when his father was killed at Jarnac. Next came the mounted German reiters, flying in the wildest disorder. Finally there were a few infantry, sick, discouraged, without food, mostly without weapons.

Between this beaten remnant of an army and complete annihilation stood Count Louis of Nassau and the splendid Huguenot cavalry, the only fighting unit of Coligny's forces that was still organized and effective. Repeatedly that cavalry charged the Royalists and forced them to abandon their pursuit of the fleeing Huguenots. Coligny himself had been hit in the cheek bone with a pistol ball. He had lost much blood and was in excruciating pain.

Like English gentlemen on a lark, the Devonian troop entered Niort with trumpets blowing and the black pennant flying. But they soon put their trumpets away and entered into the deadly business of saving what lives they could. They probably joined Nassau's rear guard and took part in those heroic charges that Ralegh remembered forty years later with so much admiration. In the next few days the magnitude of the disaster became apparent to Ralegh and his Devonian cousins; and they watched with awe the unbelievable recovery of Coligny through his raw courage and iron will.

There is no first-hand evidence for Ralegh's part in the French Wars of Religion except for his own testimony, written some forty years later, when he was a prisoner in the Tower of London, working on his *History of the World*, an incomplete work which ended during the account of the Roman Empire. Yet it contains many references to Ralegh's experience in France, for as he wrote of ancient empires and kings, their battles and the decisions by which those battles and empires were preserved or lost, he returned again and again for illustrative analogies to the French Wars of Religion. One cannot reconstruct the Battle of Moncontour and the subsequent events from Ralegh's history, but once they are reconstructed, many passages in the *History* take on new point and meaning. By placing the events of the French wars alongside passages in the *History* one can come to understand what Ralegh's experiences in them must have been like, and also what he came to feel and think about warfare and national policies in the light of them.

The first thing he became aware of was the superior qualities of Coligny, who came to represent for Ralegh the man of virtue *par excellence*. Even the death of Condé at Jarnac, he thought, had its compensations because it left Coligny in sole command. Condé was believed by some to be the bravest man in Europe; those who had read their Aristotle considered him simply foolhardy, His only notion of tactics was to set a lance, dig both spurs into his horse's side and charge the enemy where he was strongest. The Huguenot cavalry of lesser French nobility loved his hot-blooded ways and followed him with élan. But such a man was a dangerous leader for the side that always had to fight with the smallest numbers. As Ralegh said in his *History*,

I remember it well, that when the Prince of Condé was slain after the Battle of Jarnac (which prince, together with the Admiral Châtillon, had the conduct of the Protestant army), the Protestants did greatly bewail the loss of the said prince, in respect of his religion, person and birth; yet, comforting themselves, they thought it rather an advancement than a hindrance to their affairs, for so much did the valour of the one outreach the advisedness of the other, as whatso-ever the Admiral intended to win by attending the advantage, the prince adventured to lose by being over-confident in his own courage.

Coligny was known throughout all of Europe. As Admiral of France, he had already planted the first French colonies in the New World. But he was known still more for the iron will and incredible courage he had displayed, even before the wars of religion began, in the siege at San Quentin, where he had held off the huge Imperial armies long enough to buy with blood the time France needed for survival. Finally taken prisoner, he was sent to two years of imprisonment in the Netherlands. It was said that he went into captivity there a Catholic and emerged in 1559 a Protestant. In prison he had pored long over the Bible and, coming to know the Huguenots, was attracted to their moral austerity. He also pondered Theodore Beza's powerful phrase that the Church of God was an anvil that had worn out many hammers. Here, in the Huguenot movement, perhaps, was a counterforce to the House of Guise, the historical rival to Coligny's own house of Montmorency. He was, then, inclining toward the Huguenots when John Calvin sent him a letter explaining that his imprisonment was a part of God's special providence.

God has given you this opportunity to profit in his school, as though He had wished to speak to you, privately into your ear.

And so Coligny, an ambitious as well as a morally serious man, at last had become the leader of the Huguenot forces and, always with an inferior army, he had fought and been defeated first at Jarnac, now at Moncontour. Under any lesser leader those two disasters would have ended the Huguenot movement.

Ralegh arrived in time to see the end of the battle of Moncontour which haunted his memory as a paradigm of the plan and chaos of battle, its disaster and valour. It was a classical sixteenth-century field battle. At this time, the heart and core of a field army was the pikemen. The Spaniards, who were by far the most advanced tacticians and whose armies had not lost a battle for decades, believed that the pike was the queen of arms. It was a shaft, sixteen to eighteen feet long, tipped with a steel spike; it was guarded at the tip by iron plates some two feet long which were intended to hinder cavalrymen from hacking the shaft in two with their swords. The pikemen also carried short swords and sometimes daggers, the latter being 'a weapon of great advantage in pell-mell'. These weapons were used only when the opposing formations were broken or to finish off those who had fallen or who were kneeling to beg mercy which they had not, in someone's opinion, deserved. Placed in files usually sixteen men deep, the pikemen could advance on as broad a front as the commander wished. These formations, Ralegh said, were quite comparable to the ancient Greek phalanx.

The pikemen marched in ranks three feet apart and when they engaged, the first four ranks would swiftly lower their pikes to create a bristling hedge of steel. If the pikes had the courage to stand, no cavalry could break their formation: it would be easier for a naked man to burst through a hedge of thorns. If the cavalry wheeled to the rear or flank, the pikemen would pivot and face the charge. When necessary they could be manoeuvred to face all four directions at once, a self-contained unit around which a friendly cavalry could rally and in the ranks of which the arquebusiers could find shelter. In any formation they were so formidable that 'to pass the pikes' became a common phrase to indicate the surmounting of greatest danger; a woman who had nearly died in childbirth had 'passed the pikes'.

The arquebusiers carried an arquebus, a kind of primitive musket, heavy enough to require a tripod for a dead-rest, difficult to load, and very nearly impossible to aim. The word *arquebusier* was entirely too much for the English who, with their gift for rising above the perversities of other people's languages, simply called them hackbutters. A group of these hackbutters would usually be sent out in front of the pikemen where they stood in such a hopelessly exposed position that the English called them 'the forlorn hope', and the French called them the lost children, *enfants perdus*. The strategy was for the forlorn hope to volley, hoping to break the charge of cavalry or pikemen, and then retire within the hedgerow formed by their own pikes. There they would reload and fire from within the ranks.

Finally there was the cavalry, the mobile, striking force. Their commanders would survey the field, watching for signs of weakness. If the infantry were deadlocked with pikes advanced, they would skirmish with other cavalry. They also served for communications, information, and the deadly pursuit of broken troops. In France, especially, the cavalry was animated by a high sense of chivalry, gallantry, and honour.

By far the best mercenary soldiers in Europe at this time were the Swiss pikemen who had made the phalanx into an almost ultimate weapon. They hanged any comrade who displayed panic or who faltered in battle; and since they expected no mercy they continued to fight even if the battle were lost, sometimes until all were dead. They did not themselves take any prisoners, apparently caring nothing for the ransom they might gain. Any opponent who went down, nobleman or commoner, was thrust through. The French commanders considered Swiss pikemen to be the decisive factor in a battle.

The Germans, in imitation of the Swiss pikemen, developed the landsknechts who were resented by the Swiss as interlopers into their craft. Whenever these two met no quarter was given. The Swiss were more expensive than the landsknechts and they preferred to fight for whoever was most likely to be able to pay them. Naturally the constituted government always had far more resources than the rebels so the Swiss, for no political or religious reasons, were invariably found fighting on the side of authority. Those who opposed the Crown took second best, the landsknechts.

The great question of strategy was how to break the pikes. Once battle was joined, artillery was useless in the field; it slew friend and foe impartially. But there were two principal devices that were sometimes successful. The first was to choose a battleground in which the terrain was broken by rivers, entrenchments, or any kind of barricades, artificial or natural. Then the lines of the pikemen might be dented and the cavalry, or the infantry with swords, might break in. Another device was a fancy manoeuvre called the *caracole* which was performed by German reiters mounted on horses and armed, not with lances but with two pistols and a sword. When the pikes formed their phalanx, the reiters were to advance within firing range. The first rank would aim and discharge pistols, then wheel and go to the rear where they re-loaded. The next rank would then come up and fire and so on. In theory it sounds admirable, but La Noue, the French Huguenot leader, had no use for it, for he had seen it fail primarily because it didn't take into account human nature under the stress of combat; it was natural for the reiter to snap the shots off too quickly and then get out of danger. As La Noue observed, there always seemed to be more horsemen going to the rear than there were coming forward.

Coligny, then, had secured enough money to hire 6,000 reiters, about 5,000 landsknechts and had some 2,000 Huguenot cavalry, many of them of noble blood and all of high courage. With this army he intended to challenge the throne of France.

He was in the field by June 10 when the Royalist armies were in such low morale that the Cardinal of Lorraine said later that if the Admiral had immediately sought out the Royalist army, he would have beaten it. Instead, Coligny had halted to try to take the fortified city of Poitiers. But as Ralegh commented in the *History*,

The malice of a great army is broken, and the force of it spent in a great siege. This the Protestant army found true at Poitiers a little before the battle of Moncontour; and their victorious enemies, anon after, at St. Jean d'Angely.

Coligny knew what the siege was doing to his army. 'These great cities,' he said, 'are the sepulchres of armies.' He would have moved on but a large proportion of his cavalry were noblesse from Western France and they insisted on reducing Poitiers as a means of insuring the protection of their homes and lands. Ralegh was correct; the battle of Moncontour was lost at the siege of Poitiers.

By the time the two armies faced each other at Moncontour on September 30, Coligny had only 4,500 reiters, 5,000 landsknechts and his cavalry to face a force of 18,000 foot and a cavalry equal to his own. The odds were bad. Consequently he had chosen a battle field where there was strong defensive ground flanked on one side by a wood and on the other by a river, believing that this position might offset the strength of the Swiss pikemen. For two days the armies skirmished and shifted their positions, seeking tactical advantage. On October 2, Tavannes, the Royalist general, gained a position that partially outflanked the Huguenots, and Coligny had to move. He should have moved under the cover of darkness, but he was Admiral of France and his cavalry were gentlemen; honour forbade sneaking away from the field in the night. Ralegh quoted La Noue as saying,

Staying upon our reputation in show not to dislodge by night, we lost our reputation indeed by dislodging by day; whereby we were forced to fight upon our disadvatage and to our ruin.

Then Ralegh commented,

And yet did that worthy gentleman Count Lodowick of Nassau, brother to the late famous Prince of Orange, make the retreat at Moncontour with so great resolution, as he saved the one half of the Protestant army, then broken and disbanded, of which myself was an eye witness; and was one of them that had cause to thank him for it.

Though Ralegh was not in the battle itself, he did take part in the retreat when he learned that it is better to engage at some slight disadvantage than to be caught out of battle order. But the fault was not Coligny's.

On the morning of October 3, when it was light enough for honour to sleep, Coligny gave the order to move. Immediately the landsknechts and five cornets of reiters refused to march until they were paid. It had become customary for unpaid mercenary troops to refuse battle, but it is difficult, in this instance, to follow their logic: the Admiral obviously did not carry that much money around with him, and the delay occasioned by their insubordination brought their own lives into the gravest danger. For two hours Coligny pleaded, persuaded, and promised. Finally the Germans agreed to fight and then wasted a few more minutes while they prostrated themselves and kissed the earth. Their Teutonic passions now purged, they marched out, but before they could reach the ground from which Coligny intended to fight, the Royalists pressed in and Coligny had to turn for battle.

Then the Royalists halted and there was a four-hour delay while, once again, forces were shifted as commanders sought tactical advantage. In that interval Coligny gave an order that was later strongly criticized. With his troops were the two young princes in whom resided the future of the Huguenot cause; Coligny ordered them to the rear with an escort of 150 lances. It was a sensible thing to do, but it should have been done much earlier, for now it suggested to the troops that the Admiral's confidence was shaken.

The Royalist plan was for the Swiss pikemen to advance against the Huguenot foot. The Duke of Guise was to refrain from battle; he and his light horse were to stand in reserve and make their charge when it appeared that it might be decisive. So Ralegh commented,

A great and a victorious advantage it hath ever been found, to keep some one or two good troops to look on, when all else are disbanded or engaged.

Now the battle was ready. The Royalists advanced. Tavannes had noticed that when the Huguenot army was marching, before he had forced it to turn at bay, the pikes had wavered, and he thought his cavalry might break them. He sent his cavalry forward, but the Huguenot artillery had the range and cannon-balls began dropping among the horse. It was time for the charge; the Royalist horse 'drank the cup' and ran full tilt against the Huguenots, clearing away the forlorn hope but pulling up short of the pikes. Immediately the Huguenot cavalry counter-charged. Now there was shock and turn and charge again. Soon the field was covered with broken squadrons attempting to rally and re-group. Tavannes then sent his Swiss infantry forward, pikes lowered, forming a phalanx behind which his cavalry could re-form. Louis of Nassau realized that the decisive moment had come. Unless his reiters could perform the *caracole* effectively and stop the Swiss, the battle was finished. As he led the reiters forward in good order, Marshal Biron charged them from the flank; his charge spilt them; they wavered and fled the field, having scarcely fired a shot.

Observing the events, the Duke of Guise, in reserve with his light horse, charged the landsknechts who broke and gave up the battle. They tried to surrender, throwing down their weapons, falling to their knees and crying, '*bon papiste, bon papiste, moy,*' which simply gave the Protestant Swiss one more reason for slaughtering them. Those who had any wits left ran for their lives. Perhaps a thousand escaped into the woods. Of the remaining 4,000 the Swiss spared not a man. They surrounded the terrified landsknechts with their phalanxes and detached squads who threw aside their pikes, seized dagger and sword, and began the slaughter. Methodically they stabbed and slashed, piling up the dead, slipping and falling in the blood, pausing only to rest

37

the sword arm. Louis of Nassau and his cavalry were helpless. They could not charge the steel hedgerows; they could only turn and leave the field with the screams of dying men in their ears. When it was finally over, the landsknechts had kissed the earth for the second time that day. It would be a long embrace and they were still unpaid.

Judged by any ordinary standard, Coligny was now a thrice-beaten man; his army, like his face, was shattered. But destiny might be overcome by virtue, that manly combination of grace, intellect and valour. Coligny was a man of such virtue and he did force a capricious destiny to relent. First he seized a chance opportunity. Some of the Huguenot cavalrymen had intercepted messengers from the king carrying 30,000 francs intended for the Swiss pikemen. The money was taken to Coligny who offered all of it to the reiters if they would stay with him. When they considered the alternative, a three-hundred-mile dash across France, without supplies and without pike support, they decided to take the cash and to heed, for a little longer, the rumble of the drum.

Meanwhile some hackbutters and landsknechts were straggling out of the woods and into the open country south of the battlefield. The Royalist cavalry began to run them down, putting the edge of the sword into their necks or through the skull. It was then that Louis of Nassau began the heroic counter charges which won Ralegh's admiration. Louis held back the pursuit for two days and allowed what was left of the army to re-form at Niort, thirty-five miles south of the battlefield. And there, on October 5, the band of Devon horse, trumpets blowing and pennants flying, joined that shocked and beaten army.

A French historian said that the English were graciously received by the young princes. The reality may have been somewhat different. Elizabeth had sent 100 men, some of them striplings, scarcely any of whom had seen combat. And they they came bearing the standard, *Let valour end my life,* a powerful reproach to men who had fled a battlefield, leaving 4,000 comrades to be slaughtered. In that beaten army, in the general atmosphere of depression and guilt, every group and every man must have been struggling with individual griefs and personal doubts, but the two young princes must have borne the heaviest burden. Boys of seventeen, princes of the blood, they had intended to prove their courage; instead they had left the field surrounded by a bodyguard, and now in the usual search for someone to blame, their names were prominent in the grumbling and the cursing. Coligny himself was in terrible pain. He had lost at St. Quentin, he had lost at Jarnac, and now he had lost at Moncontour – each time heroically, but still he had lost. Coligny and the Protestant cause in France appeared to be finished.

But in Coligny was the mysterious inner force which great leaders are able to manifest in catastrophe; that quality, that force, fascinated Ralegh. All his life he talked about it and once, in accounting for the exploits of Alexander the Great, he tried to define it. His words apply equally well to Coligny at this moment.

For so much hath the spirit of some one man excelled, as it hath undertaken and effected the alteration of the greatest states and commonweals, the erection of monarchies, the conquest of kingdoms and empires, guided handfuls of men against multitudes of equal bodily strength, contrived victories beyond all hope and discourse of reason, converted the fearful passions of his own followers into magnanimity, and the valour of his enemies into cowardice; such spirits have been stirred up in sundry ages of the world, and in divers parts thereof to erect and cast down again, to establish and to destroy, and to bring all things, persons and states to the same certain ends, which the infinite Spirit of the Universal, piercing, moving, and governing all things, hath ordained.

That infinite spirit of the Universal which moves and governs all things is the Stoic *logos* or, in simpler terms, Destiny which has her favoured children. Coligny was one of these. And Ralegh, having watched Coligny, for the rest of his life was to believe that a child of Destiny who was also a virtuous man could triumph over an adverse fortune as Coligny now did.

At this point, Coligny made some bold decisions. Instead of holding up in La Rochelle where he would be secure but would lose any chance to take the initiative again, he went straight south where he could establish a strong defensive position along the river Charente, supported by the Huguenot strongholds of Cognac, St. Jean d'Angley, and Angoulême. Then, leaving his defeated infantry in St. Jean, he continued on further south with the reiters and the cavalry. The pursuing Royalists, unwilling to leave strongly garrisoned towns to their rear, delayed for six weeks to besiege St. Jean. Then they granted it surrender on honourable terms. Ralegh later recalled that surrender bitterly.

I was present when De Piles related the injury done unto him. He had rendered St. Jean d'Angely to the French king, Charles the Ninth, who besieged him therein. He rendered it upon promise, made by the faith of a king, that he should be suffered to depart in safety, with all his followers. Yet in the presence of the King himself, of the Duke of Anjou and his brother, general of his army, of the queen-mother, and of divers dukes and marshals of France, he was set upon and broken in his march, spoiled of all that he had, and was forced to save his life by flight, leaving the most of his soldiers dead upon the place.

So the thousand infantry that escaped at Moncontour were slaughtered here by the broken faith of a king. It is the rusty sword, Ralegh later said, and the empty purse that will enforce a prince to keep his treaties; nothing else will. St. Jean d'Angely had given him cause to know.

Meanwhile, seeing his enemy losing advantage as he had done by besieging Poitiers, Coligny daringly took the offensive once more. Allowing the Count Montgomery to choose any seventy men and whatever mounts and weapons he wished, he sent him south to rally the support of the Huguenot nobles and raise an army which could hold off the Royalist forces entrenched near the Spanish frontier and, at the same time, to prepare a refuge for Coligny's army. With his black standard fluttering, Montgomery rode southward. But he did not merely organize the Huguenots for defence: he raised an army and besieged and took the Royalist city of Navarrens. Even one of Montgomery's enemies later called his actions the most valorous and notable exploit in all the French wars. He was worthy of his shield.

Coligny's army, however, following Montgomery south, was in difficulty. Ralegh had once heard the Admiral say that whoever would shape the beast of war must begin with its belly. That belly now was lean: there was no food, no supplies. The horses were unshod, many of them so footsore they could hardly walk. Nevertheless Coligny, the man of demonic will, by 350 miles of forced marches across a network of rivers, brought his army in thirty days to Montaubon. There he crossed the Garonne and joined forces with Montgomery. Young Ralegh was one of those who endured with Coligny that long retreat from Niort to Montaubon, which later came to be called 'The Voyage of the Princes', a romantic name for the desperate retreat of a defeated army under a wounded general.

In the following weeks, the Huguenot armies ravaged the country south of the Garonne. The troops now were angry and revengeful; discipline broke down; there was slaughtering and pillage. It has been said that in the first religious war the soldiers behaved like angels, in the second like men, in the third like beasts. This was the third. In the first war, La Noue had said, the Huguenot soldiers did not have a single box of dice or pack of cards. There were no camp followers and no swearing. Coligny had remarked, 'Very fine provided that it lasts. But I have my fears that our people will shed their virtue in the course of two months, and have nothing left but their bad qualities. As an old infantry colonel, I cannot but remember the proverb, "Young hermits may become old devils." ' And as La Noue himself admitted, his infantry had soon lost its virginity. Having observed all this, Ralegh later wrote, 'The greatest and most grievous calamity that can come to any state is civil war . . . a misery more lamentable than can be described.'

He did not exaggerate its savagery. When the Catholic garrison at Navarrens surrendered, Montgomery, desperate and revengeful, slaughtered them all. Montluc retaliated by slaughtering the Huguenot garrison at Mont-de-Marsan. When Montluc's soldiers stormed the walls at Rabastens, where he was hit in the face with an arquebus shot, women joined men on the ramparts and threw stones down on the attackers. When the fortress fell, Montluc killed both men and women. In justification he wrote in Machiavellian terms,

Do not think I caused this slaughter to be made so much out of revenge for the wound I had received as to strike terror into the country, that they might not dare to make head against our army. And in my opinion all soldiers in the beginning of a conquest ought to proceed after that manner . . . He must bar his ears to all capitulation and composition.

Through it all Ralegh was watching, learning. His actions in Ireland would soon show what he had been taught.

By the middle of December, Coligny's wound was healed; his morale was high and he wrote to the commander of the Huguenot garrison at La Charité that he would resume the offensive in the spring. Coligny never limited his ambitions: like all French military men he was obessed with the symbolic idea of Paris. To hold Paris was to win a national victory; he was not going to settle for a regional one.

In the spring, when the roads were firm enough to support his troops, he took with him those German reiters who were left, the Huguenot cavalry, including the little English troop in which Ralegh was serving, and 3,000 hackbutters mounted on farm horses and country nags. He moved northward with incredible speed, precipitated and won the battle of Arnay-le-Duc, marched within sight of Paris, and then made overtures for peace. Forced to accept, Catherine de Medici signed the Peace of St. Germain on August 8, 1570. From that time until his murder on St. Bartholomew's Day, 1572, Coligny was the dominant force in the government of France. His success as a child of Destiny against devastating odds had secured for French Protestants a permanent place in the life of the nation. To be sure, toleration would be revoked, offered, denied again and then again, but the cruelties and devastations of the civil wars had given rise to a strong third party of *politiques* who were extremely sceptical about holy wars and who resisted the partisan zeal of both sides. Ultimately it was their influence that would make a permanent religious settlement possible.

But that settlement did not come at once. Catholic resentment of Coligny was probably the immediate cause of the St. Bartholomew's Massacre, of which the Admiral was principal victim. And as the bitterness subsided and Henry of Navarre became heir to the French throne, he realized that he could hold it in peace only if he abandoned the Protestant faith for the Catholic cause. He counted costs and did so. The Protestants were furious, Elizabeth calling it an 'abominable act'. Ralegh too commented on it in connection with the Israelite, Jeroboam, who, for political reasons, had set up the golden calves. This, said Ralegh, was an act of *Raggione del Stato* (as Machiavelli called actions of pure political expediency), the same sort of motive that led Henry of Navarre to change his religion. This severe stricture is his only surviving comment on that monarch with whom he made the Voyage of the Princes.

When Ralegh's life was nearly over, when he was sated with the cruelty of wars and the things he himself had seen and done, he wrote in a disillusioned vein of wars of religion and the motives of men like Coligny who waged them. We are all 'comedians' in religion, he said. We profess Christian love and charity but that is not how we act. Many men colour their ambitions by pleading religious duty; therefore discreet young princes 'should beware of yielding hasty belief to the robes of sanctimony'.

The Civil Wars in France, which occasioned such 'barbarous murders, devastations, and other calamities', were

begun and carried on by some few great men of ambitious and turbulent spirits, deluding the people with the cloak and mask only of religion, to gain their assistance to what they did more especially aim at. It is plain the Admiral Coligny advised the Prince of Condé to side with the Huguenots not only out of love to their persuasion but to gain a party.

But this is what he felt much later; at the time he was himself one of the turbulent spirits. La Noue once complained that young men read too much of Amadis de Gaul and old men too much of Machiavelli, suggesting that the young, having read

43

chivalric adventures wanted to leave home and join wars for glory; and that the older had forgotten all morality in the pursuit of their ambitions. By this standard, Ralegh came to France a young man and left it an old one.

Later Ralegh filled his *History* with reflections and reminiscences. He said nothing about Ireland; that was a running sore he didn't wish to touch. He had much to say about the New World, about being a courtier, and especially about the war against Spain and the coming of the Armada. But more than any single one of these the French Civil War came to his mind. He had been young and impressionable. He had seen at first hand what a child of Destiny could do. Coligny had dreamed of colonies in the New World, a dream Ralegh was later to pursue for England; Coligny had shaken the throne of France; his virtue had forced Destiny to relent and he had ended his life valorously. Again and again as one reviews Ralegh's life, he is reminded of parallels in the life of Coligny who must have exercised an incalculable influence on the young Englishman.

Forty years later, as he lay in the Tower repenting the impassioned brutalities he had witnessed or committed, when his heart had grown larger with compassion for the suffering of mankind, Ralegh made his final comment on soldiering in the French Wars.

It was not ignorance made Montluc, Marshal of France, confess that if the mercies of God were not infinite, none of his profession could expect any.

3

Interlude in England

Ralegh was with Coligny's army until the Peace of St. Germain in 1570. Five years later, when he was twenty-three, he was back in England. No one is sure where he was in the interval. One writer said that Ralegh had served in the Low Countries under his half-brother, Humphrey Gilbert. In the year which he is said to have served, however, his name is found on the rolls of Oxford University, but frequently names were carried on that roll when the man named was absent. Richard Hakluyt, who knew Ralegh well, said that he had been in France all this time, and we can best assume that Ralegh was living there at the time of Coligny's death and that he continued to serve the Huguenots afterwards.

In 1575 Ralegh was in London, enrolled in the Middle Temple, one of the Inns of Court, where prospective lawyers lived and received their training. Later he said that he had never read a word of the law. Although the statement savours a little of Ralegh's tendency to heighten the fact in order to improve the phrase, it is probably close to the truth. His neglect of his studies had consequences when he was tried for treason which seem, in retrospect, nightmarish.

Many of those who enrolled in the Inns of Court had no intention of being serious students of the law or of entering the profession. The landed gentry went there to learn just enough law to conduct their affairs, to judge the validity of threatened suits, to have some feeling for contracts and tenures. For these, the Inns were a club, a place to take their meals, converse, to see plays and perhaps write them, and, incidentally, to do a little roistering. Shakespeare's Shallow and Silence those two devastating caricatures of provincial justices of the peace, had both been there, as had their friend, Jack Falstaff, and their recollections, heightened by memory, give the flavour.

Shallow: I was once of Clement's Inn, where I think they will talk of mad Shallow yet.
Silence: You were called 'lusty Shallow' then, cousin.
Shallow: By the mass I was called anything; and I would have done anything indeed too, and roundly too . . . I may say to you, we knew where the bona-robas were, and had the best of them all at commandment.

One of the bona-robas, handsome ladies with light reputations, could never abide Master Shallow, but they all appear to have liked Falstaff, who had broken Skogan's head at the court gate on the very same day Master Shallow had fought with one Sampson Stockfish, a fruiterer. Falstaff sums up their memories of Inns-of-Court days in one brilliant line:

We have heard the chimes at midnight, Master Shallow.

And so had Ralegh.

Ralegh's years in the Middle Temple, according to one of his early biographers, were 'turbulent and irregular'. Both the records and the tales that survive bear it out. In a tavern once Ralegh had become annoyed with a 'roaring boy' such as Ben Jonson later satirized in *Every Man out of his Humour* as Carlo Buffone. He seized the man and sealed his upper and nether beard with sealing wax. In later life, when Ralegh was unhappy with the pranks of his oldest son, his wife reminded him that the boy came by his behaviour quite naturally.

In 1577 two of Ralegh's servants defied the watch and were arrested. In 1579 he and Humphrey Gilbert were brought before the Privy Council and put under surety not to engage in further acts of piracy. In 1580 Ralegh duelled with Sir Thomas Perrot and both were committed to the Fleet prison for six days. A month later Ralegh was in the Marshalsea prison for duelling with one of the Wingfields.

46

Though much of Ralegh's work gives the impression of a melancholy and brooding man, at the Inns of Court he gained a reputation as both swordsman and wit. Part of the equipment of a 'wit' was the ability to write a poem on occasion, and he did so for a member of the Inns, George Gascoigne, who having fought in the Low Countries, had adopted the motto, *Tam Marti Quam Mercurio* to indicate his equal devotion to Mars and Mercury, to arms and arts. In his faltering pursuit of Mercury he had written a satire, *The Steel Glass*, in rigid and clumsy blank verse. When Gascoigne asked some friends for prefatory verses, Ralegh responded in couplets as stiff and wooden as the lines of Gascoigne. It must have been his first attempt; otherwise we would have to assume that he was being ineffective out of courtesy. In his poem Ralegh successfully ignores Gascoigne's strictures on the follies of ambition and contemplates, rather, the discomforts ambitious men are subject to.

> But envious brains do nought (or light) esteem,
> Such stately steps as they cannot attain.
> For whoso reaps renown above the rest,
> With heaps of hate shall surely be oppressed.

Religions have been founded upon less prophetic insight than Ralegh displays in these uninspired couplets. The pains of ambition and the 'heaps of hate' he would soon know for himself. Ralegh must have liked Gascoigne for, when the old warrior died, his young friend borrowed his motto, used it on his own coat of arms and in his life and person fulfilled its promise.

Of the recorded episodes of Ralegh's years at the Inns of Court, the one which resulted in his being forbidden, along with Humphrey Gilbert, to engage in further piracy is the most significant because it involved Ralegh in Gilbert's bedraggled career of abortive projects, and because it was one of the first important steps in the colonizing of the New World. The promising young Gilbert had been introduced by Kat Champernowne Ashley to the service of the Queen early in her reign, and obviously stood high in her favour. He had served under Sir Henry Sidney for three years in the Irish wars, where he had earned a reputation for quixotic courage and pathological ferocity. On the strength of his reputation, Elizabeth sent him to the Netherlands in command of 1,500 men to re-inforce the tiny English garrison which found itself in some trouble. The best commander likely could not have succeeded in this difficult situation, but Gilbert was a particularly bad choice. He had succeeded in Ireland against poorly equipped and undisciplined Celtic troops by the one strategy he knew: charge and hack away. But in the Netherlands he was opposing highly skilled strategists, trained troops, and a terrain criss-crossed by dikes, canals and rivers. He set his troops to beseige the city of Goes; there Mondragon, a brilliant Spanish strategist, having led his men under cover of darkness through eight miles of shallow water, surprised Gilbert completely. Without even giving battle, the English troops fled in disorder amidst appalling slaughter.

Gilbert probably never recovered from this debacle. Afterwards, he always lacked inner assurance; the soldiers and sailors felt in him a sense of strain, a certain desperation that smelled of danger. Men didn't like to serve under him and Gilbert came to feel that somehow his own courage had been impugned and therefore must constantly be validated.

Smarting under this disaster, he returned to England with his head full of plans to retrieve his fortune. One of these plans was deserving of respect and ultimately earned a place in history. For many years the merchants of England had wanted to get to Cathay in order to trade woolens, hides and manufactured goods for spices, jewels, gold, silks, and other exotic goods. There were at that time two known ways to get there, one around the Cape of Good Hope and through the Indian Ocean, the other around Cape Horn and through the Straits of Magellan. Both were very long, highly dangerous and rigorously controlled by the Spanish and Portuguese navies. Neither, therefore, was practical for English trade. But there were believed to be two other routes, untried but theoretically possible, which looked attractive. Both were in northern waters, above the line which bounded Spanish territory. The 'Northeast Passage' through the Arctic seas had been attempted by the Willoughby expedition and found disastrous: the ships had been iced in, the crew starved, and their bones were still bleaching somewhere in the snow fields of Lapland. The other unknown route was thought to be possible through the Strait of Anian, a wide waterway running from Newfoundland across the continent of North America to the present site of San Francisco. North of the strait

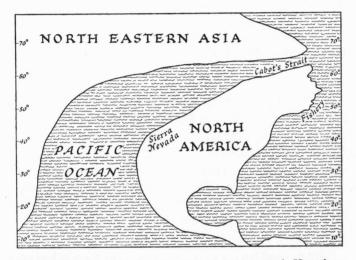

This map first drawn by Sebastian Cabot helped persuade Humphrey Gilbert that he could sail directly from Newfoundland to the Pacific, passing near Cathay.

was Cathay, the inhabitants of which would need English woollens.

The Strait of Anian, unfortunately, did not exist. But in 1576, the year after Ralegh returned from France, Gilbert wrote a book which proved that it did. He began his *New Passage to Cathay* like a scholar, citing Plato, Ficino, Aristotle and others whose words could with ingenuity be explicated into supporting his position. He explained the sea currents and the motions of the heavens. Then putting scholarship aside, he delivered the clincher; the wealth of the East was infinite, the Northwest Passage was the road to find it. English goods could be sold in Cathay and, for trifles, England would secure valuable commodities. The situation, he says, is the same as that once faced by the Castilian monarchs when Columbus made his proposal.

> This discovery hath been reserved for some noble prince or worthy man, thereby to make himself rich and the world happy.

He concludes with a flourish that is still stirring.

> And therefore give me leave without offence, always to live and die in this mind, that he is not worthy to live at all, that for fear, or danger of death, shunneth his country's service and his own honour: seeing death is inevitable and the fame of virtue immortal.

Gilbert's work almost immediately elevated him to the rank of England's best expert on the New World. Not surprisingly, therefore, when in 1578 he asked the Crown for Letters Patent authorizing him to discover, explore, and settle America, they were quickly granted. They expired in six years; he had until 1584 to plant his colony. This was the first significant proposal advanced in England for the colonization of the New World and Gilbert promptly put it into action.

He mounted a formidable expedition of ten ships fitted out with enough food for a year of voyaging and then called on his Westcountry relatives for help. Sir John and Adrian Gilbert, his brothers, subscribed in the venture. Walter Ralegh's brother, Carew, agreed to be captain of the *Hope of Greenway* and Walter himself became captain of the *Falcon*, a ship which belonged to the Queen and probably represented her stake in the venture. It is difficult not to feel significance in the fact that the Queen's ship was assigned to Ralegh; it may indicate that he knew the Queen and was known by her a few years earlier than has generally been thought. Certainly if he had not before, he would now come in for some attention from the Queen. Elizabeth was sensitive about her property, especially naval vessels; the captain of one of them would be an object of her concern.

There was the usual delay in fitting out the ships and, as frustration mounted, Henry Knollys quarrelled with Gilbert and, taking three ships, sailed out on his own privateering expedition. The seven remaining ships were scattered twice before they finally cleared harbour on November 19.

It was Gilbert's 'weird' to be plagued by having his exploits, which were usually failures, memorialized by bad poets. Thomas Churchyard, whose verse hobbled on blistered feet, wrote what, with some truth and much charity, may be called a long poem to be read at an entertainment given to the Queen in 1578 after the ships had departed. Sir Humphrey Gilbert and his friends were gone, he said, but whither no man knew. And that was true. Gilbert had been clever at confusing the issue: he had started rumours that he was going to the *Terra Australis Incognita*, to Newfoundland, to the Spanish West Indies, to Florida and to Carolina. Not even the Spaniards could find out where he really was. With Gilbert on the voyage was

> Ralegh ripe of sprite
> And rare ripe many ways.

Some believed these brothers were after gold. O no! Churchyard exclaims; they are driven by love of God and country to seek fame and their country's good.

Not having any idea what the brothers were really doing, he resorted to his poetic imagination and produced a flight of fancy as he pictured the 'noble pilgrims'.

> They feed on biscuit hard,
> And drink but simple beer,
> Salt beef and stockfish dry as keck
> Is now their greatest cheer.
>
> And when seasick (God wot) they are,
> About the ship they reel,
> And stomach belcheth up
> A dish that haddocks seek.

Churchyard then made the alarming promise that when the adventurers returned he would produce an entire book that 'to the lofty skies' would raise their 'rare renown'.

The voyage was plagued from the start by bad luck, or was it ineptness ? Gilbert himself put into an Irish port to revictual and ultimately returned to England, where he found that Carew Ralegh had arrived ahead of him, the *Hope of Greenway* having sprung a leak. The impatient captain of the *Red Lion* slipped away, probably to join Knollys, leaving only Ralegh and three other ships to carry out the venture. After one or more of the remaining ships had apparently deserted to engage in piracy, Ralegh, 'to do something worthy honour' set a course for the West Indies.

But he never arrived. Somewhere at sea he met Spanish warships. All that is known of the encounter is preserved by a Westcountry historian who was always tender of Ralegh's reputation.

Infinite commodities in sundry respects would have ensued from that voyage if the fleet had, according to appointment, followed you, or yourself had escaped the dangerous sea fight, wherein many of your company was slain, and your ships therewith sore battered and disabled.

That is, there were plans of great significance and scope which failed to be carried out only because of desertions and a sea-fight which went badly. In May, 1579, Ralegh was back in England with the Queen's ship damaged. Elizabeth disliked having her possessions decrease in value, but it appears that she blamed Gilbert, not Ralegh, for the fiasco.

Not even the piracy was successful. Either Knollys' or Ralegh's group took two prizes, one French and one Spanish. Both had been taken on the civilized side of the line and the Spanish ship really belonged to the Flemish. That was when the Privy Council ordered the prizes returned and put Gilbert and Ralegh under surety not to engage in further piracy.

About that time Gilbert and Ralegh were ordered to use their remaining warships to intercept James Fitzmaurice Fitzgerald, an Irish rebel believed to be on his way from Spain to Ireland to raise a rebellion. Had they succeeded, the history of both Ireland and Ralegh would have been far different, but again they failed. Fitzmaurice landed in west Ireland and there the long, desperate Desmond rebellion began.

Gilbert began to get the reputation of an unlucky sailor, a bad name to have among the superstitious brotherhood of the sea. The Spanish ambassador wrote Philip that not a single sailor in the Gilbert-Ralegh expedition had been paid. Obviously Gilbert had intended to make enough money from piracy to pay for the voyage, and he might have done so if it had been better managed.

What was the intent of the first Gilbert-Ralegh expedition? It remains one of the most fascinating puzzles of Ralegh's life. Quite obviously it was something more than an exploring probe. Later when Ralegh wished to find a site for a colony, he sent only two small ships to explore, followed by five to colonize. Here were ten ships assembled, well-armed and supplied. Yet there is no evidence that there were any colonists aboard. The best guess is that they intended either to attack Spanish shipping or to raid Spanish towns in the New World. If their plans had succeeded, these impecunious projectors might then have coasted up the eastern seaboard of the present United States to look for colonizing sites. They then likely would have hunted for the Strait of Anian and finally returned to England by way of the Grand Banks. But nothing had worked out. In all the sea-going history of England, few voyages were such complete failures. About the only gain from the entire venture was that England was spared Churchyard's book.

Humphrey Gilbert was becoming a desperate man. But Ralegh, in his ingenious way, salvaged something from the debacle. Without previous experience in leading naval expeditions, he had made it part way to the West Indies, had engaged in a serious fight and had, at least, returned alive. Now he turned his intellectual energies toward mastering the art of navigation and naval warfare. To assist him in his long-neglected studies, he employed a young man named Thomas Hariot, who would one day prove to be England's finest mathematician as well as Ralegh's lifelong friend. And it was also at this time that Ralegh, smarting from his humiliation by Spanish gunners, determined to design and build a galleon, a warship that could, if necessary, stand alone against a fleet of Spanish sail.

Shortly after the Gilbert-Ralegh fiasco, Sir Francis Drake made a far different return to England. He sailed into Plymouth harbour having drawn a 'long liquid line' about the world. The belly of the *Golden Hind* was heavy with gold and silver, with jewels and spice; when Elizabeth realized that she would receive about 1,200 per cent return on the money she had invested in the voyage, she sent Drake word that he might keep 10,000 pounds for himself, the equivalent, perhaps, of a quarter of a million dollars today. She also knighted him.

Englishmen flocked to the harbour to see the *Golden Hind* and it became a kind of national shrine. Overnight Drake was England's greatest sea-faring hero. It was suitable that he should become captain of one of Her Majesty's ships of the line and he chose the *Revenge*, a 500-ton galleon which he believed to be the finest fighting ship in the world.

Drake, in one stroke, had achieved everything Ralegh wanted: the smiling favour of his Queen, the adulation of the people, money, and a great fighting ship. Drake had executed a difficult mission with astonishing technical perfection. Ralegh had not. Ralegh's scheme may very well have been imaginative and daring, but his first great effort had been swallowed up in the shadow that lies between the conception and the execution. His money was gone; his reputation was below the horizon. Destiny had smiled on Drake and frowned on him. But Destiny sometimes yielded to virtue; Coligny had taught him that. There were other fields of honour and opportunity. Ireland, now seething with rebellion, was one of these, a promising place for an impecunious young captain who thought of himself as a child of Destiny.

4

Ralegh in Ireland

What attracted Ralegh to Ireland? Among other things, certainly, the chance to make a name and a fortune. Being a second son, he would inherit no estate. Like many of the Westcountry gentry, he had made some money from privateering, engaging in legalized piracy under letters from the Huguenots or William of Orange, but he had sunk it all in Gilbert's venture. He would never re-coup on a captain's pay in Ireland; he knew that. But he also knew that on November 2, 1579, the Earl of Desmond had been proclaimed a traitor and his lands escheated to the Crown. Through those lands, a great river, the Blackwater, ran placidly to the sea. There was much timber; the streams were stocked with fish; the soil was rich and deep and there were minerals beneath it. Compared with the lean land from which he came, Ireland was a voluptuous country. Energy and intelligence could make an Irish estate into one of the finest in the kingdom.

Besides, in those green lands, the Ralegh family had already made an investment in red blood. In 1569, the year Ralegh went to France, an entire band of his kinsmen and neighbours left the Westcountry and founded an English colony in Munster. Sir Peter Carew, a near kinsman, was in charge of the colonists; Ralegh's cousin, Richard Grenville, went and also a distant cousin, Warham St. Leger, who was to become Ralegh's life-long friend.

This colonizing was a grim affair, for colonists acquired land only by ejecting the Irish inhabitants, who then faced starvation. What Ralegh later wrote in his *History* about the difficulties of colonization could apply either to America or Ireland.

Certainly the miseries of war are never so bitter and many as when a whole nation, or a great part of it, forsaking their own seats, labour to root out the established possessors of another land, making room for themselves, their wives and children . . . In these migrations, the assailants bring so little with them, that they need all which the defendants have, their lands and cattle, their houses and their goods, even to the cradles of the sucking infants. The merciless terms of this controversy arm both sides with desperate resolution.

And it was so in Ireland. When the Irish became hungry enough, they massacred Carew's colonists and he retaliated swiftly, brutally, putting men, women, and children to the sword. James Fitzmaurice Fitzgerald countered by burning the entire south country; if Irishmen could not eat, Englishmen should go hungry too. Famine had received another invitation to Ireland; as usual she would come.

To rescue his Devonshire friends and kinsmen, Lieutenant-Colonel Humphrey Gilbert was sent to Munster and, in six weeks, through terror and cruelty, he pacified the land. Apparently conceiving himself as another Tamburlane, he would summon a castle to surrender. If it did, he treated its inhabitants honourably; if not, he refused to parley again or hear any entreaties; he would sack the city or castle and slaughter everyone within it, even the babies.

Gilbert's final act of terror was pathologically sadistic. Every night when he made camp, he had the heads hacked off the bodies of all who were slain that day. Of those heads, he made a double row which lined the path to his tent. Any Irishman, or woman, who wished to speak with him had to walk that grisly gauntlet, then enter the tent, fall on his knees, confess himself a traitor and sue for mercy. These tactics earned him a knighthood in England and the everlasting contempt and hatred of the Irish. But by means of those tactics he achieved the swiftest pacification any Irish rebellion had ever known.

When Ralegh went to Ireland, ten years after this rebellion, he defended Gilbert's tactics and was apparently prepared to adopt them. But still later, when he wrote the *History* and was obsessed with the theme of human cruelty, without mentioning

Gilbert or Ireland, he made comments that contemporaries would likely have recognized as applicable to his desperate half-brother. One such comment concerned Cassander, who had adopted tactics of terror similar to Gilbert's.

His carefulness to destroy those women and children whose lives hindered his purpose, argues him to have been rather skilful in matters of arms, than a valiant man, such cruelty being a true mark of cowardice.

Again, in writing of the Romans, without mentioning Gilbert, Ralegh comments on tactics like his.

It was the manner of the Romans, as often as they took a town by assault, to put all that came in their way to the sword, whatsoever they were, without regard. This they did to make themselves terrible, and the better to work such impressions in the minds of those with whom they had to do, they used often times to kill the very dogs and other beasts that ran athwart them in the streets, hewing their bodies asunder, as men delighted in shedding of blood.

Some think, Ralegh writes, 'by cruelty to change hatred into fear,' but he believes it is a bad policy.

Anyone who knows Gilbert's unquenchable anxiety about people's opinions of his ability and courage, will suspect that Ralegh had him specifically in mind when he wrote,

He that suspecteth his own worth, or other men's opinions, thinking that less regard is had of his person than he believeth to be due to his place, will commonly spend all the force of his authority in purchasing the name of a severe man . . . and the fear wherein they live, which are subject unto oppression, carries a show of reverence to him that does the wrong; at least it serves to dazzle the eyes of underlings, keeping them from prying into the weakness of such as have jurisdiction over them.

So Ralegh thought later. But when he arrived in Ireland, he was aware that his Westcountry kinsmen still held title deeds to Irish lands; he knew that Gilbert had won the favour of the Queen by suppressing a rebellion there; and he knew that an estate and a title awaited the man who could solve, even in some degree, the incredible tangle of what had been known for a century as 'the Irish problem'.

Throughout Elizabeth's reign, Ireland posed a serious threat to England's security, a threat that neither Elizabeth nor anyone else found a way to remove. The stubbornly independent Irish created continual difficulty; they were Celtic and Catholic and intractable, always rebelling or threatening to rebel somewhere or other. But worse than that, in their hostility to England they stood ready to invite the Italian, the Frenchman, the Spaniard to their shores, anyone who would fight with them against England. And since the entire naval strength of England was insufficient to secure the Irish sea coast against invasion, Ireland was an inviting door, open to England's most formidable enemies. If Philip of Spain ever accepted the invitation and secured a fortified port on the south or west coast of Ireland, England's flank would be exposed, she would lose control of her northern sea routes to America and the Grand Banks and, most frightening of all, the wild Irish kerns might be turned into disciplined soldiers. England's position would then be desperate; there was stark truth in the old proverb:

> He that will England win,
> Let him in Ireland begin.

England's first problem, then, was to gain a secure hold on Ireland and she seemed unable to do it. The basic difficulty was the incompatability and mutual incomprehensibility of two cultures, Celtic and Saxon, with different institutions, ways of life, and habits of thought. More specifically, it was impossible to impose order on a country that was disorganized to the point of chaos and constantly torn by local raids and feuds. There was, for instance, neither a central ruler nor a central city, conquest of which would transfer control to a conqueror. Nor was there any unifying principle of social order, even in the holding and transfer of land. Ireland did, to be sure, have its own institutions and modes of order, but they were decentralized and tribal.

The ancient Irish system of land tenures, for example,

was wholly unlike England's where all land in theory belonged to the Crown and was granted in perpetuity to subjects if they were loyal. The Crown's control lay in its power to escheat the land of a traitor and sell it or confer it upon a faithful subject. In Ireland, on the other hand, each great chief was independent and absolute in his demesne, which was peopled by tenants who were, in fact if not in name, serfs: they worked the land, turned over its produce to the chief, and received from him enough to maintain life. Even on adjoining lands outside his demesne, a great chief had the oppressive rights of 'coign and livery', the power to require freeholders to feed and billet troops and horses. A yeoman farmer might see the whole product of a year's work confiscated in a week if war demanded it. And warfare was perpetual. Tenants thus impoverished would take to the hills in despair, to raid, to steal, to live by their wits. So chiefs often unscrupulously exacted coign and livery simply as a means of expropriating lands. And there was no appeal, for although written laws existed, they gave no protection because illiterate people could not find out what they were. Besides there was no formal system of courts to make judgments and no machinery to enforce them. And so, as a contemporary, Sir John Davies, said, the chiefs ate up the people as though they were bread.

Although the chief held his land absolutely, the lack of a clear law of succession added to the confusion. On the death of a chief, the law of tanistry came into effect, providing for an election in which all those of the blood royal were eligible. As the chief grew old, his potential successors began to plot, hire assassins, or lead raids to demonstrate their courage and fitness as warriors. 'Struggle for lordship,' wrote a contemporary historian, 'was the curse of the country.'

Confusion at the death of a chief was compounded by the custom of gavelkind, which required then a fresh division of the lands among all those eligible, including the numerous illegitimate children. Nor did the custom of fostering and gossip simplify matters; children were given or sold to foster parents, to whom they owed fierce, unquestioning loyalty in whatever mischief might be undertaken.

59

The lowest social unit was the *creaght*, a restless wandering group whose life depended on its small herd of cattle; their one pre-occupation was to keep them from raiders and warlords. They lived in huts of wattle and daub which they would abandon at need and move on. The kerns who herded the cattle could neither read nor write; they did not even have any formal religious instruction. They wore their hair in a thick bush, a shock of which, called a 'glibb', hung down before their eyes to hide them – the English believed – so that they could lie undetected. They were naked as needles under their mantles, which served both as clothing and bed.

Another great problem of this chaotic society was the Red-shanks or gallowglasses who had originally been imported from Scotland by Irish lords as mercenary warriors. By Elizabeth's time many of them were marrying and settling land, but were no less devoted to a life of warfare. When a fight was in prospect, they would mutter dark Celtic charms, make crosses in the earth, arm themselves with wicker shields and swords, spears or bows and arrows and, wailing their weird war cries, clashing their swords, would run like a mob full at the enemy. It can be imagined what happened when they ran against the pikes, firmly set and trained to stand fast.

The recreation of the chiefs was indistinguishable from their business: raiding for cattle, burning crops and houses, raping women and terrorizing the kerns. And they paid Celtic bards to glorify these deeds. As one disgruntled Englishman put it,

> Now when their guts be full,
> Then comes the pastime in,
> The bard and harper melody
> Unto them do begin,
> This bard he doth report
> The noble conquests done . . .

Above all else the chiefs desired immortality in verse. And so past raids were immortalized and future ones inspired. This glorification shocked England's gentle poet, Edmund Spenser. Taught in the classics, he believed that the true poet was an ethical philosopher, a man who glorified action directed by reason. But these Celtic bards praised lawless and unchecked violence. What, Spenser thought, can be expected of a land where the poet maintains disorder by glorifying it?

All of the English defensive policy in Ireland, then, was based on the belief that Ireland was a chaos, without social cohesion or rule of law, a land in which all estates of men were governed by appetite and passion. Before anything else, they believed (Spenser among them), this chaos must be reduced to order by force; the sword must precede the judge, not in indiscriminate slaughter, but to establish the authority of the Queen firmly. That is why men like Gilbert and Lord Grey felt justified in carrying out what can only be called massacres.

Two other methods, both less drastic, had also been tried. In order to stabilize land tenures, Henry VIII had required the largest estates to be surrendered to the Crown in order that he might re-grant them and bestow English titles of nobility on large landowners. Now if these Irish noblemen committed treason, their lands would be forfeit to the Crown. But this device, while it did strengthen the English position, also created new bitterness and grievance, for the intricate puzzle of Celtic land law made it inevitable that the great nobles were given some lands that the lesser chieftains had some claim to. Later, Ralegh's proposals for settling these still-live grievances brought him the attention of the Queen.

The attempt to settle the Irish problems by colonizing also raised unforeseen troubles. Large estates would be granted to English nobles, like the Westcountrymen who settled in Munster, and they, with some retainers, would move to Ireland to establish an enclave of English life. But soon the curse of the land began its work and Ireland started to absorb them. The new colonists put their children at the breasts of Irish foster-mothers and in a generation or two English became an alien language. Their very names disappeared. Veres became McSwynes, Fitz-Ursulas became MacMahons. They became as lawless as the natives and even became infected with 'Irish filthiness'. You could tell a man had English blood, it was said, if he changed his shirt as often as four times a year. 'It is the fatal destiny of that land,' wrote Spenser, 'that no purposes whatever which are meant for her good will prosper.'

The fear that Ireland might become England's Achilles' heel was intensified when in 1570, a most critical moment in Anglo-Irish relations, the Pope had issued a bull excommunicating Elizabeth, freeing her subjects from 'all manner of duty, fidelity, and obedience'. He further commanded, under threat of a curse, that none of her subjects should 'dare to obey her or any of her laws, directions, or commands'. This bull promoted a discontent among English Catholics that was not immediately dangerous, but in Ireland it invited the dreaded invasion of the Catholic monarch of France or Spain.

In 1569 the intransigent James Fitzmaurice Fitzgerald had burned Munster; ten years later Gilbert and Ralegh had been ordered to intercept him on the high seas and had failed. Now he was in Ireland and the threat of foreign invasion was a terrifying reality. The King of France had refused Fitzgerald's offer of the kingship of Ireland, but the Pope himself, who agreed to consider Philip II of Spain the rightful heir of Ireland, had promised his support and appointed Dr. Nicholas Sander as Papal Legate of Ireland. In July, 1579, Sander and Fitzmaurice landed at Dingle Bay with only a small force of Spaniards, Irishmen, and Englishmen, but with pikes and calivers for 5,000 men, intending apparently to turn gallowglasses into soldiers. Sander promptly distributed copies of the bull excommunicating Elizabeth and a proclamation which stated that the Pope had appointed Fitzmaurice to fight 'against a tyrant which refuseth to hear Christ speaking by his Vicar'. That was enough to stir up action. John and James of Desmond rose in revolt, burned the crops, drove off the cattle, raided settlements, set the bards to work glorifying the rebellion and prepared to drive the English out of Ireland.

The English Council in the Pale took counter-action. First, they ordered that all harpers and bards should be executed so that the newest exploits of the Desmonds would not be sung to the people. Then, having mustered all able-bodied men in the

Pale, they fought a series of indecisive actions. But in some of these, the rebellious Irish came on in good formation, displaying some knowledge of tactics and modern weapons. When the Earl of Ormonde, head of a great Irish clan, took the field on behalf of the Crown, he refused to engage with rebels who were so well-trained and re-inforced with foreign troops; his gallowglasses, he said, could not stand up to them.

The firebrand, James Fitzmaurice Fitzgerald, had been in Ireland only a few months when he annoyed one of the Burkes who promptly shot him dead. But the rebellion continued in a confused and inconclusive way. However they tried, Ormonde and the English could not bring the Irish rebels to open, decisive battle: instead, they would abandon their towns and cities, fade into the misty bogs or the hills, and strike from ambush. The English could not march against them effectively because they barricaded every path with interlaced trees and timbers until half the island was deforested. When they were beaten, they hid, listening to the minstrels and nursing their hatred of England, awaiting the promised foreign aid.

In England rumours had been circulating that a large force of trained Spanish troops might land in Western Ireland – as many as 5,000, a number almost as great as the entire English and loyal Irish forces combined. The Crown, seeing full-scale rebellion already in action and fearing a massive invasion, decided to send a new Lord Deputy to Ireland, a man with a reputation for efficiency and severity, Lord Grey de Wilton, whose father had suppressed the Prayer Book Rebellion so ruthlessly. Grey brought with him a twenty-eight-year-old poet and soldier of fortune as assistant secretary, Edmund Spenser. And another young poet and soldier of fortune, Walter Ralegh, accompanied him in command of a hundred foot soldiers. Grey arrived on the east coast of Ireland on August 12, 1580, grimly determined to repel the invasion and settle the Irish question.

Exactly one month later the long-expected foreign invaders arrived at St. Mary Wick, nearly Dingle Bay on the west coast, a town whose name had been vulgarized to Smerwick. But the huge Spanish army the English had expected did not appear: the invaders consisted of no more than eight hundred men, mostly Italians recruited by the Pope, neither highly disciplined nor very valiant. This pitiful force of strangers had come to help the Irish, assuming that they were going to a civilized country with an organized government, where they would be fed, supplied and re-inforced. But with their Roman concepts of order, they were doomed in that twilit Celtic world. Their only hope for success, or even survival, would have been to melt into the hills and join the roving bands in their guerilla warfare, for they got no help from the disorganized Celts, and soon faced a vastly superior force, equipped and trained for siege warfare. And they made the fatal mistake, relying on continental theories of warfare, of entrenching and fortifying Smerwick, preparing to withstand a siege.

Against them with 1,600 men marched the Earl of Ormonde, whose puzzling loyalty to the Crown was explained in Ireland by saying he had slept with the Queen. (Poor Elizabeth. Someone was always explaining her policies in terms of the bedroom. Not that she cared.) And in support of Ormonde, Lord Grey marched quickly with a troop of 600 foot and 200 horses. Of one of these bands of foot, Ralegh was captain.

As they were marching overland, Ralegh noticed that as soon as the English broke camp and moved on, the Irish came in as scavengers to take whatever was left. He therefore secured permission from Grey to lie in ambush when the rest of the army marched out. As he had expected, kerns flocked into the camp and Ralegh made them prisoner. One of them carried on his back a bundle of withies, that is, bands made of twisted willows which were used as halters for the horses. Ralegh asked the kern what the withies were for and he replied, 'To hang English churls.' It was the kind of answer Ralegh might have admired from an Englishman, but he had learned from his half-brother that natives must be dealt with firmly. He therefore simply replied that they would serve equally well to hang an Irish kern. The plucky Celt soon dangled.

When Grey arrived at Smerwick, instead of attacking

64

immediately, he began putting siege trenches around the city and awaited the arrival of Admiral Winter who was bringing seige guns from England. The guns arrived and the trenches were pushed to within one hundred yards of the garrison. Then Grey summoned the garrison and its officers came out to parley. Grey asked under whose commission they had come. They replied that they were serving under the Pope who had given Ireland to King Philip and had sent them in defence of the Catholic faith. It was, the English thought, a haughty speech; it was also clear that the invaders intended to fight.

When the parley ended, the battering began. Seige guns were mounted on both sides of the town, which was caught in a merciless cross-fire. After four days of continuous bombardment the walls were battered and an assault by the English was imminent. Then the garrison asked for a parley and Grey refused it. They then requested liberty to depart 'with honour' and return to Italy. Grey denied this and all other conditions; if they wished to surrender, it must be unconditionally. Later it was said, and the Irish believed, that Grey had promised them their lives; and the 'faith of Grey' is still an Irish phrase for a broken promise. But Spenser was there and heard it all; he was later emphatic and emotional in support of Grey's version.

Finally the Italians asked for a truce until morning. Grey agreed provided that hostages were left to secure it. It was done. That night the Italians, who had sensed the flint in the Puritan Grey, uneasily hung out a white flag. 'Misericordia, misericordia,' they cried. It was unfortunate for them that they begged their lives in the language of Babylon, for Grey then realized that the Lord of Hosts had delivered the enemy to him and that he was, for this occasion, to be a vessel of wrath.

Captain Wingfield entered the fort and directed the Italians to remove all their armour and stack it neatly. Across the top of it they laid their pikes. In the morning, Grey asked who had the ward of the day among his own troops. Captain Ralegh, was the reply, and Captain Mackworth. Grey gave his orders. First two men, one Irish and one English, who had assisted Dr. Nicholas Sander and thus had fought against the armies of the

Lord, had their arms and legs broken. Then they were hanged. Some pregnant females, lascivious women of Canaan, who had serviced the lusts of the invaders were hanged too.

With the preliminaries out of the way, Grey ordered Ralegh and Mackworth to put the remainder of the Italian troops to the sword. The two captains repeated the order to their companies and the business began. Two hundred men, fully armed, marched among the now disrobed Italians. Each soldier had to kill four, that was the simple arithmetic. Bones turn the edges of swords and so they did as they had been taught in their basic training. They slashed to the left or right side of the neck just above where it joins the shoulder or they made a quick thrust to the belly.

When men face death and can only helplessly wait for it, many of them lose control of the sphincter muscles of bladder and bowel. It is sad and degrading. Some of these men, we may suppose, pleaded, some prayed, some fell to the ground and closed their eyes, some stood scornfully, some clasped crucifixes or feverishly turned their beads. Most of them fell with the first thrust but few died then. They had to be dispatched. The officers would simply indicate where more needed to be done and it was hack, cut, and thrust again.

Those who did the killing were men too. It is one thing to kill in the heat of battle when fear begets anger; it is another to cut down an unarmed man. Some of the executioners must have become physically and noisily sick; possibly some fainted. The captain observes, turns a corpse over with his foot, orders a man who is holding back to get on with it. Finally it was all done: no more misericordias, merely silence. The bodies were stripped and lay naked on the sand 'as gallant goodly personages as ever were beheld'.

Now the bodies must be buried. A trench was prepared and the corpses dragged along and flung into it. Corpses are offensive. They make noises that would have embarrassed them moments earlier; they refuse to close their mouths; they stare impolitely; the hands and legs indulge in strange grotesqueries. It is necessary to cover them quickly with the earth that impartially receives all her children and hides their ugliness and shame.

The massacre shocked Europe (all massacres shocked Europe). As usual, Elizabeth had known nothing of it; naturally she disapproved publicly. But the truth is that she wrote Grey commending him on that piece of business but complaining because certain officers had been spared for ransom instead of being killed. Now Elizabeth was not a cruel woman: as the Duke of Sussex once said quite truthfully, Elizabeth had 'never showed herself extreme to any'. That she should have written such an uncharacteristic letter is a measure of her fear and frustration at her failure to cover England's unprotected flank in the west; she seemed to be able to deal with everything else.

One cannot help wondering: when the slaughter began, when steel was proving again its superiority to flesh, did the eyes of those two young poets meet, Spenser and Ralegh, both eager for glory and for Irish lands, those two inheritors of the classical tradition that man's duty was to increase the quotient of rationality on earth? And if their glances touched, what did each man see? They never really met, so they said, until nine years later. And Ralegh never wrote or spoke a word that has survived about his part in the massacre. But the most moving theme of his *History* is human cruelty. When he came to write it, he had had occasion to suffer it personally and to understand it better. His part in the massacre at Smerwick is the ugliest thing he ever did. To know that is to know the worst.

After the massacre, things were relatively quiet. As Ralegh lay in garrison at Cork with leisure to consider ways of bettering his fortunes, he found reason to suspect that the Lord Barry, an Irish nobleman with an English title, was not loyal to the Crown. From his strategically located estate on the Great Island of Cork Harbour and the adjacent mainland, Barry's followers were making raids against the English. When he could not induce the Earl of Ormonde to act, Ralegh rode to Dublin and presented his case directly to Grey and the Irish Council. He not only accused Barry, but asserted that an

English president was needed in Munster to replace Ormonde. He recommended his brother, Humphrey Gilbert, whose mere presence, Ralegh assured them, would end the rebellion. The Council decided to give Barry Castle into Ralegh's keeping and assigned some horsemen to support his company of foot. But Ormonde, not liking the arrangement, got the orders altered, and Ralegh complained angrily that Ormonde did not want any Englishman to have anything. Ormonde, he charged, was a man of inordinate ambition and really wanted Barry's estate for himself: 'I think that all is too little for him.' But Ormonde, anxious to further a reasonable Irish policy, resisted confiscation and, instead, delivered the castle into the custody of Barry's loyal mother. This so outraged Barry that he burned his own estate and set fire to the crops. He was then proclaimed a traitor and his estate escheated to the Crown.

As it turned out, Ralegh's anger was not only understandable but justified. He was young and impatient, to be sure, and always believed he could do a better job than those over him. But Barry did prove to be the traitor Ralegh said he was, just as Ormonde's policy proved hapless. But Ralegh was not without self-interest too, and he continued to cast covetous eyes upon the Barry estate. On May 1, 1581, he wrote Lord Grey that he had already done some rebuilding at Barry Castle and had left a guard there. If Lord Grey should think Ralegh worthy to keep the castle, he would, at his own cost, 'build it up again and defend it for Her Majesty'. But Barry Castle eluded him for another seven years.

Enough stories survive from Ralegh's days in Ireland to show his qualities as a fighting man and a captain, courageous, resourceful, and sometimes foolhardy. Once when he was returning from Youghal to Cork he blundered into a trap that had been laid for him by John Fitzedmund Fitzgerald, who was also Seneschal of Imokellie. Ralegh had a few Irish foot soldiers and six horsemen, two of whom were regular cavalry and four of whom were mounted shot. He was riding out in front with the rest straggling along behind. He forded a river ahead of his troop and, in this exposed position, the Seneschal, with twelve horse, charged him. Ralegh turned and raced for the river but was cut off. In the melee Ralegh broke away, rode through the river and out the other side. In the meantime, his men, seeing the fight, came running forward. The first man there was Henry Moyle, a Devonshire man. Moyle plunged into the stream where his horse reared and threw him. He called out to Ralegh to save him; Ralegh turned, seized his horse by the bridle and brought it to him. Moyle, dripping wet and overcharged with adrenalin, made a mighty leap on to his horse's back which carried him clear over the horse and into the mire on the other side. Moyle's horse ran off and was taken by the Irish; Ralegh was now faced with the Seneschal's twelve horsemen. He held his ground, protecting Moyle, a loaded pistol in one hand, his staff in the other. The first one to come at him would be dead, and the Irish hesitated long enough for his straggling troop to reach the river. The Seneschal then turned and rode off.

Later, at a formal parley where Grey and the Earl of Ormonde were present, Ralegh taunted the Seneschal with cowardice. The Seneschal was silent, but one of his men finally spoke up to say that his master had been a coward that day but would not be again. Thereupon the Earl of Ormonde offered an immediate challenge. He and Ralegh, he said, would meet the Seneschal and the Earl of Desmond at the same ford. If he preferred, the Seneschal could bring two men with him or four, or whatever number he pleased and Ralegh and Ormonde would bring the same number. Again there was no answer. Later Ormonde and Ralegh sent the Fitzgeralds a formal challenge, but it was never answered. The English could not comprehend such conduct; they would die rather than refuse the field of honour. But the Irish didn't care about English customs; besides they knew they were at a tremendous disadvantage in such an affair. Their Irish cobs were too small to run success- fully against English war horses. Besides, since the Irish saddles had no stirrups, Irish cavalry could not set their lances in rest; rather, in a most awkward manoeuvre they struck backwards over their shoulder with the spear. In any kind of confrontation of horse, the English simply swept the Irish horse away by the force of their charge. If there had been a meeting at the ford, the Irish rebellion would likely have ended right there with the deaths of the two leading spirits of the rebellious Fitzgeralds.

Repeatedly Ralegh and his band gambled against the odds. In the autumn of 1581, with eight horse and eighty foot, he routed David Barry, who had hundreds of men. Ralegh cut off one band of Barry's footmen and charged them with only six horse. The kerns turned and fought well, killing five of the six horses and wounding Ralegh's horse so that it went plunging out of control among the Irish troops. His life was in extreme peril. But he had risked his life at the ford for his men and most soldiers will return that kind of decency. Nicholas Wright, the only man left with a horse under him, charged the six footmen who had surrounded Ralegh and scattered them. Then James Fitzgerald, a loyal Irishman, came to the rescue of Ralegh, along with one of his kerns. The action was hot and the fighting was hand to hand. The kern went down and Fitzgerald was being pressed hard. Ralegh cried out, 'Wright, if thou be a man, charge above hand and save the gentleman.' Wright charged, cutting down one of the Irish and scattering the rest. Then his horse fell and Ralegh's band were now all on foot. A number of them were killed and two were taken prisoner, but Ralegh and the others finally fought their way out and made it back to the garrison.

John Hooker, a contemporary Westcountry historian, says that Ralegh performed many such feats but one, especially, he thinks, deserves 'commendation and perpetual remembrance'. Since the English had suspicions about the reliability of Lord Roche, a supposedly loyal Irishman, Ralegh was ordered to bring him into Cork to be questioned by the governor of Munster. Irish intelligence being much better than the English, both the Seneschal of Imokellie and David Barry knew that Ralegh would be marching on Roche's castle. They took positions between Cork and Roche's estate, one with 800 men, the other with 500, to wait for Ralegh and his ninety soldiers. Then Ralegh showed the quick wit and adaptability to Irish warfare that made him a successful captain. Roche's castle was twenty miles away. Ralegh ordered his men 'upon pain of death' to be ready to march by ten of the clock that night. In darkness, in complete silence, he and his men threaded their way through the ambush and arrived in the early dawn outside Roche's castle. Surprised, some five hundred of the townsmen armed themselves and, in general disorder, advanced on Ralegh and his men. Ralegh set his troops in battle order and held off the townsmen with his pikes and hackbuts while he and five other men parleyed at the gate and were admitted.

With Irish gallantry Roche called for dinner. While the host and his unexpected guests parleyed, Ralegh's men slipped out of the battle line, a few at a time, and entered the castle. The townsmen ceased to be alarmed after a time and began to disperse. Soon all of Ralegh's men were inside. Then Ralegh informed Roche that he and his lady must accompany him to Munster. Roche politely declined, but Ralegh told him that he had no choice; he called his troops and Roche submitted. Now Ralegh had to get his captives back through the ambush. Again he marched at night in a severe storm, stumbling over stones and through bogs. One soldier died from a bad fall and all were exhausted, but the prisoners were brought safely to Munster. Ralegh had surprised the Irish by using their own tactics against them. Roche, incidentally, was acquitted and he and his sons remained loyal subjects of the Queen.

Despite the chivalric derring-do, Ralegh was restless in Ireland, partly because he felt that he was wasting himself in a futile endeavour. Even if he had had good troops, fighting the Irish, with their dispersed guerilla tactics and their willingness to destroy their own land, would be a slow, wasteful and indecisive process. And with the kind of soldiers he was given, even qualified success seemed hopeless. Men of any kind were hard to get, for the Irish service had a particularly vicious reputation. When volunteers were inadequate, the justices of the peace back in England were supposed to draft suitable men. But not seeing much point in sending fine boys to die of Irish fever, they usually rounded up the unemployed and drifters or raided the local jails. When he had been in Ireland a year, Ralegh wrote,

There is great need of a supply in Munster, for the bands are all much decayed . . . Besides, the men are such poor and miserable creatures as their captains dare not lead them to serve. If Your Honours beheld them when they arrive here, you would think them far unfit to fight for Her Majesty's crown.

Even these men were hard to hold once they had arrived for, as Sir Henry Sidney said, all places on earth had to give way to Ireland when it came to hardships for soldiers. There was much swamp and bog; victuals were scarce and unreliable; there were strange diseases and it was well known that for every ten soldiers who landed there, only five would return. It is small wonder that desertion was a major problem: great armies simply melted away. It was the curse of the land.

Ralegh also complained bitterly to the Earl of Leicester that he would like better things to do; if his Lordship knew of something significant, Ralegh would perform it.

I will be found as ready, and dare do as much in your service, as any man you may command; and do, neither, so much despair of myself but that I may be some way able to perform as much.

Were it not that Lord Grey is a servant of Leicester's, he continued, he would disdain the Irish service, 'as much as to keep sheep', which gives not only his view of Ireland, but also something of his real feeling about pastoral life which, like other poets of his time, he occasionally celebrated in his verse.

He also wrote a discontented letter to Walsingham emphasizing that things were going badly in Ireland. The Earl of Ormonde, he said, was far too lenient; he had been Lord General of Munster for two years and there were now 1,000 more traitors than when he took office.

Would God the service of Sir Humphrey Gilbert might be rightly looked into; who, with the third part of the garrison now in Ireland, ended a rebellion not much inferior to this, in two months.

The truth is that Ormonde was both effective and severe in the field but he had sympathies with Ireland which made him wish to try for some solution less drastic than extermination.

Ralegh cannot bear to take the Queen's shilling, he tells Walsingham, and not do the Queen's work; she is abused in Ireland. 'I will rather beg than live here and endure it.' These letters are pure Ralegh; they show his discontent, his thwarted ambitions, the feeling that his talents are being wasted and, in the background, in occasional eloquent phrases, a hint of the horror of English policy in Ireland: Ireland is a 'common woe', a 'lost land'. Still, he does not fail to mention that he would like to get Barry Court and the Island.

By this time, between Grey's harshness and Irish retaliation, the land of Munster was devastated, the castles burned, the cattle driven off and the people starving. Edmund Spenser saw and recorded it.

Munster . . . was a most rich and plentiful country full of corn and cattle . . . yet ere one year and a half they were brought to such wretchedness as that any stony heart would have rued the same. Out of every corner of the woods and glens they came creeping forth upon their hands, for their legs would not bear them; they looked like anatomies of death; they spake like ghosts crying out of their graves; they did eat the dead carrions, happy where they could find them; yea, and one another soon after, insomuch as the very carcasses they spared not to scrape out of their graves; and if they found a plot of watercresses or shamrocks, there they flocked as to a feast for the time, yet not able long to continue withal; that in short space there were none almost left, and a most populous and plentiful country suddenly left void of man and beast; yet, sure, in all that war there perished not many by the sword, but all by the extremity of famine which they themselves had wrought.

The misery is unspeakably tragic, beyond comprehension. Fynes Moryson recorded a scene, later, in Tyrone's rebellion from which even Dante would have shrunk.

Three children (whereof the eldest was not above ten years old), all eating and gnawing with their teeth the entrails of their dead mother, upon whose flesh they had fed twenty days past, and having eaten all from the feet upward to the bare bones, roasting it continually by a slow fire, were now come to the eating of her said entrails in like sort roasted, yet now divided from the body, being as yet raw.

In the late autumn of 1581, after a little more than a year in Ireland, Ralegh returned to England, apparently because Elizabeth and the Privy Council sent for him. Grey and Ralegh were continuing to differ about Irish policy and so both were heard. Ralegh had more wit than Grey and was more articulate, and the Queen, who was inclined to notice handsome men, was much taken with him and his point of view. Grey favoured complete subjugation of the Irish and Anglicization of the country, an expensive policy that required a large standing army in Ireland, a constant supply by sea and a drain on the Treasury. He probably thought it unfair of Ralegh to appeal to the parsimony of the monarch 'who was never profuse in delivering out of her treasure', and who had always rather give grace than cash.

For Ralegh urged a policy that was less costly and somewhat more humane. It was based on one of the oldest, simplest and most effective strategies: divide and conquer. The essence of Ralegh's proposal was that the lesser Irish chieftains might be split away from the rebellious noblemen. He was aware that the lesser chiefs had grievances: they were still bitter because they felt they had been unfairly dealt with when Henry had regranted the land. And their grievance remained fresh because of the oppressive exactions of the overlords. Ralegh argued that the lesser chiefs supported the rebellious overlords reluctantly and out of fear that Elizabeth might pardon them; then they themselves could expect to be burned out and slaughtered by the pardoned earls, if they had not been faithful to them. On the other hand, if Elizabeth could persuade the lesser chiefs that their lives and properties would be protected by the Crown and that the rebelling noblemen were irrevocably doomed, then they might defect and bring their gallowglasses to the support of the government. The Irish, under Ralegh's proposal, would be given a larger part in determining their own destinies and in sharing

74

the expenses. It is impossible to say whether it would have worked out that way; at least it was a new idea in a situation which had not seen many tried.

Ralegh had earlier pushed past Ormonde, governor of Munster, to Lord Deputy Grey at Dublin; now he had pushed beyond Grey to London and apparently felt free to continue to do so. In January, 1582, William Cecil wrote to Lord Grey that Ralegh had made another of his thrifty suggestions: he thought that the cost of maintaining 500 soldiers in Munster might very well be shifted from the Crown to the Earl of Ormonde. In the following April, Elizabeth wrote Grey an unusual letter which indicated that even though Grey was angry and sensitive about him, she nevertheless intended to further Ralegh's career in Ireland. The band of Captain Applesey, who had died, was to be put under Ralegh; by giving him double the number of men that normally served under a captain, the Queen would also double his pay.

Our pleasure is to have our servant, Walter Ralegh, trained some longer time in that our realm for his better experience in martial affairs, and for the special care we have to do him good in respect of his kindred that have served us, some of them (as you know) near about our person.

To placate Grey, she indicates that it is in gratitude to Kat Ashley that she forwards Ralegh's career.

Grey's attitude, as would be expected, was straightforward and impolitic. Ralegh's plans, he said, were easy enough to scheme up but impossible 'for others to execute'. And when he heard that Ralegh was to return to Ireland, he candidly wrote William Cecil, 'I like neither his carriage nor his company; and therefore, other than by direction and commandment, and what his right can require, he is not to expect at my hands.'

But Ralegh did not return to Ireland. In her letter to Grey, Elizabeth had instructed that Ralegh was, temporarily, to appoint a lieutenant in his place while he was 'for some considerations by us excused to stay here'. Those considerations kept Ralegh more or less in the Queen's unstable grace for about seven years, a long sabbath of courtship and poetry, jest and serious conversation, duties of state and defence of the realm.

Meanwhile, in Ireland, the Earl of Desmond was captured on November 9, 1583, and beheaded. The Earl of Ormonde presented his head to Elizabeth, who had it impaled high over London Bridge. And long after Elizabeth died, it was said in Ireland that the ghost of the earl, mounted on horse shod with silver shoes, would rise at night from the waters of Lough Gur. When the wind from the ocean swept through the western valleys, it faintly carried along the fierce cries of the Desmond gallowglasses. Ralegh may have heard them; certainly no man in England listened more keenly to the winds that blew from that lost land.

5

Utopia in the New World

While Ralegh was in Ireland and for a year after his return to England in 1582, Gilbert was devoting immense energies towards utilizing his Letters Patent for colonization in the New World. It was partly through his brother, Gilbert, that Ralegh began to see and respond to the lure of America; he would be involved in the planning and financing of several expeditions, however, before he would actually voyage to the western world himself, seeking the golden city of Manoa.

What Gilbert intended was nothing less than the establishment of a new commonwealth in North America. His scheme, though typically grandiose, was also highly imaginative and surprisingly well thought out. His first need, of course, was money, everything he owned having been lost in the earlier venture. And he thought he saw a way to get it. The English Catholics, persecuted and oppressed by the harsh recusancy law of 1581, began to seek asylum elsewhere, and like the French Huguenots before them, they began to think of the New World as a haven. Some of them approached Gilbert who, for an undisclosed consideration, assigned to them 9,000,000 acres of land between Florida and Cape Breton.

When the Spanish ambassador heard of the plans, he persuaded the Pope to oppose them. Under pressure, English Catholic priests then withdrew their support and transmitted the ambassador's threats and warnings, reminding the prospective colonists of how Spain had slaughtered the French interlopers in Florida. Reluctantly the Catholic gentlemen dropped the project. But Gilbert was still determined to plant a colony before his Letters expired in 1584. He would manage it without the Catholics – although he could not refund their money.

Ralegh was determined to participate too. He had by now designed and built the *Bark Ralegh*, a ship of 200 tons, fast and heavily gunned, twice as large as the *Falcon* in which he had been beaten by the Spanish warships. He equipped the ship at his own expense, and Gilbert made it the vice-admiral of his fleet. It cost Ralegh some 2,000 pounds, which entitled him to about a half-million acres in his brother's commonwealth.

Gilbert's project aroused great enthusiasm in England, where many felt that the nation already had delayed too long in building an overseas empire. A Hungarian scholar at Oxford, Stephen Parmenius, wrote an *Embarkation Ode* in elegant Latin hexameters that conveyed the thrill of adventure that the English felt about the project, and brought into relation with it the haunting classical vision of a perfect way of life, the Golden Age. In those happy days long past, men had lived simply and peacefully off the fruits of the earth. They did not dye their clothing, wound the breast of Mother Earth with the plough, dig for minerals, or build ships to carry on trade. But since then, civilization had produced increasing deterioration in moral fibre and in the social climate; the Golden Age had degenerated into one of silver, then bronze, finally iron, the age in which mankind now obviously lived when Astrea, goddess of justice, had fled to the heavens. But Greek thought was cyclical: someday the Golden Age would return. This idea, which springs from the pastoral nostalgia which continually afflicts mankind, was rife in Renaissance England and men wondered if it might not be realized in the New World. After all, there were resemblances between Indians and men of the Golden Age; since they did not wear clothes, they could not dye them; they were resplendent, as John Milton was to say, in their 'first naked glory'. They did not value gold or money and they had no plows. By noticing only these negative similarities, for a time Englishmen were able to see what they wished to see, that America was a natural setting for Utopia.

Parmenius begins with a tribute to Gilbert, that lasting

ornament of the British race who will discover in the New World a land where the Spaniards do not practice bloody cruelties in the name of religion. There he will find a people sprung from mother earth who still retain the purity of their ancient manners. United under Gilbert's benign rule, the citizens of this new country will know neither fraud nor guile; they will find happiness in a virtue measured not by birth but by worth; there will be neither rich nor poor and liberty will flourish. But men usually pay dearly for confusing fantasy and reality. Parmenius became so enchanted with this vision that he offered his services to Gilbert and sailed with the expedition. On it he lost his life.

Nor was Parmenius the only poet of the occasion. Half the seadogs of England turned versifier for this event. John Hawkins' verse limped through the familiar arguments: religion would be brought to the natives, England's problem of overpopulation would be solved and, best of all, those who furthered the expedition would reap a 'private gain'. That was poetry the seamen could understand.

Even Sir Francis Drake was moved by the Muses. Though his lines are stilted, their sentiments express the man.

Who seeks by worthy deeds to gain renown for hire;
Whose heart, whose hand, whose purse is prest to purchase his desire:
If any such there be that thirsteth after fame,
Lo! here a means to win himself an everlasting name.

After much poetry and many delays, Gilbert's five ships were ready to sail; all he needed was Elizabeth's permission. At the last minute, swayed by some dark intuition, she refused to give it, for Gilbert, she said, 'was not a man of good hap by sea'. And she was right, though it was rather late to say so. But Ralegh, now on his long leave from Ireland, was high enough in the Queen's favour to persuade her to let Gilbert set out. Through Ralegh she sent him a talisman, an anchor guided by a lady, a traditional emblem signifying hope. It could, however, be interpreted to mean that Elizabeth herself would be the guiding spirit of the voyage. Through Ralegh she also wished

Gilbert 'great good hap and safety to your ship, as if herself were there in person, desiring you to have care of yourself, as of that which she tendereth'. And she demanded Gilbert's picture so that she might better remember her absent courtier. It was Elizabeth at her most gracious. All of this Ralegh sent Gilbert in a letter, and committed him 'to the will and protection of God, who sends us life or death as He shall please'.

On June 11, 1583, Gilbert set out towards Newfoundland, but Ralegh was not with him; Elizabeth would not permit him to sail with his ship. Two days later, the *Bark Ralegh* turned back. Her captain alleged that she had the plague aboard, but he refused to let Gilbert inspect the ship for himself. The truth probably was that the ship lacked victuals and supply which had either been eaten up during the long delay or else pirated ashore and sold, an example of the usual slack discipline in naval affairs that only Sir Francis Drake seemed able to cope with. Since Ralegh's ship was the largest and best in the expedition, its loss was deadly serious. As the remaining ships voyaged west they sailed into a fog and the *Swallow* seized the opportunity to slip away and do a little privateering. It was her raiding of a French fishing vessel, according to the captain of the *Golden Hart*, the godly Edward Hayes, that brought the entire venture into disfavour with Almighty God.

Though the expedition was to end in tragedy, Gilbert's conduct of it was full of unconscious comedy, for he was at once grandiose, self-important and humourless. At times it was pure comic opera. The expedition crossed the Grand Banks, swarming with fishing vessels of many nations, and in the harbour of St. John's, Newfoundland, which they approached on July 30, they found more ships that had put in for repair and refitting or were drying their fish on land. The English fishermen, who by general consent were delegated to enforce the unwritten rules by which the international fleets worked in harmony, refused Gilbert permission to enter the harbour. But Gilbert, grand as Alexander, was not to be denied his kingdom. He ordered battle stations and prepared to fight his way in. First, however, he sent the 'admiral' of the harbour a message that he carried a commission from Elizabeth. Immediately the English fishermen gave the signal to enter and the expedition sailed grandly in, so preoccupied with the importance of the occasion that Gilbert's own ship, 'by great oversight' hit a rock and grounded. The English fishing vessels towed her off, but it was not a good omen.

Gilbert's very first act, before he had even taken formal possession, was to impose a tax on every ship in the harbour, payable in biscuit, fresh fish, lobsters, and 'sundry delicacies'. The following day, Sunday, the English merchants took Gilbert and his men ashore and showed them their 'garden', a grove of wild raspberries, roses, and many other flowers, 'nature itself without art'.

Having solemnly 'explored' a harbour in common use for seventy-five years, grounded his ship and taxed the fleets, he came to the climax of the comedy the next day. He assembled all the merchants and fishermen he could dragoon and read them his royal commission. Then, after cutting a piece of turf and breaking off a twig, he lifted them up, one in each hand, and took possession of all land within six hundred miles in every direction for himself, his heirs, and his assigns forever. He now owned a piece of real estate twice the length and four times the breadth of the British Isles and almost as large as the Russia of his day. For a Dartmoor boy it was a great moment.

He then proclaimed that in his territory, now under the laws of England, three statutes would take effect immediately. All public exercise of religion would be according to the Church of England which meant that all fleets other than English would have to worship on the high seas. Second, anyone who attempted to dispute Her Majesty's right (or Gilbert's) to the territory would be guilty of treason and suffer the penalties thereof. The third, he must have felt, was pure gallantry. From observing Ralegh and other witty courtiers, Gilbert had learned that Elizabeth loved the gracious act, the personal tribute. Now he too would play the *preux chevalier*. Looking very stern, he said that if anyone spoke anything tending to dishonour the Queen his ears would be cut off and his ship confiscated. His auditors probably nodded and smiled; it must be true what they had heard about the goings-on in Elizabeth's bed chamber, with Gilbert's brother, among others. Finally Gilbert granted lands to the fishermen and merchants sufficient for the drying of their fish and charged them a fee for it. Then, having levied and collected another tax, he prepared to depart. With that part of his venture the fishermen cooperated happily.

Meanwhile some of his miners had been bringing in samples of ore containing what the miners were sure was silver. Edward Hayes doubted it and wanted the refiners to test it, but Gilbert shrewdly told him that it was not wise to refine it with so many aliens around. The best course was to take some ore aboard and try it when they were under way. Hayes was content.

But many of the crewmen were not. Among them were jailbirds and pirates, lazy and unmotivated, who had not been impressed with the noble charade of turf and twig or the shipping aboard of a single bin of ore. There were rich prizes all over the Banks and they meant to have a few. So many of the sailors deserted; some seized a fishing vessel and went off to raid. Others fled ashore and hid; some shipped aboard fishing vessels and went home to England. Many were sick; some died. Gilbert finally decided to send the *Swallow* home with the sick and to continue his voyage with the three remaining vessels. He then transferred his Admiral's flag to the *Squirrel*, a little pinnace of ten tons, no larger than a lifeboat, in order that he might explore the shoreline, looking for estuaries, or bays or islands where he could build the first English village in America.

The three ships sailed south along the unknown, uncharted shores of the stormy and rockbound North Atlantic coast. Since Gilbert was gone most of the time in his pinnace, the *Delight* had little to do but stand off shore and wait for him. The sailors grew bored and soon there were sounds of revelry, the trumpets, drums, fifes, cornets and hautboys. It struck the Puritan Hayes that the *Delight* was like the swan that sings before its death. And his premonition was right. On August 29, the wind rose, there came rain with a thick mist; the *Delight* struck, foundered, and went down with all hands. The ore was lost and the charts;

all the tools were gone and most of the supplies. Now Gilbert had only his pinnace and the forty-ton *Golden Hart*. For two days he bravely coasted through the rain and fog, risking his remaining ships to find survivors. There were none.

The two little boats turned eastward into the lowering Atlantic. On September 2, Gilbert stepped on a nail and came aboard the *Golden Hart* to have the surgeon dress the wound. Hayes urged him to stay in the larger boat. Certainly it would have been a normal procedure to transfer the Admiral's flag from the pinnace; as Hesiod had said, it was fine to admire a small ship as long as one's cargo sailed in a large one. But after so many failures, Gilbert suffered that old inner fear of not measuring up, that need to validate his courage once more: there had been the failure at Goes; the disaster of his first naval expedition which had led the Queen to think he was not a man of good hap at sea; the wholesale desertions of his men; the smiles behind his back when he had officiously annexed Newfoundland and defended the Queen's honour. No, if he left the pinnace, men would say that he lacked courage and he could not endure that. So he stayed with the little *Squirrel*, he and Hayes agreeing to carry their lights all night so as not to become separated.

It became apparent that Gilbert was profoundly depressed; he was distressed for the loss of his men, his book, his notes, and most of all for the loss of his ore. Just thinking about it, he flew into a rage and beat his cabin boy nearly senseless because, when Gilbert had told him to bring the ore off the *Delight*, back in the calm harbour at St. John's, the boy had forgotten to do so. Hayes continued to beseech Gilbert to join his ship, but Gilbert replied with a certain nobility, 'I will not forsake my little company going homeward, with whom I have passed so many storms and perils'.

North of the Azores they ran into an evil storm; St. Elmo's fire flamed on the yard arm; the seas swelled and rolled. The pinnace, at one moment, would be flung high on a crest and then would dip out of sight in a trough. Through it all, Gilbert sat on deck reading his Bible. He had found a phrase for the occasion and whenever the two ships came within hailing distance he would cry out, 'We are as near to Heaven by sea as by land'. It probably did not occur to him that they were also as far. About midnight the lights of the pinnace disappeared; the Atlantic had swallowed her; she was under with all her crew.

Gilbert's cheerful godliness in the face of death impressed his countrymen and purchased him a good deal of forgiveness for his cruelties and failures. For although he had failed again, he had died bravely in a great undertaking. He deserved something better than the hapless poetical tributes that immortalize his deeds like the one from the pen of a Westcountry admirer whose facts were awry but whose sentiment was impeccable.

> T'was but three days from Newfoundland,
> When overboard he falled,
> And as he was a-going down,
> Upon the Lord he called.

A more fitting tribute may be found in Hesiod: 'It is an awful thing to die among the waves.'

On September 22, 1583, the *Golden Hart* made Falmouth Harbour and within the week Ralegh had news of his brother's death. Once again he undertook to salvage what he could from Gilbert's failure. Immediately he asked the Queen to transfer to him the Letters Patent for colonizing North America. When the matter came before the House of Commons for approval, a remarkably constituted committee was appointed to study it; there were Richard Grenville, Ralegh's cousin; one of the Devonshire Courtenays, a neighbour; Sir Francis Drake, Sir Philip Sidney and some others. With such a Westcountry committee to make the recommendation and with the Queen urging approval, the outcome was inevitable. In March, 1584, Ralegh received exclusive rights to the North American continent north of Florida and within one month his reconnoitring expedition was on its way. Ralegh himself stayed in England, but increasingly he looked toward the west where even now his ships were seeking the unknown shores.

6

The Queen's Lover

Just two years before Ralegh was assigned the colonizing rights to the North American continent, he had scarcely known the Queen in any personal way. Now he was enjoying the royal prerogative and the royal smile more than any other man in England. It was April of 1582 when Elizabeth had given the first clear sign of her favour: for 'special considerations' she excused Ralegh from returning to Ireland and kept him at her court. Court rumours spread quickly and soon the Prince of Orange in the Netherlands was aware of Ralegh's privileged position for he asked him to convey a secret message to the private ear of Elizabeth urging her to help the Protestants in the Netherlands. In selecting his message, Orange must have had in mind the plainly dressed girl who, on learning of her accession to the throne, had piously quoted the psalms: *a domino factum est et mirabile in oculis nostris* – this is the Lord's doing; it is marvelous in our eyes. Or the girl who at her coronation cherished the English Bible that the Lord Mayor of London gave her, reverently kissing it and laying it on her breast. He must not have been aware that the now brilliantly educated and gorgeously dressed Queen disliked canting Puritans and distrusted those who quoted scriptures to their own purposes. 'Say to the Queen for me,' Orange said to Ralegh privately, '*Sub umbra alarum tuarum protegimur*;' we are defended under the shadow of thy wings. As Jehovah was to Israel, he implied, so Elizabeth was to the Netherlands. He misjudged the effectiveness of his Biblical message, but not of the messenger. Ralegh had become the new royal favourite.

How he first became her favourite no one knows. It may be,

as a pleasant legend has it, that once when the Queen came to a 'plashy place' a handsome, unknown young courtier had spread his rich cloak for her to walk on and she was moved by his gallantry and his looks. Since both the act and the response are quite in character the story is not improbable. Or it may be that it started when Ralegh wrote a line of verse on a window with his diamond. He must have heard the story that when Elizabeth had been imprisoned for complicity in Wyatt's rebellion, she had expressed her courageous resolution by scratching on the window pane with her diamond ring,

> Much suspected, by me
> Nothing proved can be,
>   Quoth Elizabeth, prisoner.

Anyhow, it is told that as Elizabeth was watching him once, Ralegh carved on the window with his diamond the line,

> Fain would I climb, yet I fear to fall.

And Elizabeth wrote under it,

> If thy heart fail thee, climb not at all.

But it is more likely that Ralegh's views on Ireland and his skill in presenting them first won Elizabeth's notice. But all of these stories suggest what the whole course of their relations demonstrate: more than anything else it was the quality of Ralegh's mind that attracted Elizabeth, his vigorous wit and the strength of his intellect. It did no harm that he was dashing and handsome, but of her other lovers Hatton was handsomer; Essex and Leicester matched Ralegh in looks and carriage, and they also had what for Elizabeth was a strong and mystical attraction, that of noble blood. But none of them could equal Ralegh in intellectual gifts.

When Ralegh and Elizabeth first became aware of one another, he was a vigorous thirty and she a mature forty-nine, a Queen who by sheer force of intellect and character had ruled

86

England for about a quarter of a century, unifying a torn and disrupted land by arousing an almost fanatical devotion to her person and maintaining the little country's independence in the midst of growing empires eager to swallow it. She accomplished this by skilled diplomacy based in part on her use of the possibility of making alliances through marriage. She had held out hopes of achieving that mystical body of hers, composed of a maidenhead and an empire, to Philip of Spain, the Duke of Anjou, his brother the Duke of Alençon, Prince Charles of Sweden, the Duke of Saxony, and the Archduke Charles. Coyly she would hint that perhaps, at last, this particular suitor was the one who would win it all, but each in turn finally went home denied. It was a pleasant game, sometimes exciting, and it kept Elizabeth in a strong position to bargain for the power and security of England. But it was a lonely life for a woman who desperately needed devotion and even love.

None of these official suitors gave her the personal affection she craved, but her emotions found outlet in a series of passionate attachments to handsome and brave young men: her relations with them, though never sexually consummated, were genuinely love affairs. For Robert Dudley, Earl of Leicester, whom she had known since she was eight years old, she had first developed a real passion. She loved him deeply and for many years. Her passion for him was so apparent that the ordinary people could be forgiven for feeling that the Virgin Queen was ill-named, as did a Cornishman who went to a tavern to console his disillusion in drink, and finally blurted out bitterly, 'Sir Robert doth swive the Queen'. Sir Robert should live so long. For it had soon become apparent to Dudley as it was to the Court that the Queen could be wooed physically only up to a point: she remained clinically a virgin, although she was not emotionally frigid. She wished to be courted passionately and physically; a stirring in the codpiece made her know that she was desired. And she liked to give something of herself. She made display of her elegant, slender fingers and white arms; during one interview, the French ambassador noticed, she took her gloves on and off 'a hundred times'. Her skin was white and her breasts symmetrical and firm and she occasionally, after the fashion of the time, displayed part or all of them so conspicuously that the French ambassador goggled and tattled around. Francis Bacon summed it up tersely.

She suffered herself to be honoured, and caressed, and celebrated, and extolled with the name of love; and wished it, and continued it, beyond the suitability of her age.

Desiring love, she encouraged her lovers; they became ardent, she became cool; finally, if they threatened or stormed, she dismissed them. She was, they said, 'apter to raise flames than to quench them'. To all she made her silent plea: give me pleasure but take none.

Why, then, was she a virgin? One explanation that passed current in the taverns was given by Ben Jonson to Drummond of Hawthornden. Well into his cups and enjoying shocking his delicate-minded host, Jonson said that the Queen was a virgin by necessity; she had a heavy membrane which could not be broken although, he said, taking another drink, for her pleasure she had allowed many men to try.

But it was not a physical membrane that deterred Elizabeth from physical love; it was a dark shadow that lay athwart her mind. Before she was three years old, her mother had been beheaded, for adultery according to the official explanation. When she was eight, her mother's cousin, Catherine Howard, who had become her step-mother, was also beheaded in the Palace Yard. Those two women, nearest her in blood, had given a man his will and apparently, in consequence, had been marked for death.

When she was a young girl, while Edward was on the throne, Lord Seymour had cast covetous eyes upon her and her claim to the throne. As she was a ward living in his home (he had married another of her stepmothers) he had occasion to smack her buttocks, peek inside her robes, and romp in her bedroom before she arose. It was only horseplay in which Lady Seymour herself frequently had joined. But suddenly Lord Seymour was arrested for treason and found guilty. And it was said that Elizabeth was part of the plot, having been his paramour and being with child by him. She denied it indignantly, and fortunately her denial was true, or she would have gone to her grave in two pieces as had Anne Boleyn and Catherine Howard. The shadow of the axe had fallen across that slender, white neck by reason of charges of fornication; deep in Elizabeth's mind, sexuality became associated with the danger of violent death. A powerful, hidden fear was the membrane that could not be broken.

As early as the age of eight, after she had seen Catherine Howard beheaded, she had said that she would never marry. And there were other known signs and hints: her periods were irregular and frequently she missed them altogether. She had once said that her true colours were black and white, the colours of a nun's habit. And she had been born under the sign of Virgo, on the eve of the Feast of the Nativity of the Virgin. And sometime in her reign she came to sense the mystical power of the concept of virginity: as a nun becomes the bride of Christ, as the Doge of Venice weds the sea, so she would wed England.

> Here is my hand
> My dear lover, England,
> I am thine both with mind and heart.

Being Elizabeth's lover, though it offered prestige, power, and a means to wealth, was a difficult career, as Leicester was the first to discover. For Elizabeth was not only demanding of affection and jealously possessive; she expected her lovers to be in character and conduct worthy of the kingship they likely would never attain. There were rumours about the court that Leicester would divorce his wife and become King-Consort of England, but his hopes died when his neglected and distraught wife, Amy Robsart, fell down a staircase and broke her neck. There is no evidence that she was pushed, but half England thought she was. Clearly, after that, it was out of the question for Elizabeth to marry him. When Leicester failed badly in his conduct of an expedition in the Netherlands, she was merciless, as she was later still with Essex after his tragic debacle in Ireland. For both of them, her own hurt was deep, for she loved them; but she was also, and first, the Queen.

After Leicester, Christopher Hatton had been the Queen's lover. He was even taller and handsomer than Leicester, and danced a fine galliard. His passion excited Elizabeth but, as his pathetic letters show, he had no idea of the game he was playing. After all, Elizabeth was then only thirty-one years old, and he apparently believed that fulfilled love and even marriage were possible. Healthy, normal male that he was, he had no touch of subtlety in his mind, and he never understood the woman he tried to love.

When Elizabeth reached forty, still unfulfilled, she became spinsterish, irritable; she shrilled when frustrated and slapped the servants who had offended her. She was almost ten years older when Ralegh first excited her; for the first time she loved a man whose mind was a match for her own. From the very first he must have understood both the Queen's need for devotion and affection, and that hidden fear that kept her from ever enjoying them. At thirty, he was still suffering that long agony of the loins; at almost fifty, she was an ageing professional coquette. But she listened to his ideas with a kind of awe; it was said around the court that she thought Ralegh was an oracle.

Ralegh's intellect flashed with fire and imagination and, at the same time, it was tinged with the grandeur of philosophic gloom. He was haunted by great themes: the decay of ancient empires, the founding of new ones; the savagery of Time and the puzzles of Destiny. He knew of strange lands, the customs of the people who lived there and the medicinal properties of exotic plants. He understood the new naval strategy almost as well as Drake and was much more articulate about it. He had learned the new science from Thomas Hariot; he belonged to a group of religious mystics who paradoxically celebrated the divine darkness. He had lived in France; he knew the sad slaughters in Ireland and all of these experiences, touched by his imagination, lost their triviality and ugliness and took on poetic qualities. They became parts of larger patterns and designs; they took on meaning and life.

One interest he shared with Elizabeth was the new poetry; he was a friend of poets and a poet in his own right. Among other things, they both took delight in the new vogue of pastoralism, derived from the recently rediscovered idylls of Theocritus of Alexandria. The pastoral convention, which describes life through an image of the idealized existence of literate and artistic shepherds in a lovely landscape of timeless spring, is the playful wish-fulfillment of a sophisticated and complex culture, an imaginative vision of something like an unspoiled Eden, a Golden Age of simple purity and beauty. The Greeks placed the vision in Sicily where, as they fashioned it in their art, the flocks were always milky white, the shepherd boys passed the pleasant days playing their pipes and engaging in singing contests; their lives were filled with music and poetry and innocent love. And above all, in the pastoral convention, Time, which wastes and devours everything, seemed to be stopped. It was a highly artificial and stylized convention, in which the poet could express his wistful longing for a better world, and, at the same time, through symbols and obliquity of expression, say something about the sadder world of time and change in which he really lived. And the convention lent itself pleasantly to games of love and allusive compliment. There was something in the convention that especially appealed to the most brilliant and complex societies: after the time of Theocritus it had been revived in the Naples of Vergil, the Florence of Petrarch, the Paris of Francis I, and now in the England of Elizabeth.

Ralegh enjoyed the convention, but was amused by its artificiality. In reality he could think of nothing more contemptible than the keeping of sheep, but he was happy to use the fiction to tease and play with Elizabeth in the pastoral mode. And she had developed a pleasant little conceit. It occurred to her that her Watar, as she called him in his own Westcountry dialect, had much to do with the ocean; he was, in fact, obsessed with oceanic enterprises, so she began to call him the Shepherd of the Ocean. The ocean is ruled by the moon and so Elizabeth became, for Ralegh, the goddess of the moon, the virgin huntress, Diana. Ralegh wrote her a little poem on the theme.

> Praised be Diana's fair and harmless light,
> Praised be the dews wherewith she moists the ground;
> Praised be her beams, the glory of the night,
> Praised be her power, by which all powers abound.

> Time wears her not, she doth his chariot guide,
> Mortality below her orb is placed,
> By her the virtue of the stars down slide,
> In her is virtue's perfect image cast.

'Time wears her not.' Elizabeth inwardly knew that it did, but she would not say so; Ralegh knew it too, and later he would say it, but in her fifties that was the poetic theme that gave Elizabeth most pleasure, and as she aged she wished to hear it more and more. In the poetic pastoral world, she could pretend it was true.

But Ralegh did not always speak of her as Diana. Of the moon's three faces, Diana is the cool, chaste one, but there was also the gentle, feminine face of Cynthia, who had once dipped to earth and kissed the sleeping shepherd boy, Endymion. Since Cynthia's heart, unlike Diana's, could be touched by mortal love, that is what Ralegh usually called her – Cynthia, the Lady of the Sea.

It was in this pastoral mood that Ralegh's friend, Christopher Marlowe, wrote *The Passionate Shepherd to His Love*, in which he caught one perfect moment of youth and rescued it from time, a May morning filled with dancing and music and longing.

> Come live with me and be my love,
> And we will all the pleasures prove
> That valleys, groves, hills and fields,
> Woods or steepy mountain yields.

> And we will sit upon the rocks,
> Seeing the shepherds feed their flocks,
> By shallow rivers, to whose falls
> Melodious birds sing madrigals.

And I will make thee beds of roses,
And a thousand fragrant posies,
A cap of flowers, and a kirtle,
Embroidered all with leaves of myrtle.

A gown made of the finest wool,
Which from our pretty lambs we pull;
Fair lined slippers for the cold,
With buckles of the purest gold;

A belt of straw, and ivy buds,
With coral clasps and amber studs;
And if these pleasures may thee move,
Come live with me, and be my love.

The shepherds' swains shall dance and sing
For thy delight each May-morning.
If these delights thy mind may move,
Then live with me and be my love.

As Ralegh read Marlowe's poem, his critical and sceptical mind noticed at once that the pastoral promise depended on the absence of that great eroder, Time. What would happen if time were set ticking again? And he penned a reply to be spoken by the worldly-wise beloved.

If all the world and love were young,
And truth in every shepherd's tongue,
These pretty pleasures might me move
To live with thee, and be thy love.

Time drives the flocks from field to fold,
When rivers rage, and rocks grow cold,
And Philomel becometh dumb;
The rest complains of cares to come.

The flowers do fade, and wanton fields,
To wayward winter reckoning yields;
A honey tongue, a heart of gall,
Is fancy's spring, but sorrow's fall.

Thy gowns, thy shoes, thy beds of roses,
Thy cap, thy kirtle, and thy posies
Soon break, soon wither, soon forgotten,
In folly ripe, in reason rotten.

Thy belt of straw and ivy buds,
Thy coral clasps and amber studs,
All these in me no means can move
To come to thee and be thy love.

But could youth last and love still breed,
Had joys no date, nor age no need,
Then these delights my mind might move
To live with thee and be thy love.

Here in two exquisitely fashioned poems are juxtaposed the artifice of wish and the fact of reality, the hope of youth and the disillusion of age. And it is typical of Ralegh that, given the choice and time to meditate, he should look through the dream to the waking world.

The kind of intellectual play Ralegh and Elizabeth enjoyed was not limited to pastoralism. Once he made the apparently absurd wager that he could weigh smoke. When the Queen accepted, he weighed some tobacco in a balance, put it in his pipe and smoked it; then he knocked out the ashes and weighed them. The difference in the weight, he said, was the weight of the smoke. The Queen laughed and paid the wager, remarking that she had known many (it was the alchemists she meant) who had turned gold into smoke; Ralegh was the first to reverse the process.

But such wit play gives no indication of the depth and range of Ralegh's mind or his intense interest in the new ideas that were unsettling men's whole conception of the world, their place in it, and God's relations with it. The improved tools and methods of observing and measuring natural phenomena and testing these observations by experiment were laying bare new facts that seemed to shake the foundations of knowledge: as John Donne would soon be saying, the 'new philosophy calls all in doubt'. Ralegh's acquaintances included some of the most advanced English thinkers, and his writings show that he was aware of the issues and their implications.

Until the new science shattered it, the world picture of the Renaissance, much of which derived from Aristotle, was a poetic concept of the universe as a highly complex unity in which everything was inter-related. It was like an immense artistic creation, constructed by repetition and variation of a few basic patterns, so that valid analogies were everywhere perceptible, and the world was best understood in terms of analogical relationships. For instance, it was believed that all matter was composed of four elements and of these the entire mutable world was made; the eternal heavens, however, were composed of a pure, unchanging fifth element. On this foundation a series of analogies were constructed. There had been four ages of the world; the fifth age would be perfect and millennial. There were four liquids or humours in the body, the balance or imbalance of which determined states of feeling or health; when perfectly harmonized, they formed a stable organism, something like a fifth essence. Our world moves through four seasons; there are four quarters of the compass, four letters in the Hebrew name for God and so on. That there were seven planets likewise suggested many spiritual sets of seven: there were seven deadly sins and seven cardinal virtues; the sacraments of the Church were seven, as were the days of the creation; the very life of man passed through seven ages. And everything in the universe had its mysterious reflection in the life of man.

That universe was conceived as seven concentric spheres of pure crystal which carried the planets in their orbits around the earth, the abode made for man, which was the centre and focus of the whole great world. From large to small, the world operated on similar principles or patterns so that the great world of the heavens, the political world of the state, and the microcosm, man, worked by analogous laws and were mutually dependent and mutually explanatory. As the sun rules the planets and the king rules the state and reason rules man, God directly ruled the empyrean or realm of fire. Further, the pure love of God was the force that moved the *primum mobile*, the first mover; as it turned continually toward the fountain of love, swinging its great wheel through the sky, it imparted motion to the sphere beneath it, which in turn passed it on to the next and so on down. Man, then, was tightly integrated into a universe mysteriously similar to his own body in its operations, and through the workings of the universe he was linked directly with the love of God. It was a lovely, secure and orderly world.

But in its tight interlockings, this universe is like the Prince Rupert's drop, a bead of glass in such state of internal tension that if one corner is chipped away, the bead flies apart. So if one segment of this map was shown to be false, if one analogy proved untenable, doubt was cast on all the rest and on the theology to which it was related. Hence the new science seemed alarmingly subversive, and as soon as men like Hariot could calculate, even roughly, the speed of sun and moon, it became evident that the prime mover would have to turn at incredible speeds. When Kepler estimated that it would have to travel 7,500,000 miles in a twin pulse-beat, he concluded that it simply could not exist. Similarly, Ralegh, in his *History*, flatly denied the existence of the prime mover, and he also said that there was no crystalline heaven and no element of fire. If that were so, what had been considered the basic laws of the universe were broken.

The scientific temperament that led men to weigh smoke and devise experiments to prove that fire was not an element, that led them to scrutinize the planets through telescopes and calculate their speeds, led them also to calculate the time necessary for civilizations to take form, for cities to rise and decay, for the growth of the arts of government, for the diversification of peoples and languages. Hariot's calculations of these matters led him to question the accepted chronology of the Old Testament because it did not allow enough time; consequently he was accused of denying the word of God. When Ralegh came to write his *History*, having been taught by Hariot, he encountered similar difficulties in trying to make the happenings of the world fit into a Hebrew chronology. But he was not the iconoclastic sceptic he has sometimes been made to appear; he did try to make it fit. He was not a Galileo or even a Hariot, but he was more at home in their universe than in that of Aristotle and Ptolemy. And of the Englishmen who were exploring this new universe, he was the only one who was personally close to

Elizabeth. He could bring to her an adventure more exciting than the exploration of new lands – a glimpse into the new worlds of science and the intellect.

The group of intellectuals with whom Ralegh was informally associated – men like Hariot, Marlowe, George Chapman, and Walter Warner – were interested not only in the new science but also in that approach to religion which is not disturbed by scientific innovation or even by tricks of reason and logic: the way of the mystic. Partly because of the general suspicion directed at the new science, partly because of Marlowe's delight in saying things to shock the pious, the group acquired an un-merited reputation as anti-religious sceptics and iconoclasts. Marlowe is reported as saying, for instance, such outrageous things as that Moses was a mere juggler, 'and that one Hariot, being Sir W. Ralegh's man, can do more than he'. Marlowe also said that the New Testament was written in filthy Greek. A phrase of Shakespeare's came to be associated with them – the school of night – which to some carried overtones of the devil, witchcraft and other nonsense. But if they were concerned with darkness and night, it was the mystical way of union with God in that dazzling light which, being incomprehensible to mind and senses of mortals, seemed to be a darkness.

Every religion with a mystical strain in it is likely to contain some form of this vision of night. Mystics have always be-lieved that God must be approached by the *via negativa*, the negative way, that is by thinking of what he is not rather than what he is. The reason is simple. They believe that if a horse, for example, could reason about God, it would form an image in its mind of a perfect horse. So man, unable to escape the limitations of his own rational intellect, assigns to God exten-sions or perfections of human attributes. The God who can be approached through the positive way is simply an idealized man. The mystics cannot possibly allow such an image, for they conceive of God as totally other. Always, therefore, they have defined God by negatives. The Chinese Taoist says that the name which can be named is not the Eternal Name; the way that can be known is not the Eternal Way. And the Hindu sage sits in contemplation, whispering to his own ear, *neti, neti,* not that, not that.

Philo Judaeus of Alexandria, the source of the mystic strain in Western religion, likewise defined his Unknowable God in negative terms: unborn, incomprehensible, invisible, and ineffable. But Philo did more: he gave the tradition its central metaphor. Remembering that on Mount Sinai Moses had found God in a storm cloud, he said that those who love God, in any age, must penetrate into the 'darkness' where God is.

This idea and the image that embodies it run like black threads through mystical Christianity. God is the dark cloud of Unknowing, and the Divine Darkness is 'the unapproachable Light in which God dwells'. As Lord Herbert of Cherbury was later to phrase it,

> . . . thy blackness is a spark
> Of light inaccessible, and alone
> Our darkness which can make us think it dark.

The central poet of the 'School of Night' was Ralegh's close friend, George Chapman. He believed that inasmuch as the Essence of God was darkness to us, the poetry which celebrates that Essence should also be dark and obscure to empty and dark spirits; however, those with a 'light-bearing intellect', would not need a lantern to find their way in it. Chapman does not celebrate the darkness of Chaos nor the darkness found in the minds of 'passion-driven men'. Rather he celebrates the 'sacred night', he strikes 'that fire out of darkness, which the brightest day shall envy for beauty'.

Chapman's friend, William Warner, a pedestrian poet, puts the familiar doctrines of the School of Night in simple, comprehensible terms. 'God's nature,' he says, 'is past all kenning.' He is unmovable, un-begot, unchangeable, unpassive, unmaterial, uncompounded and infinite. 'Lord,' he apostrophizes, 'Darkness is thy covert.'

Ralegh, too, accepted the premises and the imagery of the negative way. 'Of that infinite power,' he says, 'we can comprehend but a shadow.' And his memorable definition of God, is that of the mystics: 'God is a light by abundant clarity invisible.'

This belief that God cannot properly be defined in positive terms explains a conversation Ralegh once had with a minister of the Gospel who was dining in his company at the home of Sir George Trenchard. When Ralegh innocently asked him what God was, the divine returned him Aristotle's definition that God was *Ens Entium*, Pure Being. Ralegh tried to get him to explain the meaning of the term, but the man was incapable of anything more than stock answers. Ralegh did not press it very far, but graciously asked the parson to say grace 'for that, quoth he, is better than this disputation'. Some scholars have quite mistakenly cited this episode as an illustration of Ralegh's scepticism; it is rather an illustration of his mysticism.

But, after all, the end the mystic seeks is not intellectual clarity but ecstatic experience; he seeks, in the words of Sir Thomas Browne, 'ingression into the Divine Shadow', to become one with the love that moves the sun and all the stars. Most mystics have believed that this ecstasy must be prepared for by a special purification. Chapman states this explicitly: we must be 'frozen dead' he says, 'to all the lawless flames of Cupid.' Although it cannot be known for sure, there is reason to suppose that others of the School of Night, including Ralegh, flirted for a time more or less seriously with this idea. When Shakespeare came to satirize the group he certainly said as much. It would have been a sensible mystique for the lover of a maiden Queen and would have provided another subtle link between the Queen and the low-born Ralegh. He was a complex combination of mystic and scientist, poet and swordsman, explorer, colonizer and wit. In his universality, in his inclusion in one personality of so many disparate strains, he was unique in England. Elizabeth not only enjoyed this versatility, she also made good use of it.

Ralegh rose by his own wits, it was said, and also by the royal prerogative, in line with Elizabeth's policy of paying her servants 'part in money, and the rest with grace'. With her tightly restricted funds, she could not directly grant largess, but she found many ways of conferring prerogatives from which her favourites could make money.

Ralegh himself never received a penny from Elizabeth or the crown; but he did receive abundant grace. In 1583 he had built the *Bark Ralegh* and invested heavily in Gilbert's colonial enterprise, but he had lost all his money, and he had no income, then or now, except from privateering. For years he had held licenses from both the Prince of Orange and the Prince of Condé which entitled him to prey legally upon Spanish shipping. It was a good source of income but irregular.

Elizabeth realized that if Ralegh was to serve her court he needed regular income, so in May of 1583 she gave him her first really substantial gift, the farm of wines. This meant that any vintner retailing wine in the territory he had been assigned would have to pay him one pound each year for the privilege. Not wishing to levy and collect this business tax himself, he underlet his rights to a London merchant for about 700 pounds annually. Thus, for the first time in his life, he had a substantial fixed income. But the merchant realized that if he authorized a few new outlets he would collect more for himself and soon Ralegh was complaining that he was being mulcted. The revenue from the grant had increased but he was still receiving only the original amount. Since the agreement he had made was binding, however, he asked the Queen to terminate his patent which also terminated his contract with the merchant. Then Elizabeth re-granted him the privilege and soon he was making some 2,000 pounds a year from it.

A year later Elizabeth gave Ralegh a license to export broadcloths, a privilege hitherto enjoyed only by such distinguished public servants as Cecil and Walsingham. Once again Ralegh himself would not directly engage in trade: he would simply sell the right of export to the Merchant Adventurers for a fixed sum.

Elizabeth soon realized that Ralegh needed a town house. Traditionally the See of Durham had maintained a large mansion for the use of the Bishop of Durham in London. Half of it was already being leased to one of Elizabeth's courtiers. She used persuasion to get the other half leased to Ralegh, and he kept forty men and their horses there. Only the right of a hundred roses a year from the famous rose garden was reserved to the disgruntled bishop.

In 1585 Ralegh was made Lord Warden of the Stannaries. The stannaries were the tin mines in Devon and Cornwall, and the Lord Warden presided at the Stannary Parliaments, collected the taxes on tin and was in charge of the Cornish militia. This was an important duty of state. One citizen, however, was outraged by the appointment. He wrote William Cecil pointing out that the Cornish tin miners were 'a rough and mutinous multitude, 10,000 or 13,000 strong'. Ralegh, he believed, was not reliable enough to be given such a responsibility. He went on to say that Ralegh was cursed by the poor because his license to export cloth had brought many to poverty. The complaint is overstated and ultimately proved unjustified. Ralegh performed his duties as Lord Warden in a highly competent way, was loyal to the tinners, constantly supported their causes to Parliament and the Queen and finally won their complete affection.

In the same year he was appointed to an even more sensitive and responsible office; he was made Lord Lieutenant of Cornwall. The office was a relatively new one which had either been conceived or greatly expanded as a result of the Prayer Book riots of 1549. One of the vexing problems of Tudor administration was how to mediate between the central government and the shires. From time immemorial the Justice of the Peace had been the officer of the Crown for the shire, but the justices had neither the status nor the power to carry the increasing burdens of office. Some high official, therefore, would be appointed Lord Lieutenant, generally a nobleman or even a member of the Privy Council. Ralegh was the only mere knight to hold such a position at this time. One responsibility of the Lord Lieutenant was to collect the subsidies; that is, when Parliament granted the sovereign additional monies, he had to see that all the property of the shire was assessed and evaluated and that the taxes on it were levied and collected.

More important duties of the Lord Lieutenant were to ensure the political stability of the country, to enquire into treasons, rebellions, riots, murders, and felonies. There had long been a rule in England that troops could not be levied to fight outside their own counties except in case of invasion. But when invasion threatened, it was the Lord Lieutenant's task to raise an army to meet the attack wherever it occurred. By the time Ralegh was given this assignment, war with Spain was imminent and his duties were urgent and specific, for Cornwall was the most exposed part of England, the most vulnerable to attack. He was to survey the coast, identify the most likely landing area for invading troops, fortify them, and make plans for counter-attack. He was to see that all castles and strongholds were furnished with ordnance and ammunition. The beacons were to be kept in readiness; turnpikes erected, fords and passages fortified. As Francis Bacon observed, Elizabeth never allowed her personal predilections to impede state affairs. Ralegh's appointment to this office, therefore, is a clear sign of her confidence in his abilities as organizer and administrator. She knew well enough that the day was not far off when the safety of England might rest with the energy and courage of the Lord Lieutenant of Cornwall.

In the same year, Ralegh was also made Vice-Admiral for Devon and Cornwall, the Crown's representative for the navy in those counties. His duties were to procure supplies and ordnance, attend to the condition of the harbours, impress men for royal service and to see that the Royal Navy in those two counties was fit and battle ready.

In March, 1585, Elizabeth knighted Ralegh and early in 1586 designated him as captain of her guard. His duty was to maintain a small, valiant force of men whose sole function was to guard the Queen's life. Ralegh himself was to stand at the door of her antechamber during working hours, within sight and probably within hearing of all the business transacted in the Presence Chamber.

With duties of such magnitude it is plain why Ralegh never accompanied his colonists to Virginia. He had work enough for a dozen men, work of high importance; one need not rely solely on the theory of a repining Queen to explain his presence in England.

Meanwhile, he was prospering in fortune by acquiring land. In 1586 he was given a grant of land in Munster. Each grantee was to receive 12,000 acres, but Ralegh appears to have received several such grants, as well as the College of Youghal, the See of Lismore and other buildings, castles and lands. When Anthony Babington was convicted of treason and his lands were escheated, Ralegh was granted his three manors in Lincolnshire, Derbyshire, and Nottinghamshire. Finally, in 1591, he cast covetous eyes on the fertile and beautifully situated estate of Sherborne. It consisted of a castle, a park, and several adjacent manors in the shire of Dorset. For hundreds of years it had belonged to the See of Salisbury, and it was said that a medieval bishop named Osmund had placed a curse on anyone who alienated the estate from the See or who profited by its alienation. A man from the Westcountry, it might be thought, would have taken such a curse seriously. Later on, perhaps, Ralegh did, but at the time he was content to take a 'lease' for ninety-nine years at an annual rental of 360 pounds. It was worth much more and ninety-nine year leases usually meant permanent ownership.

So that was what it meant to love a Queen: exclusive rights to colonize the New World; 80,000 acres in Ireland; financial privileges in cloth and wine; access to the royal presence, a city home and a country estate torn from the churches that owned them, and finally to become the most important official in the Westcountry.

It is little wonder that as the self-confident and sometimes arrogant but low-born Ralegh rose in power, prestige, and fortune, he aroused envy and made enemies. Soon after he became conspicuous in the Queen's grace, the Earl of Oxford taunted him with 'jack' and 'upstart', and other nobles of the court liked to sneer at his Westcountry accent and his birth. Ralegh would have been happy to have run a sword through some of them but he was forbidden to duel. He could speak, however.

103

If any man accuse me to my face, I will answer him with my mouth, but my tail is good enough to return an answer to such as traduce me behind my back.

Actually Ralegh came from a family whose name was alive in the time of William the Conqueror. And he set the antiquary, John Hooker, to searching out his pedigree. Hooker found that a Sir John De Ralegh had married the daughter of D'Amerie Clare, who was descended from Henry the First. So Ralegh discovered that he came from a royal line; he was a long-lost Plantagenet.

His clothes, too, antagonized many people. One of his portraits shows him wearing a suit of silver armour and he glitters with diamonds, rubies and pearls. A Jesuit, who called him the 'darling of the English Cleopatra', said that the pearls in his shoes alone were worth 6,000 pounds. But his clothes were not mere vanity; like his search for a royal ancestry they were a statement of his ambitions and that is why they were so resented. Aristotle had said that magnificence, a certain greatness in doing, was the mark of nobility and royalty. And although the Puritans were constantly preaching about the ungodliness of brave apparel, men of the court, like Shakespeare's old Polonius, thought it sensible to dress expensively if one had the purse for it.

For many years, England had tried to pass and enforce laws against excess in apparel. Parliament had many of the godly in its ranks who were worried about offending God; but others had more practical concerns. They thought that dressing beyond one's station tended to break down what they considered to be a proper distinction of classes. The fact that Parliament continually passed and re-passed such laws indicates that people were not paying much attention to them. In 1585, in Ralegh's first Parliament, there was again a committee appointed to study sumptuousness of apparel. It must have been widely enjoyed when Mr. Speaker appointed Ralegh a member of it. There is nothing to indicate that his work on this committee was particularly brilliant.

His privileges of farming wine and exporting woollens, like his flamboyant dress, added to his growing unpopularity. Merchants who were competing in order to survive resented having to pay a tax of dubious legality to a decorative courtier who contributed nothing to their product or their business. His readiness to draw his sword, the suspicions about his religious orthodoxy all were against him, but mainly it was that his star rose too fast; he had gone from commoner and soldier of fortune to court favourite in a mere two years. By 1587, Sir Anthony Bagot said that Ralegh had become 'the best hated man of the world in court, city, and country'. And Richard Tarleton, the clown and jester of Shakespeare's company, bitterly remarked, 'The knave commands the Queen'.

But Ralegh worked hard for Elizabeth's favours and gave England good value for them. In 1602, shortly before the Queen died, Ralegh wrote to Robert Cecil,

It grieves me to find with what difficulty and torment to myself I obtain the smallest favour. Her Majesty knows that I am ready to spend all I have, and my life, for her in a day . . . For all I have I will sell for her in an hour and spend it in her service.

It was true. Elizabeth never had a courtier as willing as Ralegh to spend his private fortune in public service. But it is also true that Elizabeth and Cecil had long since concluded of Ralegh what he had once said of Ormonde, that nothing less than all would ever satisfy him. He never appears to have been particularly grateful to the Queen in spite of his willingness to die for her. Later in the *History*, he wrote, possibly with himself in mind,

It is the disease of kings, of states, and of private men, to covet the greatest things, but not to enjoy the least; the desire of that which we neither have nor need, taking from us the true use and fruition of what we have already. The curse upon mortal men was never taken from them since the beginning of the world to this day.

But for now the days of his adventuring are over. For twelve years, he himself was to say, he was the lover of a Queen who showered largess upon him which she expected him to earn and repay with interest. Robert Cecil said of Ralegh that he could 'toil terribly'. From 1583 to 1593 was the decade of his labour.

7

Ralegh and the English Navy

One of Ralegh's most important tasks, in the decade of his labour, was to help formulate England's naval policy. Soon Spanish pikemen and European land battles would be relatively insignificant, and the future of Europe and especially America would be decided by the fighting fleets. Spain's naval strategy was traditional and unimaginative; so was the design of her ships. In England, however, new ships were being designed and their qualities dictated a new naval strategy. Ralegh was not the principal architect of that policy which had its beginnings in the time of Henry VIII. Drake, Hawkins, Frobisher and the Howards were also passionately committed to it. But Ralegh become the recorder of that policy; he wrote the most articulate prose about it; and it is to his prose, therefore, that we turn when we wish to learn about it.

By 1575, the year Ralegh had enrolled at the Inns of Court, England and Spain had developed different kinds of fleets and different theories of naval warfare. The Mediterranean, a relatively calm sea, offers no unusual threat to vessels of light construction. The Mediterranean powers, therefore, tended to build galleys, vessels some 160 feet long and only 25 feet wide, the ratio of length to beam being about 7 to 1. These long, narrow ships were slow in turning and not very manoeuvrable; therefore there had been little change or development in the naval tactics employed in battles between fleets of galleys.

The advantage of the galley, which its proponents thought decisive, was its motive power, human muscles flexed under the whips of the galley masters, pulling fifty oars, twenty-five on each side. By means of its oars, the ship could move in any weather except the high seas; and if there was a wind, it could unfurl two or three lateen sails which would increase its speed. The prow of the galley was a great beam tipped by a metal beak, a kind of giant pike. The galley would bear down on another ship, ram it, throw grappling irons across the enemy's hull, and put soldiers aboard where they would fight a land battle on the deck of a ship using pistols, swords, cutlasses, daggers, hackbuts, bows and arrows and even large stones flung from stations built on the masts high above the decks.

But every weapon has its disadvantages and those of the galley were formidable. Because both sides of the deck were occupied by galley slaves, no guns could be mounted broadside; the ship could deliver fire only from the prow and the stern. Two of the small cannons had to be kept trained on the slaves, once action was joined, to keep them from desertion or mutiny. And the galley could not stay long at sea. There were fifty-eight effective fighters aboard her and another 200 non-effectives who manned the oars and the ship's stations. There was little storage space; no substantial supply of stores could be carried; there was no way of caring for sick or wounded. Therefore galleys could fight only limited engagements, generally of a few hours, and then had to retire.

The Battle of Lepanto (October 7, 1571), the culmination of the use of the galley in naval warfare, had an immense although indirect influence on the naval struggle between England and Spain. It was a decisive engagement between Spanish and Turkish cultures and between the Christian and Moslem faiths. Suleiman the Turk had pushed through Hungary and was threatening Vienna; early in 1571 he had assembled in the Gulf of Corinth a large Turkish fleet. The Christian forces were led by one of Europe's most dashing heroes, Don John of Austria, who had assembled his armada in a great crescent. On the right wing were fifty-three galleys under Gian Andrea Doria; on the left wing were fifty-three more under the Venetian Barbarigo. In the centre was Don John himself with seventy galleys. Half a mile back was a reserve of thirty-seven galleys under Alvaro de Bazan. These ships all advanced in a long line which measured five miles from the extremes of left flank to right. This kind of naval manoeuvre, Ralegh later noted in his *History*, was exactly comparable to the French cavalry charges which he had participated in. There were no tactical manoeuvrings; the ships simply came head on at one another.

The Turks opposed the Christian formations with a slightly larger number of galleys, some 270 to the Christian 220, and both sides used their galleys primarily as troop transports. They were simply platforms by which land soldiers could be transported to an oceanic battle field. The Christian ships were jammed with 20,000 land soldiers; on Don John's ship alone there were 400 hackbutters. The Turks had only 16,000 troops but these included 6,000 Janissaries, men of proved courage and prowess who had taken religious vows to fight to the death.

Out in front of his charge, Don John sent six galleases, much larger ships, some 220 feet between the uprights. They were worked by a crew of sixty oars who rowed under cover. Above the heads of the oarsmen a deck had been built which supported a tier of guns and, fore and aft, great superstructures or 'castles' had been built. Behind the castles of each ship, 1,000 men were sheltered. Each gallease had a massive ram on its prow and its mission was to plough through the Turkish formation, breaking its line and making it easier for the Christian galleys to close and board.

And so these two fleets came together. There was almost no artillery fire; no galleon or sailing vessel of any kind saw action; the two navies rammed, grappled, and fought as though Humphrey Gilbert or the old Prince of Condé had devised their tactics. The Turks were armed primarily with bows and knives and they wore no armour. The Christians had hackbut support and wore morions and breastplates. As usual the side with the better weapons won. The Turkish fleet was practically annihilated.

Seldom has there been such rejoicing in Christendom. When the Pope saw Don John after the battle he greeted him with the Biblical phrase, 'There was a man sent from God whose name was John'. And the artist Vasari painted a picture of the battle on the entrance wall of the Vatican chapel. The opposite panel remained empty for a year and then was filled in with the depiction of another Christian triumph: the murder of Coligny.

It is one of the great ironies of history that the victory of Lepanto doomed Spain. It locked the Spanish mind up in the tactics of galley warfare, even after their fleet was composed of galleons, and made Philip think of naval engagements as religious crusades in which the will of God was more important than good sailing or accurate artillery. Spain never recovered from its greatest naval victory.

Up in English waters, shipbuilders faced a different problem. The lightly constructed galleys, built low to the waterline, were vulnerable to the white leopards of the wild northern seas. And the galleases, with their high superstructure, would roll and wallow; they could not ride out a tempest; for that heavily timbered ships and re-inforced canvas sails were needed. And sometime in the reign of Henry VIII the remarkable decision was reached to abandon oars altogether and build galleons, vessels propelled by the wind; it was the beginning of a courageous new policy for there is no deeper or more irrational human fear than that of being unable to move when an agent of destruction is advancing. The abandonment of oars meant that sailing vessels might lie becalmed while the galleys approached, rammed, grappled and boarded. Everyone agreed that the chief disadvantage of the new galleon was its vulnerability to the whims of Aeolus.

But the advantages! What fighter could have resisted them? The old 7 to 1 ratio of length to beam was reduced to 3 to 1. The galleons were about 100 feet long and some 30 feet wide. This meant that, with a wind, they could turn twice while a galley was turning once. And all of the decks could be used to support tiers of artillery. The new theory of naval warfare in northern waters was not to ram and board but rather to develop competent gunners who, while their captain was outmanoeuvring the enemy, could fire and sink the hostile ships.

Francis Drake was a great believer in gunnery practise. He sent his ships out in good weather or bad to shoot at targets until the Lord Admiral chided him for his prodigal use of the Queen's ammunition. To those who thought that the galleon might lie helpless while the galleys came to destroy it, the theoreticians of the new strategy had a confident answer. The calm sea made the best gun platform and consequently made artillery fire more accurate. All the motion a galleon needed to defeat a galley was enough to turn her broadside to the approaching enemy, and that was not difficult. She could be warped from an anchor or towed round by a long boat with twenty good men at its oars.

Just before Elizabeth's reign began, when the English had lost Calais to France, English seapower had been unable to drive off the blockading French fleet and supply the port. The loss of Calais created a profound crisis of confidence concerning the Navy which had been allowed to deteriorate during the reigns of Edward and Mary. One of Elizabeth's first acts, therefore, had been to appoint a committee to recommend a sound naval programme. That committee had cautiously advised the building of four huge ships somewhat after the model of the large Portuguese galleons of 1,000 tons or more; but the heart of the recommendation was for twenty galleons of around 500 tons each, swift, manoeuvrable, and heavily gunned. To objections continually raised that these little vessels would be outgunned by the Portuguese giants, Ralegh made a convincing reply. A galleon delivers a broadside, then heels about in order to present the other broadside to the enemy. While it is turning the guns that have already been fired are being re-loaded. The swifter English ships, he said, could turn twice as fast as the lumbering Portuguese galleons; therefore with half the number of guns, the smaller, swifter ships could deliver the same firepower as the larger ships and still retain many other advantages.

The reason for building the Portuguese (and later the Spanish) warships so large was that they were still conceived, after the manner of galley warfare, as floating platforms designed to carry soldiers. The sailors were to sail the ship and man the artillery, but the chief Spanish tactic was still to board and fight hand to hand. Therefore their vast galleons still carried super-structures to serve as fortress walls for their soldiers and they filled their ships with men. That was a dangerous thing to do, sanitary arrangements being what they were. All ships gave part of their holds up to ballast; a walled-off area under decks would be filled with rocks to bring the ships a little lower in the water and give them stability. Above the ballast were the cook shack and the privies, and all the waste of the ship, incredible as it seems, ran not out into the sea, but down in the hold. The ships soon became floating privies; after a few weeks at sea they stank like a beached whale. Then it was essential to find a harbour, carry out the old ballast, clean the ship and wash her down. For as the waste accumulated in the dark hold, the rats would poke their whiskered noses into it; they lived in and on human excrement. At night they would come up on deck, seeking out the ship's stores, running through the galley and pantry. Every disease, every form of bacteria that any man carried, was soon boiling in the blood of the rats which vectored it right back to the men. Dysentery was always expected; the plague or typhus were dreaded, and when they broke out, the entire crew of a ship might be sick at once and half of them, or even more, might die. Few British sailors were killed in the actual fighting against the Armada; they died like cattle of ship's fever that followed when they choked the seaports with their foul ships. And so the fewer men on board the better and the English naval strategy of manoeuvring and cannonading meant that there needed to be no soldiers aboard their galleons; the old guard of the British Navy, however, never fully accepted that fact.

To carry out the tactics of the new warfare, one thing was essential: to seize the wind gauge, that is, to be upwind of the enemy. This was important for two reasons: first, powder was not smokeless and a bombardment sent smoke rolling down-wind, choking and blinding those who had lost the wind gauge and who could no longer see to manoeuvre their ships or sight their guns. And the one who had lost the wind could only run downwind before the enemy unless he had a faster ship which could sail around her pursuer and recover the wind. The ship that had the wind gauge could wheel, come head on, retire, present the broadside, and harass, harry, and drive the other ship before it.

At the beginning of Elizabeth's reign, as a result of the committee's investigation, an ambitious naval programme had been conceived, but there was never any money to further it; ten years later England had only two new galleons. Elizabeth was not too worried, for she was, at this time, planning no offensive naval warfare. Rather her principal strategy was to disrupt French and Spanish commerce. Therefore she granted commissions and letters of reprisal to swarms of privateers who were to give one-tenth of their booty to the Lord Admiral of England for the building and maintaining of the Navy. It was difficult to get pirates to pay an honest tithe, but the English government worked strenuously at it.

After the Crown was paid and the other expenses met, the crew and captain divided what was left. Clearly, therefore, the fewer in the crew the better, and that was the reason why no soldiers were carried on privateering vessels. In order to make more money, the sailors were willing to sail the ship and do the fighting too. A quite unexpected bonus was that, as the number of men was reduced, the risk of infections and plagues was reduced also. Fewer men meant less costly voyages and, as the ships were able to carry more supplies, their capability for staying out at sea was greatly increased. The Hawkinses of Plymouth had been privateers on a grand scale; Drake and Ralegh now had privateering ships continually at sea. These Westcountry men knew the advantages of smaller crews, smaller ships and larger guns. What they learned from privateering they were adapting to England's naval policy.

Ralegh believed that during the decade of the 1570s, two of Her Majesty's galleons could have defeated one hundred Spanish warships. Inasmuch as the Spanish navy, at that time, consisted almost entirely of galleys, he was probably right; certainly the statement is evidence of his confidence in the new strategy. That strategy was furthered in 1577 when John Hawkins came forward and offered his services to the Crown; he said that Navy funds were being embezzled and mismanaged, that he could build ships for one-half of their present costs and supply them better and more cheaply. William Cecil and Elizabeth believed him and named him Treasurer of the Navy. Immediately Hawkins swept with a long broom, alienating both the traditionalists in the navy and also the merchants who had been gouging the government. More important, he worked for a navy which completely embodied the new designs and the new tactics. In 1582 he got William Cecil to agree to a standard manning table for the galleons of one man to every one and one-half tons of ship's weight; and in 1585 he reduced this further, one man to two tons. A galleon like the *Revenge* would have only 250 men aboard her, whereas a Portuguese galleon might have 1,500 or more. Hawkins realized from his privateering that by reducing manpower, he could pay better and attract a better class of sailor. Also there would be less sickness in the fleet. So he laid down more ships like the *Revenge* and, at the same time, called in old ships and re-modelled them, making them smaller and faster.

But now the Spanish Navy was also beginning to stir. In 1580 when the King of Portugal died, his kingdom and his galleons came to Philip of Spain. A year later Philip laid down nine new galleons in the Biscay yards. In 1583 the Spanish under the brilliant Santa Cruz, met the French Navy, defeated it, and captured all of the Azores Islands. The English became uneasy and the traditionalists in the British Navy, at this critical moment, brought charges of corruption and incompetence against John Hawkins. The walls of England's defences, they said, were rotten and loose-timbered.

Elizabeth was deeply concerned. Immediately she appointed a committee of her best sea-dogs to investigate: Walter Ralegh, his brother Carew, Fulke Greville, Francis Drake, Martin Frobisher and others. These men visited the shipyards and went aboard the ships; they reviewed designs of galleons; they listened to the theories of Hawkins and his critics and returned a report to Elizabeth which said that the English navy was seaworthy and battle ready, that its tactics and strategy were superior. But they also warned that more galleons must be built to meet the new threat from Spain. Elizabeth immediately provided the funds to refurbish old ships and lay down new ones.

By now Ralegh had the funds to begin building the galleon he had been designing in his mind ever since his first defeat by Spanish warships in 1578. In his theory of ship design he differed a little from Hawkins and Drake. They were the practical privateers who wanted a fast, hard-hitting ship, all bone and muscle. But Ralegh agreed with a contemporary writer who had argued that a ship of the Queen's navy should not be 'too low for disgracing'. Rather it 'should carry such grace and countenance as to terrorize the enemy'. It was Aristotle's idea of magnificence again, the belief that something should be sacrificed in efficiency in order to achieve an appearance consonant with the honour of a great Queen.

So Ralegh built his ship about 100 tons larger than the *Revenge* with enough superstructure to give her grace and countenance. When the Spanish invasion was imminent he gave his ship to the Crown, receiving no payment until five years later. And when the Admiral of the Fleet, Lord Howard, looked over the Royal Navy, he chose for his flagship the *Ark Ralegh* and renamed her the *Ark Royal*. And he wrote to William Cecil,

I pray you tell Her Majesty for me that her money was well given for the *Ark Ralegh* for I think her the odd ship in the world for all conditions . . .

By 'odd' he did not mean queer; he meant unique. And he went on to say that she seemed to be the fastest ship afloat. 'We can see no sail, great or small, but how far soever they be off we fetch them and speak with them.' It is tantalizing that he said so little. We do not know the especial features in design that made her unique; we only know that she was one of history's great ships and that, for a decade, she led the English navy into battle.

And we know why Ralegh named her the *Ark*. In the *History*, he says that in all time there was never a ship 'so capacious nor so strong to defend itself . . . as the ark of Noah, the invention of God himself'. This is an example of Ralegh's poetic nature triumphing over his sceptical intellect. A glance at the Bible would have shown him that the ark was built on a length to beam ratio of 6 to 1 as were Spanish galleys. And it had a very high superstructure like Portuguese galleons. Ralegh's ark could have weathered much heavier seas than Noah's, could have sailed infinitely farther and could have blown the original Ark out of the water. But he was a poet, and it pleased him to think that like Noah he had built a ship which would triumphantly survive whatever destruction lay ahead.

8

The Land of the Virgin Queen

None of Ralegh's labours can approach in significance his great unwearying efforts to colonize in America. From 1584 until he died, he spent his treasure and gave the full force of his feverish intellectual energy in various attempts to win the New World from Spain and make it part of an English empire. He had probably first become interested in the possibilities of the New World when he had served in France under Admiral Coligny who had planted the first French colonies in America. And from members of the Admiral's expedition, he came to know the difficulties that had beset Coligny, and would beset him, in the founding of new colonies.

The first problem was that Spain and Portugal had arrived first and had established cities, roads, naval bases and army garrisons. Further, Pope Alexander VI, wishing to avoid a possible clash between the two Catholic powers in the New World had issued a bull of May 4, 1493, intended to prevent further difficulties. In this bull the Pope ceded to Spain

all islands and lands found and to be found, discovered and to be discovered, to the west and south by making and drawing a line from the Arctic or North Pole to the Antarctic, or South Pole, which line shall be distant an hundred leagues west and south of any of the islands which are commonly called the Azores or Cape de Verde.

The Pope concluded this amazing document by saying that if any man presumed to infringe the rights therein conferred he should incur the indignation of Almighty God and the apostles Peter and Paul.

The bull itself was a bad legal document. It had drawn a line

117

a hundred leagues west and south of 'any' of the Azores islands. No one could actually draw such a line unless a specific island was named, but Spain and Portugal agreed on a meridian 370 leagues west of Cape Verde. This gave Spain the West Indies, Florida, Mexico and the west coast of South America. It gave Portugal one-third of present-day Brazil and then, going eastward, the African coast and the East Indies.

But there was an even greater ambiguity in the document. Spain was to have all lands west and south of a meridian if the language of the document was to be taken literally. But north and south have no meaning with reference to a meridian. The document could be construed to mean that two lines should be drawn, a meridian 100 leagues west of the Azores and a latitude 100 leagues south of those islands; some who took the bull seriously so interpreted it. Such an interpretation left everything north of the modern state of Florida outside the lands ceded in the Pope's bull and therefore open to exploration.

Before allowing Gilbert and Ralegh to sail back in 1578, Elizabeth and her government had developed a realistic policy: they agreed among themselves not to attempt to colonize any place where a Christian king had already taken possession, had made settlements, and had effective control of the territory. Without publicly admitting its validity, they would tacitly observe that mystical latitude the Pope had drawn and colonize north of it. Ralegh's continual suggestions of settlements south of that line, in Guiana, they resisted; but when he and Gilbert proposed colonies north of Florida the English government agreed and ignored the Spanish ambassador's contention that the territory of Florida extended north to the Arctic circle.

Coligny's first mistake, as the English saw it, was that he had planted his first colony in Portuguese territory, his second and third in Spanish territory. All of those colonies had been under continual military threat and the final one was massacred by the Spanish.

His second mistake was that his colonists, primarily Huguenots looking for religious freedom, had brought no equipment with which they could plant or reap. Instead, conceiving themselves as traders, they brought shiploads of cheap trinkets which they bartered to the Indians for food. The Indians, who were themselves surviving only marginally, simply could not support the additional burden of feeding Frenchmen who, as John Hawkins said, wished to live in America by the sweat of other men's brows.

Ralegh knew that Spain and Portugal intended to keep the New World free from intruders, and that if he ventured out there he had better be prepared for rough play. More important, he knew that there was a limited future in defrauding the natives: colonists, in order to keep the friendship of the Indians, must carry or plant their own food. Further, he realized that there needed to be a systematized trade; the New World must yield something to the old. The old world, in turn, to win the new, must make a national effort backed with ample resources. That was the kind of effort Spain had made, and Spain had been richly repaid.

Seven months after Gilbert's death, one month after he received his Letters Patent from Parliament, on April 27, 1584, Ralegh despatched two barks from a Westcountry port. Their captains were Master Philip Amadas and Master Arthur Barlow; their pilot was the highly skilled Portuguese, Simon Fernandez, who had made a voyage of reconnaissance to the New World for Humphrey Gilbert in 1580. Before the ships left, Ralegh gave his captains 'instructions and commandments'.

They have perished; but from what the captains did we may assume that they were told to proceed to the coast of North America and find an island or islet easily defended; they were to attempt to trade with the natives and to make a survey of the goods available there for barter; they were to plant some crops, not for food but to find what English seeds would grow in the soil of the new land; and finally they were to bring home some natives who could be taught the English language and the Christian faith, and who could be made into the Queen's loyal subjects. They would then be available as interpreters and as factors in trading negotiations when the main colony was planted.

After touching at the Canaries the ships sailed to the West Indies and then north along the American coast. On July 2, the land breeze brought them the scent of a 'delicate garden abounding with all kind of odoriferous flowers'. Two days later they made landfall at Wokoken, an island which is part of a long sand reef off the coast of North Carolina. Immediately they lifted up turf and twig and took possession of the land for Ralegh in the name of Queen Elizabeth. He now owned the North American continent if he could hold it against the Spaniard.

After the ceremonies were completed, the explorers 'viewed the land'. The place was overrun with wild grapes. Arthur Barlow had never seen anything in the vineyards of Europe to compare with this. Grapes even grew down to the beach where 'the very beating and surge of the sea overflowed them'.

All this was propitious, for England imported so much wine from Spain as to cause an unfavourable balance of trade. Since claret and port could be profitably freighted a long distance, wines might be the commodity that could make the American venture a success financially.

For two days the little party lay at anchor; on the third a canoe with three Indians appeared. The three English leaders rowed out to meet the natives, exchanged greetings and invited them aboard. They were timid, but one Indian came. He was given a shirt and hat which pleased him, then a drink of wine which delighted him so much that he got in his canoe and soon returned with it full of fish. This, the captains thought, showed a disposition to trade.

The next day some forty or fifty Indian men came aboard. They were 'very handsome and goodly people and in their behaviour as mannerly and civil as any of Europe'. The leader, Granganimeo, made 'all signs of joy and welcome', and soon the English and the Indians began trading; the colonizers could not resist repeating the mistakes of Coligny's men by taking advantage of the natives. Barlow was delighted when Granganimeo's simple heart was so overcome with the glitter of a tin dish that he gave twenty deer skins for it. Excited with his bargain, he

THE LAND OF THE VIRGIN QUEEN

took the dish, punched a hole in it, hung it around his neck and said it would defend him against the arrows of his enemies. Next a copper kettle went for fifty skins which were worth, Barlow says, fifty crowns. The Indians wanted most the hatchets, axes, and knives, and when Granganimeo saw some armour he wanted it badly enough to offer a box of pearls for it. But Barlow refused because, more than pearls, he wanted the knowledge of where they were obtained. In his report to Ralegh he claimed that he had found out the location of the pearl fisheries and that he had communicated that information privately to Ralegh.

Trade bred confidence and soon Granganimeo brought his wife and children aboard. The lady was wearing a necklace of pearls and Granganimeo had on his head a broad plate of 'gold or copper', impossible to identify because it was unpolished metal. Ralegh's captains made every effort to get the Indian to remove the plate and let them examine it, but he would not. Finally they were allowed to feel it; it was malleable; and with that broad hint, Barlow, in his report, dropped the subject of gold.

The expedition then sailed north some twenty miles to Roanoke Island where they saw their first Indian village. They were hospitably entertained by Granganimeo's wife, and Barlow was so impressed with the 'love and kindness' shown to his men that he concluded, as Parmenius had done before him, that the ancient myth of the golden age was already a reality in the New World.

We found the people most gentle, loving and faithful, void of all guile and treason, and such as live after the manner of the golden age.

But the Indians gave the white men a friendly and hospitable reception not because their natures were unspoiled by a vicious society but because they believed – until they came to know their guests better – that they were supernatural beings. Marvelling at the whiteness of the skins, they thought their visitors were reincarnated men who had come from the pale world of shades. The fact that the visitors had no women with them and refrained from attempting to possess the bare brown flesh they saw all around them supported that theory. Besides, it was ripe and lush summer; fish were plentiful; crops were growing; food was easy to get. It was a pleasure to share it with visitors who brought excitement and wonder into their lives and offered tin plates and copper pots in exchange for the common objects of their routine lives. But amidst all this friendliness, Barlow maintained an unusual degree of caution. He never allowed his men to go unarmed among the Indians nor would he allow them to sleep in native houses.

Barlow carefully noted that the Indians had poor weapons: their breastplates were of wood, their swords of wood hardened in fire; they carried war clubs which had a staghorn in the end; and their arrows were small, barely powerful enough to kill a naked man, certainly not one who wore armour.

Barlow and his men sowed some peas into the ground. In ten days they were up fourteen inches. They had seen enough; the natives were friendly and a colony would be able to grow its own food on Roanoke Island. Barlow reported enthusiastically that the 'soil is the most plentiful, sweet, fruitful and wholesome of all the world'.

In the same ten days that the peas were growing, Barlow persuaded two lusty warriors, Manteo and Wanchese, to return to England with him where, shortly after his arrival, he gave Ralegh his written report. Ralegh presented it to the Queen who read with approval the news about grapes, pearls, the fertility of the soil, the willingness of the natives to trade, and their golden-age dispositions. But Elizabeth's critical eye could not have failed to notice that the explorers had found no safe harbour even for small ships. Vessels larger than 100 tons, unable to cross the sand reef, would have to ride at anchor, vulnerable to hurricanes and other hazards. Also Barlow's caution among the Indians spoke much more eloquently than did his report of the continual civil wars the Indians were engaged in. The country had been ravaged by cruel and bloody feuds characterized by treachery, surprise, broken faith, and perpetual hatreds. Besides, he said, the Indians worshipped 'idols' which were 'illusions of the devil'. Barlow had intended to convey a picture of a land flowing with grape and money, possessed by a gentle, loving people who desired to trade and were extremely inept at it, the very thing England was looking for. There were overtones in his picture, however, which might have suggested caution.

While Barlow was in America Ralegh was making larger plans for his colonization. Always in his mind was the contrast between the effective efforts of Spain and the fumbling inadequacies of England and France. It was the small scale of Coligny's and Gilbert's enterprises that had foredoomed them. Ralegh had a friend in France, an English clergyman named Richard Hakluyt who, like Ralegh, had known personally a number of the French colonists from the Florida colonies. Like Ralegh also he had a passionate sense of mission about the New World, so Ralegh asked him to come to England and prepare a treatise which would persuade Elizabeth and her councillors that it was in England's vital interests to make a national effort in America. It was to be no proposal for an exotic trading post, for a little highly publicized adventuring, but for an empire that would match, and ultimately overmatch, that of Spain. Even before Amadas and Barlow had returned, Hakluyt had completed his *Discourse on Western Planting*, written 'at the request and direction' of Walter Ralegh.

Much of what he said had all been heard before about converting the heathen, employing idle men and finding the Northwest Passage. But in pursuit of Ralegh's larger aims, he asserted that an American colony might make England a self-sustaining nation. Wine, olive oil and silks, which were now imported, could be produced in America. Also gold, silver, copper and pearls are to be found there. He insisted that the people were gentle and obedient (both Barlow and Hakluyt probably had instructions from Ralegh to emphasize this point), but obedient or not, will they or nil they, the natural inhabitants, with whom England will make every effort to trade peaceably, will if necessary be forced to surrender the 'natural commodities of their lands' and Englishmen will become 'great gainers'.

Most important of all, Hakluyt mapped out a comprehensive attack on the Spanish empire which, if successful, would simply drive Spain from the New World. The black legend of Spanish cruelties ensured, he said, that the natives, given a chance, will revolt and willingly join their English liberators (all his life Ralegh thought of himself as the humane emancipator of the Indians). Once a good base has been established in the middle of North America, the English can raid northward against the fishing fleets and southward against the West Indies and the Spanish Main. Hakluyt boldly suggested that then the English may with impunity violate the Pope's line and Spanish territories.

If you touch Philip [in the Indies], you touch the apple of his eye; for take away his treasure, which is *nervus belli* and which he hath almost [entirely] out of his West Indies, his old bands of soldiers will soon be dissolved, his purposes defeated, his powers and strength diminished, his pride abated, and his tyranny utterly suppressed.

But if England did not drive Spain from the New World, if she did not plant in North America immediately, Hakluyt was convinced that the Spanish would soon occupy all of the American territories.

Elizabeth had read Hakluyt's *Discourse* when Ralegh brought her the report by Barlow which so fully (and perhaps suspiciously) confirmed Hakluyt's arguments. Since the emoluments from the Crown had not yet started to flow into his pockets, Ralegh himself had no money, and so he urged Elizabeth to take a personal interest in the venture. He tempted her with a brilliant stroke. Would Her Majesty allow the new land to be called, after her, Virginia? Elizabeth, smiling, nodded approval. Immediately the northern boundary of Florida retreated from the Arctic Circle where Spain had placed it and came to rest around the 31st parallel where it is today. The North Atlantic coast, from Florida to Newfoundland, had a new name and Elizabeth was part of the New World forever.

While the new land bore the name of Elizabeth, the legal title to it remained with Ralegh if Parliament would confirm his claim. In February, 1585, that title was confirmed but hedged with a few restrictions: he could not take imprisoned debtors, wives, wards or apprentices to the new colony. Shipping and supplies must be paid for; they could not be requisitioned by the authority of the Crown. All of this Ralegh agreed to; shortly thereafter Elizabeth knighted him and he had a seal made of his coat of arms with an inscription, 'Lord and Governor of Virginia'.

Knowing that Ralegh desperately needed money to further the American enterprise, and believing that he was entitled to it, Elizabeth began to supply it through the farm of wines, the license to export cloths and other privileges. Ralegh knew that these gifts were to be used in the service of the nation and that is how he used them.

Elizabeth, then, would support the colonizing plan, but only indirectly and cautiously, for she was not ready to defy Spain openly. The official responsibility was to be Ralegh's. But his urgent duties in England demanded his presence there, even without Elizabeth's reluctance to expose her favourites to hazard. He was therefore forbidden to lead the expedition in person. He would set the goals and formulate the plans, but he must find a deputy to carry them out. He needed a man in whom he could place entire confidence, and he selected his cousin, Richard Grenville of Cornwall, who in certain ways resembled Sir Humphrey Gilbert, a man of unqualified, even fanatical courage. Although more self-assured than Gilbert, like him he had a tendency to near hysteria in moments of crisis. He was a most formidable captain. Ralegh approached his stern, combative cousin and asked him to take the general charge of the voyage. Out of 'the love he bare unto Sir Walter Ralegh, together with a disposition he had to attempt honourable actions', Grenville agreed to hazard himself in the second Virginia voyage.

Because Elizabeth had provided no money, although she did provide a ship, Grenville was expected to take enough from piracy to pay the costs of the voyage and, if possible, return a profit to the investors. Those accompanying Grenville were not given land grants; rather they were to be paid wages and given a share in any profits. This first colony was not an attempt to establish English homesteaders in a new land but to make enough money by piracy, trade, or by finding gold or pearls, to make future large-scale colonizing a possibility.

The ships left England on April 9, 1585, with Grenville as Admiral aboard the *Tyger*, the Queen's ship. There were six other ships, including the *Roebuck* which Ralegh had built, and two small pinnaces. The company was a remarkable one. Ralph Lane, who was to have charge after the colonists arrived, was the Queen's equerry and had commanded troops in Ireland and the Low Countries. There was Thomas Cavendish who was later to circumnavigate the globe; and in a brilliant stroke, Ralegh had persuaded Thomas Hariot, an authentic scientist, to accompany the expedition and make a survey of the plants and mineral wealth of the New World.

On the 12th of May, Grenville came to an uninhabited harbour in Puerto Rico where he built a fortified camp, and constructed a pinnace to replace one which had been lost on the voyage. When it was completed, on May 29, he sailed out and captured two frigates filled with rich freight and prominent Spaniards, all of whom were later ransomed 'for good round sums'. Already Grenville was making the voyage pay.

After a stop at the port of Isabella in Hispaniola where the colonists took seeds, roots, and cuttings of many plants, including sugar cane to transplant in Virginia, the expedition made landfall on the North American coast on June 20. The ships were almost wrecked on the Cape of Fear but on the 26th Simon Fernandez brought them to anchor at Wokoken. Three days later the *Tyger* struck a bar and sank. Though she was re-floated, it was still a grave misfortune, for it was now too late to plant crops, and the *Tyger* carried almost all of the provisions for the coming winter. The colonists now had food enough only for twenty days, which placed them in the position that Coligny's Florida colonies had once been in: they must either live off the natives or starve.

Despite their bad luck, the colonists showed great energy.

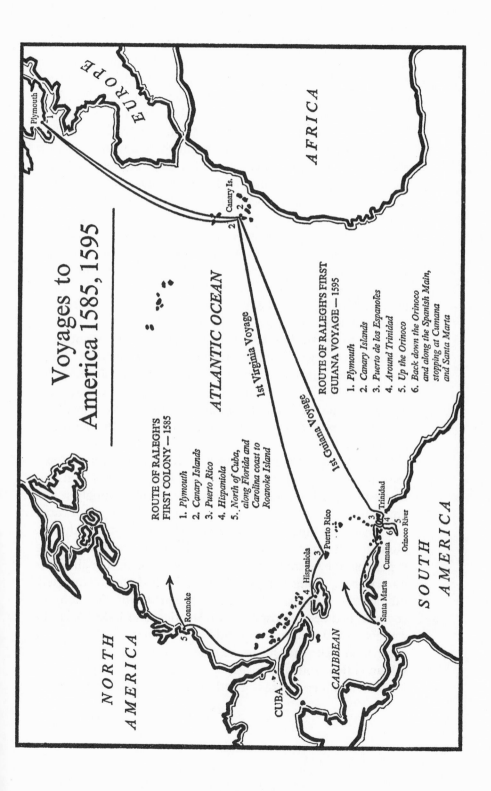

Voyages to America 1585, 1595

EUROPE

Plymouth

AFRICA

Canary Is.

ATLANTIC OCEAN

1st Virginia Voyage

1st Guiana Voyage

ROUTE OF RALEGH'S FIRST COLONY — 1585

1. Plymouth
2. Canary Islands
3. Puerto Rico
4. Hispaniola
5. North of Cuba, along Florida and Carolina coast to Roanoke Island

ROUTE OF RALEGH'S FIRST GUIANA VOYAGE — 1595

1. Plymouth
2. Canary Islands
3. Puerto de los Españoles
4. Around Trinidad
5. Up the Orinoco
6. Back down the Orinoco and along the Spanish Main, stopping at Cumana and Santa Marta

NORTH AMERICA

Roanoke

Hispaniola

Puerto Rico

Trinidad

Cumana

Orinoco River

Santa Marta

CUBA

CARIBBEAN

SOUTH AMERICA

With the assistance of Manteo and Wanchese, they began to explore creeks and estuaries, and took small parties to the mainland. On one of these trips, Grenville and a party of three boats were exploring the main; somehow an Indian managed to steal a silver cup from one of them. Grenville, who had served in Ireland and had been taught there how to deal with native thievery, demanded that the cup be returned immediately. When it was not, he burned a village and destroyed all the corn planted around it. Transplanting these Irish tactics to the New World was a bad start.

When the explorations were concluded, the colonists decided that it would be safer to establish themselves on Roanoke Island than to attempt a village on the mainland, for the island offered a natural defence. There they settled and, in about two months, Grenville left them with a promise that reinforcements and supplies would reach them by the following Easter. He then returned to England by way of the West Indies. Off Bermuda he overhauled a large Spanish freighter of 300 tons, the *Santa Maria*. The ship's manifest indicated that she carried gold, silver, pearls, ginger, cochineal, and other cargo to the value of 120,000 ducats. Grenville himself, with a prize crew, took over the *Santa Maria* and brought her into Plymouth on September 18.

Ralegh, who had been nervously awaiting word, hurried down to secure the cargo. Rumours had already reached London that it was worth half a million pounds, but, disappointingly it was not. Grenville said there was no gold or silver; the main cargo was sugar and ginger which he valued at only 50,000 ducats. However, that, along with the other booty he had taken, made it possible for Grenville to give each of the investors all of his money back, along with some gain; he had thus completely fulfilled the dual task Ralegh had assigned him. A colony of 107 men had been transported to America, and Ralegh's credit was good for future ventures. Still he could not resist the role of persecuted Celt: the Queen, he complained, had taken for herself an entire cabinet of pearls.

On September 3, 1585, a little more than two months after

Queen Elizabeth in her glory. To her right is visible the ships which had vanquished Spain's Invincible Armada. Below is her crown, emblem of sovereignty temporal and spiritual; her right hand rests on the globe delicately but with assurance. From the garments encrusted with jewelled ornaments looks out the woman who commanded Ralegh's devotion and from whom he hoped advancement. The painter gives no hint that Time is eroding her charm and her power. *(By permission of Francis Tyrwhitt-Drake)*

Robert Devereux, second Earl of Essex, to whose career Ralegh found his fortunes ironically bound. First the younger and high-born Essex took Ralegh's place in Elizabeth's affection and favour. Having shared the command of the expedition against Spain, they had to share even less comfortably the glory of the victory at Cadiz. Sometime friends, they were divided by rivalry for power, and the catastrophic fall of Essex brought Ralegh first into bitter unpopularity and later into jeopardy of his life. This portrait shows the handsome, intense, and unstable hero soon after his triumphant return from Cadiz. *(The National Portrait Gallery, London)*

the colonists arrived, Ralph Lane sent a letter home to Richard Hakluyt which buttressed the Hakluyt-Barlow arguments. He reported again on the great numbers and the size of the grapes; he said that he had found many kinds of flax, one of which was like silk. The sugar cane from the West Indies was growing and he affirmed optimistically that everything England received from Spain, France, Italy, or the East Indies could be found or grown in Virginia. The people were 'most courteous' and they needed English woollens. The air in America was wholesome; he had no sick men.

To conclude, if Virginia had but horses and kine in some reasonable proportion, I dare assure myself, being inhabited with English, no realm in Christendom were comparable to it.

The one unmistakable stroke of genius which Ralegh showed in this venture was his persuading Thomas Hariot to go to America as a kind of second in command, for Hariot played the most important role in the relations of the colonists with the natives. He began by showing the Indians some sea compasses, the loadstone, a perspective glass (precursor of the telescope), burning glasses, fireworks, clocks and so on. These were the instruments and inventions that were revolutionizing Elizabethan technology and when the Indians saw them, they thought they 'were rather the works of gods than of men', and Hariot said, it led the Indians to feel that God must especially love such people to have taught them so much. The Indian fear of Hariot's magic made it easier for him to teach religion to the natives and helped keep them in fearful wonder.

He set up his perspective glass in such a way that, by concentrating the rays of the sun, it would start a fire several yards away. One of his glasses was apparently so made that if the viewer stood close, he would see things in their usual size and appearance. If he stepped back, however, the image would suddenly be gigantic. While the *wiroan* was still shaking his head in disbelief, Hariot could shift the focus further outward until suddenly all images would be reversed, and people, trees, and animals would all be standing with their heads downward, their feet pointing up.

At these tricks, and similar ones performed with a loadstone, such as picking up iron with a magnetized sword, the Indians were properly amazed, and it was a good thing; the survival of the colonists would soon depend on the superstitious awe which Hariot had engendered. For soon food became scarce. The coastal Indians were not good hunters; their weapons were poor and they took large animals only occasionally. Their diet was mainly fish caught in weirs, and crop foods which they had stored. Never having been taught Puritan thrift, they stored enough maize only to see them through the winter and to provide seed for the next spring. They had no provisions for long visits from pale visitors. Nothing except a fear more terrible than that of starvation could induce them to part with their seed corn.

Further, the Indians had little else to trade with; their supply of skins was small and they had already lost their taste for trinkets: copper utensils were what they wanted most. Before long they became shrewd bargainers: they demanded many utensils for a little food until they had all the utensils they wanted and the colonists were growing more desperate for food all the time. Then it occurred to the crafty and disillusioned mind of the chief of Roanoke Island, Pemisapan, that he should continue to accumulate copper, that the mainland Indians might want it as badly as his people had, that with it he might effect an alliance that would see the white interlopers destroyed through the agency of their own copper pots.

Meanwhile the colonists were not enjoying their journey into the golden age. Many who were city-bred longed for the taverns, the bull-baitings, the plays and other amusements of London. Not finding them they sulked and lazed, pampering their bellies, as Hariot said. Many of them had come hoping to find gold and silver; when the first explorations failed to find it, they lost interest and simply existed from day to day without any effort to learn the language, teach religion, or fulfill any of the high aims of Hakluyt's *Discourse*.

The leaders of the colony, however, Hariot and Lane, tried to live by the spirit of the Ralegh-Hakluyt pamphlet, to avoid Spanish cruelties, and to win the natives by kindness. Accompanied by a small group of soldiers, they travelled from village to village, surveying the land, the flora and fauna, and visiting the people. In many villages, 'subtle devices' were practised against them, but the colonists, seeking 'by all means possible to win [the Indians] by gentleness', never retaliated. And then Hariot began to observe a pattern. Wherever the colonists practised the Christian faith and did not retaliate, a strange sickness came upon the inhabitants of the town, and people began to die 'very fast'. It was as though the psalm was being fulfilled, 'Vengeance is mine, saith the Lord, I will repay'. As the Indians too discerned this pattern, they came to feel that the god of the white men had given them skill to kill whom they would at any distance and without weapons. One old chief believed that the souls of the white men who had been killed by the Indians came back and mysteriously afflicted the transgressors. When the Indians perceived also that the exploring groups did not attempt to force or persuade their women, the belief grew that the white visitors were something other than human.

But as the winter wore on and food for 104 men was increasingly difficult to find, frustrations grew on both sides. The Indians likely observed that those pale celibates, before many months had passed, were merely pale; and for men from the spirit world they had uncommonly large appetites which their god seemed incapable of satisfying. Among the colonists doubts about the New World were growing; even Lane was dubious. It read very well when Hakluyt wrote about establishing new industries, but when had Englishmen ever cultivated grapes and made wine from them? It was an art that took generations to learn; and there was no real hope of making silk or cultivating olives with inexperienced men; all of that was simply visionary. The conviction grew on Lane that there were only two practical hopes for his colony; he must find either a rich mine or a passage to the South Seas. Once he had arrived at this decision, he forgot agriculture and gambled the future of his colony on explorations.

He sailed up the Chowan River; at the village of Chawanoac,

he found the largest Indian tribe yet discovered. Its chief, Menatonon, could put 700 braves in the field. Lane, with his small company, was worried and, as a precaution, seized the chief and held him, releasing him only when his favourite son, young Skiko, was given as hostage and sent back to Roanoke as security for the safety of the expedition.

And Menatonon told Lane some things he wanted to hear. Because the English were newcomers, they had not yet learned to evaluate Indian stories; they were inclined to be as credulous, in their own way, as the Indians themselves. To the northeast, Menatonon said, three days by canoe and four days over land was an island in a bay where there was a great quantity of pearls; all the better sort of Indians were bedecked with them and their houses and beds were garnished with them. It was, he said, a wonder to see. Menatonon warned Lane that the King of Pearls would bring many warriors into the field to resist him. Lane thereupon resolved that if the supply ships which Ralegh and Grenville had promised him not later than Easter arrived on time, he would march northwards, erecting a series of forts as he went. He would build these forts near Indian cornfields in order that the men detailed to hold them could eat. At the Bay of Pearls he would erect a strong fort and then bring all the Roanoke colony northwards to this new site which would have been somewhere on Chesapeake Bay. That would have been a much better site for a colony and would have provided a sheltered harbour which was the most pressing need. But the failure of Ralegh's relief ship to arrive on time nullified the plan.

Menatonon told Lane other interesting things. Up the Roanoke River there was, he said, 'a marvellous and most strange mineral, which the Indians called wassador'. This was the word for copper but Lane, who wished to believe something more, said that it was also the name Indians gave to all minerals. Menatonon described wassador as 'very soft and pale', and said that it could be panned in an almost pure form in a deep pool where the river fell from high rocks and hills. It sounded as if it might be grains of gold carried down by the river; even if it were

132

not, one of Lane's assayers told him that any copper which savages could melt must be 'one of the richest minerals in the world'. With all this information, Lane returned to his base on Roanoke Island and made immediate plans for exploring the river. And he had one other incentive. Menatonon told him that thirty or forty days' journey up the Roanoke would bring him close to the sea. Because no one had any knowledge whatever of the interior of the continent, Lane believed, or at least hoped, that such a journey might bring him to the Pacific where, conceivably, a deep port would open the way to the Indies of spice and mine. At one stroke he might find both the Pacific harbour and the gold.

Lane prepared two boats, taking the little food he had been able to barter from the Indians, and with forty men, nearly half of his entire company, he set out on the expedition that would probably determine the success or failure of the colony. This was the opportunity Pemisapan had been waiting for, and he showed a certain primitive genius in the way he plotted the destruction of the colonists. First he travelled up the Roanoke River, along the route which Lane planned to take, telling the Indians that Lane intended to kill them. Their only hope, he said, was to abandon their towns immediately, taking all their food with them. Such a policy was disastrous for Lane, for he depended entirely on being able to secure food along the way. His expedition crossed Albemarle Sound and travelled up the Roanoke River a total distance of 160 miles from Roanoke Island. At that point he had two days' supply of food left. He therefore stopped and called his men into council. Lane said he thought that the Indians had probably enticed them into a trap with the intent of starving them; he believed, therefore, that it was wisest for them to return. Actually, he inwardly wished to continue, but thought it best, in case things went badly, to be on the record with the contrary opinion. The vote was 38 to 2 to continue up river; someone pointed out that there were two mastiffs which, if necessary, could be boiled with sassafras and eaten. This was the only time on the entire voyage that Lane's men showed enthusiasm. The scent of gold was in their nostrils.

133

Two days later all of their food was gone. They heard some savages calling, to Manteo they thought, who answered them. Soon they heard a song which they believed to be a song of welcome. Manteo, however, perceiving that it was a war chant, shouted a warning; immediately there was a volley of arrows.It is a commentary on the prowess of the Virginia Indians that not a single colonist was hurt. The voyagers replied with musket fire which drove the Indians into the woods. But it meant the end of the voyage. The colonists ate the mastiffs and hastened back down stream. On Easter eve, Lane said, 'they fasted very truly', one of his few essays into humour. Finally they found some weirs and helped themselves to the fish, just in time, too, for some of the light horsemen were 'far spent'. The next day they arrived home.

In the meantime, Pemisapan, never expecting to see them again, had been engaging in psychological warfare on Roanoke Island. He told the remaining colonists that Lane and his men were all dead. He also denounced the god of the white men and blasphemed Christ, saying that a god who couldn't feed his worshippers wasn't a true god. Upon his return, Lane discovered all of this and more. Gradually he saw the outlines of the conspiracy.

A month or so earlier, in March, Pemisapan had proposed to the Indians on Roanoke Island that they all flee to the main land leaving the island's crops unsowed, and that in the future they should refuse to sell any food at all. This would have meant starvation for the colonists, for they had not a single grain of corn to put in the ground for themselves, and they never had been able to make the reed weirs in which fish were snared, a surprising incompetence in Lane's technicians. This proposal of Pemisapan's, however, had been opposed by his aged father, Ensenore, primarily because of superstitious fear. Having seen Hariot's magic and having seen the sickness strike those who injured the white man, he thought it too dangerous to risk provoking their god. So Ensenore prevailed and the Indians had planted some corn for the colonists on Roanoke Island; it would be ripe around July 1. That was still ten weeks away when Lane unexpectedly returned in the middle of April, discrediting Pemisapan and justifying the counsel of the sage Ensenore. But a few days later, on April 20, Ensenore died and Pemisapan was free to try again. In the meantime he had persuaded Wanchese to join him against the English and these two devised a new conspiracy. Recognizing that with Lane's return they now needed a substantially larger number of braves, they began bargaining with the surrounding tribes: copper kettles for copper warriors. Soon they had seven or eight hundred braves ready to assist them.

Under the guise of funeral obsequies for Ensenore, the Indians were to gather on the mainland across from the island. Then a score or so of braves, chosen for their courage and strength, would come over to Roanoke in the dead of night and set fire to the houses of Lane, Hariot, and the other leaders of the colony. When the sleepers awoke, they were supposed to run out of their houses 'of a sudden amazed', in their shirts and without arms. There each would be met by a destroying angel who was to knock out his brains with a stag-horn war club. When the leaders went down, a signal would be given and the war canoes from the mainland would ferry all the braves to the island where they would massacre the remaining colonists.

It was a good plan and should have worked. But there was one hitch: the young prince Skiko. Lane and his men had treated the young blood with consideration and respect and he had come to like them. Two weeks before the scheduled attack, he revealed the entire plot.

After the death of Ensenore, Pemisapan had taken his braves to the mainland. The colonists were in such desperate need of food that they were sending to him every day now; he never quite denied them altogether, but he gave as little as he dared. June 10 was the day the natives had appointed to rid themselves of the intruders whom they had come to detest. But on the night of May 31, Lane decided to act. He intended that night to make what he called a 'canvisado', actually a *camisado*, a tactic developed by the Spaniards in which men dressed in white shirts made an attack on the enemy in the dark of night, the

135

white shirts serving for identification. But that afternoon some of his light horsemen had surprised a canoe full of natives, captured them and cut off their heads. This alarmed the others who scattered and thereby rendered the *camisado* unlikely to succeed.

So Lane decided to turn Pemisapan's own strategy against him. The next day he took twenty-seven of his best men and rowed to the mainland. Then he sent for Pemisapan and seven or eight of his *wiroans*, the leaders of the uprising. Before the Indians arrived, he gave his men a watchword. They were to listen for it and when they heard it, they were to open fire on the natives and kill them all. Lane, the Puritan, had been terribly offended by Pemisapan's blasphemies; it seemed to him that Jehovah and Dagon were met again, this time in Virginia. When the chiefs were assembled, he gave the password: 'Christ, our Victory.' Immediately the colonists slaughtered the chiefs, all except Pemisapan who, though wounded, only pretended to be dead. Suddenly he jumped up and ran off toward the woods pursued by an Irishman who soon emerged from the forest with Pemisapan's head in his hand.

One week later, twenty-three sail appeared off the island. No one knew whether they were friendly or whether the King of Spain, once again, had sent a force to clear the intruders from the kingdom the Pope had given him. It turned out to be Sir Francis Drake, who had been plundering the Spanish Main. Elizabeth had at last given her permission for a raid against the Spanish Empire in reprisal for Philip's seizure of some English merchant ships. Drake had sacked San Domingo and Cartagena, receiving ransom for both cities, and then, surprisingly, he sailed up the coast of Florida and attacked the Spanish colony at St. Augustine, burning the fort and driving the survivors into the interior. Since that attack promised no hope of booty, it was likely carried out at the request of Ralegh, in order to remove the threat to the flank of Virginia.

So Drake arrived in Virginia at the critical moment when the colony was shaken by the attempted massacre, its hopes disappointed, its incentive gone. Drake tried to save Ralegh's colony. He offered to leave enough supply to keep Lane until August when Lane had intended to return to England anyway. That would give him the summer in which to explore; to try once again for the *wassador* or to find a route to the sea. He also offered to leave ship captains who knew good harbours, who would help find one for the site of the next colony, and who could then bring them all back to England. He also volunteered guns, oarsmen, ammunition, and clothing, and finally he offered the *Francis*, a bark of 70 tons; she was small enough to avoid shoals and bars, but large enough to transport the colony north to Chesapeake Bay.

It was all agreed upon when, on June 13, a bad storm swept up the Carolina coast; there were waterspouts and hurricanes. Cables snapped, anchors were lost, the pinnaces and many of the small boats were driven into shore and beaten to pieces. Only by skill and good luck were the larger vessels saved. On June 16, when the storm cleared, Lane saw, in disbelief and dismay, that the *Francis*, with all the stores which Drake had given him aboard, and a number of his colonists too, was crowding full sail eastward for England. It is surprising that a ship under Drake's command should have been guilty of such a breach of discipline. But the sea-captains were independent men; and when they had called a council and had the full voice of crew and passengers, no court in England would hold them guilty of malfeasance.

Drake still tried to save the colony. He offered another ship, but she was too big to be brought inside the reef at Albemarle Sound; she would have to lie at anchor in the road. Lane realized that she was also too large to use in exploring the coast; it would be difficult to load and unload her while she was lying out at sea. Besides, even to a moderate Puritan, the storm looked like the finger of an angry God. So Lane called an assembly, reminding the colonists that Ralegh had promised them relief by Easter; it was now past the middle of June. He suggested that with the increased hostilities against Spain it would be unlikely that England could spend much money or thought on the colonists. He therefore proposed returning to England

137

with Drake. The company 'readily assented' and began to fetch their baggage off Roanoke Island in the small boats. The wind came up again, the ships began to pitch and roll, and the sailors, angered at the many risks they had already undergone for the colonists, threw overboard the chests, books, writings and valuables, including a string of pearls Lane had intended for the Queen. Then Drake's fleet, with all the colonists aboard, stood out at sea.

Seventy-two hours later, Ralegh's first relief ship appeared and dropped anchor. Two weeks later, Richard Grenville arrived in the *Tyger* accompanied by other vessels. Bad winds, sickness, any of the hundred reasons that inevitably delayed naval expeditions in the age of Elizabeth had delayed Ralegh's ships. Had they arrived a few hours earlier, the colony could have been removed to Chesapeake, founded on the shores of a good harbour, and given food for a year. Destiny had beaten Ralegh by the margin of three days and nights.

The first relief vessel had spent a few days looking for the colonists and finally returned to England with all its provisions, the voyage a total loss. When Grenville arrived, he was completely puzzled. He found the houses intact and the walls of the fort unbreached but there were no settlers, and he could learn nothing from the Indians, most of whom had fled anyway. He decided that Roanoke Island must be held and so he debarked fifteen men and left them a two-years' supply of food. It was a major error in judgment, for as soon as Grenville's sails dipped under the horizon, the Indians attacked the colonists and killed two of them. The other thirteen put out to sea in a boat and were never seen again.

On his way home Grenville again looked for prizes. He found one ship with a cargo of sugar, ginger and hides. He sacked some towns in the Azores and brought home some booty and prisoners for ransom. He had not made enough on this trip, however, to repay the investors; and the government, as well as the promoters, were beginning to make a pessimistic assessment of the situation. The colonists had found no mine. The obedient and courteous savages had proved cunning and hostile. The religious instruction had been superficial and unsuccessful. In one year, it appeared, the English had managed to make themselves and their religion almost as badly hated as the Spaniards. They had kidnapped Indians, robbed their weirs, spoiled their cornfields; they had treacherously murdered their chiefs in the name of Christ, the very thing Parmenius had pointed to as the essence of Spanish cruelty. No one had really meant it to be that way, but again, between the conception and the execution there had fallen the shadow.

An anonymous account said that the hand of God had come on the colonists for the outrages and cruelties which 'some of them' had practised against the Indians. And yet the same account showed no basic disillusionment; it concluded sadly by saying, 'And so they left this Paradise of the world'. The idea that America was the land of the golden age simply would not die. Twenty-three years later, Michael Drayton used almost the same phrase in his *Ode to the Virginian Voyage.*

> You brave heroic minds,
> Worthy your country's name,
>   That honour still pursue,
>   Go and subdue,
> Whilst loitering hinds
> Lurk here at home with shame . . .
>
> And cheerfully at sea
> Success you still entice,
>   To get the pearl and gold
>   And ours to hold,
> Virginia,
> Earth's only paradise.

Gold, pearls and paradise. Visions are indestructible.

Back in England, many of the returned colonists were bitter. They spread rancorous stories about the New World and scoffed at its potential. Ralegh, who was determined to send out a new colony and who still hoped for support from private or state sources, determined to counteract these libels against the land which he had never seen but in which he had so much confidence. And so he urged Thomas Hariot to write a comprehensive report that would inspire confidence in the new land and make a permanent addition to the nation's literature. That report was completed and published in 1588.

Hariot gave a survey in depth of the resources of Virginia; it has been called the first statistical survey on a large scale in the English language. Concerning precious metals he is very reserved. There is rich iron ore; he himself has seen copper plates and some silver, and that is all he will say. Clearly he did not share the fantasies about gold and pearls.

The most interesting section in his report is the one on 'The Nature and Manners of the People'. For the first time an Englishman wrote about the religion of the Indian without indignation. Because Hariot was neither shocked nor repelled, he saw beyond the savagery and superstition into what appeared to be the rudiments of a natural religion. For example, he said that they have 'one only chief and great God, which hath been from all eternity'. He also pointed out that the Indians believed in the immortality of the soul, including a kind of heaven and hell, and believed also that they would ultimately be sent to one or the other as a judgment for their life on earth. This belief, he said, made the common people respect their governors and also motivated them to take 'great care what they do, to avoid torment after death'.

Hariot can be called a Deist only in the loosest sense, but the spirit of Deism animated his view of the native beliefs: a people using the light of natural reason, without special revelation, had arrived at some central religious truths. They had discovered some of mankind's common notions.

Hariot had applied himself as diligently as any man could to learn the Indian language so that in every town he came to, he could speak intelligibly of the Bible and 'the true doctrine of salvation through Christ'. He was not deluded about the ability of the savages to comprehend what he said. They were able to realize that the Bible was holy; they would hold it to their breasts, kiss and embrace it; they would stroke their bodies with it as though it were a charm. Frequently Indians joined the colonists in singing psalms and praying; when they were ill they requested the colonists to pray to their God, which they did, said Hariot, and often with good effect. Hariot's recital of his missionary work among the Indians, set forth in the simplest terms and without self-praise, is wholly convincing and sufficiently answers the charges of atheism levelled at him when similar charges were later directed against the School of Night. And his insistence that English missionary work could only be effective as Englishmen came to understand the language and convey their meanings better is the most sensible thing that had yet been said concerning the conversion of the heathen.

When Hariot's report was written, it might have appeared that the English had done little in the New World. But that would be a superficial view. In 1586, Davis had sailed the straits between Baffin Island and Greenland. Near the Arctic Circle, he had seen a mountain shining like gold; he named it Mt. Ralegh. Southwards was a less glittering headland which he named Cape Walsingham. Davis Straits, Mt. Ralegh, Cape Walsingham and Virginia: English place names were being transplanted to America.

Any man in England who could read, and many who couldn't, knew of Roanoke, Chesapeake, and Secotan, of Granganimeo, Pemisapan, Metanonon and Skiko. Any wild thing loses a little of its wildness when you have its name. Merchants, eager to trade, were reading Hariot's report. A few Indian words had come over into English; some English words were circulating in the strange guttural of Virginia. In the deep woods, brown and white flesh had coupled. John White had painted the villages and people of the New World; those paintings were reproduced in Hariot's report. Manteo, who always remained loyal to the Queen, had told the Indians about England. In many ways the old world and the new had mingled.

If there was to be profitable trade between the two nations, a commodity was needed which could be cheaply freighted and sold at a profit in England. Such a commodity existed and Hariot had described it.

There is an herb which is sowed apart by itself and is called by the

141

inhabitants Uppowoc: . . . the Spaniards generally call it Tobacco. The leaves thereof being dried and brought into powder, they use to take the fume or smoke thereof by sucking it through pipes made of clay, into their stomach and head; from whence it purges superfluous phlegm and other gross humours, and openeth all the pores and passages of the body.

Through the use of this herb, Hariot says, the Indians have avoided entirely many diseases which afflict the English. And he explained how tobacco was used for sacrifice, to quiet storms, and to pacify the gods. When the Indians wished to dedicate a new fish weir, or when they had escaped from danger, they would throw some tobacco up into the air and always with 'strange gestures, stamping, sometimes dancing, clapping of hands, holding up of hands, and staring up into the heavens, uttering therewithal, and chattering strange words and noises'. But when James of Scotland, the world's leading authority on witchcraft, read that passage and realized that tobacco was a tool of the Devil, an agent of sorcery and witchcraft, he hardened his mind against the man who had been responsible for its popularity at Elizabeth's court.

But Ralegh himself loved all the strange new things that came to him from America. The words intrigued him and the people and the adventures. He would have liked pearl and gold and a passage to the Orient. But he was still fascinated with tobacco and the potato and other herbs. He knew a place in Ireland, in the deep soil by the Blackwater River, where they might grow. He would see. He had a silver pipe cast for himself and, in his usual manner, made it into his own personal symbol. When he lighted it, the ladies would squeal and run away in pretended fright or annoyance; and an old servant allegedly threw water on him when he saw smoke pouring from his nostrils. But many others were being soothed and then captivated by the Indian medicine and soon they were willing to lay down an ounce of pure silver for a few dried leaves.

Three members of the expedition, it was said, had become Americans: Lane, Hariot, and the artist, John White. But even of those three only one, the artist, was willing to return. In the other members of the expedition there had not yet arisen that ambiguity of emotion that includes a willingness to leave the English sky and taverns, the noise and bustle of the streets and ports, and live in the new land. It was still alien. Virginia was an inspired name for a beautiful land, but it awaited a people who would pay the price of exile for it.

Mastering his intense disappointment at the failure of his first great expedition, Ralegh began to lay plans for an entirely different kind of venture. He sent out a third colony, but shortly after it arrived in Virginia, the Spanish Armada sailed against England. The New World would now have to wait, while great matters were settled in the old.

9

Ralegh and the Armada

A good historian, a little pressed for space, might write an adequate history of the Spanish Armada without mentioning the name of Ralegh. And no one was ever more keenly aware of it than Ralegh himself. But he did play an important role in that event although, for him, an unusual one. For once, the great actor was entirely behind the scenes, contributing intellectual and physical energy and the resources of his ships. And if Fate and Philip had played a slightly different and wiser game, Ralegh might have been the pivotal figure in the invasion.

By 1586 Ralegh had built himself a small navy. The *Ark Ralegh* was nearly finished; there were two barks of 200 tons each: the *Bark Ralegh* and the *Roebuck;* and there were a number of pinnaces, two of which, the *Serpent* of 35 tons, and the *Mary Spark* of 50 tons had, on a privateering venture, brought back to England, for ransom, the distinguished Spaniard, Don Pedro Sarmiento de Gamboa, whom Ralegh liked and with whom he entered into some interesting intrigues. Sarmiento told him about a vast, unsettled and relatively unexplored wedge-shaped kingdom lying between the Orinoco and Amazon rivers. The stories he related fired Ralegh's imagination and ten years later, when he wrote about it, his prose still rang with the exultation he had felt.

Many years since, I had knowledge by relation of that mighty, rich and beautiful Empire of Guiana, and of that great and golden city, which the Spaniards call El Dorado and the naturals Manoa.

And despite all the mighty events that intervened, that relation

Ralegh burns St. Joseph and captures Berreo and Jorges. *(Radio Times Hulton Picture Library)*

The Ark Ralegh, built to Ralegh's specifications and at his expense, became the Ark Royal flagship that for years led the English navy to victory. *(Radio Times Hulton Picture Library)*

John White, who accompanied Ralegh's expedition to Virginia in 1585 as artist, made paintings of the dwellings, clothing, and modes of living of the Indians there. Here he depicts their manner of fishing, trapping the fish in reed weirs and spearing them from the wooden dug-out 'cannows'. He shows a variety of edible and useful fish, including sea crabs with long spiky tails. These they fastened to sticks to make points with which to strike fish and take them up into the boats. *(Radio Times Hulton Picture Library)*

haunted Ralegh like a wild vision; it never let him rest. No other man in England responded to it as he did; none ever really believed in it except himself and probably his dog-like follower, Lawrence Keymis.

Conversation between Ralegh and Sarmiento covered other matters. Ralegh spoke of the design of warships and indicated that he might be willing to sell one of his smaller vessels to the King of Spain. Sarmiento quickly seized that gambit and said that if Ralegh, without disloyalty of course, wished to serve the King of Spain he would be rewarded with good Indian gold; further, Sarmiento pointed out that monarchs always tire of favourites. When Elizabeth tired of Ralegh, he said, Spanish friendship would keep him from falling into insignificance. He could still be an English statesman with the support of English Catholics and the prestige of his friendship with Philip. Ralegh indicated an interest.

There was nothing unusual about this. For years John Hawkins had taken money from Spain under the pretence that he would, in some fashion or another and at some time or another, serve the Spanish king. Naturally he reported everything to Elizabeth and her Privy Council who looked upon his arrangement as a valuable source of information; also they appeared to be amused to see a belligerent Puritan supported by the Catholic king. Similarly, Ralegh reported his conversations to Elizabeth who thought that Sarmiento might be useful. War appeared imminent and Elizabeth wished to avoid it if she could. There still might be a chance to draw back. Therefore, at her direction, Ralegh released Sarmiento without ransom in order that he might carry private intelligence from Elizabeth to Philip. Half way across France he was arrested by the Huguenots and imprisoned; the Spanish ambassador notified Ralegh who immediately wrote to Prince Henry of Navarre with whom he had voyaged once and asked him, on behalf of Elizabeth, to release the Spaniard. It was done and Sarmiento delivered his message. Whatever it was, it did not succeed.

Elizabeth was also taking other measures that might prevent or delay a general war. If Ralegh had been managing Philip's affairs, the Spanish strategy would have hinged on a decisive naval engagement. Once the English fleet was destroyed, and not until then, he would have landed troops. But Philip was conditioned in older modes of warfare. His success, he thought, depended only on his own fleet holding off the English while the Duke of Parma's army was ferried across the English Channel from the Low Countries in barges and flat-boats. The English did not think it conceivable that Spain would send her castellated galleons up the sleeve of the channel unless she had a deep-water harbour for them to anchor in and adequate fortification to protect them once they were there. Such a harbour could be one captured from the English such as Plymouth or Falmouth, or more likely, it could be one in the Low Countries. As yet Philip had no such harbour; unless he obtained one on the coast of the Netherlands, the Duke of Parma's army, with its barges, would be confined to inland waterways. When the barges emerged into the estuaries and started for the open sea and England, long before they would come under the protection of the guns on the Spanish galleons, the Dutch Sea-Beggars, in their small, shallow-drafted privateering vessels, would set the Spanish soldiers swimming.

And so Elizabeth expected a Spanish attack on one of the fine harbours: Sluys, Ostend, Brill or Flushing, and the Earl of Leicester and his army were, at all costs, to prevent the success of such an attack. Early in 1586 Parma was besieging Rheinberg; Leicester's army was at Arnhem. A council of war wisely decided that the allies could not hope to match the Spanish infantry in an open battle. It was decided, therefore, that Leicester would try to force Parma to abandon the siege of Rheinberg by making a diversionary attack on Goes and Zutphen. And the diversion was successful. Parma immediately marched to the relief of the two cities. Awaiting him was a small body of English cavalry, among them Sir Philip Sidney, the gentle knight, mirror of chivalry and the glass of manners. There was also another young man, Robert Devereux, Earl of Essex, scarcely older than Ralegh was when he first came to France.

As the relief column neared Zutphen, the English cavalry,

awaiting a chance for action in a heavy fog, could not see them. Suddenly the fog lifted and, as if led by the Prince of Condé, they charged wildly and bravely, scattering the Spanish cavalry. But immediately the Spanish infantry threw up the steel hedge of pikes behind which the hackbutters and musketeers volleyed. A musketball entered the left thigh of Sir Philip Sidney, shattering the bone. The English withdrew, Zutphen and Goes remained in Spanish hands, and a few days later Sidney died of gangrene. England mourned as she has seldom mourned. Elizabeth especially was distressed at the loss of so much brightness and, to conceal her pain, she spoke of that inconsiderate fellow, Sidney, who had got himself knocked on the head.

Many poets, and many who were not, wrote commemorative verse, seeking apparently some national catharsis, to find meaning in the meaningless, to soften the tragedy by ennobling the death. Among those who wrote were Edmund Spenser and Fulke Greville as well as Ralegh. Ralegh's poem was not one of his best; it was long and loosely structured, lacking a firm, powerful movement of passion through to the end. Nevertheless Ralegh's poem contained the noblest verse written about the knight who more than any other Englishman had made the Platonic and Christian ideal of inward grace an actuality and not a courtly mannerism.

Whence to sharp wars sweet honour did thee call,
Thy country's love, religion, and thy friends:
Of worthy men, the marks, the lives and ends,
And her defence for whom we labour all.

There didst thou vanquish shame and tedious age,
Grief, sorrow, sickness and base fortune's might:
Thy rising day saw never woeful night,
But passed with praise, from off this worldly stage . . .

What hath he lost, that such great grace hath won,
Young years for endless years, and hope unsure,
Of fortune's gifts, for wealth that still shall dure,
Oh happy race with so great praises run.

An even greater disaster for England than Sidney's death occurred a year later when the Duke of Parma, in one of the most brilliant exploits in the history of a brilliant army, captured both the deep-water ports of Sluys and Ostend. Now, Parma thought, he would not even need the Spanish galleons. He would build his barges and some night, when there was a moon and the sea was calm, he would advance silently across the Channel; his pikes would be marching on London before England knew she had been invaded. He confided his plan to the King who wrote in the margin of his letter, 'It won't work'. With Dutch Sea-Beggars all over the seas, with every Lowland citizen a potential spy, an operation of that kind could never be kept secret. Philip was right: naval force was needed. The big ships would have to pay a visit to England where Philip had once been king; they would blockade the Channel and behind their protective screen, the Spanish pikes would be ferried across to the nation that had seen no invasion by sea for over 500 years.

But the issue of war or peace had been decided even before Leicester lost the deep-water ports. When the Babington Plot was discovered, the most frightening plot ever laid against Elizabeth's life, necessity had overridden choice and events went forward in a lock step. For one by one the leaders of the Protestant world had been assassinated; they had fallen to the muffled face and the dagger or to the mob and the sword. In Scotland, the Regent Earl of Moray had been killed in 1570.

> Ye highlands and ye lowlands,
> Where hae ye been?
> They've slain the Earl of Moray
> And laid him on the green.

It had been Coligny in 1572; and an attempt on the life of William of Orange in 1582 had barely failed. And then it was learned that Philip of Spain had set a price on the head of Orange, a fantastic one, enough to corrupt a hermit. It was suspected that he had done the same for Elizabeth. When a potential assassin had enquired of the Papacy if he would be absolved for murder if it was Elizabeth's life he took, a Papal secretary, with or without authority, had assured him that he would, and so Elizabeth remained the isolated leader of the Protestant world, vulnerable, fragile, and without issue, unwilling to take the precautions for her personal safety which the government thought necessary. She had been deprived of the traditional moral sanctions of the church against murder, and had been made the prize target in all Europe for bounty-hunters.

From 1569 there had been a series of plots to murder Elizabeth and put Mary Stuart on the throne. None of these plots had been well planned; not one was really feasible. But then neither were the plots that had killed the other Protestant rulers. All plans might fail except one and Elizabeth would still be dead. By 1584, Parliament, now desperate, passed the startling Bond of Association. The signers of that Bond included all members of Parliament, in which Ralegh was then serving, and many thousands of other substantial citizens. The signers agreed that they would prevent the succession of any person by whom or in whose interests the death of Elizabeth should be procured, and they further pledged themselves to pursue that person to death. Naturally they had in mind Mary Stuart and any of her English Catholic allies, but the Bond touched James, her son, for he too stood to benefit from Elizabeth's death. Elizabeth calmly insisted on a qualifying phrase stating that those excluded from succession must be 'assenting and privy' to the murder. With that qualification it passed the house and, almost immediately, the Parry plot was discovered. In 1586 came the Babington Plot, in which a young Catholic gentleman with five accomplices had again cooked up what was coming to be the standard plot: a foreign invasion, a rising of the English Catholics, both to be signalled by the murder of the Queen. The Babington plotters had asked support from Philip of Spain and he, the cautious, the prudent, was at last ready to act.

As the affair is so much in God's service it certainly deserves to be supported, and we must hope that our Lord will prosper it, unless our sins are an impediment . . . Perhaps the time at length has arrived when He will strike.

Babington wrote a letter to Mary, informing her of the plot. Walsingham intercepted the letter, read it, and then sent it on, realizing that a kingdom now hinged upon Mary's reply. Her answer, if and when it came, would establish whether she was 'assenting and privy' to the contemplated murder of the Queen. The foolish Mary, thinking her letters safely hidden, smuggled out a reply which Walsingham promptly seized. The plot, she said, including the murder of Elizabeth, was very much to her liking.

Once those words had been written, despite Elizabeth's persistent protection of the life of Mary, it is hard to see what could have stopped the events that followed. They marched like Swiss pikes. Mary was tried before a commission of forty-six peers and councillors and found guilty; the whole affair was exposed to the English nation and now everyone believed not merely that she had engaged in this plot, but that she had also been privy to all the others. When the commission found her guilty, it was now a matter for Parliament. The Members met in joint session and lords and commons petitioned unanimously for the head of Mary Stuart. Although Elizabeth wavered and excused, tacked and veered, the execution was finally carried out. *Mortui non mordent.* The dead do not bite.

Now whatever reservations Philip had previously felt about attacking England were gone. Mary Stuart on the throne would have meant far too much power for France. But before she died, Mary had bequeathed to Philip her inheritance both in Scotland and in England; by the law of God and nations he now could make some claim to being rightful ruler of both countries. A few years earlier he had been only a claimant to the throne of Portugal. His pikes had trailed into Lisbon, and Portugal was his. He would now see what could be done in the north.

In the north, there were a few matters to be cleared up. Babington's lands were forfeited to the Crown. And the Captain of Elizabeth's Guard, Sir Christopher Hatton, was going to be the new Lord Chancellor. As England entered her period of greatest peril, Elizabeth needed someone to guard and preserve England's mystical bride. As she considered the men who had the courage, the intelligence, the good sword arm and the un-compromising devotion, she decided upon the flashing courtier from Devon with the rustic speech. She bestowed upon him Babington's lands and symbolically delivered her body into his protection. He, in turn, gave her the *Ark Royal* and pledged his own life; for years to come Ralegh and the *Ark* were the chief symbols of England's defence of the monarch.

And now there was work to be done. Elizabeth named a Council of War to plan the defence of the realm. Ralegh was on that council and so were Richard Grenville and Ralph Lane, his companions in the founding of the first colony. And there were Lord Grey; Sir John Norris and Sir Roger Williams, who had become brilliant tacticians fighting in the Low Countries; Sir Richard Bingham, who had fought with Ralegh in Ireland, and others. Ralegh's influence in the selection of this committee is obvious, and it may be the closest he ever came to what he so long wished to be: a trusted councillor and a maker of England's policy.

While helping plan the defence of the realm, Ralegh became convinced of a number of matters that later all became part of the doctrine of British sea power. He perceived that it was impossible to fortify adequately all the harbours and potential landing places in a country with a long shoreline. Certainly some defences should be erected, but the English navy was the only thing that could prevent the Spanish navy from landing troops. And as he thought of Parma with his 20,000 undefeated Spanish veterans, marching with pike and musket against London, against trained bands of citizens equipped with halberds and bills, who did not know the use of hackbut or musket and who had never mastered the intricacy of the pike manoeuvres, he had terrible misgivings. He knew that the English fleet must destroy the Spanish fleet; there was no other safety or deliverance.

The Council of War surveyed the English harbours, all convinced and Ralegh especially, that Philip must seize a port, throw a screen of soldiers around it and hold it from counter-attack in order that he might establish a regular line of supply along which would flow ammunition, material for repairs, medicine and food. He never recovered from his astonishment that Philip would do otherwise. Twenty years later he wrote,

For to invade by sea upon a perilous coast, being neither in possession of any port, nor succoured by any party, may better fit a prince presuming on his fortune, than enriched with understanding. Such was the enterprise of Philip the Second upon England in the year 1588, who had belike never heard of this counsel.

Ralegh was unworried about the deep-water ports which Parma had seized in the Low Countries. If the Spanish galleons ever entered one of those unfortified harbours, the English navy would have Philip where they wanted him. But he did worry about landings in England. Milford Haven at the mouth of the Bristol Channel was vulnerable, but so were Plymouth, the Isle of Wight, The Downs, Margate, the Thames and Portland: all of these, Ralegh thought, should be fortified. But more than the others, Plymouth appeared to offer the likely place for Spain to land. Before committing a fleet to the Sleeve with a southwest wind blowing that would send it right on to the North Sea, Philip must have an anchorage somewhere. The Council therefore recommended strong fortifications in Plymouth harbour and a force of 5,000 men in Devon and Cornwall to resist a landing. Portland was the next likely possibility, they thought, and a force of 2,700 men from Dorset and Wilts was to be stationed there. And then, taking their cue from Irish warfare, they ordered that if the Spaniards succeeded in landing, no matter where, the country was to be devastated, crops wasted and burned and every animal driven off or killed. There would be no royal road to London.

Separately from the Council, Ralegh petitioned William Cecil for cannon for Portland and Weymouth. In December, 1587, he was in Cornwall and Devon levying footmen and horse, arranging for beacon lights to be prepared, erecting the turnpikes and barriers that would delay the Spaniard, and devising the tactics that would finally annihilate him. Had the Spaniard, at a critical moment, chosen to enter Plymouth harbour, as he might well have done, the response of the shore batteries and the troops might have decided the entire invasion. Whichever way it went, it would have been Ralegh's responsibility.

In the meantime, Drake and the sea-hawks, Ralegh among them, were urging the Queen to take the offensive. A year earlier she had turned Drake loose and he had made tactically flawless raids on Cadiz and Corunna, smashing up ships, capturing and burning the barrel staves in which the Armada would have carried its food and water, and his action, undoubtedly, had delayed the sailing of that vast, unwieldy fleet. Now the hawks were pointing out that, in Ralegh's phrase, 'the same winds that bring in the enemy bind our shipping'. In other words, the following winds that would bring the Spaniard north would blow the English ships back into their own ports. This meant that in any action in the Channel, the Spaniards would have the weather gauge. The English superiority, which lay in their ability to manoeuvre, to stay out of range and bombard the floating castles crowded with men and horses, would all be lost. The English fleet could either run with the wind before the Spaniard or drop sails and wait to be rammed, boarded and burned.

Drake wanted to attack the Armada in its own ports as he had done a year earlier, or else to go south of Lisbon and wait for the fleet to come out onto the high seas. Then he would have the weather gauge all the way to England; he would harry the Spaniard, shoot their wooden castles to splinters, fill them with holes at the waterline and not a ship would ever reach the Channel. Ralegh concurred wholeheartedly and later, sitting in the Tower, he wrote for the benefit of Prince Henry, with this and other incidents in mind:

If the late Queen would have believed her men of war as she did her scribes, we had in her time beaten that great empire in pieces and made their kings kings of figs and oranges, as in old times. But Her Majesty did all by halves.

It was a shocking thing for Elizabeth and her Council to require the fleet to station itself in the Channel, the wind against it, like a line of cavalry defending a mountain pass. It was bad tactics. But as it turned out, Drake's proposal to meet the Armada on the high seas might have been worse. For when the Armada arrived and action was joined, the English ships used up all of their powder and shot in one day. That kind of cannonading was something entirely new in naval warfare. No one could have foreseen it and no one did. Because they were fighting near home shores, the English ships were continually resupplied by the pinnaces and were able to continue fighting through many days of action. If Drake had closed with the Armada in the Bay of Biscay he would soon have found himself without shot and powder and the Armada would have been between him and England.

And there was more to it than that. Elizabeth realized, as Ralegh and Drake never did, that the fighter with the best chance in her age was the one who countered. The one who thrust was vulnerable in a hundred ways he could not control; he would meet many enemies before he even saw his foe and the least of them might destroy him. Philip discovered that. Disease broke out in his fleet; supplies spoiled; wrong sizes of shot for the cannon were put aboard some ships. Everything went wrong. And when the Armada was ready to sail, the great Admiral of Spain, the Marquis of Santa Cruz, died. Imperturbably Philip thanked his hidden God for not allowing the Admiral to be taken when the fleet was under way.

Philip now had to choose a new commander and he finally lighted on the Count Medina Sidonia, a strange anti-hero in a heroic age, but a man who, in an odd way, commands respect. The Count's response to Philip's solemn call was an urgent request to remain uncalled. He always became seasick, he said, and he always caught a cold away from home. A better man and a better admiral should be chosen. Those who like the tone and flair of Drake and Ralegh have abused Medina Sidonia in his own time as well as in ours. But he saw himself in an unheroic and even comic light; he was intellectually honest, and as it proved, very brave. There is something in the man the modern temper feels a little closer to than it can ever feel for his almost superhuman adversaries.

Medina Sidonia had never commanded a fleet before, but he had the one quality Philip wanted most: he was religious, a man of good life and habits, the kind of man Philip would be pleased with if Philip were God. And Philip was counting on God; he knew well enough that he would need a miracle to win. One of the highest officers in the Spanish fleet was asked, before the Armada sailed, if he expected to beat the English in the Channel. He answered that he did because God would arrange the battle so that the Spaniards could grapple the English ships and board them. God, he said, could do this in either of two ways: by controlling the weather or by taking away the wits of the Englishmen. Their only hope of victory was in coming to close quarters. So, he said, we sail against England confidently hoping for a miracle. Dogged by the victory of Lepanto, the Spaniards marched armed soldiers, horses, hackbutters and pikemen aboard the castellated galleons; they sailed out to fight another land battle on the sea.

Philip was doing everything he knew to get God committed. The Pope himself christened the fleet 'The Invincible Armada'. Before the fleet left Spain, both the heavenly and earthly treasuries of the Church were opened, and plenary indulgences were granted to all who assisted the Armada in the execution of the Pope's bull against Elizabeth. This was a nice touch, aimed at the loyalties of Chatholic subjects in the Low Countries, in Ireland, Scotland and England. It was said in England that the Pope had also contributed a million of gold to the enterprise; the truth is that he had offered to do so when the first Spanish soldier set foot on English soil, a qualification of some magnitude.

Philip issued orders that all sailors and soldiers were to confess their sins and receive absolution before sailing. Once aboard there was to be no swearing, and the ships were searched to make sure that no women had been stowed away. In addition, Philip placed great reliance on the talismanic charm of sacred symbols. Always the Virgin had been considered the destroyer of heresies. It was said that in the days of Arius and Nestorius she had, single-handed, vanquished those abominable devia-

155

tions, and it was believed that she would similarly vanquish the heresies of Luther and Calvin. Representations of the Virgin were generally carried by Spanish pikemen; they carried such a banner when they sacked Antwerp. A verse in Latin had been introduced into the Rosary from a medieval anthem, 'Praise the Virgin Mary who alone overcomes all heresies'. There was an entire school of Counter-Reformation art which showed the Virgin triumphant. In a chapel of the Cathedral of Naples, Calvin and Luther are represented in recognizable form as fallen, overcome by a young hero who bears the banner, *Semper Virgo, Dei Genitrix, Immaculata.*

And so Mary was the destroyer of heresies, but it is impossible to destroy heresies, it seems, without destroying heretics and so the Protestants, fearful and resentful of the Virgin, had retaliated, especially in the Low Countries but also in England, by tearing her images out of the churches, plunging daggers into them, stripping off her clothes while shouting obscenities and insults.

Philip had designed for the Armada a great banner thirty or forty feet across consisting of the Royal Arms of Spain supported by a crucified Christ on the one side and the Virgin Mary on the other. This standard had been consecrated at a Mass in two separate churches in Lisbon before the fleet sailed, and it bore the motto: *Exsurge Deus et Vindica Causam Tuam.* Arise O God and vindicate thy cause. It was a dangerously ambiguous motto, the kind of thing one might have expected from the oracle at Delphi, for if the battle went badly for Spain the Protestants could say that the motto had been fulfilled – and that is precisely what they did say.

Elizabeth countered with a prayer of her own appointed to be read in all of the churches, 'O let thine enemies know that thou hast received England'. On both sides, but especially by Philip of Spain, the will of God was considered the decisive factor.

The Armada of some 130 sail set out from Lisbon on May 30 and slowly tacked northwards along the Portuguese and Spanish coasts. Off Cape Finisterre the ships were scattered by a storm but ultimately they gathered and lay in Corunna harbour for another month. All this time more food spoiled, more ships sprang leaks and more men came down with dysentery and ship's fever – the cruel typhus. On July 22 the Armada sailed again. When English soil was first sighted at Lizard Point, the great banner of the Virgin was run up and unfurled from the mast. And Medina Sidonia had another standard which he was saving for his first encounter with the English, his personal emblem which was to be flown from the mast of his flagship, the *San Martin*. It represented a crucified Christ with the Virgin at one side and Mary Magdalene at the other. He raised it when he sighted Lord Howard in the *Ark*. And so the ships named after the Virgin, *Our Lady of the Rose*, *Our Lady of the Rosary*, and those named after saints, *San Philip*, *San Martin*, *Santa Ana* and the others brought to England, for the first time, the destroyer of heresies who had been fearfully known for so long in the Low Countries. England, thinking of herself as the heir of ancient Israel, met those ships with the *Ark* and the *Rainbow*, symbols of Israel's deliverance. It promised to be an interesting contest, although one doesn't envy God's position.

The initial advantage lay with Spain. Howard, Drake, Hawkins and Frobisher, each in command of a squadron, all lay cooped up in Plymouth harbour. Lord Henry Seymour's squadron was up near Dover guarding against any surprise Parma might attempt with his fleet of barges. On July 29, Drake and Howard received word that the Spanish fleet, with sails furled, was waiting off the Scilly Isles. That was at three o'clock in the afternoon; the tide was then coming in with a current of more than one knot. The ebb tide, with an equally strong current, would be moving out of the harbour about ten o'clock that night. The wind was still from the southwest, which meant that the sailing ships could not use their sails, but would have to be warped out to sea. That would be no easy matter. The Spaniards then had about twelve hours in which to exploit their tactical surprise. If they had decided to attack the English fleet, they presumably would have employed the tactics of Lepanto and sent in first their four great galleases, the giant ships equipped with both sail and oars. They could move in any weather and would have been the only ships inside Plymouth harbour that were manoeuvrable. Whether Ralegh's shore guns could have sunk or disabled them before they came among the English galleons is conjectural. It was, however, the last opportunity to employ the gallease in naval warfare.

But the Spaniards chose to wait. Later Medina Sidonia was blamed for it all, and with stoic resolution and unconsciously comic self-deprecation he took the blame. But he was under strict orders from Philip to avoid a fight until he had joined with Parma's troops at Sluys. To have gone into Plymouth harbour would have been a defiance of orders that even a Santa Cruz, even a Drake, might have hesitated at. Not more than two or three of his ships could have gone in at a time; inside the harbour it would have been pell-mell. And there was a decisive policy consideration. The Spaniards assumed that only Drake was in Plymouth harbour and that the other three squadrons were at sea. If one or all of those squadrons had come up on the rear of the Spanish fleet while it was engaged at Plymouth, it would have been a fight to the finish and Parma and his barges would be left to rot on the shores of Sluys. Medina Sidonia lost a great opportunity, but given his information and prior orders from Spain, he really had no choice.

While the Spaniards were in council, the English were painfully warping their ships out to sea. The little flyboats, with men at the oars, would carry two or more anchors out as far as the cable would allow and drop them. Then the sailors aboard the galleons would fall to and, with ropes, pull their ships up to the anchors; then the process would be repeated. With the tide helping, the fleet made it out of the harbour and around the point of Rame Head where it anchored. While it was still moonlight, the ships began beating out to sea, a difficult feat of seamanship made possible only by the excellent sailing qualities of the ships which were able to manoeuvre near a coastline and in the teeth of a wind. A drifting fog concealed them and when it lifted, the Spanish saw, to their consternation and dismay, that the English had the weather gauge and were ready to give battle. It was difficult to see now how the miracle that would enable the ships of the Armada to ram and board would ever come about. This was the decisive manoeuvre of the battle and the best sailors aboard the *Armada* must have seen the outcome before a shot was fired.

On Saturday the Spanish ships were sighted from the shore and Ralegh's beacons flared along the coasts of Cornwall into Devon and on to Portsmouth where they began burning in a long line inward, flaming all day and through the night until every farmer, and shepherd, every cloth weaver and landowner in England knew that to the south of them, in the Channel, the stakes of empire were being waged at last.

The next day, Sunday, the English fleet, in the rear of the Armada and with the weather gauge, began the cannonading. The fleets exchanged broadsides; there was much smoke and a number of hits but few casualties. Elizabeth's scribes had insisted that Lord Howard cumber his ships with some musketeers, and he had instructions from the Privy Council to close in and board where possible, a suicidal galley tactic which would have deprived him of all his advantages. But it was an instruction he had no intention of obeying.

After the first day's fighting, on Sunday, July 21, the Armada drifted past Plymouth without any indication that it wished to seize the harbour. The southeast wind was still blowing; the ships could not return, so Ralegh, with his troops, marched toward Portland to see what would happen there. On the 23rd the fleet also sailed past Portland Bill and Ralegh's coast was safe. There would be no landings and no fighting in Cornwall or Devon, so he was free to join the English fleet and he did, but his presence there made no difference. He had no command, and the master of the ship he boarded paid no attention to him. The gunners performed as they would have if he had stayed in Plymouth. But in England's most terrible moment, he had placed his body between England and the Spanish fleet; he had, at least, made a gesture.

In the meantime, one of Ralegh's ships was playing a part in one of the fascinating by-plays of the battle. Captain Jacob Whiddon, who had captured Sarmiento in 1586, was sailing the

Roebuck assigned to the squadron of Sir Francis Drake. His job was to bring supplies and ammunitions from shore to ship. On the first day of the battle, Sunday, the flagship of Pedro de Valdes, *Our Lady of the Rosary*, accidentally collided with another Spanish ship and lost her bowsprit. When she was drifting out of control, Medina Sidonia courageously offered to take her in tow with his flagship. He was dissuaded, however, by his officers, and so *Our Lady of the Rosary* drifted to one side and out of the battle.

Lord Howard held a council of war that night and decided to hang close on the Armada's heels as it slowly drifted with the wind up channel. Sir Francis Drake, with the *Revenge*, was given the honour of leading the English ships. He was to put a lighted lantern on his stern and the rest of the fleet would guide on him. Some time during that night Drake did the most astonishing thing of his life and only his uncritical admirers have been able to excuse him for it. Without a word to Howard, he doused his lantern and veered off to port, saying later that he had seen some dark ships passing in the other direction and thought they might be part of the Spanish fleet tacking around the English flank to recover the wind gauge. There were, in fact, some darkened ships passing in the other direction but they were unarmed merchant vessels. What makes Drake's story more than a little fishy is that when dawn broke, the *Revenge* just happened to be within hailing distance of *Our Lady of the Rosary* and when her captain found that the great Drake was summoning him to surrender, he thought it not inconsistent with his honour to do so. Drake's action put Howard and the *Ark* in the greatest jeopardy, for Howard, losing Drake's light, saw a Spanish poop lantern and thought Drake had outdistanced him. With the *Bear* and the *Mary Rose* he closed up and sailed all night cradled in the arms of the Spanish crescent. Drake, in the meantime, had taken the richest prize of the entire battle and sent it home in charge of Captain Whiddon and the *Roebuck*.

And so the battle went on up the Channel, Medina Sidonia running low on ammunition and supplies and unable to obtain any word from Parma as to where or when he would meet him. He kept asking for support, for ships to take off his wounded, and for supplies but Parma could send nothing out of Sluys because the Dutch Sea-Beggars were swarming all around the port. Moving slowly, keeping a tight formation, Medina Sidonia arrived at Calais on Saturday, July 27, and dropped anchor. He could go no further until he heard from Parma; if he drifted on, he would be in the North Sea and, with his ammunition depleted and the wind still from the southwest, all opportunity for convoying Parma's troops to England would be lost. He could never run back through the Sleeve, so now he would simply have to anchor and take his punishment.

Now the second decisive moment of the battle had arrived. The Spaniard was anchored close in to the shore, in a tight formation. It was a highly suitable place for the English to employ the tactic of the fire-ships. Vessels piled with pitch and tar and freighted with gun powder had been prepared in English ports, but there was no time to send for them. There was a need for immediate action and Drake, seeing that need, offered one of his own ships of 200 tons to be converted to a fire-boat on the spot and Hawkins seconded with an offer of one of his. In a moment there were offers of six more. These eight ships were loaded with combustibles and their guns were double-shotted. When the flames reached the powder, those guns would explode. The sails of the fire-ships were shaken out, they were given to the following wind, and their helms were tied to a course that would send them directly into the Spanish formation.

Medina Sidonia saw the fire-ships coming, fired a gun to warn his fleet, slipped his cables, and stood out to sea. But for the first time the admirable Spanish discipline failed. Many captains simply cut their cables and ran before the wind. The current was moving strongly toward the Flemish coast and the wind, rising into a gale, was driving them in the same directions. The fire-boats burned no galleons but they scattered them and delivered them, many now without anchor cables, to the hazard of wind and current.

Lord Howard, meanwhile, lay at anchor and waited for the

dawn. Some time before it was light enough to resume battle, two visitors came aboard with a message from the Queen: Sir Walter Ralegh and Richard Drake. Their instructions were the last angry sputter of the old guard. A naval battle had been going on for days and more shot and powder were being expended in one day than had ever before been used in an entire engagement. Three or four Spanish galleons were captured or sunk, but the fleet was still intact. The Council and the Queen were increasingly alarmed by the failure of Howard to grapple and board and to use his military forces. It looked to them more like a naval ballet than a naval battle, 'a morris dance upon the waters', someone called it. The new tacticians, of course, found aesthetic as well as military pleasure in the way things were going, but Elizabeth did not. Her message, delivered through Ralegh, was 'to attack the Armada in some way, or to engage it, if he could not burn it'. Of all the tasks he ever performed, Ralegh must have liked this one least, because he could not conceivably have agreed with the order. But possibly because of this order, or more likely because he had already perceived that his cannonading, to be effective, must be at closer range, Howard decided to move in on the Armada. He drove ashore the *San Lorenzo*, one of the great galleases, and spent several hours boarding and looting her while his entire squadron stood by. That seemed to be what the Privy Council wanted, but it was a sorry tactic which allowed the rest of the Spanish fleet to escape into the North Sea. The danger to England was now over. All that remained was to see how badly the Armada could still be hurt.

This last day of the battle was frightful. Drake, Hawkins and Frobisher closed to within 'half a musket shot' and poured broadsides into the Spanish fleet. The high castles were blown to splinters, the slaughter of soldiers on the crowded upper decks was so bad that blood was seen spilling out of the scuppers. Every first-line ship was leaking and the Spanish sailors and soldiers who had not been killed were sick, disabled or disheartened. At four o'clock in the afternoon a squall came up which separated the fleets.

As if by a miracle, the Armada escaped going ashore on the Zeeland sands, and ultimately about half the ships, punished and suffering to the limits of human endurance and beyond, rounded Scotland and set a course west of Ireland that would bring them home. Medina Sidonia, humiliated, blaming himself for everything, finally brought the crippled fleet back to Philip who was dutifully grateful to the Almighty for not letting all of it be destroyed. He would try again. Perhaps his talismans were now powerful enough; certainly his ships were not. He would build some new galleons after the English style; he would name them for the Twelve Apostles. Perhaps it was not suitable, after all, to name ships for the Holy Mother.

Back in England there was much criticism of Howard's conduct of the war. Ralegh defended the Lord Admiral in some of the most stinging prose he ever wrote.

Certainly he that will happily perform a fight at sea must be skilful in making choice of vessels to fight in; he must believe that there is more belonging to a good man of war upon the waters than great daring; and must know that there is a great deal of difference between fighting loose, or at large, and grappling. The guns of a slow ship pierce as well, and make as great holes, as those in a swift. To clap ships together without consideration, belongs rather to a madman than to a man of war; for by such an ignorant bravery was Peter Strozzi lost at the Azores, when he fought against the Marquis of Santa Cruz. In like sort had the Lord Charles Howard, Admiral of England, been lost in the year 1588, if he had not been better advised than a great many malignant fools were that found fault with his behaviour. The Spaniards had an army aboard them and he had none; they had more ships than he had, and of higher building and charging; so that, had he entangled himself with those great and powerful vessels, he had gravely endangered the kingdom of England.

Ralegh also knew that King James of Scotland had earned England's gratitude at that moment. When his mother had been beheaded a year earlier, the hot bloods of Scotland were telling him that they would follow him to London at the head of the greatest army ever raised in Scotland. And so Ralegh wrote, in his *History*,

But had the Duke of Parma, in the year 1588, joined the army which he commanded with that of Spain, and landed it on the south coast, and had His Majesty at the same time declared himself against us in the north, it is easy to divine what had become of the liberty of England.

And he was right. There was something Ralegh may not have known, however. When the beacons flared through the night telling the nation that the Armada had come to England, Elizabeth sent a special courier riding through the night to Edinburgh. He arrived soiled with travel but wasted no time on amenities. He immediately saw the King privately and delivered a message from the Queen. It was a promise of some kind that Elizabeth, with her usual mingling of audacity and caution had not written down; there was no document, no seal, simply the word of a Queen given when the Spanish knife was at her jugular. To this day no one knows what that promise was. Elizabeth never revealed it and James, too, was silent. But he did not move against England and he never complained later.

Thinking at first that the Armada would go to Denmark to refit, Ralegh urged the Queen to order close and continuous pursuit. But soon cargo was seen floating in the North Sea, with horses and asses swimming far out of sight of land, while the Spanish ships crowded on sail and hurried north. Then everyone knew that the battle was over at last and that the Armada knew that it was beaten. One problem remained. What would happen if the ships stopped at friendly Irish ports, landed Spanish pikemen and raised a rebellion there ? That contingency must be taken care of. And so the Queen ordered those redoubtable cousins, Ralegh and Grenville, to go to Ireland at once and see that the harbours were made unsafe for enemy ships. By then, however, another cousin, Sir George Carew, was sending word from Ireland that the main body of the fleet had avoided the coast altogether, that the ships that had come in were being torn apart by sea and rocks, and that the enemy were suffering miseries 'to be pitied in any but a Spaniard'. Sir George was able to mop up several hundred Spanish sailors and soldiers, but hundreds more, with Irish help, escaped into

Scotland; some eventually got home. Ralegh and Grenville sailed to the east coast of Ireland and there, realizing that danger was past, devoted most of their time to looking after their Irish enterprises.

There was much glory all around. Hawkins and Frobisher, who had led squadrons, were knighted aboard the *Ark* by Howard; Sir Francis Drake received the prize money from *Our Lady of the Rosary*; Ralegh, however, received no prize money, no compensation and no glory. As time went on the victory assumed epic proportions; quarrelling and differences were forgotten, for a time, in England, and on the Continent a new alignment of feeling toward Spain and England and a new set of attitudes were slowly being born. The victory was regarded by the Protestants as a religious triumph. Roger Williams said that the nation had been saved by divine intervention. The Zealanders struck medals which bore on one side the inscription, 'Glory to God alone'. The English medal bore the legend, 'He breathed and they were scattered'. And Philip reportedly said, 'I sent my ships to fight against men and not against the winds and waves of God'.

And so the legend grew among Englishmen. The spoiler had been spoiled. The destroyer of heresies and all the Spanish saints had assembled an Invincible Armada off England's shores. And the hosts of Israel had gone out to meet them, led by the *Ark*. Ralegh had given England the symbol of her victory.

10

American and Irish Colonies

Ralegh's first American colony had been intended as a probe, not as a permanent settlement. It consisted of fortune-seekers, under military command, who were to explore and survey the country, hoping to find gold or pearls, silk or some other product that could be profitably traded. But all the time that colony was out, Ralegh and his friends had worked on a scheme for permanent settlement in America. Under that scheme, married men would be recruited to take their families to the New World with them. Simply by agreeing to go, a householder would be granted five hundred acres of land in America; with a little money to invest, he could own an enormous plantation if he could expel any native claimants. These settlers were to be organized as a chartered company with rights of self-government, and some members of that company were to remain in England to keep the colonists supplied and, in general, to look after their interests and welfare. While Ralegh still held title to the continent, he had relinquished a good deal of authority over the new colony; it was to be a self-governing corporation in which he had a large investment, a personal interest, but no longer a sole command.

About the time Ralegh was planning this colonization, Cecil and Walsingham were working out a scheme for settling English colonists on the escheated Desmond estates. They probably consulted Ralegh because their plan incorporated some of Ralegh's ideas for the 1587 colony in America. They envisioned a stable society of English settlers living under English law, strong enough to protect themselves against Irish rebellions without requiring the Crown to keep an expeditionary army in the field. It was believed that in time, when the wasted lands could be reclaimed, the settlers should be able to pay taxes and Ireland should begin to contribute to the maintenance of the kingdom.

Under the provisions of the plan, large grants of land, up to 12,000 acres not counting wasteland and bog, would be given to powerful 'undertakers', men of means and enterprise who, in turn, would lease to freeholders, tenant farmers, shopkeepers, craftsmen and others. The undertaker had to agree to bring in a certain number of tenants, according to the size of his grant, and these tenants were to receive land rent-free for the first few years. After that they would pay nominal taxes.

Ralegh was working, then, on the plans for permanent colonies in Ireland and America at the same time, but the opportunity in Ireland came first. In June, 1586, when Ralegh was 34 years of age, just about the time that Lane and his men were returning with Drake from Virginia, the settling in Ireland began. Ralegh was originally granted 12,000 acres; but in close association with him were Sir John Stowell and Sir John Clifton who also had 12,000 acres each. There is some reason to suppose that Ralegh secured their land for them and that, in some way, it was ultimately to come to him. If so, he had not long to wait, for his partners soon became impatient and left Ireland.

Their reason for leaving was the usual Irish chaos. There were in Ireland no land-office records; many claims to the land had always been hereditary, traditional and verbal after the Celtic fashion. Anglo-Irish landowners and even Irish landowners who had not been attainted started endless lawsuits, some refusing to leave the land until the suits had been settled. As a result, the 'pioneers' became disgruntled and began to drift back to England.

But the English government was determined to succeed in Ireland this time. A new commission was sent from London to make a definitive survey of lands and then to make definite assignments. This was just at the time when Ralegh was about to become Captain of the Guard, when the Babington lands were being given to him and when he was in the highest favour with the Queen. It is no accident that the commission began its survey in the vicinity of Youghal and Lismore where Ralegh's lands lay. The survey proceeded well and on February 27, 1587, Ralegh received a Privy Seal warrant giving him title to 42,000 acres of arable land and probably an equal amount of waste land. No other concession in Ireland approached it in size; he secured the best land on both sides of the Blackwater River, including one 'decayed' town, a number of castles, the barony of Inchiquin, and White's Island, the former seat of the Barrys which he had long coveted and which was now his at last. The land was heavily forested and there was evidence of mineral wealth. Under the Geraldines, there were popular rights to the fisheries and to the gathering of food from the waters. But Elizabeth reserved these rights exclusively to Ralegh. For this empire, he was to pay nothing until 1591, half-rent until 1594, and then a full rent of 233 pounds per year, about a tenth of what he could make on one reasonably successful privateering venture. And there was one further concession. The Queen agreed that an extra cavalry company should be sent to Munster to protect the intended settlers. It was a wise concession, but it angered the central government in Dublin and when Sir William Fitzwilliam became Lord Deputy in 1588 he was excessively annoyed that Elizabeth's sumptuous favourite should so far have abused his favour as to have created what was practically a state within a state.

Within two years, most of the Irish seignories were relative failures. Richard Grenville's was succeeding reasonably well; Warham St. Leger's also. But Ralegh's colonies were thriving; it appeared as though, with proper attention and a little luck, he might achieve, for the first time, the age-long aims of English settlement in Ireland. And Ralegh acted like a man who intended to succeed. In the autumn of 1588, when he and Grenville had convoyed troops to Ireland to meet any belated threat from the Spanish Armada, he had stayed to inspect his Munster properties. And when, in 1589, the Crown required reports on the success of the colonization, Ralegh replied that he had settled 144 men of whom 73 had their families with them, almost half of the 320 tenants he was expected ultimately to place under his grant. On the other twenty-three seignories there were only 500 settlers altogether; most of the holdings were failing or had failed and the Irish were drifting back either to occupy the land again or to become rent farmers. In that year the Queen became angry with her former lover and wrote a letter to the Lord Deputy saying that Ralegh was to surrender all of his lands except the original 12,000 acres. But that letter was never sent, probably because if Ralegh's colony went under the entire plantation scheme in Munster would fail.

In that year, 1589, possibly in May, Ralegh left the Court and went to live in Ireland. It was said that he had been chased out of England by the Earl of Essex. The Lord Deputy of Ireland, Fitzwilliam, apparently thought so for he soon entered into a bitter quarrel with Ralegh. In 1586 Ralegh had acquired the lease of Lismore from a man who claimed title to it. But another title was in the hands of Sir William Stanley who had once done the Crown good service in Ireland. Since that time he had gone to the Netherlands with Leicester and been made the governor of the town of Deventer. The Dutch had objected strongly to this appointment because Stanley was a devout Roman Catholic. But Leicester had haughtily replied to all objections that he knew whom to trust among his own officers. It was unfortunate that he didn't for Stanley had long wrestled in his conscience with the intricate problem of loyalty and when he finally decided that it belonged to the Church, he accepted also the Pope's bull of excommunication against Elizabeth and, as a logical corollary, turned Deventer over to the Spaniards. For this service he refused an offer of money, saying that his reward was a conscience finally at peace with itself. Stanley's wife, left destitute in Ireland, appealed to the Lord Deputy who favoured her suit. Ralegh believed that Fitzwilliam made this decision not because he felt any sympathy for the widow or believed in the legality of her case, but rather because he had heard Ralegh was in disgrace at Court and now vulnerable. Ralegh, therefore, wrote a scathing letter to his cousin, Sir George Carew, one that shows his arrogance and his blind pursuit of his own interests at their worst. His 'retreat' from the Court, he says, was only to look after a prize that one of his ships had brought to an Irish port.

If in Ireland they think that I am not worth the respecting they shall much deceive themselves. I am in place to be believed not inferior to any man, to pleasure or displeasure the greatest; and my opinion is so received and believed that I can anger the best of them. And therefore, if the Deputy be not as ready to stead me as I have been to defend him – be it as it may.

As for the suit over Lismore, he said that he would 'shortly send over order from the Queen for a dismiss of their cavillations'. The legal dubiety, as far as the ambitious Ralegh was concerned, was merely a cavil. And he concluded his letter with a curious touch that reveals the cynical and disillusioned courtier. 'The Queen thinks that George Carew longs to see her; and therefore see her. Farewell, noble George, my chosen friend and kinsman, from whom nor time nor fortune nor adversity shall ever sever me.' It was a strange mixture of meanness and generosity of nature in the same letter.

The Queen may have been annoyed with Ralegh, but she was furious with Stanley, who had brought the English into contempt among their allies, and she wrote Fitzwilliam that a traitor's wife was to have no favour. The legal issue was never tried; it was simply settled by royal fiat.

And another traitor's wife was proving troublesome. Eleanor, Countess of Desmond, had written to William Cecil,

I am enforced through extreme poverty to make my moan unto your Honour. At this present my misery is such that my five children and myself liveth in all want of meat, drink, and clothes, having no house nor dwelling wherein I with them may rest.

But none of her husband's vast estates, out of which Ralegh's colony had been carved, ever returned to her. Ultimately she was awarded a pension of 200 pounds a year. When Ralegh was sent to the Tower, in later years, as he reviewed the history of the world he began to see recurrent and cyclical patterns. What men did or what nations did was frequently returned upon them. Bitter deeds bore bitter fruit. And one day Ralegh would have the time and occasion to reflect that by his own admission the wife of a traitor had no rights. In just a few years his wife would write a letter to a monarch who found women distasteful and who, like Elizabeth, believed that the estates of traitors should be bestowed on personal favourites.

I beseech Your Majesty, in the mercies of Jesus Christ, to signify your gracious pleasure concerning myself and my poor children: that whereas Your Majesty hath disposed of all my husband's estates to the value of four thousand pound a year, so that there remaineth nothing to give me and my children bread . . .

Like the Countess of Desmond she would receive a pension for her moan, but the lands were gone forever.

Ralegh had not been tender with the truth when he wrote to noble George. He was, clearly enough, in the Queen's disfavour although no one knows quite why. The most likely explanation is simply a quarrel somehow related to Elizabeth's infatuation with Essex. He had not come to Ireland merely to plant potatoes and tobacco in his garden at Youghal, although he did that too without the slightest awareness of the econonic revolution that would some day result from that act of curiosity.

And so it appeared that despite the opposition of Dublin, Ralegh's Irish colony would succeed. The American colony was a more difficult matter. When the new colonists were recruited, it was found that only two of the former colonists were willing to return, the artist John White and the pilot Fernandez. The artist was chosen as governor and twelve councillors were elected to assist him. It was agreed that the new colony would be planted north of Roanoke Island somewhere on Chesapeake Bay; the most important criterion for the new site was a deep-water port. On January 7, 1587, Ralegh issued a charter authorizing the new colonists to found the city of Ralegh in Virginia. Originally 150 men subscribed, a few of whom were willing to risk their wives and children. But some subscribers died, others withdrew; eventually eighty-eight men, seventeen women and ten children, along with two Indians, the long-faithful Manteo and another one named Tawaye, sailed to Virginia by way of the West Indies where they were to water and collect livestock and plants. They were to proceed first to Roanoke, recover the fifteen men left by Grenville a year earlier and erroneously presumed to be alive, and then install Manteo as Ralegh's representative and as lord of Roanoke Island. With a friendly dukedom on its flank, the expedition was then to proceed to Chesapeake and found the new city.

Predictably, the expedition made a late start, not leaving England until May 8. Soon White, an intellectual whose intentions soared beyond his abilities, quarrelled bitterly with the pilot and, because he lacked the strength of Drake or Grenville, the quarrelling was never resolved; it merely grew into bitter and divisive hostilities. Fernandez leisurely plodded along from island to island and did not make landfall in Virginia until July 16. On July 22 the old site at Port Ferdinando was reached, too late for planting crops. Fernandez anchored in the road while White, with forty men, put off in a pinnace for Roanoke Island. Once White and his men were aboard the pinnace, Fernandez hailed him, told him that a council of his sailors had agreed that it would endanger the ships to go to Chesapeake now and risk the autumn Atlantic storms. Therefore the entire colony would be put ashore at Roanoke Island. It was completely and unbelievably counter to Ralegh's explicit instructions.

The Indians had never returned to Roanoke Island; it was deserted. The colonists immediately began to restore the houses and fell timbers for a palisaded fort; White and Manteo sailed over to Croatoan where they wished to establish friendship with the tribes and find out what had happened to the fifteen men Grenville had left a year earlier. The Indians at first expressed great anxiety lest the colonists take their winter's supply of maize. White promised them that he would not touch it and the Indians, much relieved by his promise, freely volunteered the information that the Grenville colony had put to sea in a small boat and had not been seen again.

After White returned to Roanoke Island, he faced his first

major difficulty. One of his men had gone out alone to fish for crabs; he had been surprised by a group of Dasemunkepeuc braves and killed. This was the tribe which had attacked Grenville's men and White believed that he must now exact reprisals or be vulnerable to further attacks. Therefore, one morning before it was light enough to see clearly, he surrounded the village and began firing at some Indians out in the fields. One was slain before White discovered his tragic mistake. The Dasemunkepeucs, after killing the white man, had abandoned their village and fled inland. The Croatoans, discovering the empty village, had sent some of their own men north to gather the maize and pumpkins that had been left in the fields. White had killed a brave from Manteo's own tribe. He extended a formal apology which, after explanations, was apparently accepted by the tribe. Those who know something of Indian psychology will be inclined to wonder about the extent of the forgiveness on the part of the dead man's family.

On August 13, Manteo was christened and ceremoniously given the title of Lord of Roanoke Island. On the 18th the wife of Ananias Dare, who was Eleanor White, daughter of the governor, gave birth to a daughter, Virginia Dare, the first English child born in the New World.

The colonists now found themselves in a rather bad position. White's promise not to take food from the Indians was considered binding. And Fernandez had failed to take on enough livestock and salt in the West Indies to see the colonists through the winter. There must be new supply from England if they were to survive. Of the twelve assistant governors, nine were with the colony and three had remained in London for the very purpose for which they would now be needed. But the colonists were alarmed and suspicious, and, in a council, they insisted that White himself return to England and be personally responsible for the return of the supply ship. White begged to be excused; his return, he said, would disgrace him. Finally all the colonists signed a statement certifying that he was returning at their insistence.

His pride assuaged, he left the little colony. By now it was secure behind a palisade inside which, mounted on thick wooden platforms, were heavy cannons and lighter field guns. There was an agreement that the colonists would explore inland and, if they found a suitable site, move some fifty miles northward. White then embarked, set a course for England, waved goodbye to the anxious colonists including his daughter and grand-daughter and then turned his eyes eastwards. No white man ever saw those colonists again. They became the lost colony.

When White returned to England he asked the investors for supplies and begged Ralegh to use his influence. Ralegh immediately appointed a pinnace to go to the New World with the necessary salt and livestock; further he wrote a letter to the colonists saying that he would send a sizeable expedition with both men and supplies the following summer. The pinnace never sailed; no one knows why.

The following spring Ralegh organized another relief expedition, this time under the dependable Grenville, who again was sailing aboard the Queen's ship, the *Tyger*. In March, 1588, when Grenville was ready to sail, the Privy Council, under the threat of the Spanish Armada, forbade the voyage. Grenville appealed, requesting that the vessels unsuited for naval service be allowed to go. The Privy Council agreed and White, on April 22, set out in two small pinnaces. He had with him fifteen additional colonists and a limited amount of supplies. The captains of the pinnaces turned to piracy for which their ships and crews were unsuited. The pinnace on which White was sailing was captured and stripped by a French privateer; it had to turn back. A month later the other pinnace also returned, never having reached Virginia. By then the Armada was assembled and ready to sail from Lisbon and all other naval business in England was at an end until that dread issue was resolved.

Early in 1589 Ralegh again, with Hakluyt's help, got nineteen men together, mostly London merchants, who agreed to sponsor the colony. They were formed into a 'free corporation' of the City of Ralegh. They were to share the rights of the colonists, were privileged to establish new settlements, and were given the right to trade, without taxes or customs, in any part of the territory which was settled under Ralegh's patent. Ralegh reserved for himself one-fifth of any gold or silver found in the colony and the title to the New World still belonged to him. But this move was an attempt to free himself from further responsibility for the colonists. His interest in Virginia had waned; his mind was now occupied with the former Desmond estates in Ireland; and within the year he began speaking openly about Guiana and El Dorado.

But he could not excuse himself quite so easily. The London merchants could not raise money for America from investors; and the continued threat from Spain, despite the defeat of the Armada, was enough to keep English vessels tied up in their own harbours. White had nowhere to turn except to Ralegh who, this time, went directly to the Queen. With her consent, he was allowed to strike a bargain with an English privateer whose vessels were being held up in the English ports. If this privateer would execute a bond for 3,000 pounds guaranteeing that he would take White, some new colonists and some supplies to Virginia, his ships would be released.

The bargain was made, but the bond was never taken. Such administrative inefficiency was routine. When White arrived at Plymouth, the captains rudely refused to take any supplies aboard except one chest; nor would they allow any of the proposed new colonists to sail, not even White's cabin boy. White now had to decide whether to return to London, appeal through Ralegh again and find adequate shipping or whether he should simply sail back to the colony and take his chances. He decided on the latter course.

The privateers chased prizes all summer long; and only when autumn storms were sweeping up the coast did they anchor off Port Ferdinando. Again cables were snapped and anchors lost; the sailors threatened and complained and wanted to sail home immediately. White pleaded and finally Captain Cook joined him in persuading them to allow one boat with seven men to go ashore on Roanoke Island. As the boat approached the shore, in the darkness, the men saw fire on the island and believed, therefore, that they would find the colony safe. They stood offshore through the night, sounding trumpets and playing familiar English tunes.

The next day they went ashore to discover that what they had seen was a grass fire and some smouldering stumps; the houses had been taken down, apparently to salvage the timbers, but the palisade was still up. It had not been breached and inside it were the heavy cannon, still in working condition. This indicated that the colonists had moved a considerable distance and could not carry them along. On a tree they found carved the letters C R O and in another place the full word C R O A T O A N, indicating that the colonists had abandoned the dangerous plan of moving northwards into unknown territory and had gone south among the friends and kinsmen of the new Lord of Roanoke. And White had arranged with them before he had gone back to England that if they moved under duress or were in danger, they were to carve a cross above the letters which indicated their destination. There was no cross and so at least all the omens so far were hopeful.

The next morning White and Cook secured consent to sail to Croatoan, but their ship broke a cable and lost another anchor. Now, out of four anchors, only one was left; the weather was worse; food was scarce and so, as a compromise, a council decided to go to the West Indies to winter and then return the following spring. But it didn't work out, and the ship returned to England, arriving on October 24, 1591. It was White's last trip to Virginia.

After that there were undoubtedly good intentions of having various ships stop, on various occasions, and search for the colonists. It could be believed, if one wished to, that the colony was flourishing somewhere in the interior. But those who had read Lane's account would not be likely to think so. Ralegh believed that he had relieved himself of both responsibility and guilt but the matter preyed on his mind. Finally in 1602 he sent out a final ship to search for the colony. At that time he made his famous statement that he would yet live to see Virginia an English nation. But the expedition found nothing.

The lost colony now became a matter for legend. One of

176

those, stubbornly persistent and romantic, insists that blue-eyed children and Indians with light hair were later seen in that region. There are two other possibilities, however. One is that the colony, in despair, went aboard the remaining pinnace, sailed for England and died fearfully among the waves. The other is that Powhatan succeeded where Pemisapan had failed and that within a few months of their arrival the colonists had fallen to the tomahawk and the knife.

In the third and final edition of his essays published in 1625, Bacon has an essay 'Of Plantations'. It is full of wisdom about not expecting immediate profits, about the necessity of choosing substantial men for the venture, the inherent failure in a policy which entertains the natives 'with trifles and gingles' instead of using them 'justly and graciously'. He does not mention Ralegh or any of those associated with him in that venture, but he must have expressed what many Englishmen had thought, not only about Ralegh's lost colony, but also about Jamestown.

It is the sinfullest thing in the world, to forsake or destitute a plantation once in forwardness; for besides the dishonour, it is the guiltiness of blood of many commiserable persons.

Ralegh who had forsaken Roanoke and James who had 'destituted' Jamestown were both safely dead.

II

The Lovers' Quarrel

As Ralegh had once been warned by the noble and sagacious Sarmiento, court favourites are subject to caprice. Elizabeth's first capriciousness toward Ralegh was caused by a young nobleman who, at the siege of Zutphen when Sidney was so senselessly slain, had charged the pikes and lived. He had been knighted for bravery on the field by the Earl of Leicester and was a knight-banneret at the age of 19. He was Robert Devereux, Earl of Essex, tall, broad-shouldered, with auburn hair, an impulsive, generous manner and probably the best swordsman in England. Ralegh's eyes were close-lidded, somnolent, the eyes of a man brooding on some hidden matter. Essex was wide-eyed, ingenuous, outgoing, naive. Both men possessed great reserves of energy, both had strong personal magnetism, but it was subdued and suppressed in the one, flamboyant and sparkling in the other.

Like Ralegh, Essex could write graceful verse; it lacked the penetration, the curious intellectual ingenuity, the counter-thrust that Ralegh's mind gave almost any idea, but it was limpid and graceful and his prose was vigorous and clear. Unlike Ralegh, Essex had been formally educated at Cambridge, and the stamp of the Greek and the Roman classics was on his mind and on his behaviour. The Queen, it was said, loved him 'for his goodly person, his urbanity and his innate courtesy'. Perhaps the ultimate attraction was the mysterious bond of noble blood. The Queen had always been determined to keep the peerage and the circle of nobility more select than her father had done. For most of her reign, William Cecil was the only man elevated to the peerage for political services to the state and he

178

was given only the lowest rank. The almost incalculable services of men like Norris and Vere, as Ralegh bitterly remarked, were never rewarded by the Queen except with grace and affection. Ralegh was keenly aware of the limitations of his own relatively humble birth; he had spoken about it with Edmund Spenser who understood it too and had little consolation to offer.

> In brave pursuit of honourable deed,
> There is I know not what great difference,
> Between the vulgar and the noble seed,
> Which unto things of valorous pretence
> Seems to be born by native influence.

By the end of 1587 Essex had participated in one valiant charge, not unlike a dozen Ralegh had made in France or Ireland, but, because of his birth he was Master of the Horse, a rank comparable to that of Lord Admiral, and he had also been made Knight of the Garter. Elizabeth's new favourite made no effort to conceal his contempt for his upstart rival. In the summer of 1587 the Queen, for some trivial and forgotten court matter, had snubbed Essex's sister who also happened to be the wife of Sir Thomas Perrot with whom Ralegh had fought a duel back in his Inns of Court days. Essex was outraged; he immediately assumed that Ralegh was the cause. He stormed past Ralegh who stood at his post as Captain of the Guard and who could not, officially, hear or see what went on in the Queen's chamber. There Essex carefully raised his voice so that Ralegh must hear him and spoke of him as a knave and wretch. The Queen calmly replied that Essex had no reason to 'disdain' Ralegh; she used the word several times and it was the warmest thing she said in Ralegh's behalf. Even that was too much for Essex who, as he proudly told his followers later, described to the Queen what Ralegh had been and what he was. Ralegh soon found a way to answer Essex and in 1588 there was the inevitable challenge to a duel. The Privy Council forbade it and anxiously tried to keep Elizabeth from hearing of it.

Later that summer, when one observer had remarked that

Ralegh was the most hated man in the Court, another wrote of the Queen and her new lover.

When she is abroad, nobody near her but my Lord of Essex, and at night my Lord is at cards or one game or another with her, that he cometh not to his own lodging till the birds sing in the morning.

One game or another. Undoubtedly Elizabeth was playing a game, a very old one by now and not at all what the writer of the innuendo supposed. She was fifty-four and the game was passionate flirtation and virginal slumber. No man could endure it indefinitely: Leicester had finally married again, much to the Queen's outraged anger; Ralegh, in the School of Night, had his retreat into mysticism and science. And Essex's turn would come, but now he carried all before him. His passion, his grace, his courtesy made him not only Elizabeth's favourite but the entire Court's as well. And even the commoners of England delighted in him; he had the flair the public responds to.

When Ralegh could no longer endure Elizabeth's unconcealed infatuation with Essex, he fled to Ireland, ostensibly to manage his colony there. His enemies, naturally, said that the Earl had chased him out of England. But Ralegh had another reason for leaving the Court and going to Ireland in 1589. He intended to write for Elizabeth England's first great epic poem, a tribute to which she could not fail to respond. For although his countrymen were producing the most brilliant drama since the Greeks and lyric poetry to equal the sonnets of Petrarch or the songs of Provence, England had never produced an epic worthy of the name. In the classically oriented schools of England, where Homer and Vergil were considered the summit of all art, that failure seemed a special reproach to the nation. Previous attempts at epics had resulted in clumsy, tedious poems devoid of the noble fire that immortalized the deeds of ancient heroes and provided ideals of conduct and manners for the generations that followed. Ralegh intended to write an epic in twelve books in the pastoral mode. Elizabeth would be Cynthia; he would be the Shepherd of the Ocean. He would call it *The Ocean to Cynthia*. He would build for Elizabeth a monument in rhyme of the kind Horace had talked about, stronger than bronze, higher than a pyramid.

First, however, he wrote two smaller poems, one a sonnet about a hermit who, disappointed in love, retires from the world.

Like to a hermit poor in place obscure,
I mean to spend my days of endless doubt,
To wail such woes as time cannot recure,
Where none but Love shall ever find me out.

My food shall be of care and sorrow made,
My drink not else but tears fall'n from mine eyes,
And for my light in such obscured shade,
The flames shall serve which from my heart arise.

A gown of grey my body shall attire,
My staff of broken hope whereon I'll stay,
Of late repentance linked with long desire,
The couch is framed whereon my limbs I'll lay.

And at my gate despair shall linger still,
To let in death when Love and Fortune will.

The line about 'late repentance linked with long desire' is so tersely apt that one wonders if it is merely a conventional tribute to the ageing beauty or whether Elizabeth had in fact once created and sustained in Ralegh that cage of Little-Ease where love hungers for fulfilment.

In the other poem, counterpointing an artificially naive metre and tone against sophisticated content, Ralegh adapts, from an old ballad called 'Walsingham', the conventional pattern of interrogation and reply. As a pilgrim returning from Walsingham is asked if he has seen the speaker's queenly love who has abandoned him, the brevity of earthly love is poignantly contrasted with the eternality of that true love man vainly hungers for.

Know that love is a careless child,
And forgets promise past;
He is blind, he is deaf when he list,
And in faith never fast.

His desire is a dureless content,
And a trustless joy;
He is won with a world of despair
And lost with a toy.

Of women kind such indeed is the love,
Or the word Love abused,
Under which many childish desires
And conceits are excused.

But true love is a durable fire,
In the mind ever burning;
Never sick, never old, never dead,
From itself never turning.

The message to Elizabeth was clear and phrased with poetic intensity. Whether she heard, or what she felt, no one knows.

These poems are among the handful of Ralegh's best, but compared to what he had intended to write they were trifles. And the excellence of the short, quintessential lyrics, sprung from an immediate emotional impulse, did not augur well for the large, sustained structuring of an epic. Ralegh's greater visions, his grand designs, found their realization not in poetry but in prose. There he was a master.

Ralegh's epic poem is as much a puzzle as the rest of his life. The fragment that remains was found among the papers left by Robert Cecil. It consists of what is called the eleventh book of *The Ocean to Cynthia* and a scrap of a twelfth book, a few lines called *Entreating of Sorrow*. We do not even know what the design of the entire twelve books was. What remains is a protracted but not very convincing moan about Cynthia's displeasure and Ralegh's remorse. Perhaps he intended, in the unwritten first ten books, to strike the epic note of action: to sing of colonies and naval battles, of the faded glories of ancient Britain and the new glories under the Queen and Huntress chaste and fair. But that is mere conjecture. What remains is all tentative and incomplete. Even some of the quatrains are left unfinished; there are ellipses to indicate either a turn in thought or a void to be filled in later. The metre is too rough in places even for intentional dissonance and the thought is sometimes

obscure, although more from fragmentariness than profundity.
It professes, of course, to be about Cynthia, but what is
valuable in it is the revelation of Ralegh's tortured frustrations,
his discontent. He is

> Slain with self thoughts, amazed in fearful dreams,
> Woes without date. . . .

In the artifice of the poem he feels this way because he has
offended Cynthia. The reader suspects deeper and more
opaque reasons. There are many noble lines which touch themes
that engaged Ralegh almost obsessively: the failure of great
undertakings, time's persistent, quiet obliteration of human
passion and accomplishment, the desire for transcendence.
Occasionally the tone is elevated by genuine passion.

> To seek new worlds for gold, for praise, for glory,
> To try desire, to try love severed far,
> When I was gone she sent her memory,
> More strong than were ten thousand ships of war,

> To call me back, to leave great honour's thought,
> To leave my friends, my fortune, my attempt,
> To leave the purpose I so long had sought,
> And hold both cares and comforts in contempt.

Elizabeth is 'a vestal fire that burns but never wasteth'.
Reason tells him that his own flames of desire which rise from
the sight of her external form cannot last, that such love is slave
to age and vassal to time. But his heart tells him otherwise.
Elizabeth's beauty cannot be touched by time; as the moon-
goddess Cynthia she is above the earthly sphere of mortality
and mutability.

But despite arresting lines and phrases, the poem suggests
not so much a vision partially captured as an attempt to revivify
the mingling of Platonism and sensual love that Petrarch had
introduced and his followers had exhausted. Its day was over
and Ralegh's lack of conviction about it is evident. Far from
reassuring the fifty-seven-year-old Queen, his strained verses

could only have distressed her. It is a rather embarassing performance as it reveals both poet and man. But the two 'trifles' remain among the most touching poems ever written for Elizabeth. The persistent pattern of Ralegh's life is again evident: gleams of effortless brilliance, failure in the grand design.

But Ralegh knew that Edmund Spenser, who was living on a grant of Desmond lands farther up the Blackwater at Kilcolman, had been working on an epic poem which had once been supported and sponsored by Sir Philip Sidney. One day, he packed up his own work and went up river to visit his neighbour. Spenser left an engaging account of the happy and harmonious meeting of the great poet and the would-be great poet, both of them in a kind of exile from Queen and Court. Speaking in the artifice of the pastoral mode through the mask of Colin Clout, the rustic poet of the people, Spenser tells how at Kilcolman he and Ralegh read their poetry aloud to each other.

> He piped, I sung; and when he sung, I piped,
> By change of turns, each making other merry,
> Neither envying other, nor envied,
> So piped we until we both were weary.

Both read; both listened, both praised generously.

As Ralegh listened to *The Faerie Queene*, he readily perceived that in Spenser's poem, under the guise of ancient romance, was an allegorical picture of Elizabeth, her Court, and her age. And the multiple meanings of the allegory were as complex and intriguing as the plot or the sweet, somnolent music. Here was a poem moving on levels of meaning that Ralegh's tortured introspection in *Cynthia* could not approach. He knew it well enough, and he did not resent it. Rather, he persuaded Spenser to accompany him to London to meet the Queen and have his work published, so that England and the Queen might see themselves as he had seen them, that bright afternoon at Kilcolman, caught up 'into the artifice of eternity'.

Of course there was something in it for Ralegh too. His sponsorship of this epic of the Virgin Queen and certain charming additions which Spenser, out of gratitude, would make to his poem, would help restore him to Elizabeth's favour. But in all of the association of Ralegh and Spenser there is no evidence of bargaining or a sense of value given and received; whatever mutual advantage ensued, it all appears to have been spontaneous and generous.

When the first three books of *The Faerie Queene* were published, Ralegh was very conspicuous in the introductory apparatus. First of all came Spenser's dedication of his poem to Elizabeth as Queen of England, France and Ireland; later, he added Virginia, a nice touch on behalf of his friend. Immediately after the dedication came a letter addressed to Sir Walter Ralegh. In it Spenser explained the design of his poem, ostensibly to Ralegh but actually to all of England. Next came the dedicatory poems that Spenser's friends had written at his request; among them is a sonnet by Ralegh which is easily the best of them all and indeed one of the finest poems he ever wrote. In it Ralegh sees the Faerie Queene as surpassing Petrarch's Laura; and even the great Homer is shaken by the power of Spenser's verse.

> Methought I saw the grave where Laura lay,
> Within that Temple where the vestal flame
> Was wont to burn, and passing by that way,
> To see that buried dust of living fame,
> Whose tomb fair love and fairer virtue kept,
> All suddenly I saw the Fairy Queen:
> At whose approach the soul of Petrarch wept,
> And from thenceforth those graces were not seen.
> For they this Queen attended, in whose stead
> Oblivion laid him down on Laura's hearse:
> Hereat the hardest stones were seen to bleed,
> And groans of buried ghosts the heavens did pierce.
>   Where Homer's spright did tremble all for grief,
>   And curst th' access of that celestial thief.

Ralegh's poem not only placed Spenser among the great poets, but it also replaced Laura with Elizabeth as the object of Europe's platonized but passionate adoration. It was, of course, what she had wanted all her life.

Spenser, in turn, wrote an imposing series of dedicatory sonnets to Sir Christopher Hatton, the Lord High Chancellor; to William Cecil, now Lord Burleigh, the Lord High Treasurer; to the Earls of Oxford, Northumberland, Essex, to the Earl of Ormonde under whom Ralegh had grudgingly served in Ireland, to the Lord Admiral Howard, Lord Hunsdon, Lord Grey, Lord Buckhurst, Sir Francis Walsingham and to the valiant Sir John Norris. Near the end of this formidable array of England's great men came the sonnet to his friend, Sir Walter Ralegh, the best sonnet of the lot and completely generous. Ralegh, he says, has sung the praises of Cynthia much better than he, but until he is willing to make his verse known, Spenser's will have to serve.

My rhymes I know unsavoury and sour,
To taste the streams that like a golden shower
Flow from thy fruitful head, of thy love's praise,
Fitter perhaps to thunder martial stour,
When so thee list thy lofty Muse to raise:
Yet till that thou thy poem will make known,
Let thy fair Cynthia's praises be thus rudely shown.

Spenser did everything he could to make his epic the means of reconciliation between Elizabeth and Ralegh. For the greatest of the many characters by whom he portrayed or reflected Elizabeth, Spenser borrowed Ralegh's image of her as the moon goddess, except that he took one of her other names, Phoebe, and adding to it the prefix *Bel*, created Belphoebe, the beautiful Cynthia. And until Ralegh visited him, it had not occurred to Spenser to make a place in his poem for a man he had known only as the captain of a small band of foot in Ireland. But now he invented a character, Timias, a name which derived from the Greek word for honour, and made him the personal squire of England's greatest and legendary king, Prince Arthur. To bring Timias and Belphoebe together, in life as well as in art, Spenser utilized the story that he had once heard of the trap laid for Ralegh by the Seneschal of Imokellie. In the story as Spenser adapts it, three foresters lie in wait for Timias by a 'narrow

186

ford'. As Timias enters the river, the foresters throw spears and shoot arrows at him very much as it had actually happened. In Spenser's version, however, Timias cannot attack his assailants because of a high bank on the river side. Finally, after much struggle, and with vengeance and wrath, he climbs the bank and kills his three assailants, but not before he has been wounded.

As he lies stricken and helpless, providence sends to him Belphoebe who finds the squire almost dead. She hurries into the woods to seek some healing herbs. The poet is not sure which herb she found but it was either polygony, panachaea, or 'divine tobacco' and when she applied it to the wound the squire was cured. Polygony was the name of a Greek herb; panachaea (the modern *panacea*) was a Roman herb that had once been used to cure the heroic Aeneas. Tobacco was a graceful reference to Ralegh's colonizing adventures. Thus, Greece, Rome and Virginia were brought together in the episode.

Although Belphoebe has cured Timias of the dart that had pierced his thigh, she has unwittingly, at the same time, wounded him with a dart from her eye. Timias wishes to speak of love but 'when his mean estate he did review' he kept silent and pined inwardly. Belphoebe did everything to cure him but the only cordial that can restore a lovesick heart she, as Diana, cannot give.

And so Ralegh found his place in England's epic. Perhaps his pleasure in all of this was slightly tempered. The dedicatory sonnet addressed to him, although it was the best, was not given a position of honour. And his role in the poem was a minor one. Artegal, the embodiment of Justice, reflected Lord Grey for whom Spenser always had the greatest admiration; and there were, or would be when the next three books were written, heroic reflections of Sidney, Essex, and Leicester. They were knights who portrayed valour or courtesy or temperance or grace; they were the prototypes of what young gentlemen should be; they were the gentle knights of England. To be a courageous, love-sick squire, even Arthur's squire, must have seemed a little disappointing to the man who was descended from kings and whose aim was nothing less than the overthrow of the Spanish empire in the New World and its replacement by the laws and language of England.

Almost immediately, Ralegh came back into Elizabeth's favour, partly because of Spenser's poem, but also because Essex, like the others, had tired of Elizabeth's long oxymoronic pastime of flame and frost. And so he married a warm and handsome young woman, Frances Walsingham, the widow of Sir Philip Sidney. The angry and offended Elizabeth continued Essex's responsibilities and left his honours untouched but, for a time, she brought Ralegh back to Court to amuse and divert her and guard her mystical body. To Edmund Spenser she gave a generous grant of fifty pounds a year. When she informed her Lord High Treasurer, he was dismayed. 'All that money for a song?' he asked. Yes, William Cecil, devoted, honourable and prosaic man, all that money for a song. But what a song it was.

12

Disgrace and the Tower

By 1590, after a year in Ireland, Ralegh was back at Court. The first three books of *The Faerie Queene* had been published; his Irish estates were being managed in his absence by several men he had taken into partnership. His Virginia colony had not been heard from and no relief ship had reached them. There were murmurings about that in England but Ralegh believed that the responsibility for these colonies now lay with the London merchants to whom he had assigned his colonizing rights. And his head was busy with other matters. For the first time he was heard to speak of El Dorado and the golden city of Manoa. But this was simply one of many things he talked of. In the meantime there were immediate plans that engaged his attention.

After the defeat of the Armada, Philip had begun to rebuild his navy with what was, for that slow-footed king, unusual despatch. He had contracted for twelve galleons, The Twelve Apostles, to be built somewhat on English models; nine more were to be laid down on the larger Portuguese model and he had contracted for twelve Ragusan models; it was to be a powerful new Armada. But it took time; in 1589 and 1590 his navy was weak and English privateers swarmed all over his sea routes. Over ninety prizes were brought to England that year, the greatest haul of Spanish vessels ever made, and Ralegh's ships brought in their share. A Dutch observer wrote that the English 'are become lords and masters of the sea and need fear no man'. The situation was so critical that in 1590 Philip did not allow his silver fleet to sail from the West Indies. With the stream of silver from the Potosi mines stopped at its source, a wave of bankruptcies spread over Spain and work was hastened on the new fleet.

The English knew that a year's supply of silver lay in West Indian ports and that sailing could not be delayed another year. John Hawkins therefore devised a plan that was to bring that silver to England. He would send small squadrons of fighting ships successively into the sea lanes between the Azores Islands and Spain so that no matter when the ships came they would be intercepted. Thus England's foxes would spoil the Spanish grape.

In the meantime the Twelve Apostles were slipping off the ways. The greatest of them, the *San Philip* of 1,500 tons, was already in the water. Soon the *San Andrew* and the *San Barnabe* would join her. Other ships were coming too and they were under the command of Admiral Bazan, the brother of the Marquis of Santa Cruz, a veteran of the Mediterranean wars. These ships were still high-charged and they still carried large numbers of Spanish infantry, but they were better sailing vessels than Spain had ever had, and they would be on the sea before the plate fleet would be allowed to sail. The small squadron that met Bazan had better look to itself.

In the pursuance of Hawkins' plan, early in 1591 a fleet was assembled of six royal vessels, six armed merchantmen, the ubiquitous *Bark Ralegh*, and some pinnaces for communications and supply. Lord Thomas Howard was appointed Admiral of the Fleet; his Vice-Admiral was Sir Walter Ralegh. This was to have been Ralegh's first position of command, either on land or sea, his first chance to win a greater place than that of a squire in England's epic. And then, predictably, the Queen changed her mind. Sir Walter must return to Court. This decision was probably not influenced by any remaining personal passion, but the Queen was always reluctant to hazard any of the men in whom she confided and with whom she had a personal friendship. She was a lonely woman with many worshippers but few confidants. 'Be sparing of the young gentlemen,' had always been her advice to Norris and Vere in the Low Countries, advice they no doubt received with a certain amount of reserve.

And so Sir Walter must find a substitute. Chagrined and frustrated, he turned once again to Cousin Grenville, one of the bravest men he knew, one who could be counted on to be the Queen's true sailor in any hazard. He would be captain of Drake's old ship, the *Revenge*.

Early in September news came back to England that the *Revenge*, alone, had fought the entire Spanish fleet and been destroyed while Lord Howard had refused the battle. It was also reported that Ralegh's formal challenge awaited the Admiral upon his return. But when the fleet returned, the Privy Council immediately interrogated the principal officers and also six survivors of the *Revenge*. When their story was told a different picture emerged and Ralegh immediately, possibly at the request of the Crown, wrote his first prose work, *The Truth of the Fight about the Isles of the Azores*. His account is charged with excitement; the prose is so vivid and powerful that the last fight of the *Revenge* became and has remained England's greatest naval saga, although it is now better known through Lord Tennyson's poem than from Ralegh's account on which Tennyson drew.

Lord Howard's squadron had been at sea for six months; it was too long. The rats and the microbes had formed their customary vicious alliance in the sewage of the ballast and ship's fever, typhus, that most relentless and deadly of plagues, had burned through the fleet. There was nothing for it but to find a port, carry out the filthy ballast and carry in clean rocks while the sick men lay ashore where they would not be huddled together, where they could drink fresh water and where, although the fact was lost on them, the latrines would be outside the camp area. And so it came about, as Tennyson was later to write, 'At Flores in the Azores, Sir Richard Grenville lay,' as did the rest of the fleet, when an English merchant ship, which had been courageously dogging the Spanish fleet, came scudding through the mist and the early morning darkness to report that a fleet of fifty-three Spanish sail, with twenty fighting ships (including some of the Twelve Apostles), was bearing down with the wind under full sail. There was not much time. Howard

191

fired off cannons and lowered and raised his mainsail four times, the signal to slip cables and stand out to sea. The ships, not yet fully ballasted, were riding lightly on the water and could not manoeuvre as sharply as usual. All of the ships except the *Revenge* beat out of the harbour, tacking into the wind, making a wide sweep to the northeast, hoping to come around in the rear of the Spanish fleet and thus recover the wind gauge. It was the same manoeuvre that Lord Howard of Effingham and Drake had executed successfully when the Armada had lain off Plymouth Hoe.

The question that can never be fully answered is why Grenville was late and did not join the rest of the fleet. Ralegh says that he had eighty sick men on shore and would not leave them. But the other ships also had sick men ashore. The *Bonaventure* was worse off than the *Revenge*, not having enough men to handle her mainsail until twenty men were transferred to her from one of the barks. And no one ever suggested, then or now, that Howard simply abandoned Grenville's men.

Sir William Monson, writing when the matter was no longer a national crisis, gave a different version.

But Sir Richard Grenville, being astern, and imagining this fleet to come from the Indies, and not to be the Armada of which they were informed, would by no means be persuaded by his master or company to cut his cable to follow his Admiral, as all discipline of war did teach him; nay, so headstrong, rash and unadvised he was that he offered violence to all that counselled him to the contrary.

It is doubtful that Grenville really thought the Indies fleet was approaching. Captain Middleton, who brought the news, was far too competent an observer to make such a mistake. He had seen the warships, counted them, and followed them for hours.

When Grenville finally made sail, he could not have tacked after Howard without being cut off. There was a way open, however, and that was simply to crowd on sail and run before the wind. Instead Grenville held one of those inevitable councils of war in which the Master of the ship strongly urged that sensible course. And that, said Ralegh, would have been the right thing to do. But Richard Grenville was sailing the ship which Francis Drake had immortalized. To run would be 'to dishonour himself, his country and Her Majesty's ship'. It was his 'greatness of mind', said Ralegh, his magnanimity, that led to his tragic decision. Thus, while Ralegh condemned Grenville's action, he also redeemed it.

Grenville's plan was not completely suicidal. The Spaniard was coming on in two squadrons, each stretched out in battle line with a narrow channel between them. Grenville proposed to sail through it, cannonading from starboard and larboard, thus forcing the enemy to lie back until he had sailed through the entire fleet. Then he would again have the wind gauge and could rejoin Howard. While running this fearsome gauntlet he would be exposed to broadsides from both Spanish squadrons, but fighting men are expected to take risks. There was an even greater problem, however, than the Spanish cannonading and that was the wind. It was quartering against the *Revenge* and she would have to tack. Thus her great assets, speed and manoeuvrability, would be lost.

Grenville had his way and the *Revenge* sailed into a slender blue channel which was lined with a forest of Spanish spars. As the first enemy ships came up, Grenville cannonaded with good effect; they luffed their sails and dropped to lee. It was working as he had expected. But then the captain of the giant *San Philip* executed the decisive manoeuvre. Like a galley, he drove at the *Revenge* intending to ram her; Grenville heeled about and fired the entire lower tier of ordnance at point blank range. The volley blew down some of the *San Philip's* superstructure and tore holes in her sides. But she was now on top of him and her huge sails took all the wind, leaving the *Revenge* becalmed, dead in the water in the midst of the Spanish navy.

Now Howard had to exercise an agonizing command responsibility. He, too, held a council and urged that his fleet, at whatever cost, enter that deadly channel and fight through to the rescue of the *Revenge*. Howard was a good sailor but not an experienced commander, at least the Spanish thought not.

Ralegh completely vindicates Howard's personal honour even while questioning his judgment.

It is very true that the Lord Thomas [Howard] would have entered between the squadrons, but the rest would not condescend; and the master of his own ship offered to leap into the sea rather than to conduct . . . Her Majesty's ship and the rest to be a prey to the enemy where there was no hope nor possibility either of defence or victory. Which also in my opinion had ill sorted or answered the discretion and trust of a general, to commit himself and his charge to an assured destruction, without hope or any likelihood of prevailing.

The *Revenge* was not entirely forsaken. For two hours the *Foresight* fought as near as she dared and withdrew only when almost surrounded. At the beginning of the fight, the *George Noble*, a merchant ship of London, came up under the *Revenge*'s lee and asked Sir Richard what his commands were. Grenville told the captain to save himself and leave the *Revenge* to its destiny. One other ship tried to help. When night fell, Captain Jacob Whiddon, in one of Ralegh's pinnaces, sneaked into the battle area to see if he could give any relief. When dawn broke and the Spaniards sighted her, she 'was hunted like a hare amongst ravenous hounds, but escaped'. And the rest of the English fleet stayed outside and volleyed, keeping the wind gauge, harassing the flanks of the enemy, but failing to give any effectual help.

It was just a little after three in the afternoon when the *Revenge* was becalmed. The *San Philip* immediately grappled her and got ten men aboard. Then the grappling irons broke and seven of the Spanish soldiers were killed; the other three found cover and hid. Another of the Twelve, the *San Barnabe*, then came up and grappled. Before a ship grappled, the standard tactic was to sweep the decks of the enemy vessel with small arms fire in an attempt to force the defenders below deck. The Spanish ships all carried musketeers who poured a continuous barrage into the *Revenge*. Grenville was wounded early in the fight, but never left the upper deck. The *San Barnabe* grappled firmly and tried to board, but the English sailors, from the high works of their ship, fired muskets and threw grenades at the boarders who were repelled.

Next Admiral Arambaru came up and rammed the *Revenge*, grappling at the same time. He got some of his soldiers onto the English quarter-deck where they hauled down the ensign, killed some of the crew and fought their way to the mainmast. But in ramming, the Spanish ship had lost her prow; the stout-timbered *Revenge* had proved too tough and the Admiral had to call his men back and fall away.

Next the galleon *Ascension* came up and was followed by another ship under Don Luis Cuitino; the firing and fighting continued all night. According to Ralegh, fifteen different ships came against the *Revenge* during that long and desperate night, all attempting to board and all beaten off.

In the darkness, in the centre of the mêlée, the *Revenge* and several other ships were locked together, all entangled, all becalmed. Admiral Bazan spent the night collecting his fleet and putting it in a circle around the crippled enemy. The *Ascension* and Cuitino's ships, having lost their mobility, were thrown together by the waves and suffered heavy damages in addition to what the *Revenge* had inflicted. Both went down. The *San Phlip* was the worst hurt of the rest of the Spanish fleet but many other ships had suffered damage as the gunners of the *Revenge* continued to shoot from every gun that could be brought to bear on an enemy vessel. Of the *Revenge*'s crew, which originally numbered only 100 effectives, forty were now dead and most of the rest were wounded.

While the surgeon was dressing Grenville's wounds, a volley killed him and sent a ball through Grenville's body and another into his head. He was wounded to the death. The *Revenge* looked like a slaughter-house, her powder was gone 'down to the last barrel', her pikes, which had been used to push the boarders back, were broken; she had six feet of water in her hold, her deck was almost even with the water, all her rigging was down and she was 'not able to move one way or the other, but as she was moved with the waves and billows of the sea'.

And that was the moment, after fifteen hours of cannonading and hand-to-hand fighting, when Grenville called the master gunner to him and gave the fearful order for which his name has always been remembered.

> Sink me the ship, Master Gunner – sink her,
> split her in twain!
> Fall into the hands of God, not into the
> hands of Spain.

The gunner would have obeyed his admiral, but the captain, the masters and the others would not agree. They believed they could get terms from the Spaniard which would send back to England 'valiant men, yet living, and whose wounds were not mortal, who might do their country and prince acceptable service hereafter'. They further argued that the *Revenge* had taken three shot under water, that the repairs on the holes were so fragile that they would burst open with the 'first working of the sea', that the ship was doomed and could never reach a Spanish harbour.

Sir Richard would not hear of it; but he was too weak to enforce his will. The captain, who had most of the men on his side, was taken aboard the Spanish flagship where he asked for terms. He pointed out that Grenville had ordered the ship blown up, and that if the Spaniards did not grant honourable terms those orders would likely be carried out. Admiral Bazan realized it well enough. But beyond that, the Spaniards knew and admired gallantry; they were unquestionably touched by the heroic fight of the *Revenge* and Bazan, if he could, seemed anxious to save the life of Grenville whom he so much admired 'for his notable valour'. Bazan, therefore, agreed that the common seamen would be returned to England; the better sort also, but only after the payment of ransom. When the captain returned with these terms, Grenville and the master gunner stood alone in opposing them. The latter seized a sword and would have slain himself had he not been overpowered and locked in his cabin. The English sailors, still fearing what Grenville might do, began slipping over the side and swimming or rowing to the Spanish vessels. Admiral Bazan then summoned Grenville to come to his flagship.

Sir Richard answered that he might do with his body what he list, for he esteemed it not; and as he was carried out of the ship he swooned, and reviving again desired the company to pray for him. The General used Sir Richard with all humanity, and left nothing unattempted that tended to his recovery, highly commending his valour and worthiness, and greatly bewailing the danger wherein he was.

When Grenville was finally aboard the flagship, the Admiral thought it unsuitable to call on him in person, but all of his captains and officers came around to see for themselves the *gran cossario* who had made such an awesome fight. A Dutchman who was trading at the Azores heard the seamen's talk about Grenville's last hours and wrote about them. While supping with the Spanish captains, Grenville, he said,

would carouse three or four glasses of wine, and in a bravery take the glasses between his teeth and crash them in pieces and swallow them down, so that often times the blood ran out of his mouth without any harm at all unto him: and this was told me by divers credible persons . . .

That a dying man should have done anything 'of so hard a complexion' is obviously false; that he should even have sat at dinner is wholly improbable; and the legendary quality of this relation may impugn the accuracy of everything the Dutchman heard. But Grenville's last words, as reported by him, sound very much like Sir Richard.

Here die I, Richard Grenville, with a joyful and quiet mind, for that I have ended my life as a true soldier ought to do, that hath fought for his country, Queen, religion and honour, whereby my soul most joyful departeth out of this body and shall always leave behind it an everlasting fame of a valiant and true soldier that hath done his duty as he was bound to do.

Only that much of his statement was translated when the

account was rendered into English. But, according to the Dutchman, that was not all Grenville said.

But the others of my company have done as traitors and dogs, for which they shall be reproached all their lives and leave a shameful name forever.

The words of dying men are supposed to be prophetic. These were not. When his cousin Ralegh finished his account of the fight, Grenville's men were national heroes and the honour of Lord Thomas Howard was unscathed.

Not content with merely narrating England's most spectacular sea-fight, Ralegh went on to enlarge on one of the great and passionate themes of his life. He was England's Cato and the sombre *Carthago delenda est* of that ancient Stoic became 'The Spanish Empire must be destroyed'. The conclusion of Ralegh's account is an indictment of Spanish cruelty; he rehearsed again the black legend of Spain. There was, perhaps, something in the back of his mind. The King of Castile, he says, thinks that he has fallen heir to the whole world; he thirsts greedily 'after English blood'. But the fight of the *Revenge*, like the fight with the Armada before it, has really displayed the weakness of the Spaniard. That is all he says but the implications dovetail with some things he had recently been thinking about the great and beautiful empire of Guiana.

He concludes with a remembrance of the Queen.

We, her true and obedient vassals, guided by the shining light of her virtues, shall always love her, serve her, and obey her to the end of our lives.

Ralegh had handled a difficult task with brilliance. The loss of the *Revenge* was almost forgotten in the fierce immortality which his pen had conferred upon Sir Richard Grenville and his valorous men.

Hawkins' plan to capture the Spanish silver fleet had not worked, but it was not abandoned; rather it was decided to double the size and power of the English fleet and send it out to intercept Spain's merchant fleet which now would be laden with a two-years' accumulation of silver. If that fleet could be taken, Philip would indeed be, in Ralegh's phrase, a king of figs and oranges.

In January of 1592, the Queen bestowed what was to prove her final favour on Ralegh. For years as he had travelled between Plymouth and London he had seen, in the shire of Dorset, a large manor called Sherborne which belonged to the see of Salisbury. Ralegh looking at that manor, as Sir John Harington said, was like Ahab looking at Naboth's vineyard. He had been lusting after it for years. The previous bishop had courageously refused to lease it to the Crown and the displeased Elizabeth steadfastly refused to appoint a new bishop. After the bishopric had lain idle for three years, Ralegh sent Elizabeth a jewel worth 250 pounds and urged her to appoint a new bishop. She did, but made him consent to lease Sherborne to Ralegh for ninety-nine years at 360 pounds per year. It was said that a long time ago a Bishop Osmund had placed a curse on anyone who should alienate that land and it was to prove remarkably effective as curses go: Ralegh died on the scaffold, as did three of his successors at Sherborne; two others died in prison and one was murdered.

But Ralegh had no time for curses; he repaired the ruined castle, began building a residence in the park, and started to create a landscape that suited him. He diverted streams, planted cedars from Virginia, shrubs and flowers from tropical islands and, in a few years, had created an estate of exotic beauty. He now had, for the first time in his life, a home and an estate suitable for a man with a wife and family. The thought occured to others; it must have also occurred to him.

At the same time, the new expedition against Spanish shipping was getting ready to sail. The plan was to search for the plate fleet and then to proceed, if necessary, to the Isthmus of Panama and take the silver at its source. To do this it was planned to equip a fleet of thirteen vessels again as a quasi-private venture. The Queen, to show her approval, invested 1,800 pounds; the London merchants raised 6,000. Ralegh undertook to equip the fleet and to find the rest of the money needed. He borrowed 11,000 pounds at an interest rate that was likely around fourteen per cent; besides that he was already in debt to the Crown.

To discharge that debt he asked payment for the *Ark Ralegh;* the Crown agreed and set the price at 5,000 pounds. The detractors said that this sale was merely a pretext for giving money to Ralegh, but that is false. The sum is almost exactly what it had cost John Hawkins to build capital ships. It was a fair price.

On this new venture, Ralegh was to be Admiral of the Fleet, and he should have sailed in March. But the fleet was weatherbound in the Thames and Ralegh was terribly impatient, for more reasons than one as it turned out. 'I am not able to live,' he wrote, 'to row up and down with every tide from Gravesend to London.'

On March 10, he wrote a letter to Robert Cecil in which he says he has promised the Queen that he will not accompany the fleet if he can get the mariners to sail under Frobisher, a martinet under whom Ralegh's sailors were not happy to sail. It appears that Elizabeth had again been beset by her old fears.

At the end of the letter, Ralegh emphasizes that he is not going off to sea in order to avoid a marriage.

If any such thing were, I would have imparted it unto yourself before any man living; and, therefore, I pray believe it not, and I beseech you to suppress, what you can, any such malicious report. For I protest before God, there is none on the face of the earth that I would be fastened unto.

When Ralegh wrote this letter he had already been married for almost four months. Lies like this, gross and palpable, ruined his credit with many men; but he desperately needed to keep word of the marriage from Elizabeth, whatever it cost him, until he could get out to sea where, he was confident, he would make his fortune and put himself beyond the caprices of the Queen forever.

The girl he had married on the previous November 19 was

Elizabeth Throckmorton, one of Elizabeth's maids of honour. She had been pregnant when he married her and she was far gone with child now. She had left the Court, ostensibly to visit her brother in the country, and Ralegh knew that her condition could not be concealed long. It is little wonder that he damned the winds. Elizabeth was the daughter of Sir Nicholas Throckmorton who had served the Queen long and faithfully before his death in 1579. She was bright and vivacious, several years younger than Ralegh, who was now a man of forty. He can have had no present pleasure in his barren flirtation with the Queen, but, on the other hand, she was still the source of all good things. Ralegh knew the storm that had blown up when Leicester married; he knew that the Earl of Essex's wife had been forever barred from the Court. And he was in a worse position than either. When the earls had married, Elizabeth's fury had been abated by the nobility of their blood and the legitimacy of the relationship. But the squire of low degree had debauched a maid of honour. It would be the blow to her pride that would infuriate Elizabeth, but she would have every justification for taking out on Ralegh all the irrational fear and hatred of sexuality that went so deep in her nature.

On May 6, 1592, the fleet finally sailed with Ralegh in command. Perhaps he thought that he could slip away, as Drake so often had, but Elizabeth's suspicions had now been confirmed and she sent Martin Frobisher after him with orders for his return. Frobisher overhauled him in one day but Ralegh violated the orders as far as he dared, staying with the fleet until it made landfall at Cape Finisterre. There he stationed half the fleet under Frobisher near the coast to distract the Spaniards but not to engage them. The rest he sent out to watch for the treasure fleet at the Azores. It was too late in the season to carry out the attack on the Panamanian isthmus.

Ralegh then returned to London where he was immediately arrested and placed in the Tower. The Queen was deeply angry; she was hurt; and she never really forgave Ralegh. After all, Anne Boleyn, her mother, had been a maid of honour when Henry VIII had first lusted after her. He had left the ageing and ugly Catherine of Aragon for a bright and budding girl. And now it had all happened again, only this time to her.

But there was also real justification for her anger. Bess had been delivered of her baby on March 29. On Monday, April 10, the child was christened and, in the greatest surprise of the entire affair, the Earl of Essex stood as godfather. It was a generous thing, almost excessively generous, for him to do; it was the kind of impulsive kindness that was characteristic of him. One can only imagine how it all looked to Elizabeth, a conspiracy entered into by her two lovers to mask reality, to conceal a little longer what time had done to her.

Ralegh named his first son Damerei. The Westcountry genealogist who had found him to be descended from kings had done so on the grounds that a Sir John de Ralegh had married the daughter of D'Amerie Clare. Damerei Ralegh was to be Sir Walter's living symbol of his Plantagenet ancestry, but the child died in infancy and with later children Ralegh was content with simpler names.

Having delivered her child, Elizabeth Throckmorton returned to Court on April 25 as if nothing had happened. Everything we know of her and her huband would lead us to suspect that this kind of desperate deceit was Ralegh's idea and not hers. And by the time she returned to Court the Queen knew everything. Probably she confronted the frightened girl; at least someone got a confession from her, and Elizabeth sent Frobisher to Devon with the orders that brought Ralegh back; if he had had another forty-eight hours it is doubtful that Frobisher could have overtaken him. But he was Time's fool, so he said, and he had no choice other than to return.

Although the Queen was indignant, the rest of London fell to laughing and it was cruel sport, a national scandal with the usual round of coarse jokes and jibes. Sir Edward Stafford wrote to Sir Anthony Bacon, 'If you have anything to do with Sir Walter Ralegh or any love to make to Mrs. Throckmorton, at the Tower tomorrow you may speak with them.'

Someone invented the details of the intimate incident that had brought it all about and John Aubrey heard and recorded it.

He loved a wench well, and one time getting up one of the maids-of-honour up against a tree in the wood ('twas his first lady), who seemed at first boarding to be something fearful of her honour and modest, she cried, 'Sweet Sir Walter, what do you me ask? Will you undo me? Nay, sweet Sir Walter! Sweet Sir Walter! Sir Walter!' At last, as the danger and the pleasure at the same time grew higher, she cried in the ecstasy, 'Swisser Swatter, Swisser Swatter.' She proved with child.

Even in a new play by the young William Shakespeare, *Love's Labour Lost,* some found Ralegh's plight glanced at comically in the humiliation of Don Armado, the polysyllabic braggart whose liaison with a country wench is exposed in the public announcement of her pregnancy. Whatever Shakespeare's real intention, London was full of people who were delighted to laugh at the discomfiture of the decorative swordsman without giving a second thought to the humiliation it caused Bess.

Ralegh still had his friends. The Westcountry kin called on Bess and offered their swords to Ralegh. And the gentle Spenser wanted to do something more. His epic of England, after all, was unfinished. There was always room for another episode or two.

And so he devised an episode in which the lovely Amoret is pursued and caught by an ugly monster, Lust. Timias attempts to save her and, while driving Lust away, inadvertently wounds her. Belphoebe then appears and slays Lust with an arrow; on entering the cave she finds the squire kissing Amoret who is lying in a swoon. Belphoebe's noble heart was filled with 'deep disdain'. She reached for an arrow and would have slain them both but instead she spoke, four words, and powerful ones, too.

> 'Is this the faith?' she said, and said no more,
> But turned her face, and fled away for evermore.

The squire is so remorseful that he decides to become a hermit, an idea Spenser obviously took from Ralegh's poem, 'Like to a hermit poor in place obscure'. Timias vows never to speak to another woman; he retires to the wild forest and actually grows a 'glibb', and becomes appropriately woebegone. Naturally there must be another reconciliation between Belphoebe and Timias and it is accomplished by a charming, if unrealistic, device. A dove flies down beside Timias and the two of them engage in a duet of moan and complaint. Then Timias looks over what is left of all the bounty that Belphoebe had bestowed upon him. Among the 'relics' he finds a rich jewel, a ruby shaped like a heart which he fastens to a ribbon and ties around the neck of the dove. The dove then goes flying off to Belphoebe.

Enticed by both the jewel and the dove, Belphoebe is led to Timias. When she sees the pathetic condition of this glibbed hermit, she forgives him. The allegory is clear except for the dove and the ruby, the meaning of which will shortly appear.

If Spenser could have let it go at that, it would have been a charming episode, the tone of which was about right for the peccadillo it immortalized. After all, Ralegh was forty and Bess was at least twenty-eight; they were not infatuated children. Three years later Ralegh was to say that he was in the winter of his life. If he was ever to marry and renew the state of a family descended from kings but now decayed, it had to be soon. If Elizabeth had been sensible about love and marriage, the courtier and the maid-of-honour could have proceeded more conventionally. They paid a high price for their impatience although neither of them ever complained or appears to have regretted it.

But there was a deep puritan strain in Spenser and he was writing an epic which was to train young noblemen in virtue. Prince Arthur's squire, the 'honoured' one, had fallen. And so he would have to draw out the moral and restore the sinner to grace.

The Sixth Book of *The Faerie Queene* is the book of Courtesy. One of the chief enemies of the courteous knight is the Blatant Beast, a symbol of slander and scandal. The beast bites and carries off a lady named Serena, and Serena was Ralegh's pastoral-poetic name for his wife. The courteous knight, Sir

Calidore, overtakes the beast, rescues Serena, and puts the monster to flight.

Soon appear on the scene Prince Arthur and his squire, Timias, who has recovered the favour of Belphoebe and now stands in her grace. Timias has three mighty enemies who still seek to overthrow him: Malice, Deceit, and Detraction. These enemies, afraid to face Timias themselves, cleverly arrange to put the Blatant Beast in his way. Timias-Ralegh drives it away but not before he himself is bitten. At that moment appears Prince Arthur, who is frequently an instrument of heavenly grace. The two ride on together and find Serena who reveals that she, too, has been sorely wounded in mind and body; Timias begins to swoon and so Arthur brings them both to a chapel where a holy hermit dwells. At this point Spenser interrupts the narrative to instruct England's young noblemen.

> No wound, which warlike hand of enemy
> Inflicts with dint of sword, so sore doth light,
> As doth the poisonous sting, which infamy
> Infixeth in the name of noble wight . . .
>
> Such were the wounds, the which that Blatant Beast
> Made in the bodies of that Squire and Dame.

The hermit at first had little success in healing the wounds Scandal had made because they were festering inwardly. He then perceived that his patient needed not the skill of the surgeon but rather 'sad sobriety', that is, Timias and Serena must control 'the stubborn rage of passion blind'. And so he tells them that they must cure themselves.

> The best (said he) that I can you advise,
> Is to avoid the occasion of the ill:
> For when the cause, whence evil doth arise,
> Removed is, the effect surceaseth still.
> Abstain from pleasure, and restrain your will,
> Subdue desire, and bridle loose delight,
> Use scanted diet and forbear your fill,
> Shun secrecy and talk in open sight:
> So shall you soon repair your present evil plight.

Timias and Serena gladly accept this advice and soon they are healed. Thus Ralegh's most intimate personal life was published to point a moral and adorn a tale.

What Ralegh was really feeling through it all we know only indirectly. There are hints in some poems he wrote at this time, but not to Cynthia, the unattainable divinity of the moon whom he had flattered as superior to time and change. Now she had changed towards him, and all men could see the changes time had worked on her, but no courtier dared speak of them. After so many years of courtly trifling and poetic prevarication, it must have seemed release and relief to wed and bed, to know the warmth of human love with its imperfections and hazards, even with its brevity. And so, when he wrote poems to the real woman who, unlike a poetical goddess, walked on the ground and would get old, he touched the theme that, though it haunted him and his fellow poets, he never dared touch when addressing Cynthia. *Carpe diem,* the Romans had sung; seize today, love now, for love and beauty exist only today; tomorrow they belong to devouring Time. One of Ralegh's poems to Serena is a 'translation' of Catullus much as his 'hermit' poem had transformed Desportes.

> Now Serena be not coy;
> Since we freely may enjoy
> Sweet embraces, such delights,
> As will shorten tedious nights.
> Think that beauty will not stay
> With you always but away;
> And that tyrannizing face
> That now holds such perfect grace,
> Will both changed and ruined be;
> So frail is all things as we see,
> So subject unto conquering Time.
> Then gather flowers in their prime . . .

How different from the poems to Cynthia, where no hint either of ageing or fulfilment of love disturbs the placid artifice!

Another poem, though it does not name Serena, has the same air of being written about a loved mortal:

206

Nature that washed her hands in milk
And had forgot to dry them,
Instead of earth took snow and silk,
At Love's request to try them,
If she a mistress could compose
To please Love's fancy out of those.

After the beauty is evoked, Time enters the poem; Time, which despises nature and turns the 'snow and silk and milk to dust'. But just when the poet would conventionally urge his love to love him, some sombre shadow crossed Ralegh's mind and he pursued the cruelty of Time to its ultimate place, the 'dark and silent grave', where it, at last, 'shuts up the story of our days'. And it was these lines which rose later to his memory the night before he was to die, after he had said his last farewell to Bess.

Bess and the home they lived in, Serena and Sherborne: Ralegh loved them both far more than anything else in his life. Whatever happiness he knew it was at Sherborne with Bess.

Now, however, in May, 1592, he was suffering from his marriage, humiliated with scandal and imprisoned in the Tower. He must get out. To do so, he made two desperate efforts to appease Elizabeth which were both about the least imaginative and plainly contrived things he ever did. First he wrote a letter to Robert Cecil who was now Elizabeth's secretary in fact if not in name. Since Cecil was at this time still Ralegh's friend, Sir Walter naturally assumed that what he wrote would be shown to the Queen.

My heart was never broken till this day, that I hear the Queen goes away so far off, whom I have followed so many years with so great love and desire, in so many journeys, and am now left behind her, in a dark prison all alone.

It wasn't a bad beginning; one might almost believe a little of it if the rest hadn't deteriorated so badly.

While she was yet near at hand, that I might hear of her once in two or three days, my sorrows were the less: but even now my heart is cast into the depth of all misery. I that was wont to behold her riding like Alexander, hunting like Diana, walking like Venus, the

207

gentle wind blowing her fair hair about her pure cheeks, like a nymph; sometime sitting in the shade like a goddess; sometime singing like an angel; sometime playing like Orpheus. Behold the sorrow of this world! Once amiss hath bereaved me of all. O Glory that only shineth in misfortune, what is become of thy assurance?

There is a good deal more of this pseudo-classical fakery.

The other device Ralegh employed to catch the sympathy of the Queen was, if possible, worse: he composed and acted a pathetic scene in the Tower that even the groundlings would have found absurd. His keeper in the Tower was his cousin, Sir George Carew. Another kinsman, Arthur Gorges, wrote to Robert Cecil that a near tragedy had occurred in the Tower. From the high battlements, Ralegh had seen the gay buntings and pavilions of the barges as Elizabeth and a royal procession floated down the Thames to visit some courtier. He gazed and sighed and fell into 'a great distemper', saying that his enemies had brought the Queen within his sight to torment him. He could not endure seeing the royal barge without seeing the Queen. He would therefore disguise himself and get a pair of oars, row up to the barge, and ease his mind with one look at Belphoebe. Sir George Carew replied that he could not allow the prisoner out; it was contrary to Her Majesty's commands. Immediately there was 'iron walking' as Ralegh and Carew drew daggers. Brave Gorges stepped betwen them and received a slash on his knuckles. He later offered this scratch as proof that the episode was genuine. Ralegh was restrained and swore that he would hate Sir George Carew until the end of time.

What reveals this for the farce that it is, aside from its own improbability, is that Gorges added a postscript on a little slip of paper which was affixed to the letter with wax so that it could easily be pulled off; the letter might then be given to someone without the postscript which read, 'if you let the Queen's Majesty know hereof, as you think good, be it . . .'

These two episodes reveal a tragic deterioration in Ralegh's feelings about the Queen since the days when he had written the Hermit and Walsingham poems. Elizabeth desperately needed flattery in her lifelong struggle against time and loneliness; flattery, tempered with wit and grace, is a form of affection. But empty flattery is insulting and condescending. Elizabeth was a realist; Ralegh's crude farce was tiresome and transparent. It is a mark of Cecil's good sense that he never pulled the postscript off that letter. Elizabeth probably never saw it but if she did she also saw the postscript.

How Ralegh really felt about Elizabeth while he was suffering the disgrace to his own honour and smarting under the coarse slandering of Bess is embodied in a poem, called 'The Lie'. Savage in tone, it was obviously written from deep and bitter hurt; it stands in brutal contrast to the romantic rhetoric of the letter to Cecil.

> Go soul, the body's guest,
> Upon a thankless errand,
> Fear not to touch the best,
> The truth shall be thy warrant:
> Go, since I needs must die,
> And give the world the lie.
>
> Say to the Court it glows,
> And shines like rotten wood,
> Say to the Church it shows
> What's good and doth no good.
> If Church and Court reply,
> Then give them both the lie.

And then came a paragraph which hit out directly at Elizabeth. Not even the later cavil of the angry Essex that Elizabeth's conditions were as crooked as her carcass is quite as penetratingly cruel as Ralegh's verse.

> Tell Potentates they live
> Acting by others' action,
> Not loved unless they give,
> Not strong but by affection,
> If Potentates reply,
> Give Potentates the lie.

Not loved unless they give; no one could know it better than Ralegh or feel it more than Elizabeth.

It could be said that Ralegh wrote this bitter poem for the easing of his mind, and that he did not publish it. That is true. But the poem circulated widely: two replies were written in the early 1590's and ultimately several responses were printed. All fell short of the original and only served to publicize it. But one of them hits a curiously prophetic note.

> And when you come again
> To give the world the lie,
> I pray you tell them how to live,
> And teach them how to die.

Ralegh's release from the Tower, as it happened, resulted neither from his crude pantomime nor his pen but from the ships he had sent under Frobisher to annoy the King of Spain. While Frobisher, following Ralegh's directions, was leading the Spanish warships on a fool's chase over the seas, Sir John Borough spread the ships of his squadron over the sea lanes a few leagues west of Flores. On August 3, a vast, high-charged carrack of Portugal hove into sight. She was the *Madre de Dios* of 1,600 tons with seven decks and 800 men, 165 feet long, a floating castle she seemed to the English who cut her away from the other Spanish ships and engaged her. In addition to her cargo she had aboard many passengers including some governors and officials from the East and West Indies and many wealthy merchants. The first ships to bring her under fire were Ralegh's *Roebuck* and Borough's *Foresight*, a ship the Queen had contributed to the voyage. What happened after that became a matter for an English maritime court to decide. Borough said that the Earl of Cumberland and several of his vessels appeared on the scene when the fight was nearly over; the Earl then boarded the carrack with 360 men who immediately began to pillage, breaking open casks and chests and stuffing their pockets with gold, pearls, silver, gems and any of the more portable treasures. The Earl of Cumberland said that he had boarded only because *Roebuck* and *Foresight* were disabled and were being beaten by the carrack.

Once the *Madre de Dios* was subdued, Borough and Cumberland engaged in a violent quarrel as to who should take possession. Borough was not impressed with the noble blood of his adversary and actually was in a stronger position because he sailed the Queen's ship. He therefore took possession of the carrack 'in Her Majesty's name and right', and he added in a dispatch sent home that in spite of the pillaging he hoped the Queen would receive more profit from this ship than from any other ever brought to England.

He was right. The carrack arrived at the mouth of the Dart on the 8th of September, but people knew it was coming long before; the breeze that was bringing her north wafted the scent of her cargo all along the shores of Devon. It was as if the Spice Islands were floating into harbour. Aboard that carrack were 537 tons of East India spice, cloves, cinnamon, nutmeg, pepper, mace and benjamin. Also there were musk, amber, diamonds, crosses encrusted with stones, fifteen tons of ebony and many bales of silks, satins and tapestries. Such a treasure ship had never been seen. The scent of spice drifted into all the towns for miles around, drawing people as scented pollen draws bees. Sailors who had been at sea for five months were giving pearls to barmaids, trading pieces of amber for tankards of ale, opening caskets of silks in the harbour stores, accepting five, ten, or, at most, twenty per cent of what their merchandise was worth. The scent of money reached London faster than the scent of cinnamon came to Plymouth. Westcountry men had plundered wrecked ships and prizes for years, but had never seen anything like this. From London, goldsmiths, jewellers and merchants, their chests bulging with cash, raced for the port. Over 2,000 of them had arrived and more were coming. It was the largest and most exciting fair ever staged in England.

At last, even the government heard about it. The Queen told Robert Cecil that he must leave immediately, secure the prize, and recover whatever loot he could. William Cecil had long been grooming his son for high office, partly like Polonius, by plying him with maxims. One of these was, 'Seek not to be Essex, shun to be Ralegh', an almost cruel piece of advice for such a hopeless candidate for glamorous heroism, for while young Robert Cecil had many of his father's good qualities – patience, shrewdness, stable judgment – he also had a handicap: he was barely five feet tall and he was physically weak. The thought of going alone to the Westcountry among a mutinous and disorderly rabble made him understandably apprehensive and he asked his father to urge the Queen to release Ralegh. Sir John Hawkins wrote in support that Ralegh was 'the especial man' to control the looting. Obviously something had to be done and fast.

And so the Tower doors were opened. When Ralegh was told of the prize and he thought of the money which could rebuild Sherborne, insure the success of his Irish estates, send him to Guiana and make him prosperous forever, he became almost manic. Of those London jewellers who were buying his treasure, he said, 'If I meet any of them coming up, if it be upon the wildest heath in all the way, I mean to strip them as naked as they were born. For it is infinite that Her Majesty hath been robbed and that of the most rare things'.

Cecil arrived at Dartmouth ahead of Ralegh, turning back all he met on the road. He found one sailor with a chain of orient pearls, two chains of gold, four great pearls as large as peas, four crystal forks, four crystal spoons set with gold and stones, and two cords of musk. A corporal had a large bag of rubies; another plunderer had over 300 diamonds.

When Ralegh arrived, the mariners greeted him with such shouts and with such obvious affection that Cecil, who had seen Ralegh only as the ambitious and despised courtier, was completely surprised. He wrote to Sir Thomas Heneage,

I assure you sir, his poor servants, to the number of 140 goodly men, and all the mariners came to him with such shouts of joy, as I never saw a man more troubled to quiet them in my life.

Ralegh, playing the role of poor prisoner to the hilt, told all who congratulated him on his liberty that his freedom was only temporary, he was still 'the Queen of England's poor captive'. Cecil anxiously urged him to conceal that fact, for by diminishing his credit with the people it might make recovery of the loot more difficult. Ralegh's credit, said Cecil, 'I do vow to you before

God is greater amongst the mariners than I thought for'. Never before having seen the world of ships and sailors, of naval battles and prizes, Cecil suddenly was seeing both that world and Ralegh's place in it. And Ralegh's manic energy in attempting to recover the loot was almost laughable; he was Shylock without a daughter, moaning the loss of his ducats and working like a demon to recover them. Cecil then learned, as he later wrote, that Ralegh 'can toil terribly'.

When it was all over Ralegh generously said that Sir Robert had recovered not less than 10,000 pounds for the Queen. The merchants were sent home, depositions taken, homes and pockets searched, and finally the carrack was towed into the Thames to be discharged of cargo which amounted to 141,000 pounds. It is hard to translate that amount into modern money, but ten million dollars might be a reasonable estimate.

Now the prize was to be divided. The Earl of Cumberland had a legitimate claim that was discharged for 36,000 pounds. In the remaining cargo worth 105,000 pounds, the London merchants had invested 6,000, the Queen 1,800, and Ralegh 11,000. The Queen had provided 1,150 tons of shipping out of 5,000 tons, or about twenty per cent. Normally she would have been entitled to about fifteen percent of the prize. Ralegh was clearly entitled to two-thirds of it or more. But from that entitlement must be subtracted the costs of his freedom, of the Queen's displeasure, and of the seducing of a maid of honour. He was finally given 36,000 pounds which proved the truth of one of Spenser's Puritan aphorisms, that men buy pleasure dearly. Ralegh claimed that the enterprise had cost him 34,000 pounds, and he did not accept the settlement graciously.

I gave my ship's sails and cables to furnish the carrack and bring her home, or else she had perished. My ship first boarded her and only stayed with her and brought her into harbour or else she had perished upon Scilly . . .

He points out that he had lost 1,100 pounds in Lord Thomas Howard's voyage of the previous year when the *Revenge* was lost; he had been paying interest on a debt of 11,000 pounds and

213

finally, every other adventurer had received double his money back; only Ralegh had received no more than the return of his principal.

I took all the care and the pains; carried the ships from hence to Falmouth, and from thence to the north cape of Spain, and they [the merchants] only sat still and did but disburse 6,000 pounds out of the common store, for which double is given to them and less than mine own to me: and to the Earl of Cumberland, 17,000 profit who adventured for himself and I for the Queen.

Everything Ralegh said, allowing for some exaggeration, was true, but once again Time had made a fool of him. If he and Bess had waited just one year to begin their liaison, he would have been a very wealthy man.

But finally he managed to carry it off with a swagger. Fourscore thousand pounds, he said, was more than ever a man had given her Majesty yet.

If God have sent it for my ransom, I hope Her Majesty of her abundant goodness will accept it . . . If my imprisonment or my life might do Her Majesty more good, I protest, before God, I would never desire either liberty or further respite of breathing.

Both the noble cadences and the complaints sounded like the real Ralegh: money could move him to passionate utterance. At least he was free. Belphoebe had seen the heart-shaped ruby; it had pleased her. It should have; actually, it had cost her pining lover about 40,000 pounds.

If Ralegh had lost only his prize money it would have been bad enough, but his disgrace meant also the failure and ultimate loss of his Irish estates. The one product the Desmond lands produced which was immediately exportable was timber. By 1592, when he went to the Tower, he had invested 5,000 pounds in a sawmill and had 200 of his settlers at work felling trees and sawing them into barrel staves. These were being shipped to the Canary and Madeira Islands to be made into hogsheads in which sweet Spanish wines were returned to England. When Ralegh entered the Tower, Sir William Fitzwilliam, with whom he had quarrelled so bitterly, arrested Ralegh's partner, Henry

Pyne, on charges that he was selling heavy planking to the Spaniards for the construction of warships. He further charged that Pyne had Catholic sympathies and was a channel of information between Catholic refugees on the Continent and recusants in England and Ireland. Pyne cleared himself of these charges and, in August, just before Ralegh left the Tower, petitioned for a renewal of his trade with the islands. It was not until January 21, 1594, that the renewal was finally granted. Meanwhile the colonists in Ireland were left without their principal source of income. Besides, the Council expressed alarm at the deforesting of Ralegh's properties and determined to regulate that.

While Ralegh was still in the Tower, Fitzwilliam carried on his feud with bad results for England as well as for Sir Walter. He said that Ralegh owed 400 pounds in taxes; if they were not paid immediately, he would seize the settlers' milk cows. Ralegh replied that the debt was only some 36 pounds and that it had been paid. He proved to be right but by the time the government found it out it was too late. By then Fitzwilliam had seized 500 milk cows, in some cases taking all a settler had.

Some had but two, and some three, to relieve their poor wives and children, and in a strange country newly set down to build and plant.

The colonists became discouraged and began to drift back to England. From the Tower Ralegh wrote to Robert Cecil, 'The doting Deputy hath dispeopled me . . . It is a sign how my disgraces have passed the seas'. But he was not blameless; he had abused the royal favour, angering the Lord Deputy and refusing in his proud way to cooperate with him. When the royal favour was lost, the Deputy had retaliated.

With the income from timber in abeyance, Ralegh tried to exploit the minerals on his Irish estates. He assembled fifty Cornish miners but they never sailed. For another ten years he would hold his Irish lands, but his holdings slowly withered and their failure was apparent before Tyrone's rebellion finally ended all hope of success.

215

At home, too, there was trouble for Ralegh. Christopher Marlowe had outraged the guardians of morals and religion by saying that the New Testament was filthily written, meaning that it was in common rather than in classical Greek; it was said that he had also read some kind of 'atheist lecture' to Sir Walter Ralegh and others, that he had made an anagram of the word *God* in which he spelled it backwards and there was, of course, the famous slander that Moses, like Thomas Hariot, was a juggler. A commission was sent to Dorset to examine into Ralegh's religion, but by the time it got around to pondering these weighty matters, Marlowe had been dead for almost a year, slain in a tavern brawl, and the investigation came to nothing. It was simply one more indication in England that Ralegh was out of favour and that there were many in England who would have been glad to see him put down a little further.

The Queen would have nothing to do with him. He still held all of his offices, including Captain of the Guard, but was not permitted to exercise them. He wrote a plaintive letter to Lord Admiral Howard.

I hope your Lordship will take my remembrance in good part. And if your Lordship will vouchsafe [to ask] Her Majesty for me to attend you privately in her service, I hope I shall stand your Lordship in the place of a poor mariner or soldier. I have no other desire but to serve Her Majesty. And seeing I deserve nor place, nor honour, nor reward, I hope it will be easily granted, if I be not condemned to the grave; no liberty nor hope left that either time or the giving of my life may recover, or be a sacrifice for my offences.

Despite the Westcountry sense of injured merit and a little self-pity, his offer to serve privately is genuine and his relations with his Queen are now simply that of any loyal subject. For the first time in ten years, Ralegh is standing on his own.

In the same year in which he wrote to Lord Howard, an English privateer captured a Spanish ship which was carrying a bundle of letters concerning Guiana and El Dorado. When Ralegh read those accounts, he knew that time was short; if he meant to make Guiana into an English empire, he would have to move soon in order to beat the Spaniard.

13

The Golden Empire

The land north of Florida did not look promising for an empire which must be financed out of its own resources rather than from the treasury of England. But in South America there existed a vast unexplored land of jungle, wilderness and mountain lying between two broad, serpentine rivers, the Amazon and the Orinoco. In 1584, when Hakluyt and Ralegh were trying to interest the Queen in a state venture in Virginia, Hakluyt had mentioned the alternative.

All that part of America eastward from Cumana unto the river of St. Augustine in Brazil containeth in length along the sea side 2,100 miles. In which compass and tract there is neither Spaniard, Portingales nor any Christian man but only Caribs, Indians and savages. In which place is great plenty of gold, pearl and precious stones.

And this tract of land stretched westward to the Andes mountains. Whoever colonized it would drive an iron wedge between the Spanish empires of Peru and Mexico and would control the waterways into the interior. English warships based along this coast could choke off the flow of gold to Spain and could attack, one at a time, the Spanish-held islands and the fortified cities of the Spanish Main. The Spanish empire would then topple and the entire action could be financed by the inconceivable wealth of Guiana.

Ralegh had been thinking of Guiana ever since the time of Hakluyt's *Discourse*, but it was not until 1594 that he was ready to act. Then, out of his privateering captains, he selected Jacob Whiddon, the man who had captured Sarmiento, who had towed to port *Our Lady of the Rosary* during the fight with the

217

Armada, and who, in that wild night off the Azores, had so gallantly come to the support of the *Revenge*. To him Ralegh gave the task of reconnaissance just as he had earlier sent Captains Barlow and Amadas to the shores of Virginia before he ventured the main party.

Before Whiddon sailed, Lady Ralegh wrote a letter to Sir Robert Cecil.

I hope for my sake you will rather draw Sir Watar towards the east than help him forward toward the sunset if any respect to me or love to him be not forgotten.

Bess wanted him restored to his position at Court rather than sent off to unknown hazards in South America. There follows in the letter a passage that some have thought reflects the style of Ralegh who, therefore, must have written it in connivance with his wife.

But every month has his flower and every season his contentment, and you great counsellors are so full of new counsels, as you are steady in nothing; but we poor souls that hath bought sorrow at a high price desire, and can be pleased with, the same misfortune we hold, fearing alterations will but multiply misery of which we have already felt sufficient. I know only your persuasions are of effect with him, and held as oracles tied to them by Love; therefore I humbly beseech you rather stay him than further him. By the which you shall bind me forever.

But the supposed literary grace of the letter consists merely in some antithetical phrases in the Euphuistic style, a current Court fad for ladies; it does not sound like Sir Walter, either in matter or style; and in any case it did no good, for Whiddon sailed.

The great delta of the Orinoco was guarded by the Island of Trinidad, recently occupied by the Spaniards under Don Antonio de Berreo, who had made three major expeditions into the interior of Guiana in search of El Dorado. Berreo knew more about Guiana than any living man and he believed in the legend of Manoa with a passion equal to Ralegh's. In Trinidad, therefore, was the logical place to seek out information and native guides.

When Whiddon arrived at the island, he requested permission from Berreo to take on water and supplies. While his vessels were being laden, Whiddon traded with the Indians, listened sympathetically to their complaints of Spanish cruelty, and enquired about El Dorado. Berreo, now alarmed, remained outwardly friendly, but when Whiddon was away from his ships, he sent Indians aboard to invite the crew to come ashore and hunt deer. Eight of them, being (as Ralegh later wrote) very wise men, accepted the offer and were immediately set upon and killed. This, Whiddon realized, was Berreo's way of terminating his welcome and he immediately hoisted anchor and returned to England bringing back stories gleaned from natives and from sailors that confirmed the existence of the land of El Dorado. Ralegh immediately sought Letters Patent from the Crown authorizing him to explore and settle Guiana.

He received the Letters without difficulty, although they were significantly different from the ones given him for the settling of Virginia. Like those they authorized him to discover, subdue, and take possession of lands not already in the possession of a Christian king. And they went further. They authorized him to offend and enfeeble the King of Spain and his subjects in any way and to resist by force of arms all persons who should attempt to settle within 200 leagues of the place where he and his people might fix their habitation. He was also permitted to capture any trading ship that came within his domain. But these Letters were issued only to 'our servant, Sir Walter Ralegh'; the usual adjectives, 'trusty and well-beloved' were omitted.

Ralegh sank his entire fortune into equipping an expedition. Robert Cecil gave something; the Lord High Admiral contributed the *Lion's Whelp* which was to serve as Vice-Admiral under Captain Gifford. All the rest of the expense was apparently borne by Ralegh himself. He was to be Admiral in one of his own ships, probably either the *Bark Ralegh* or the *Roebuck*. And remembering the difficulties of exploring the shallow rivers in North Carolina, he equipped a Spanish gallego of shallow draught which one of his privateers had previously captured. She was to sail under Lawrence Keymis, a former Oxford don who was hopelessly fascinated by Ralegh and his schemes. And there was another small bark under Captains Cross and Calfield; those four ships, three of them Ralegh's, made up the entire force. Ralegh later said that had he died in Guiana, he would not have left 300 marks a year for his wife and his son Walter. As usual, he had gambled everything.

When the fleet was assembled, the winds were contrary and once again Ralegh suffered that agony of seeing his supplies dwindle, his sailors slip away, and his money dissipate. 'This wind,' he wrote to Robert Cecil, 'breaks my heart.' He was especially anxious because a number of English privateers were bound for Guiana where they might, he said, 'frustrate the Queen's purpose', if they should attempt Guiana, be driven off, and dissipate the advantage of surprise which his own lightly armed forces might otherwise enjoy. Also he believed that the success of the venture depended on an enlightened Indian policy which would encourage the natives to rise against Spain. If privateers plundered and abused the natives before he arrived, this design also would be thwarted. In January of 1595 he wrote to Cecil that all was ready and he was 'only gazing for a wind to carry me to my destiny'.

On February 6 he finally stood out to sea. Six months later, in August, he was back in England, 'withered' and a 'beggar'. He asked Robert Cecil, does Guiana 'pass for a history or a fable' ? To make it appear more like the former, he had sent the Queen a little gold, some pearls and some diamonds – or if they were not diamonds, they exceeded any diamond in beauty. There was another rare stone very much like an amethyst. Though most of his men had brought home ore samples, some of which had been assayed by an officer of the Mint and pronounced worthless, Ralegh himself had dug some gold ore out of quartz with his dagger. Three refiners, including two controllers of the Mint, had said that it was fabulously rich.

But it all sounded a little dubious and the calumniators were soon at work. Some said that Ralegh had never left England at all but had spent the six months in Cornwall. Witnesses could be produced who had seen him there. Others said that he had sailed to the Barbary Coast and had traded there for some gold ore. To convince the Queen and his countrymen that he had indeed 'passed the pikes', he wrote an account called *The Discovery of the large, rich, and beautiful Empire of Guiana, with a relation of the great and golden city of Manoa (which the Spaniards call El Dorado)*. He dedicated it to the Lord Admiral and Cecil, saying it was the only return they would get for their investment. Succeeding generations have thought it a handsome return. The late Bernard De Voto considered it the greatest piece of prose to come out of the English Renaissance and certainly it is one of the most imaginative and stirring adventure stories ever written. And soon all of Europe was reading it: there were four German editions, seven Dutch, some Latin and many in English.

To the casual reader Ralegh's account offers some difficulty. He wrote it, as he says, hastily, without taking thought for structure. It was huddled together not to please the classically fastidious, nor to instruct through pleasure, but to prove his own veracity. It is therefore a model of baroque exuberance in which four main themes are intertwined and intermingled: the legend of El Dorado and the search for the city of Manoa; the delineation of a humane policy toward the natives by which he has won their allegiance to England; the fantastic riches of Guiana; and finally, the voyage itself. His narrative can best be understood if these themes are considered separately.

THE LEGEND

First, Ralegh explains why 'in the winter of [his] life' he undertook a voyage in which he was 'accompanied with many sorrows, with labour, hunger, heat, sickness and peril'. It was only to recover his lost favour with the Queen.

If I had known other way to win, if I had imagined how greater adventures might have regained, if I could conceive what farther means I might yet use, but even to appease so powerful displeasure, I would not doubt but for one year more to hold fast my soul in my teeth till it were performed.

And this was the legend that had lured him across the seas. When the illiterate and bloody Pizarro stumbled into Peru in 1524, he found an advanced civilization which his brutal and crafy nature could in no way appreciate. There were fine roads and a highly developed system of irrigation. A regular and exact census was kept. There was taxation, but it was taken in kind, inasmuch as money was not known. And there were advanced social theories under which no man was to be overworked and no man was to remain idle. When a city became overcrowded, colonists were removed to an under-developed area where new cities were founded and ruled under the just laws of the nation. The Inca civilization has reminded more than one scholar of certain features of Sir Thomas More's *Utopia*, written eight years before Pizarro's discovery. Enthusiasm for the Inca civilization has always run high, one historian believing that 'probably never in the world has a communistic experiment, on a large scale, attained a greater measure of success'.

And although there was no money in Peru, there was much gold. The amounts were fantastically exaggerated in some Spanish accounts, but it was a fact that the walls in the Temple of the Sun at Tumbez were tapestried with plates of silver and gold. It was also a fact that Pizarro ransomed the Inca for five million in gold, a fifth of which was dutifully sent on to King Philip. Ultimately Pizarro's cruelties depopulated the Inca Empire, not entirely through slaughter. Some of the Incas, it was believed, had fled eastwards into the Andes mountains. At that point, concerning this 'lost tribe' fact ends and fancy begins. From both Sarmiento and Berreo Ralegh had heard that a younger son of Guayanacapa, Emperor of Peru, had fled eastward from Eden with several thousand warriors called Orejones. They had captured all of the land lying between the two great rivers and had founded a capital city called Manoa on a large inland lake known as the Lake of Parima. This eastward flight also explained the puzzling fact that despite all the gold ornaments and gold plates found in Peru, there were no gold mines that would supply such wealth. The Spaniard had found a mountain of silver, but all of his feverish search for gold, over many decades, had yielded little. It was believed, therefore, that the gold mines must exist somewhere in the interior and that the rivers of Guiana were the veins along which that golden stream had once flowed into the Inca Empire.

All of this Ralegh writes succinctly and in a matter-of-fact tone.

The Empire of Guiana is directly east from Peru . . . It hath more abundance of gold than any part of Peru and as many or more great cities than Peru had; it is governed by the same laws, and people observe the same religion and the same form and policies in government as was used in Peru, not differing in any part.

Ralegh was certainly attracted by the prospect of uniting forces and destinies with these civilized Peruvians. Good minds are even more fascinating than gold mines, and in Guiana he thought he would find a people with whom he could deal rationally, who would understand and appreciate English law, English arts and the English Bible. They would not be artful savages like Pemisapan and his hungry warriors. The English and Inca empires would have much to give one another. After all, Marco Polo, in Cathay, had discovered a civilization to match the brilliance of the Venetian state. Ralegh hoped to discover a civilization worthy of England.

Sir Walter tells his readers that he had personally 'been assured by such of the Spaniards as have seen Manoa, the Imperial City of Guiana', that it exceeded any city in the world for riches. And here he typically exaggerates and misleads. He had never talked to a Spaniard who had seen Manoa and, in fact, only two Spaniards ever claimed to have seen that city. Ralegh had read an account by one of them and Berreo had told him of the other.

Because nothing else was known of the fabled city, Ralegh

accepted as true the accounts written of the Inca Empire by Spanish historians and then extrapolated. If those accounts were true of the former Inca Empire, they were true of Manoa. The histories claimed that the Inca had dishes and vessels of gold and silver in his house, and in his wardrobe were giant statues of gold, one of which weighed 4,700 pounds and was worth at least 100,000 pounds sterling. 'I know,' Ralegh wrote to Robert Cecil, 'that in Manoa there are store of these.' How he knows he does not say.

The Inca had ropes of gold, heaps of gold, chests and troughs of gold and silver. And what really sent the imagination soaring in the Spanish account was a 'garden of pleasure' which the Inca had built on a pleasant island. There he had counterfeited in gold everything that lived or grew in his country. There were beasts, birds, trees, herbs, fishes, flowers, all imitated in gold and silver, all life-size and cunningly wrought, 'an invention and magnificence until then never seen'. W. B. Yeats' holy city of Byzantium, that world of gold and ivory artifice where golden birds sing on golden boughs, does not surpass this world Ralegh conceived. His prose burns with passion and belief when he tells of it. There is no caution, not the slightest qualification. And one cannot help remembering that he was a Devon boy who had lived in a land where a vanished civilization had once built a stone city and had buried gold in shining heaps beneath it. It is as though he had found, far off, an unknown and exotic land that stirred into recollection the deep and powerful boyhood images of his own country.

And Spaniards believed enough of this that they were willing to risk some toil and treasure in pursuit of it. In 1542, Pizarro had sent Orellana down the Papamene branch of the Amazon to find the new Inca. Nothing came of that. But later a Spaniard did get through to the city, so he said, the first Western man ever to have been there. His name was Juan Martinez; he was master of the munition to Diego Ordas, a Knight of the Order of Santiago. Ordas had sailed up the Orinoco River to Morequito, a native village at the juncture of the Orinoco and Caroni rivers (Ralegh calls it the Caroli). And at that place one of Ordas's ships had left a great anchor which Ralegh saw. Here was a touch of reality for the Celtic folk-mind to build on.

At Morequito, the expedition of Ordas came to an end when, through some accident, the entire store of powder was burned. Martinez, as master of munitions, was held responsible and ordered executed. At the protest of the other soldiers, however, Juan of the ill hap was finally set adrift in a canoe, without food or arms, upon the swift flowing current of that uncharted river. And here his story began. Ralegh had not only read that story, he had also talked with Berreo, who believed in it with a child-like trust. And of many strange tales, there was never a stranger one.

Some natives found Martinez drifting alone and, having never seen a white man before, they carried him into the interior 'to be wondered at'. He was passed along from town to town, ever deeper into the jungle until he came to the borders of Manoa. At the border, he was blindfolded and led along for fifteen days until he came to the gates of a city. There the blindfold was removed and he was led toward the Emperor's palace. He walked from noon until dark; the next morning he arose and travelled from sunrise until sunset before he came at last to the palace of the Inca, who immediately recognized him as a Christian and treated him well, a puzzling non-sequitur, considering what Pizarro had done to the Indians in Peru.

Martinez was entertained for several months in Manoa and finally sued for permission to leave. His suit was graciously granted and he was laden with all the gold he could carry. When he again came to the border country, the Orenoqueponi relieved him of his gold 'save only two great bottles of gourds, which were filled with beads curiously wrought'. These and his story he brought back to the Spanish Main. A written copy of that story came into the hands of Antonio de Berreo; another may still be seen in the Chancery of San Juan de Puerto Rico.

When Martinez lay dying, he called for his confessor, swore to the truth of his adventure, and gave the gold beads to the church under the wise condition that continual prayers would be said for his soul.

Martinez not only confirmed the legend of the gilded man, he added something to it. Once a year, he said, the captains, tributaries, and governors gathered to carouse with the Emperor. Not one man, therefore, but dozens of them, in an hour when the rose of wine was blooming, anointed their bodies with white balsam. Then the fine powdered gold was blown through hollow canes until all were 'shining from foot to the head'. And it was this sight, along with the gold shields and armour and the gold images in the temples, that led Martinez to give the land the name of El Dorado.

Martinez did not entirely invent his story. Undoubtedly he had heard a legend, which long before Ralegh's time and long after, circulated throughout Guiana, a legend which, in turn, may have been based on some kind of practice related, however remotely, to the one he described. It is difficult for us, as it was for Ralegh, to believe that a devout Catholic would lie to his confessor. But whereas Ralegh concluded that he must therefore have told the truth, most men would be inclined to think that fear and shame and a humiliating journey through the villages and jungles of Guiana had done something to the man's mind in which reality and fantasy were thereafter fused.

And so three men had looked for the kingdom, one had found it. Martinez was followed by Pedro de Osua, Knight of Navarre, and by others including Don Gonzales de Casada, all of whom found nothing. The latter gave his daughter in marriage to Berreo, first requiring him to swear on his honour that he would 'follow the enterprise to the last of his substance and his life'. And Berreo told Ralegh that he had spent 300,000 ducats in the quest which he never abandoned. And with all that expenditure, said Ralegh, Berreo never came as near to Manoa as he and his Englishmen had done.

After Casada, there were at least four other expeditions that tried and failed and tried again and finally there were the explorations of Berreo himself. In 1580, at the unlikely age of 60, he had started from the Western province of New Granada and followed a tributary downstream to the Orinoco which he crossed. There he saw to the west a mountain range which was barred by a steep escarpment. His men were exhausted; he was out of supplies, and he did not attempt the mountains. But he did come back with all the legends and a recommendation that Trinidad be colonized and that he be made governor of Guiana. He finally received a commission from Philip II which made him governor of El Dorado.

He made a second expedition in 1588. Again he crossed the Orinoco from the west and probed the mountains for a pass into the highlands. Again that escarpment baffled him: he needed a passage through and over it and he could not find one.

Two years later he again worked down the Orinoco to its confluence with the Caroni. By following the Caroni upstream he believed that he would find his way to El Dorado. But when he arrived there he found again that he had neither the men nor the equipment to surmount the rugged and inaccessible gorge of the Caroni where its fantastic cataract spills over great ledges. But that cataract, he believed, fell from the land of his desirings. Short of supplies, he was obliged to seize food from the natives and his men were free with the women; the natives became surly and hostile. Finally Berreo was forced to return to Trinidad where Ralegh had found and captured him. Before Ralegh had arrived, however, an old cacique called Morequito (after whom the village was called) had come to Cumana on the Spanish Main with a 'great store of gold plate'. Berreo heard of it, talked with Morequito, and sent some Spanish soldiers and a friar back to his village with him. Eventually this entire company was escorted to Manoa. That fact, Berreo told Ralegh, was certain. But then it was the story of Juan Martinez all over again. As they were returning with their 40,000 pesos of gold, they were set upon by Morequito and his men, who slew them all except one who swam the river and returned. 'I only am escaped alone to tell thee', was the recurrent theme of the Spanish search for Manoa.

Berreo then led an expedition to Morequito where he slew the cacique and put his uncle, Topiawari, in chains. He led the old man around like a dog for seventeen days until the natives could find his ransom which was 100 plates of gold. He then released Topiawari, who became the new cacique of the village of Morequito.

And so it appeared perfectly clear to Ralegh that he now knew where Manoa was. He must sail up the Orinoco to the Caroni. There he would find Topiawari, treat him kindly, win his confidence and the old cacique would show him a forgotten or hidden trail along or around the Caroni cataract. Once on top of the scarp, he would be within an easy march of one of the earth's mighty nations, and a city larger than London, richer than Cathay. That nation, by wit or valour or both, he would win for England.

And there were other things beyond that scarp; wonders in Guiana were endless. Beyond the Caroni, on one of its branches dwelt

a nation of people, whose heads appear not above their shoulders; which though it may be thought a mere fable, yet for mine own part, I am resolved it is true, because every child in the provinces of Aromaia and Canuri affirm the same: they are called Ewaipanoma: they are reported to have their eyes in their shoulders, and their mouths in the middle of their breasts, and . . . a long train of hair groweth backward between their shoulders.

Ralegh again had persuasive reasons for believing this story. Old Topiawari, when he finally met him, had given him his favourite son to take back to England. That young prince of blood had told Ralegh that the Ewaipanoma were mighty men, giants, whose bows and arrows and clubs were thrice as large as any others in Guiana. When Ralegh expressed scepticism, the boy told him with casual and evident sincerity that they were a great and mighty nation and quite a common sight. In recent years they had slain many hundreds of his father's people. If he had only known Ralegh was interested, he could have shown him where to capture one of these hideous creatures to bring back to England. Then the matter would have been 'beyond all doubt'.

Later, when Ralegh came to Cumana, he spoke with a Spaniard, 'a man of great travel', who, when he found Ralegh had been to Caroni, asked him if he had seen any of the

Ewaipanoma 'which are those without heads'. This man who
was 'esteemed a most honest man of his word, and in all things
else', said that he had seen many of them. These legends must
have set bells chiming in Ralegh's head. Giants had once built
a stone city, forgotten ages ago, on the granite wastes of Dartmoor. How Ralegh himself would have received his tales in
London it is difficult to say: but on the banks of the Caroni he
was predisposed to believed them and he did.

The story of the men with no heads raised more eyebrows and
laughter in England than any other in Ralegh's account. No one
appears to have believed it except for that beautiful creation of
Shakespeare's imagination, the fair Desdemona. When the
formidable Moor came to court her, he told her of almost as
many wonders as Ralegh had seen in Guiana. Fascinated, she
listened as Othello spoke of

> . . . the Cannibals that each other eat,
> The Anthropophagi, and men whose heads
> Do grow beneath their shoulders.

Othello and Topiawari's son both captivated their listeners.

And there were more wonders. The Amazon River, as everyone knew, was named for those wild and lovely warriors who
dwelt on its southern bank. Ralegh 'was very desirous to understand the truth of those warlike women'; he found a man, a
native cacique who had been there and could tell him. The
strongholds of these women, he said, were sixty leagues south
of the river. The Amazons refrained from the company of men
except for one month during the year, the month of April,
Ralegh believes. In that month when it is best to be in England,
and in Amazonia, the kings of the border would gather for their
intriguing ritual. The queens of the Amazons would look them
over and choose their companions; then the rest of the women
'cast lots for their valentines'. Once suitably paired off, they
would feast, dance and drink wine, much wine, the party growing in gaiety as the moon waxed. When the moon waned and
died, the festival ended and all returned to their own countries

to await the results. All the women who gave birth to sons sent them to the borderlands to be with their true fathers; those who bore girls nursed and nourished them. In the classical myths of the Amazons it had always been said that the women cut off their right breasts in order that they could better hurl the spear and shoot the bow. This, says Ralegh, 'I do not find to be true'. Obviously he was a man who appreciated symmetry.

It is on the basis of these legends, so credulously believed, that Ralegh has been called a great liar. Those who see him as a twentieth-century liberal *manqué* do not believe, somehow, that he is serious in these matters, as they ignore his devout prayers on the scaffold or the entire framework of his *History* which was written to show the providence of God in the affairs of men. But lying has little meaning in this context, the world of the folk-mind where the throat is taut, the voice hushed with wonder. And always in the background is some empirical basis, far different from the bright radiance of the legend, but some foundation on which the imagination can build its desires, an anchor rusting on a river bank.

This, then, was the dream that hounded Ralegh to his death and now, in 1595, drew him on his first disastrous voyage to the conquest of Utopia by kindness.

THE INDIAN POLICY

When Ralegh arrived at Trinidad, he immediately began to court the natives and they disclosed to him the cruel practises of the Spaniard. Berreo had executed two Indians for trading with Ralegh and some now lay in prison, half-starved, bound in chains, while the jailers dropped hot grease on their naked bodies.

When Ralegh had taken the island, he assembled all the caciques and, through an interpreter, told them that 'he was the servant of a great Queen, who was the Great Cacique of the North and a virgin'. The Great Cacique had delivered many nations from the Spaniards who were her enemies because of their cruelty and oppression. 'Having freed all the coast of the

Northern world' from Spain, she had now sent her servant, Sir Walter Ralegh, to free the Indians and to defend all of Guiana from invasion and conquest. He then showed the caciques a picture of Elizabeth 'which they so admired and honoured, as it had been easy to have brought them idolatrous thereof'. Everywhere Ralegh went he staged the same scene and delivered the same oration. As a result, all over Guiana and its borders, 'Her Majesty is very famous and admirable, whom they now call Ezrabeta, Cassipuna Aquerawana' or Elizabeth the Great Commander. It was the old flattery in a new setting, and Elizabeth may have found it a little hard to resist.

And he brought her something a little more tangible. At the ceremony on Trinidad Island, Ralegh formally annexed the island, raising a high pole bearing the Royal arms, an act authorized by his Letters Patent. By conquest, therefore, the island belonged to the Queen if she cared to have it and, of course, to hold it.

Ralegh soon discovered that the chief source of native hostility to Spain was the casual appropriation of native women. He therefore forbade any commingling of his men with the native women, and he believes that he returned with a company of men, no single one of whom had ever known a Guianan woman either forcibly or by consent. Considering the roughnecks who made up the majority of his party, this was an achievement only slightly less wondrous than the legends, especially when, as Ralegh says, many hundreds of native women came among them, some of whom were both young and excellently well favoured, all stark naked and 'without deceit', a pleasant contrast to the ladies of the Court. It was their asceticism, says Ralegh, more than anything else, that led the natives to love him and drew them 'to admire Her Majesty whose commandment I told them it was'. The Virgin Queen appeared to rule a nation of virgin soldiers and the natives were properly impressed.

Further, he would not allow his men to take anything without paying for it, not even a potato. It was hard to keep the meaner sort from thievery and so before he left any village he would assemble all the people and ask through an interpreter if they had suffered any theft or violence. If they had, the property was restored and the offender punished in the sight of all.

Everywhere, he shared food with the natives, treated them well, and gave them gifts; indeed Ralegh says (what is undoubtedly true) that he gave away more gold in Guiana than he brought back with him. It is unfortunate that this humane and generous policy is tainted. Again and again Ralegh gives the impression that he followed this policy less because it was humane than because it was expedient. He did not wish to spoil the greater enterprise and so, to be as unlike the Spaniard as possible, he seldom enquired about gold or tried to obtain it. But gold is what he was really after; he was no English counterpart of Bishop Las Casas, seeking to redeem and educate the natives. On the other hand, no one can read his account without realizing that he did treat the natives courteously, gently, without arrogance and with never a hint of condescension. He appears to have enjoyed mingling and talking with them and he had a genuine abhorrence of Spanish cruelties.

THE VEIN OF GOLD

Of all the paradoxes and contrasts in this fantastic voyage, there is none stranger than the one between the handful of dubious ore and the still more dubious gems Ralegh returned with and his depiction of Guiana as a land of untold wealth. He seldom departs from the theme for long. When he returned he imparted the vision to George Chapman who left the pursuit of darkness long enough to exult in verse about the new empire.

> Guiana, whose rich feet are mines of gold,
> Whose forehead knocks against the roof of stars,
> Stands on her tip-toes at fair England looking,
> Kissing her hand, bowing her mighty breast,
> And every sign of all submission making,
> To be her sister and the daughter both
> Of our most sacred maid.

To join London and Manoa, the daughter and sister of England

232

in a mingling of laws and arts and culture – and wealth – that was what Ralegh was after.

He had found gold in the rivers of Trinidad, but the Spaniards scorned it. Guiana was the treasure heap, 'the magazine of all rich metals', which contained more gold than the Indies or Peru. There, gold could be found in grains in the rivers. It could be found in the white spar of the rock ledges, in the images which appear to be copper but are one-third gold. There is more gold to be gained in Guiana than Cortez found in Mexico or Pizarro in Peru; the prince that possesses that land shall be lord of more gold and shall rule a more beautiful empire than either the King of Spain or the Great Turk. Yet when Ralegh wrote such things, he had never seen anything more than a naked savage living in a jungle hut.

But the theme continues. The Indians of Trinidad possess plates of gold which came from Guiana. The Amapaia, a tribe of the Orinoco, gave Berreo ten images of gold, some gold plates and gold croissants so brilliantly engraved and wrought that Berreo sent them on to King Philip. Nothing in Italy, Spain or the Low Countries could match their workmanship. By trading hatchets and knives, Berreo got images in gold of men, birds and fishes which he again sent to King Philip to justify further assistance from Spain.

In Trinidad, in 1591, a Frenchman traded a knife for a piece of gold weighing a pound and a half. This same man saw a bark of forty tons full of gold, worth two million, which came from El Dorado.

The Orenoqueponi bury jewels and gold with their dead. And when their great men die, in addition to long lamentation, they hang the corpse in the hut of death all decked with gold plates. Those fabulous graves remind one of the Devon kistvaens Ralegh knew in his youth, also supposedly full of gold. He could have robbed these graves, he said, but it would have turned the natives hostile and he wished first to find out whether the Queen would refuse or accept the whole enterprise of Guiana.

There was in Guiana a mountain that shone like crystal; Berreo said there were diamonds on it. Ralegh and his men saw hills covered with stones which sparkled and danced with the colours of gold and silver. They were not mere marcasite, which Ralegh could recognize very well, but *madre del oro*, mother of gold, which always is a certain sign of precious metal. According to captured documents, when the Spaniards had asked Topiawari how the Manoans got their gold, the old chief had replied that they went into a plain and pulled up grass by the roots. By taking the earth from these roots and washing it in water, they obtained the gold dust with which they gilded their bodies; the large pieces they wrought into eagles. A soldier had once traded a hatchet, Topiawari said, for a gold eagle weighing twenty-seven pounds.

Ralegh's lust for gold was not mere personal greed. He knew that the Spanish Empire was not maintained by means of wine and the oranges of Seville.

It is his Indian gold that endangereth and disturbeth all the nations of Europe, it purchaseth intelligence, creepeth into counsels, and setteth bound loyalty at liberty in the greatest monarchies of Europe.

The English can have equal amounts of it and more. But to invade Manoa and match the strength of the Orejones, Ralegh needs a small force of soldiers financed by the Queen. The expedition will more than pay for itself.

The common soldier shall here fight for gold, and pay himself instead of pence with plates of half a foot broad . . . Those commanders and chieftains that shoot at honour and abundance shall find there more rich and beautiful cities, more temples adorned with golden images, more sepulchres filled with treasure than either Cortez found in Mexico or Pizarro in Peru. And the shining glory of this conquest will eclipse all those so far-extended beams of the Spanish nation.

It is dizzying. The thoughts climb and soar, always circling back to what the Spaniard has won and England may win. And that Guiana has resisted the Spaniard is an indication that God has reserved this Empire for Her Majesty and the English nation.

Robert Cecil and the Queen read this intoxicated account;

234

they looked at the small heap of ore and the peculiar gems and neither ever again evinced the slightest interest in Guiana. But to Ralegh it mattered not at all. Guiana was a fire in his bones, and he would never rest until he found the Golden City.

THE VOYAGE

Intermingled with the treatise on colonial policy, the dazzling vision of wealth, and the legends is an account of an actual journey, made by living Englishmen up the Orinoco River in the year 1595. It is considerably less fantastic than the context Ralegh provided for it, but it is a strange and wondrous adventure, enough in itself to provide exciting reminiscences for a lifetime.

When Ralegh left England, he sailed to the Grand Canaries and then on to Teneriffe. There his ships were separated and Ralegh, accompanied by Captain Cross, sailed on to Puerto de los Espanoles where the Spanish colonists came aboard to buy linen. Ralegh feasted them and was generous with his good Spanish wine. They had not tasted its like for many years, and after a few drinks they became merry. Ralegh then told them a story he had carefully spread in England that he was on his way to relieve the Virginia colonies. The Spaniards seemed to believe it and uncautiously boasted of the riches of Guiana.

Ralegh sailed on around Trinidad to St. Joseph where he slew the harbour guard and marched on the town which he burned at the urging of the natives. Most of the Spaniards ran away, but he captured Berreo and a Captain Jorge whom he refers to as Captain George. Ralegh treated his captives like gentlemen and they talked freely of Guiana. Captain George told him of a silver mine on the Caroni River and Berreo seems to have told him everything he had ever heard or done; he also tried to dissuade Ralegh from going up the Orinoco at that time of year saying that the current was too swift and that the natives would desert their villages, leaving him without supplies. Ralegh presumed that Berreo had other motives than concern for his welfare.

When the other two ships arrived at Trinidad, the expedition set out to penetrate the Orinoco delta, a vast jungle flatland through which sixteen different channels, and many cross channels, linked and wound and finally flowed out to sea. The immediate problem was to decide which of these arms they should penetrate in order to find the Orinoco. Ralegh sent a small boat ahead to reconnoitre but it soon turned back for fear of hostile natives and poisoned arrows.

Immediately Ralegh's curiosity was aroused and he set out to discover the antidote for the poison. Berreo had told him that no white man had ever been able to learn it and that the natives themselves did not know except for holy men who guarded the secret and passed it on to their sons. Ralegh considered it the chief sign of his success in dealing with the Guianans that he penetrated this mystery. The poison, he learned, made men very thirsty, which was true. The antidote was to drink no liquid until the wound had been dressed. If they drink, he was told, they are dead. Fortunately he never had to test his discovery.

He soon found that his barks could not penetrate the delta; the rivers were too shallow and their entrances were barred with silt. Since the small boats were insufficient for such a long journey, he paused while the carpenters cut down the gallego so that she could move through five feet of water; he also fitted her with oars. He put sixty men in the gallego, twenty in the long boat from the *Lion's Whelp;* ten in Captain Calfield's wherry, and ten in his own barge, 100 men in all. In those boats the men had to sleep, carry their food and prepare meals, including the slaughtering and dressing of game.

Ralegh found this crowding hard to endure, for although he was an excellent swordsman and a courageous cavalryman, he was not rugged: he lacked the tough-fibred stamina that explorers need. The rude life enervated him physically and disgusted him aesthetically. He baked in the sun, was drenched in the rains; and the odour of the men and the cooking sickened him. Except for rare moments, his journey was not an exhilarating adventure but a continuous act of dogged will.

To get through the Chinese box of the Orinoco, he employed

as guide an Arwacan Indian who himself had not been through the delta for twelve years; he was young and inexperienced and, says Ralegh, of no judgment. They could have wandered forever in that labyrinth of waters 'if God hadn't sent better help'.

And certainly God moved in a mysterious way. Their young guide sent them into a channel which they named the River of the Red Cross after St. George of England. They were, Ralegh said confidently, the first Englishmen ever to enter it. They sailed past many islands and much broken ground, curiously observing the artificial towns and villages built on stilts some twenty feet above the earth. They were told that the river could rise up to the level of the floors in the rainy season and since the inundations made it impossible for the delta natives to sow, plant or raise crops, they lived on deer, fish, breadfruit, birds and fowl.

When the expedition arrived at the first village they found a naked, savage people with matted hair, like Irish kerns who had thrown away their blankets, their last tenuous hold with civilization. At this village the Indian pilot and his brother went ashore to try to get information. Immediately the Indians seized them saying they would kill them for bringing a strange nation into their territory to 'spoil and destroy them', a commentary on their previous relations with the Spaniards. The brother broke free, and being a swift and highly motivated runner, outdistanced his pursuit, coming to the creek bank and crying out that the pilot was slain. Ralegh immediately seized the oldest man he could see, thinking that his venerability might make him the most valuable hostage. He told the pursuing Indians, who had drawn up short, that if his pilot weren't returned, he would kill the old man. His colonial native policy at that moment was in some jeopardy, but he was desperate. Back in the camp, however, the diversion of the first escape allowed the pilot to break free and he, too, plunged into the jungle in a race for his life. The natives loosed their deer dogs which broke into full cry and soon the woods echoed with baying, barking, and the shrill cries of the hunters. 'This poor chased Indian' doubled and redoubled and finally, with great endurance and skill, recovered the river bank, climbed a tree, ran out on an overhanging limb and dived into the river where the boats recovered him, 'half dead with fear'. As insurance against further attack, Ralegh decided to keep the old man hostage for a while and it was a lucky stroke, or, as Ralegh believed, providential. For he was an intelligent native who had lived in the delta all his life. He knew it well and agreed to take the English through it.

On the third day, as they were toiling through swamp and jungle, on guard against poisoned arrows, fighting the tricky cross-currents, the galley stuck fast in the mud. It looked for a while, said Ralegh, as if he would have to leave ninety men there 'to have inhabited like rooks upon trees', but by throwing all ballast out of the galley, and with all their sweat and muscle thrown into the effort, they finally refloated her. Berreo had been right after all. The currents were vicious; their food was gone; no one would trade with them; and the pilot, in true Indian fashion, kept saying not what was true, but what he thought the discouraged men wanted to hear, that land was not far off. Ralegh would not turn back. The world, he said, would laugh them to scorn, and he had already heard enough of England's scornful laughter.

In this perilous situation, the old pilot, Ciawani, told them that if they would enter a branch of the river on the right hand with the barge and long boats, leaving the galley behind, he could bring them to a village of the Arwacas, where they would find food. That meant leaving all weapons behind except small arms and all except twenty of the men. They suspected treachery, but had no choice unless they wished to turn back.

According to their enigmatic guide, they would reach the village and be back at the galley by sunset. And so they entered a small river overhung with lianas and bent their backs to the oars against the current. Sunset came. They had rowed forty miles, and the oarsmen were exhausted; more and more it appeared that they were being led up a river of darkness. Ralegh must have been remembering Ralph Lane's trip up the Roanoke ten years earlier. And so he stopped and held a council of war in which it was determined to hang the guide. In extreme frustration the expression of a wish is often almost as therapeutic as its fulfilment; and the tension eased enough after the decision was made for someone to ask how they would ever get back to the galley if they killed the old man. All pondered this sober matter and receiving firm assurances once more that the village was just ahead, they wearily rowed again up that dark, flowing river.

We were very desirous to find this town, hoping of a feast because we made but a short breakfast aboard the galley in the morning and it was now eight a clock at night, and our stomachs began to gnaw apace.

At one o'clock in the morning, they heard the barking of dogs. The natives came down to welcome them, gave them food to eat and traded them bread, fish and hens. Ralegh's men loaded their canoes and next morning prepared to return to the galley. Before they left, Ralegh asked if he could meet the lord of the village, but learned that he had gone up the Orinoco to trade for gold and women. The food and this undoubted testimony of gold ahead, put heart back into his men. Later, Ralegh said, they actually passed this native chief on his way back down the Orinoco with thirty women and 'divers plates of gold'. However it was dark and they had passed him on that wide water without seeing him. The report of gold, therefore, was unconfirmed.

With their galley again stocked with food, the expedition rowed on up the delta. Then, one day, Ralegh saw his first savannah.

On both sides of this river, we passed the most beautiful country that ever mine eyes beheld: and whereas all that we had seen before was nothing but woods, prickles, bushes and thorns, here we beheld plains of twenty miles in length, the grass short and green, and in divers parts, groves of trees by themselves, as if they had been by all the art and labour in the world so made of purpose: and still as we rowed, the deer came down feeding by the water's side as if they had been used to a keeper's call.

Here for the first time, too, he saw the alligator, 'the ugly serpent, Lagarto', and when one of the young Negroes in the party jumped out of the galley to swim he was pulled under and devoured. It was a strange mixture of beauty and terror: serpents, alligators, queer fishes, and birds that were carnation, purple, crimson and orange-tawny.

As they moved through the savannahs, Captain Gifford saw four canoes ahead of him and in good spirits offered his men a race. They rowed 'at the uttermost of their strengths' and finally pulled abreast. Two of the canoes beached and their occupants ran into the jungle, leaving the canoes which were loaded with bread being taken down the river to trade. Food was low again and the bread, Ralegh said, was more welcome than anything could have been 'except gold'. Now the soldiers cried out, 'Let us go on, we care not how far'.

Their eagerness was motivated by the elusive scent of gold. For in one of the canoes, in addition to the natives, there had been three Spaniards who had all escaped, leaving behind a basket containing quick-silver, saltpetre, and other chemicals used for refining gold. Now Ralegh was tremendously excited. He cried out that he would give five hundred pounds sterling to the man who could catch him a Spaniard. His crews tumbled ashore and once again the manhunt in the jungle was on but it proved fruitless. Ralegh did not join it but stayed to interrogate the Indians, one of whom, naturally, told him what he wanted to hear. Ralegh now believed that he knew the location of a gold mine, 'though I made not the same known to all'.

Finally after fifteen days in the heat and stench, the men weary from stroking the oars twelve hours a day, the boats broke out of the delta and the men saw the mouth of the Orinoco. They beached on a sand bar where they found thousands of turtle eggs which they gathered and cooked. 'The men were now well filled and highly contented.' And there was another reason for their contentment. Far off they could see the shining mountains and beyond those mountains, in Ralegh's phrase, lay the maidenhead of Guiana.

At dawn the local cacique, Toparimaca, visited him. Ralegh entertained him with courtly grace. They drank wine and were pleasant together. Another cacique, a visitor, had a beautiful wife, tall, black-eyed, her body well padded and curved. Her hair, which was as long as her body, was done up in intricate knots. As with other beautiful women, her awareness of her own comeliness gave her poise: she did not stand in awe of her husband as other native women did. Rather she spoke and discoursed among the captains and gentlemen, drinking with them, making conversation and captivating everyone including Ralegh.

I have seen a lady in England so like to her, as but for the difference of colour, I would have sworn might have been the same.

Colour was only one of the slight differences between her and the ladies of the Court; her unabashed nakedness Ralegh does not mention, his narrative being primarily intended for the eyes of the sovereign spinster.

Five days later, they arrived at the confluence of the Caroni and the Orinoco, having made good time sweeping along the broad breast of the main river. At the little town of Morequito, Ralegh immediately sent for the cacique Topiawari, the uncle of Morequito whom Berreo had slain. He came bringing gifts, including pineapple, roots, bread and an armadillo which Ralegh describes minutely. The old cacique listened courteously to Ralegh's lecture on Elizabeth the Great and her kingdom of kindly and valiant warriors. And then Ralegh asked him the question on which everything depended. Pointing to the mountains rising up to the westward and shielded by a high escarpment, he asked who lived over there.

He answered with a great sigh (as a man which had inward feeling of the loss of his country and liberty, especially for that his eldest son was slain in a battle on that side of the mountains, whom he most entirely loved), that he remembered in his father's lifetime when he was very old and himself a young man, that there came down into that large valley of Guiana a nation from so far off as the sun slept (for such were his own words) with so great a multitude as they could not be numbered nor resisted, and that they wore large coats, and hats of crimson colour, which colour he expressed by showing a piece of red wood wherewith my tent was supported, and they were called

Orejones and Epuremei, those that had slain and rooted out so many of the ancient people, as there were leaves in the wood upon all the trees and had now made themselves lords of all . . . saving only of two nations.

It was everything Ralegh had come to hear. The Orejones from Peru, an 'apparelled people', dwelt beyond the scarp at whose foot he was now standing.

Even a less enthusiastic explorer than Ralegh would have had to believe the old man for he spoke the truth. But it was his truth, not Ralegh's. The difficulty lay in the fact that the dialogue was between men of different worlds who spoke different sounds and thought in different images.

At the head of the Caroni was a great savannah which, when completely inundated in the spring floods, resembled a lake; this was the basis in fact for the stories of the Lake of Parima. And it was true that a tribe from the highlands of Guiana had extended its frontiers at the expense of the Morequitos whom they had slaughtered. It was also true that they were a little more advanced than those whom they conquered and spoiled. Their villages, in Topiawari's view, were as much finer than his as London, in Ralegh's view, was finer than St. Ives. But Ralegh was measuring these replies in terms of an imaginative vision he had carried in his head from the Thames. And so they completely misunderstood one another.

Topiawari further told Ralegh that at the head of the Caroni were three other mighty nations whom he could count on as allies against the Spaniards, the Orejones or the Epuremei.

Ralegh thereupon organized his men into three different exploring parties and he himself led one on foot up the banks of the Caroni. Among other things, he wished to look for the silver mine Captain George had told him about. When they cleared the first ridge, the falls of the Caroni came in view.

When we [were come] to the tops of the first hills of the plains adjoining to the river, we beheld that wonderful breach of waters which ran down Caroli: and might from that mountain see the river, how it ran in three parts, above twenty miles off, and there appeared some ten or twelve overfalls in sight, every one as high over the other as a Church-tower, which fell with that fury, that the rebound of waters made it seem as if it had been all covered over with a great shower of rain: and in some places we took it at the first for a smoke that had risen over some great town.

Ralegh set out with the men to hike to the falls. It was hard going, jungle and rock, over one hill, down into a valley and up another hill. Ralegh was an 'ill footman', and he became exhausted, drained, and finally said that the men would have to go on without him. But they played the game with him which they had learned from their guide in the delta. The cataract, they said, was just over the next ridge and Ralegh, more amused than deceived, followed along and came to the falls. And he was glad he had for even the savannah country was not as beautiful as this: there were deer crossing in every path, unafraid, gentle, their soft eyes filled with curiosity; birds on every tree sang a thousand tunes no Englishman had ever heard. And every stone they stooped to take up seemed to promise either gold or silver. All of his men returned to Morequito with ore in their pockets and this, Ralegh complains, is the reason his discovery of gold has been doubted. Some of the men, with no judgment, picked up whatever glittered. And this was the ore the assayers had found worthless. But he had come across a ledge of white spar while hiking to the falls. In the veins of that quartz there was yellow ore. He had no tools with him but with his dagger and fingers he had dug and torn and hacked until he had enough to bring back to England for assay. What he had torn from the white flint was as rich as any that had ever been found.

To understand Ralegh's last tragic voyage in search of a gold mine some twenty years later, it is crucial to realize that he never really had one specific place in mind. He believed that the entire country was full of gold; it could be found in rivers, in graves; it could be had by trading and he knew of at least two mines. This was one of them. At the time he made no effort to mark the ledge or the path to it; he erected no cairns or markers, probably because he thought of this gold ore as nothing more than a confirmation of his hopes. He did not intend to return, find this ledge, break up the quartz and cart it on the backs of his men to Morequito. It would have seemed fantastic to him then, given the steepness of the terrain and the distance, even to think of it. In a land gleaming with gold, this incident seemed unimportant. After he had lain in the Tower for thirteen years, it took on different dimensions.

When the exploring parties returned to Morequito, they heard of the men without heads who lived beyond the cataract and began to consider whether they could attempt the gorge themselves. The men had no spare clothing: for three weeks, wet or dry, they had been living and sleeping in what they were wearing. And the Orinoco began to rise alarmingly. The summer rains were incessant and the great scarp began to appear formidable beyond their present means. The consensus was that they should return to their ships. Ralegh, therefore, called Topiawari and an interpreter into his tent. He sent all others outside. Then Ralegh opened his heart and his thoughts to the old man. What he needed to know, he said, was the passage that would lead him 'into the golden parts of Guiana, and to the civil towns and apparelled people of Inga'. Those people were enemies to Morequito, as were the Spaniards, and Ralegh was there to deliver Morequito and his people from both of them.

The cacique's reply was evasive. It was the wrong time of the year to go. And Ralegh did not have enough soldiers. Once, three hundred Spaniards had been trapped up on that frontier when the Epuremei set fire to the jungle grass. It was a journey of four days to the town of the Macureguarai who lived on the frontier of the Epuremei and were the nearest subject of the Inca; they wore clothing and were very rich, all the plates of gold which passed down the river having come from there. And much farther into the interior were the golden images of men and beasts, of birds and fishes.

What a tantalizing interview for Ralegh. He was within four days, he believed, of discoveries that would make the British Empire in Guiana a reality. He could not give it up. And so he asked Topiawari if he thought that the English were strong enough to take the town of the Macureguarai. Topiawari finally said he thought they were. And if the rivers remained navigable, he would himself lead the expedition. But he dared not leave his own town undefended; Ralegh must leave fifty soldiers in his village to guard it. Ralegh explained to him that he had only fifty good men with him, that the rest were oarsmen and labourers. And he hadn't enough shot and powder to leave a supply in the village and assault a town at the same time. If he left his men at Morequito without arms and powder, they would be vulnerable to the Spaniard, who even now might very well be on his way up the river to drive the English out. He knew Berreo was expecting reinforcements. Therefore, even though his nephew, John Gilbert, wanted to stay and young Grenville seconded him, Ralegh reluctantly decided that he could not attempt it. And Topiawari made one other strong point. He begged Ralegh not to invade the Epuremei and then depart from the country. If he did, those fierce warriors would slaughter him and his people if they guided or assisted the English in any way. But if Ralegh could bring enough force to maintain the borders of the Morequitos, then they would join with him in the assault, for it was the Epuremei who continually raided them and took their women. In reprisal, the two nations would march together; the English could have the gold and the Morequitans the women. It was a bargain Ralegh would have been glad to strike.

And so to preserve the greater enterprise, Ralegh determined not to attack one or two towns for immediate gain.

Therefore till I had known Her Majesty's pleasure, I would rather have lost the sack of one or two towns (although they might have been very profitable) than to have defaced or endangered the future hope of so many millions, and the great good and rich trade which England may be possessed of thereby. I am assured now that they will all die even to the last man against Spaniards in hope of our succour and return: whereas otherwise if I had either laid hands on the borderers or ransomed the lords, as Berreo did, or invaded the subjects of Inga, I know all had been lost for hereafter.

Reluctantly, Ralegh decided to return. He left two volunteers with Topiawari, Francis Sparrow, who was instructed to travel to Macureguarai and trade with those 'borderers' the merchandise which Ralegh had left for that purpose. If he could win their friendship, he was to try to go on to Manoa. And he also left a young lad, Hugh Goodwin, who wished to stay and learn the language. Sparrow ultimately made his way back to England without having achieved either objective, and twenty-two years later Ralegh's men, when he returned to Guiana, found Hugh Goodwin scarcely able to utter a word of the tongue that Shakespeare spake and probably without the faith and morals Milton held.

Ralegh was completely won over by Topiawari. He could not hope to live, he said, until Ralegh returned. Death now called for him each day (his own phrase, Ralegh assures the reader), and therefore he would send with Ralegh to the land of the Virgin Queen his favourite son who would make an alliance with the English and lead them back to the new empire.

Before Ralegh left Morequito, a neighbouring cacique named Putijma offered to bring him to a mountain (Mt. Iconuri) adjoining his town where there were stones the colour of gold. Not having the physical stamina to make the march, Ralegh asked Keymis to lead a reconnaissance. The mountain was some twenty miles downstream and fifteen inland. It was a journey that Berreo and men of his physical stamina would have made easily, but Keymis was ineffectual and weak, a man born to follow others, uncertain and fearful when he himself was in command. He found the jungle going difficult; he kept wondering if the Spanish reinforcements had arrived, if he and his men might be cut off from Ralegh's party, and so he turned back to the river without reaching the mountain. Later, when Ralegh was in the Tower, Keymis reminded him of this mine. He always swore that he knew where it was, and as years passed the conviction grew on him that it was rich and real and that he could find it. This, then, was the second mine Ralegh had in mind. But he never spoke in England, then or later, of two possible mines and a number of other interesting possibilities. He always spoke simply of 'a mine'.

As Ralegh floated down the river while Keymis was marching

inland, he saw rocks that appeared to contain gold ore. And on
the Winicapora branch of the Orinoco there was a mountain of
crystal. A mighty river fell over it, Ralegh said, sounding as
'if a thousand great bells were knocked one against another'.
On that mountain, Berreo told him, there were diamonds and
other precious stones which could be seen shining from far off.
Berreo hadn't gone there because the natives were hostile to his
Spaniards and he hadn't dared. But the friendly English should
find it an easy matter. This, then, constituted a third possible
mine.

But for this time the journey was over. Ralegh released his
noble prisoners, Berreo and Captain George. On his way north
he landed and attacked Cumana on the Spanish Main but was
driven back. He then sacked the towns of Rio de la Hacha and
Santa Marta but gained little booty. Then he thought of going
to Virginia but the weather was bad, he was exhausted and his
men had had enough. Virginia and the lost colony would have
to wait a little longer. It was the Virgin who mattered now.
Everything would depend on her reaction. And so he concludes
his narrative.

Now that it hath pleased God to send us safe to our ships, it is time to
leave Guiana to the Sun whom they worship and steer away to the
North . . . Guiana is a country that hath yet her maidenhead, never
sacked, turned, nor wrought, the face of the earth hath not been torn,
nor the virtue and salt of the soil spent by manurance, the graves have
not been opened for gold, the mines not broken with sledges nor their
images pulled down out of their temples. It hath never been entered
by any army of strength, and never conquered or possessed by any
Christian prince.

Ralegh was sure that the Inca would come to terms. He
would pay an English garrison hundreds of thousands of pounds
yearly to protect him against the Spaniards. What Ralegh
obviously meant is that he could extort that much from the
Incas. It all awaited the pleasure of the Queen.

When Ralegh returned, Richard Hakluyt wrote in support of
the venture, urging the Queen to act at this propitious moment;

and George Chapman wrote of Ralegh's sustaining 'pain, charge and peril' for the good of his country.

> Then most admired sovereign, let your breath
> Go forth upon the waters, and create
> A golden world in this our iron age.

But Elizabeth was tired; she knew that she was not Jehovah and she did not believe in golden worlds.

Ralegh is often praised for his 'colonial policy' and certainly he was the first to suggest that a European power might ally itself with natives in a benevolent policy of mutual advantage. He undoubtedly helped to set an idea working in European heads. But his policy, as his narrative reveals it, was really not much more than simple expedience. He needed native support against Spain; the only way to gain that support was through a policy of kindness.

His contribution would seem to be less tangible. He opened the wonders (and to a certain extent the realities) of Guiana to literate Englishmen. As his colonizing in Virginia had done earlier, so his voyaging in Guiana took the edge of strangeness off that fabulous land. But most significant was the effect of his personality on the caciques and their people. Whatever Ralegh may have lacked in physical stamina, he had an immense intellectual energy, a personal charm, a current of passion which the natives responded to. Something of the fire and design in his own mind he conveyed to them. For fifteen years, at various times, Englishmen returned to the Orinoco or the branches of the Amazon and when they did, their chief currency with the natives was Ralegh's name. When that name was sounded, they came over the rivers and through the jungles to see the emissaries of their deliverer. In 1604, when a Dutch boat came into the Orinoco, the natives ran toward it crying, 'Anglee, Anglee'. The legend of the gentle soldier who served the Virgin Queen took on, in the thatched villages of Guiana, the same qualities as the legend of the Epuremei. Ralegh became a legendary, almost supernatural being who had been sent among them for

248

their deliverance, and they never seemed to doubt that he would return. Like Arthur, he was a once and future king.

One can only be grateful that he was not allowed to return with an army and take the maidenhead of that wild land. It would have been like opening a kistvaen. The reality would have made him not only Time's fool but England's as well. The legends and adventure he left are worth more than the gold he sought. It is sometimes fortunate that the ultimate and inevitable triumph of reality is delayed.

14

The Fights at Cadiz and Fayal

The fight of the *Revenge* had demonstrated that if the plate fleet was to be taken it would have to be captured not off the shores of Spain where the Twelve Apostles were on convoy duty but rather where it assembled in the West Indies. While Ralegh had been in Guiana, Drake and Hawkins had led a strong naval force to the Western islands. John Hawkins died before the expedition reached the Indies; he was buried at sea and the command fell entirely to Drake. Sir Francis had not changed either his tactics or his nature and what had been imaginative and daring a few years ago now began to appear as desperation and lack of judgment. He attacked the fortified town of San Juan without understanding its defences; the engineers had erected scientific defenses which were too much for simple gallantry and assault. Repulsed there, Drake attacked two smaller towns but gained little booty. He then sailed to Nombre de Dios, joined with the Cimaroons, and marched across the isthmus to assault Panama and take whatever treasure lay stored there. But he found Panama barricaded and defended by Spanish soldiers with their usual grim efficiency, and so he was forced to retreat to his ships which were now foul and ill-supplied. He put into a small island to take on water, relieve the sickness that had broken out among his crews and to await better weather. It is poignant to contrast his youthful memories of the Indies as 'a delicious and pleasant arbor', with the appearance it presented to him when he was a sick, defeated, old man. It had become, he said, 'a vast and desert wilderness'. But he clung to the belief that his own personal crusade against Philip of Spain had providential support.

God hath many things in store for us, and I know many means to do Her Majesty good service and make us rich, for we must have gold before we see England.

One thing God has in store for all men and his 'fell sergeant' found the weakened Drake as he lay in the foul and foggy weather in his filthy ship, waiting for sunlight and a fresh breeze. He was buried at sea.

Now that *Aquines* and *El Draco* were dead, the Spaniard began to stir again. On March 29, 1596, the Archduke Albert, Governor of the Netherlands, seized Calais from the French. It was the strongest fortress on the French coast; it lay only a few miles from Dover in the narrowest part of the channel, and it was the kind of fortified harbour Philip had needed in 1588. For once the men of action had their way and England assembled the strongest and best equipped force Elizabeth ever sent against Spain. Its object was to land an expeditionary force on the Spanish coast and to destroy Spanish warships and supporting vessels in order to forestall another Armada. There were seventeen ships of the royal navy, including eleven galleons, supported by forty-seven armed merchantmen and pinnaces. The Dutch contributed eighteen warships, small but fast and heavily gunned. And more than 6,000 troops were assembled under Vere. England could not have made a better effort.

The expedition was under the joint command of the Earl of Essex and Lord Charles Howard of Effingham, each of whom was to command a squadron of vessels; in addition there were to be two more squadrons, one under Lord Thomas Howard and one under Vice-Admiral Sir Walter Ralegh sailing the *Warspite*. The equipping of this expedition presented the largest and most difficult problem of logistics and supply yet attempted in England, even greater than that of 1588 because of the expeditionary force. Much of the task of equipping the expedition fell to Ralegh and the principal burden of impressing men to sail the ships seems to have fallen on him. He writes of 'dragging in the mire from ale-house to ale-house' in the seaports, rounding up the stragglers and deserters, toiling terribly once more.

The hatred of the Essex faction toward Ralegh was always excessive, even in that age of superb hatreds. They now were saying that he was purposely delaying the expedition out of his own 'pregnant design' which presumably was a desire to see the Earl of Essex fail. Before most of the Earl's various ventures, Ralegh was credited with seeking their failure; the supporters of Essex apparently felt some doubt about their impulsive, generous and weak hero, and needed to prepare a scapegoat in case of failure.

When finally the fleet assembled at Plymouth, Ralegh and Sir Francis Vere quarrelled bitterly over precedence, both touchy over honour and both quick to set the iron walking. Young Arthur Throckmorton, Bess Ralegh's brother, intruded into the quarrel with such hot words that the Lords ordered him to leave their presence. He was allowed to sail at last, after the quarrel was sensibly composed by Essex and Howard who gave Ralegh precedence at sea and Vere precedence on land.

The fleet set sail for Cadiz Harbour, arriving there on June 20 and achieving good tactical surprise. But by the time it was ready for action, the Spaniards had formed a plan of defence which consisted of sealing off the mouth of the harbour with four of the Twelve Apostles, including the *San Philip* and the *San Andrew* which were chiefly responsible for the capture of the *Revenge*. In front of the warships was a fleet of galleys. Both galleys and galleons were to some extent under the protection of land guns on both sides of the harbour.

To understand the English strategy, the confusion, and the course of the battle, it is necessary to have in mind the general layout of the harbour, and it can be reasonably well simulated by the holding out both arms fairly close together and making a fist with the left hand. Between the arms lies the deep but narrow harbour; the left arm is a long sand spit which connects the town of Cadiz with the mainland; the fist is the town itself and the knuckles are fortifications set on steep and rocky cliffs. The right arm is the Spanish mainland. Essex and Lord Howard disagreed sharply on strategy. Essex wanted to break through the Spanish galleons, fight and win a naval battle

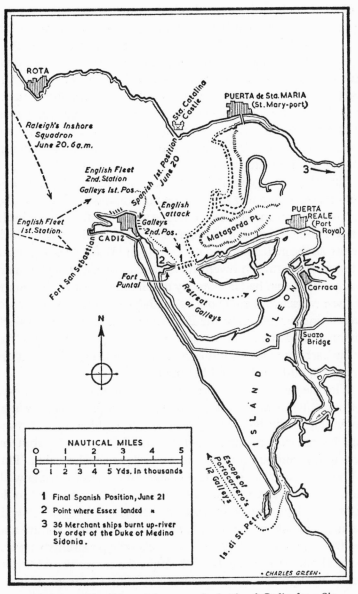

Map of the disposition of forces at the battle of Cadiz from Sir Walter Raleigh *by Philip Magnus, by courtesy of the publisher Wm. Collins Sons & Co. Ltd.*

and then launch his troops from the quiet waters of the inner harbour. Howard had been cautious in 1588 and he was older now; he did not want to force an entrance past the land guns and come to anchor in a harbour where his fleet would be immobile and vulnerable, as he thought, to the galleys and the guns. And so, at a conference of war attended only by Essex and Howard and the Secretary, it was decided over Essex's strong objections, to attack from the sea; Essex would send men ashore near the town of Cadiz and Howard would cover his rear by landing further south on the sand spit.

But things went wrong. The winds were high; there had been some chase of Spanish ships in the night and when dawn broke, both the squadrons of Essex and Howard were off the town itself. Lord Thomas Howard, as ordered, was blockading the harbour mouth so the galleons could not escape and Ralegh was stationed a few miles north to prevent the escape of the richly laden merchant vessels that had been ready to sail to the East Indies. Some of these vessels did come out of the harbour, hugging the coast line, trying to sneak past the English and out to sea, but Ralegh saw them and chased them back. He lost them in a bank of fog at the harbour's mouth, but as they were now safely bottled up, he sailed south and joined the main fleet.

What he saw when he arrived there sickened him. Essex was putting fully armed soldiers into small boats in choppy water. Some of the boats had already swamped and soldiers were drowning. Ralegh was an inexperienced naval commander, but no man in England knew better the theories of naval warfare. This action was against all the rules and against common sense as well. Howard and Essex were doing just what Philip had tried to do in 1588, to land troops without first securing a harbour. Even if the men got ashore they would be exposed to naval gunfire and fire from the fortress, and there was also the possibility that if a storm should scatter the English ships, the troops would be left ashore unsupplied. It was against any sound concept of naval strategy to land troops on a foreign shore before the enemy navy had been engaged and defeated.

Ralegh came aboard Essex's ship and tried to dissuade him

from landing his troops; Essex, however, said it was Howard's strategy, Howard's decision, and his own honour would be touched if he failed to land his men now. Presumably it was not dishonourable to expose them to drowning and defeat. Ralegh, generally poised in a crisis, never showed to better advantage than now. He was courteous to the Earl, but persuasive and tenacious.

. . . in the presence of all the colonels [I] protested against the resolution; giving him reasons, and making apparent demonstrations that he thereby ran the way of our general ruin, to the utter overthrow of the whole armies, their own lives, and Her Majesty's future safety. The Earl excused himself, and laid it to the Lord Admiral, who (he said) 'would not consent to enter with the fleet till the town were first possessed'. All the commanders and gentlemen present besought me to dissuade the attempt; for they all perceived the danger, and were resolved that the most part could not but perish in the sea, ere they came to set foot on ground; and if any arrived on shore, yet were they sure to have their boats cast about their heads; and that twenty men in so desperate a descent would have defeated them all.

Essex would not himself approach Howard again, but he asked Ralegh to do so. And Howard did change his mind, probably not so much from the force of Ralegh's argument as from the fact that the seas were still rising, and his own cautious nature had taken alarm. When Ralegh rowed back to Essex's ship, he could not wait even to come aboard, but stood up in his boat and shouted *Entramos*; the Earl took off his hat and flung it into the sea, a gesture that typified everything about him that Englishmen loved: courage, exuberance, and energy.

Once the decision was made, the fleet should have forced an entrance to the harbour immediately. But all of the ships waited while the soldiers were brought back on board and then they weighed anchors and moved toward the harbour mouth, where another council was called. Essex favoured moving in, even though it was near sunset; Howard was opposed and Ralegh's support of Howard decided the issue. The English waited for morning light. This decision has been criticized; certainly it is open to question. Drake, it is said, would have sailed in immediately and so he would, but his tactics, once so successful, were now also open to question. Howard's problems were real: there was no plan of battle, the harbour was small, and the English could not sail in haphazardly and choke it with their ships. But what weighed most of all, undoubtedly, was the recollection of the fire-ships and their success against the Armada. If the English had gone in and won a quick, decisive victory, that would have been brilliant strategy. But if night had caught them in the harbour, the galleys could have been converted into fire-ships and rowed against them in the darkness; and it is difficult to see how the English could then have defended their ships from the flames.

That night Ralegh wrote a letter to Lord Howard suggesting a battle plan. There were four of the Twelve Apostles in the harbour and he wanted to capture them all. Knowing that they would burn themselves rather than yield, he suggested that when the cannonading had cleared their decks, two large flyboats, pulled by oars and filled with soldiers, should be assigned to board each galleon. This was agreed on and Ralegh then asked the honour of leading the attack. It was granted. Later that night, however, Lord Thomas Howard protested to the Lord Admiral that his rank and experience warranted him precedence. For whatever reason, the Lord Admiral appears to have changed his mind and given Howard the honour.

Ralegh, however, remembering his 'great duty to Her Majesty', weighed anchor with first light and got a good start on the rest of the fleet. The Spaniards, meanwhile, had thought better of their battle plan and had withdrawn the galleons and galleys into the narrowest neck of the inner harbour. There the four great Apostles lay, broadsides presented, to meet the onset of the English fleet. As Ralegh sailed into the harbour, the land guns opened fire as did seventeen galleys which now lay close in to shore under the protection of the fort. Every time they cannonaded, Ralegh replied with a flourish of trumpets, 'disdaining to shoot one piece at any one or all of those esteemed dreadful monsters'. He had one purpose; to take the *San Philip*

256

and the *San Andrew*. The ships behind him, however, paid some attention to the galleys which, after a few rounds, fled behind the galleons, again proving that they were useless in combat against heavily gunned ships.

Now, 'being resolved to be revenged for the *Revenge* or to second her with my own life', Ralegh came to anchor and began firing at the galleons. Sir George Carew (cousin George) came up on one side and Lord Thomas Howard and Sir Francis Vere on the other. There seems little doubt, in retrospect, that Ralegh dropped anchor too soon and the others followed suit. He was undoubtedly advised to do so by the ship's captain and the master gunner, but the command responsibility was his. It was, however, his first naval command and he made the same mistake Lord Howard had made seven years earlier in the first week of the fighting with the Armada.

Hearing the cannonading, the Earl of Essex in the *Repulse* thrust up through the fleet and anchored near Ralegh. The cannonading of these five ships, which were later joined by Captain Cross in the *Swiftsure*, continued against the four Spanish galleons for two hours. The Spaniards returned the fire and their volleys of cannon and culverin were coming as thick as musket shot. Ralegh's ship took a number of hits and he became alarmed, fearing that she might sink. He got in a skiff and went again to Essex's ships, pointing out to the Earl that the fly-boats, which were to board the Spanish galleons, had not arrived. He, therefore, requested permission to use the Queen's ship to ram and board; the *Warspite*, he said, might as well burn as sink. Essex replied that he would second whatever Ralegh did with his life and upon his honour. Again, Ralegh's inexperience in naval combat nearly led him to surrender his greatest advantage, superior gunnery; if he had actually tried to board immediately he might have been beaten, but the circumstances made boarding impossible.

By now the harbour was so choked with English sail that no more ships could enter. Lord Howard, therefore, left the *Ark Royal* and came aboard the *Nonpareil* which was under the command of his kinsman, Lord Thomas Howard. While Ralegh was speaking with Essex, Sir Francis Vere decided to move in closer; he did this, said Ralegh rather touchily, because 'his esteemed great valour' had been offended at having to fight behind Sir Walter for so many hours. It is more likely that Vere's captain and gunner perceived that closer action was called for. When Ralegh came back aboard his own ship, he found that two other warships had thrust up ahead of him, those of Essex and Lord Thomas Howard. Vere, in the meantime, had fastened a rope to Ralegh's ship and was warping up. Ralegh cut the warping rope with an axe and Vere fell back. A modern naval commander could only be appalled by these schoolboy tricks, this overriding concern for personal glory in a major engagement of national forces, but Elizabeth had been putting up with it for years.

Ralegh managed to take the lead again; then he turned the *Warspite* athwart the channel so that none could get past him. He then cannonaded for another hour at closer range until he believed he could successfuly board. Then he laid out a warp alongside the *San Philip* and hauled himself up 'to shake hands with her'. Lord Thomas Howard, at the same time, was warping up on another galleon and Essex on yet another. English gunnery had been superior; for over three hours the Spanish sailors had taken a fearful pounding. Seeing the English galleons so close, they broke and gave up the action. The four Apostles slipped their cables and immediately all ran aground 'tumbling into the sea heaps of soldiers, so thick as if coals had been poured out of a sack in many ports at once; some drowned and some sticking in the mud'. The *San Philip* and the *St. Thomas* set themselves afire. English sailors got aboard the other two galleons, however, and ultimately brought them back to England. As the two great ships burned, Ralegh watched in horror.

The spectacle was very lamentable on their side; for many drowned themselves; many, half burnt, leapt into the water; very many hanging by the ropes' ends by the ships' sides, under the water even to the lips; many swimming with grievous wounds, strucken under water, and put out of their pain; and withal so huge a fire and such tearing of the ordnance in the great *Philip* and the rest, when the fire came to them, as, if any man had a desire to see Hell itself, it was there most lively figured.

The English, said Ralegh, spared the lives of all, but the Dutch, who had done nothing during the battle, carried too many scars to permit their being magnanimous with Spaniards: they made an indiscriminate slaughter until Ralegh and the Lord Admiral forbade it.

The naval battle over, the troops landed in a secure harbour on quiet waters and took the fortress and the town of Cadiz. In this land action, Essex displayed great courage. Ralegh did not participate. Near the end of the naval engagement a shell had landed near him on the deck of the *Warspite* driving large splinters into the calf of his leg; he was in terrible pain and would limp for the rest of his life. He, therefore, took no part other than asking to be carried ashore. Once ashore, his torment was too great for him to stay long. He glimpsed the inside of the town and saw that the soldiers had broken all discipline and were looting and sacking; there was nothing he could do but return to the ship. The land victory was won.

The naval action, however, was not entirely complete. Far inside the inner harbour were the merchant ships laden with cargo. The next morning Ralegh sent to the Lord Admiral and suggested that those ships be secured at once, and they should have been. However, there was much confusion and he never received an answer. That afternoon, the merchants of Cadiz and Seville called on the Lord Admiral and offered a ransom of two millions if he would spare their fleet. While Howard was considering that offer, the Duke of Medina Sidonia, who was in charge of coastal defense and who was still busy at his role of luckless non-hero, arrived and ordered all the merchant ships to be burned. Soon flames were enveloping two Lisbon galleons, three Levanters, three new treasure frigates, thirty-four ships of the *flota* and many smaller vessels. That bonfire completely dislocated the Spanish trade with America and bankrupted all the merchants whose ships were burned. It was a sacrifice scarcely equalled in naval history. It cost the King of Spain about 40,000,000 ducats, but beyond that, the expedition had achieved its main objective: it was unlikely now that Philip would invade England in 1596.

On the way home from Cadiz, Essex proposed going to the Azores and attempting to take the Plate Fleet. Ralegh vigorously opposed him, alleging infection on his ships and want of supply. The two quarreled and later Ralegh was much blamed by the Essex faction for preventing what, they said, would have been the certain capture of the fleet. The decision, actually, had not been Ralegh's to make: it was made, as usual, by the entire council, but Ralegh was blamed.

When the fleet returned to England, Vere termed the whole action 'mere summer bravery'. It was much more than that, although a soldier could scarcely have been expected to understand the economic disruption caused in Spain by the loss of fifty naval vessels. It was true that the taking of the town of Cadiz itself had been of no importance except that Bishop Ossory's library was stolen and taken back to England where it became the foundation of the Bodleian at Oxford University.

In the immediate afterglow all were generous with one another. The Lord High Admiral wrote,

I can assure you, there is not a braver man in the world than the Earl of Essex . . . The chiefest for the sea service, besides the Earl were the Lord Thomas Howard, Sir Walter Ralegh, and my son Southwell.

And Ralegh wrote of Essex,

The Earl hath behaved himself, I protest to you by the living God, both valiantly and advisedly in the highest degree without pride, without cruelty, and hath gotten great honour and much love of all.

One of the Essex faction wrote to another that he would be glad to know Ralegh better for he had behaved with great valour and judgment.

The unusual concord didn't last long. Soon Ralegh had

written an account of the affair which made him look much better than anyone else and Essex, at the same time, was blaming him for the 'failure' of the expedition.

In one thing Ralegh remained constant. He was Time's fool and Fortune's tennis ball. Of all who sailed on the expedition, only he, so he wrote, had received nothing.

The town of Cadiz was very rich in merchandise, in plate and money; many rich prisoners given to the land commanders; so as that sort are very rich. Some had prisoners for sixteen thousand ducats; some for twenty thousand; and besides, great houses of merchandise. What the generals have gotten, I know least; they protest it is little. For my own part, I have gotten a lame leg and a deformed. For the rest, either I spake too late or it was otherwise resolved. I have not wanted good words and exceeding kind and regardful usance. But I have possession of naught but poverty and pain.

It was all true and it was very like Sir Walter, the aggrieved Celt, to say so.

THE ISLANDS VOYAGE

Ralegh's career now entered a new phase; he was performing better than when he was the Queen's favourite. He was being heard now in Parliament where his voice was not as soothing to the royal prerogative as were those of Robert Cecil and Francis Bacon. There was a new and becoming independence in the positions he held and he showed a new confidence in his own abilities.

The victory at Cadiz had driven the Spanish empire to the brink of revolution and internal chaos. National pride had suffered most; the proud Spanish nobles were humiliated and exasperated with Philip's ineptness and the self-abasement of Medina Sidonia. Many bankrupt merchants were pleading vainly for state reimbursement for the loss of ships and cargoes. Essex received a letter from one of his informants in Spain:

In the Court great rumours, mutinies, privy meetings of the grandees, deliberations either to take the Prince from his father and proclaim him king or the King from his favourites.

261

Philip was goaded into an outraged frenzy. He brandished a candelabrum above his head and swore he would pawn even that if necessary to secure his revenge.

In September of 1596, England received firm intelligence that a number of Spanish officers had landed in Ireland; it was known that the Earl of Tyrone was, once again, at the very edge of rebellion. It was learned further that a new Spanish fleet was being assembled. The Queen appointed a Council of War as she had in 1588. Essex was its leading spirit; Norris and Vere were appointed to serve with him. Essex enlarged the Council, specifically asking for Sir Walter Ralegh and Sir George Carew. Again and again their service to the nation drew Essex and Ralegh together. If they had been different men, if either had been less ambitious or more politically mature, they might have formed an alliance or a personal friendship that would have drastically altered their personal destinies and perhaps the course of English history. But nothing less than all would satisfy either man and so it was their 'weird' to come together in crises and then, in more peaceful times, to resume their feuds, always egged on by the intrigues of jealous and ambitious subordinates.

When the Council of War first met, Essex had prepared the agenda in an impressively efficient manner. He had devised eleven questions on which he wanted every man's opinion. They included such items as whether the new Spanish Armada would sail immediately or in the spring; whether it would be a raid in reprisal for Cadiz involving the sacking of coastal cities or whether it would be an all-out invasion; what measures should be taken in either case and where the nation should concentrate its stores and men. Essex himself believed that there would be an invasion and that Philip, having learned something in 1588, would first seize a harbour, possibly Plymouth, in which case he thought the Spaniards could be blockaded, starved, and compelled to surrender. He recognized, however, that Philip might seize a port on the French coast, Brest perhaps, for use as an advance base. Lord Willoughby thought that Ireland, Scotland, or the Low Countries would be the point of attack. Lord North felt sure that Spain could not muster enough force to invade and believed that either Southampton or the Isle of Wight would be seized and sacked or held for ransom in reprisal for Cadiz.

Ralegh's opinion, as usual, was both original and positive, too positive as it turned out. Convinced by his own naval theories, he believed that Spain would never again attempt an invasion without first winning a naval battle which would give her command of the seas.

I hold it for a principle that there is no enemy so ill-advised as to offer to hold any place or piece of ground upon this coast, when Her Majesty, with the help of the Low Countries, may command the sea. The reasons are manifold, manifest, and therefore superfluous to insert.

It is amazing to see such rational and logical policy issue from the mind of a man who, eighteen months previously, had listened so avidly to Topiawari's son and the cacique who had been to Amazonia. And Philip was no less a contradiction than Ralegh: generally he acted without passion; rashness was a trait he eschewed above all others. But like Ralegh he had his vulnerable side; always Philip believed that he had a secret weapon in the will of God, which shifted all balance of power to his own war plans. And so Ralegh's position was theoretically impeccable but practically wrong, for Philip did intend to seize Falmouth and hold it for an invasion port. Old William Cecil was the only one who correctly guessed his intentions, even naming the port.

Sir George Carew disagreed with Ralegh and, in general, supported the suppositions of Essex. The majority, therefore, held that Philip would come at once; that he would seize Plymouth, Southampton or the Isle of Wight which towns were therefore to be strongly garrisoned. Troop ships were to be assembled at Gravesend in order to ferry troops across the Thames if necessary, and the naval forces were to stand by to blockade or sink the enemy fleet.

In this plan, Ralegh did not concur and he drew up a separate plan of his own which has been lost. It was based on the undoubted fact of England's naval supremacy and probably involved taking the offensive, either with a raid on the West Indies, or a diversionary raid on the Azores with the ultimate objective of taking the Plate Fleet. If Philip had been a different king, Ralegh's plan might have been the best. But, as a matter of fact, Philip had already ordered his fleet to sail in October whether it was ready or not.

The Adelantado of Castille, who had now replaced Medina Sidonia, had all of his captains and pilots take an oath and subscribe their opinions in writing that the fleet could not succeed in its present state of readiness. Philip nevertheless repeated his orders with great severity and, at the very end of October, at the last allowable moment, the Adelantado put to sea. His fleet was struck by a gale which English ships might have ridden out; but Philip's ships still lacked something in seaworthiness, and the seamanship of his crews in stormy waters could never match the English. Before the storm subsided, seven galleons and twenty-five armed ships were wrecked or driven ashore with the loss of two thousand men. The king who always calmly and rationally held that men must never attempt to anticipate the will of God had once again tried to leave his Deity with no alternative, and that *deus absconditus* had replied by remaining hidden.

This new disaster almost ruined Philip. He declared bankruptcy which immediately created a panic on every exchange in Europe. He tried to settle his debts with the bankers for forty-five per cent. When, in desperation, they pleaded for fifty-five, he repudiated everything. The war against heresy, he said, satisfied his conscience and justified the necessity of his action. So Philip would not be getting any more money from the bankers. Now his empire depended on the flow of Indian gold. How eagerly Ralegh and Essex must have thought of that fleet and what its capture would now mean both to Spain and to England. All the men of action thought it was their chance to strike the decisive blow and in January, 1597, they persuaded Elizabeth to order the mobilization of the Navy. But now England, for the first time, began to experience some difficulties with civilian support of the war against Spain. The London merchants and the citizens of the maritime counties balked at raising more funds. Essex, at the same time, was sulking because Robert Cecil had been named First Secretary, the position once so admirably filled by his now aged father. Then Elizabeth appointed Lord Cobham as Warden of the Cinque Ports; Cobham was close to Ralegh and Cecil and a member of the anti-Essex faction. It appeared that the angry Essex now might leave the Court altogether.

The Queen therefore called him in and soothed him, and on April 18, Cecil and Ralegh dined with Essex and agreed to support him and forward the enterprise. In return, Cecil was to be made Chancellor of the Duchy of Lancaster and Ralegh was to be given the contract for supplying the six thousand soldiers that would be mobilized for the expedition. Ralegh probably fulfilled more contracts for supplying naval vessels than any other man in England, and he made a good deal of money doing it. But in all the charges that were later brought against him, even his bitterest enemies never suggested that he had not fulfilled his contracts fairly and honourably. For several months he, Cecil and Essex worked together to mobilize the army and prepare the fleet for combat.

By the beginning of April the battle plan was formed and preparations were well advanced. The plan showed that Elizabeth's 'scribes', as Ralegh called them, had been heard; the largest part of the fleet was to be placed on the defensive along the English coast. It was to be supported by a fleet of oared galleys, a strange anachronism, but they were obviously intended for close work in the harbours if an invasion fleet should drop anchor.

A smaller fleet was to sail for Spain under Lord Thomas Howard with Ralegh as Vice-Admiral. But the fighting men managed to convince the Queen that the offensive action needed the main force; the battle plan was therefore continually modified until it was finally determined that a large fleet with six thousand soldiers aboard would sail under the sole command of the Earl of Essex.

Now that the friendship of Essex and Ralegh appeared firm,

Essex employed all of his grace and charm to persuade the Queen to bring Ralegh back to Court and allow him to perform his duties as Captain of the Guard. For four years, those duties had been carried out by a substitute. The Queen finally gave way and Ralegh returned but now on an entirely different basis: he was counsellor and admiral in his own right and by his own abilities. Now perhaps both Ralegh and England could forget the humiliating Throckmorton episode, although Spenser had done his well-intentioned best to see that it would be remembered forever.

Finally, about the middle of May, the fleet was ready to sail. There were seventeen royal ships, including the two captured Spanish galleons, the *St. Matthew* and the *St. Andrew*, which were now to sail against the king who had so piously conceived and built them for the destruction of heretics. There were also twenty-two Dutch men-of-war, numerous transports and pinnaces, and the army of 6,000 men. Essex showed again that under favourable circumstances he could act the statesman. Realizing that the enterprise might be jeopardized by the bad blood between Vere and Ralegh, a leftover from the Cadiz action, he called them together and asked them to shake hands. Both men agreed that honour had not been touched and therefore did so willingly.

Now the men of action were to learn some of Philip's lessons; they were to fight some of his old enemies. First, there were adverse winds. It took two months for the fleet to assemble at Plymouth. There it was organized into four squadrons under Essex, Lord Thomas Howard, Sir Richard Levenson and Ralegh. George Carew was vice-admiral in the captured *St. Matthew* and Arthur Gorges was captain of Ralegh's *Warspite*. This was the trio that had once staged that unsuccessful little melodrama in the Tower.

Essex had clear and explicit instructions. He was to proceed to Ferrol where the Spanish fleet had assembled for repair after the late storm. He was to attack that city, as he had Cadiz, both by sea and by land, with the objective of destroying the Spanish fleet by fire or by cannonading. Destroy the ships. That primary

266

task was stressed and repeated. If he found the fleet on the high seas rather than in Ferrol, he was to engage and destroy it. Once the Spanish fleet was destroyed and the danger of invasion was over, he was to proceed to the Azores to intercept East Indian carracks or the West Indian treasure fleet, weather and other circumstances permitting. He was also authorized to seize and hold the island of Terceira, the central island in the Azores group and one of the largest. It looked as if Elizabeth at last meant to expand her empire and begin to contain Spain by establishing permanent bases outside the Channel for the English fleet.

On July 10, the fleet stood out to sea; the next day a gale came up and Ralegh became separated from the fleet and from most of the ships in his squadron. The reason was that the two Spanish prizes sprang leaks and were in difficulty. Again the lack of seaworthiness in Spanish galleons was demonstrated. When the weather moderated, he and the two Apostles, along with the *Bonaventure*, which had stayed with him, went on for Finisterre. The gale, having slackened for a day or so, rose again and never abated for a week. On board one of the ships, a young poet named John Donne, who was also on the Cadiz voyage, was powerfully stimulated by the force and fury of the storm.

> Then like two mighty kings which dwelling far
> Asunder, meet against a third to war,
> The south and west winds joined, and as they blew
> Waves like a rolling trench before them threw . . .
> Lightning was all our light, and it rained more
> Than if the sun had drunk the sea before.
> Some coffined in their cabins lie, equally
> Grieved that they are not dead and yet must die.

Donne pictured the shaking of the masts, the snapping of the tackle, the holds filled with water, the men weary with pumping, the ordnance breaking loose, until finally, unless God says 'another Fiat', there shall be no more day.

After a week of such battering, the squadrons had lost all

cohesion. Ralegh, still an inexperienced seaman, was the first to turn back to port. He did so, he said later, only because his ships were in some trouble, and he had been told that he was farthest out from England. He assumed, therefore, that if, as he returned, he sighted no other English ships, it would mean that they had come into port ahead of him. He ran before the wind and arrived, his sensitive honour deeply hurt, to find out that he alone had come back. But he was also concerned about Essex. Knowing the Earl's valour and refusal to admit failure, he was afraid that he would fight the seas until he was lost. But Essex returned to Falmouth only one day after Ralegh had arrived at Plymouth, his flagship in such bad condition that he had to transfer to another vessel. Ralegh generously wrote Cecil a letter to be shown to the Queen.

[He] put into Falmouth in great extremity and imminent peril of sinking in the sea, which I knew would betide him ere he would yield to either seas or winds . . . There could not be more done by any man upon the earth, God having turned the heavens with that fury against us, a matter beyond the power of valour or will of man to resist.

Cecil showed the Queen a part of Ralegh's letter but not the part that told of the dangers for fear she would lose heart and cancel the enterprise. Elizabeth wept with joy to hear that Essex was safe. The Earl himself, in the meantime, had ridden to Plymouth where he dined with Ralegh aboard the *Warspite* and threw all of his energy into getting the fleet to sea again.

The best sailor of them all, Lord Thomas Howard, had not returned. And in a few days there came from him a note, simply saying that he was near Corunna and waiting for the rest of the fleet. Essex kept whatever chagrin he felt to himself and sent pinnaces to Spain with orders for Howard to avoid action until the rest of the fleet rejoined him. He was either to keep out of sight off Finisterre or else fall back towards England. Thus he could watch the Spanish fleet without being overwhelmed by superior numbers.

Essex, supported by Ralegh, had the fleet ready to sail again within a week. Many of the ships, unfit for duty, had to be left behind, and there had been sickness and desertions, but Essex believed that he now had a fitter fleet, a better striking force than before. The storm had eliminated the weaklings. He intended to sail to Corunna, meet Lord Thomas Howard, and seek out the Spanish fleet. If they met it on the sea they would engage. If not, they would harry the coasts and attempt to lure the fleet out. All talk of invasion by sea and land was dropped. Finally it was agreed that once they had succeeded in engaging and sinking the Spanish fleet, or if they determined that it was unable to put out to sea, they would go to the Azores and make a search for treasure fleets. Elimination of the idea of invasion from the battle plan suggests that many of the troop ships were disabled and, likely, the plague had broken out among the soldiers. In either case, it was to be primarily a naval task force that put out to sea the second time.

Again the winds were wrong; sickness broke out, desertions, even among the gentlemen, increased, and the last stroke of bad luck came when Lord Thomas Howard sailed into port on July 31. He had interpreted the instructions to fall back toward England as permission to return home. He too, likely, had damaged ships and sickness aboard. But he brought news that Essex and Ralegh were glad to hear. Howard, with his small squadron, had cruised off Ferrol before he had received Essex's orders not to engage, and had defied the Adelantado to come out and fight. Since he did not come, he must not have been ready. If he could not put out to sea yet, Ralegh and Essex could safely proceed after the treasure fleet. The capture of the fleet would both finish Philip and pay a handsome return to the adventurers that would justify the action. 'We must have gold before we see England,' Drake's last despairing cry, was now the chief motivation of the task force.

And so a new council was held in which it was determined to sail to Havana and intercept the treasure fleet there. Such an action would require only 2,000 troops and there were victuals enough already to supply the smaller force for the six months the journey would take. All agreed to this except Sir Francis Vere who felt that it was unwarrantably risky when Spain was known to be assembling an offensive armament. Essex and Ralegh were sufficiently dissuaded that they journeyed to London together to secure the Queen's approval. The Queen received her once and present favourites graciously, but when they returned to the fleet they said no more about the Indies. That is not to say that they changed their own minds in the slightest, but they dared not digress too far from the Queen's adamant orders that the Spanish fleet must first be destroyed.

By now it was necessary to disband more troops because of sickness and consequently to devise another plan of battle, a plan this time to enter Ferrol harbour and attempt to destroy the Spanish fleet with fire-ships. Since the *St. Matthew* and the *St. Andrew* had proved themselves relatively useless as fighting galleons, it was proposed to use them, along with some smaller ships and fly-boats, to burn Philip's latest hopes. The Queen approved, provided that Essex did not lead the dangerous exploit; Ralegh's safety being no longer a matter of personal concern to her, it was settled that he would lead.

When the wind finally came round, the transports were not ready and Essex had to disband the rest of his soldiers except for 1,000 veterans from the Low Country wars. Now about all the fleet could do was take to the seas and improvise a campaign. Essex informed the Privy Council of the situation and left without awaiting a reply. Robert Cecil was sure that nothing would be accomplished. It was too late, he thought, for the Spanish fleet to sail against England, the carracks were undoubtedly already home and the task force, with most of the soldiers disbanded, was too weak to take any of the islands. The pragmatic Cecil, as it turned out, was wrong on all three counts. But in his belief that the Earl was trying to salvage his honour in some way he was correct.

Essex intended to proceed to Cape Finisterre, just south of Ferrol, so that any wind which brought the Spaniard out would also give the English the weather gauge for the long pursuit toward the Channel. But again there was a bad storm and again the two Spanish ships were the first to suffer. The *St. Matthew* was so badly disabled that Essex personally urged Sir George Carew to abandon her, but that stout Devonshireman would not. Instead he took her into a French port and ultimately back to England where he found another vessel and rejoined the fleet. The *St. Andrew* also had not ridden the storm well and had been separated. Thus with both of the large proposed fire-ships gone, the English were discouraged from entering Ferrol Harbour.

Off Corunna, a further misunderstanding set the commanders at cross-purposes. Ralegh's mainyard broke in two and Essex, in the *Repulse,* sprang a bad leak. Ralegh flew his distress signal and Essex ordered him to proceed to the second appointed rendezvous, which was off Lisbon. At least that was what Ralegh thought. Essex said his signals had been misunderstood and that he had actually ordered Ralegh to run in under Cape Finisterre. Ralegh said that he could not have sailed eastwards anyway with his mainmast broken. The confusion increased when Essex hauled up to fix his leak and the other ships followed Ralegh south, including the rest of the smaller fire-ships.

When Essex arrived at Finisterre and found that Ralegh and the bulk of the fleet had gone to Lisbon, all of his old suspicions were aroused. Ralegh, he thought, was attempting to take the leadership of the expedition from the Earl and cover himself with glory as he had at Cadiz. Essex called a council of war in which it was agreed that Ralegh's absence justified disobeying the Queen's order to destroy the Spanish ships first of all. Sir Thomas Monson and others asserted that with the fleet now at their disposal, they could not hope to do more than intercept the Plate Fleet. Essex listened but immediately sent a report to the Queen in which he used Ralegh's absence as his excuse for altering her orders, but he in no way cast blame on Ralegh's behaviour.

Ralegh, meanwhile, was trying desperately to get some intelligence concerning either the Spanish warships or the treasure fleet. And he got some, but it was false information deliberately intended to mislead him. An English bark had come with some third-hand news that the Adelantado had sailed for the Azores to convoy the treasure fleet. And Ralegh, in whom belief so quickly followed hope, made no effort to check the report, but simply dispatched it to Essex who, as eager and incautious as Ralegh, replied that he was off the Azores and that Ralegh was to follow. The truth was that the Adelantado was still in Ferrol making every effort to sail against England while the English fleet was being decoyed out of the way.

Ralegh finally rejoined Essex on September 15. The two men dined together and Ralegh satisfied him, for the time at least, that he had acted not from design but rather from necessity. Arthur Gorges, who was also present, said that Essex 'seemed to be the joyfullest man living'; and he assured Ralegh that he had never for a moment believed the aspersions and insinuations of his own followers. Essex offered to send another dispatch to the Queen, clearing up the matter of Ralegh's absence at Finisterre, but Ralegh insisted that it was unnecessary. If any damage had been done by the previous report, it could be repaired when they returned. The important thing now was for these two greyhounds to catch the hare.

And once again they were baited with false information. They captured a pinnace from the Indies whose prisoners told them that the *flota*, if it sailed that year, would sail south of the Azores and avoid them altogether. It was, therefore, decided to disperse the squadrons and cover a wide sweep of the sea. Small vessels were to ply back and forth conveying information, and a set of signals was devised to be used when the Spanish fleet was sighted. The most westerly island in the main group was Fayal; it was also one of the two most strongly defended. Because it would provide an excellent outpost from which the fleet could be intercepted, that island was to be taken by Ralegh and Essex.

Ralegh requested permission to take on fresh water as the other ships had already done while waiting for him to join them. The Earl granted it and said that Ralegh, after watering, should follow him to Fayal. Then in the middle of the night Ralegh received new orders from Essex: he was to weigh anchor immediately, proceed to Fayal and water there. Ralegh complied and arrived at Fayal, finding to his complete surprise, that Essex was not to be seen. What happened to Essex will never be known; he did not explain then or later. However, without communicating with anyone he had suddenly veered off, apparently at the receipt of some fresh information. The excitement was feverish; it was now believed that the treasure fleet was near the island; the treasure of the Indies, for the first time in history, was within the English grasp.

For three days Ralegh lay off Fayal awaiting the Earl. In the meantime, murmurs aboard his ships had grown into taunts. His men felt that their inactivity was dishonourable and so Ralegh called a council. Two Portuguese had swum out to the English vessels, and given them full information on the strength of the fort; Ralegh believed that he could take it with the force he had. The followers of Essex, however, were arrogant and stubborn; they would not consent to any landing in the Earl's absence. So Ralegh waited a fourth day. Still Essex did not come. Ralegh, therefore, determined that he would land with a hundred pikes and muskets and form a bridgehead which would protect him while he watered. This at least was within his province and certainly Essex, who had ordered him to land and water at Fayal, could not object to that. And it is unlikely that he would have.

But as Ralegh prepared to land, he was seen from the fort and a detachment of Spanish soldiers was sent down to intercept him and put him back in the sea. When Ralegh saw the troops, instead of withdrawing, which might have been prudent, he asked his fellow captains for reinforcements. Several of the Low Country officers requested permission to accompany him with their highly trained and valuable soldiers. But Ralegh said he would risk none of the Earl's men in the landing, only his own. However, if he secured a beachhead he would send for them.

He thereupon embarked 260 of his men in small boats and approached the reefs that guarded the shore. Upon that shore, the Spaniard awaited him. It was a dangerous landing and Ralegh knew it. He ordered his pinnaces to move in and give him a preliminary bombardment behind which he could bring in his forces. But the mariners on the pinnaces were not professionals and the musket-fire alarmed them. They simply would not go in close enough to be effective.

Ralegh taunted them, spoke all the 'disgraceful words' that his tongue could find, a battle oration that Arthur Gorges unfortunately did not preserve. But they were men of low condition and their sense of honour did not respond to highminded upbraiding. Now Ralegh was desperate. His men were drinking the cup: the fire from shore was reaching them. It was either retreat or charge and Ralegh had been too long with the French cavalry to have many doubts as to what it became a soldier to do. And there was always a noticeable difference between his complete assurance in a land action and his usually somewhat halting command in naval battles. Here he was superb.

He commanded his Westcountry oarsmen to row straight in upon the rocks. They did so. The boats shattered on that flinty beach, two of them completely stove in, with men thrown into the water, dashed against the sides of the boats, and under continual fire. But all except a few men recovered and charged with muskets firing, pikes levelled and swords swinging. The Spaniards began to withdraw after a few moments hand-to-hand, and then broke. They threw away their weapons and ran at dead heat for the safety of the fort.

Now Ralegh had his beachhead and so he sent back, according to the plan, for the Low Country troops. Perhaps his original plan had been merely to take on water and thus save the Earl's honour; perhaps that was merely window dressing for the Earl's zealous followers. Whichever it was, he now had men lying dead and wounded on the beach, and he had no intention of forcing a second landing.

Soon he had five hundred troops on shore, all men who had faced the Spaniard in the trenches of Holland. The fortified town lay four miles away and the road by which it was reached led under two forts, both strongly gunned. Ralegh had thought the surf too risky for a man in armour and so he was wearing nothing except a gorget. In the best English tradition he led the attack with only a staff in his hand and a large white scarf knotted around his throat. Forty gentlemen seconded him in good

274

order, marching as if on parade; behind them came the troops. The gentlemen came under artillery fire from the High Fort but not a man quickened his pace. Soon they reached the cover of some rocks where they halted. The troops behind them, with great good sense, broke ranks and ran for cover, thus avoiding the devastation of artillery pieces that by now had begun to zero in.

Ralegh concealed his contempt and asked Captain Brett, a regular officer from the Ostend garrison, to call for volunteers to reconnoitre the rest of the way to the fort. They were to find the best and safest route and the troops would move up behind them. But, in the best tradition of the private soldier, not a single man would volunteer. Brett was so humiliated that he offered to do it himself. But Ralegh by now had had enough. He would go alone and signal the troops when it was safe for them to follow. The gentlemen protested; Captain Brett protested; Arthur Gorges protested. Ralegh called for a casque and cuirass, put them on, and led out, but he could not restrain Arthur Gorges and about ten of the Westcountry gentlemen, most of them distantly related to him, from following.

Soon they came under the guns of the High Fort again and large shot and musket balls began to fall around them. Gorges was hit in the leg. Ralegh was shot once through the sleeve and twice through the breeches. He stopped and pointed out to Arthur Gorges that the large red scarf he was wearing presented too good a target; he asked if Gorges would mind removing it. His cousin replied that he did not wish to do the Spaniard so much honour. and besides he had noticed that in the matter of scarves Ralegh was setting an example which he thought he should follow. And so these gallant and foolish men of Devon marched on, carried out their reconnaissance, and called up the troops which advanced under the cover Ralegh pointed out to them. The Spanish soldiers soon fled the town and ensconced themselves in the High Fort. Ralegh decided that enough had been done for that day; his men would rest until morning and then make the final assault.

At daybreak, just as he was preparing to assault, Essex and

the rest of the fleet appeared. Essex had been off on a fool's chase; that was annoyance enough. But now he saw that the ambitious poet, with a handful of men, had practically reduced the strongest island in the Azores, the only success the expedition had achieved so far. Now everything Essex had suspected when Ralegh had run off to Lisbon seemed to be justified. The man was attempting again to steal his honour which, to Essex, meant more than the Spanish purse. His subordinates poured aboard his ships, telling of their attempts to dissuade Ralegh from landing and confirming all his suspicions. He therefore summoned Ralegh aboard.

Ralegh quite naturally believed that he was being called to receive congratulations; with dismay he learned that he was to be court-martialed at sea and hanged from a yardarm. This was the end of whatever chance there might have been for these two imperious men to work together. Essex's actions at Fayal must be remembered later if one is to understand Ralegh's conduct when the Earl's life or death was being debated by the English Crown. Now, however, Ralegh showed neither fear nor anger; he simply answered the Earl on every point. First, he said, the Earl had given him orders to land and water at Fayal. That was true but of course he had done a little more than that.

The Earl's wrath was based on a legal technicality. It was an article of the fleet that no captain of a ship, if it became separated from the main fleet, could land anywhere without the General's permission under pain of death. Ralegh knew this law and acknowledged it. But he pointed out that he was not merely a captain. As Vice-Admiral he was a principal commander; if the Earl had been disabled or killed, he would, after Lord Thomas Howard, have been a successive commander of the entire fleet. A successive commander could not be court-martialed at sea. Ever since Drake had beheaded a recalcitrant officer at sea, it had been the practice, in an uneasy British Navy, to exempt 'successive commanders' from the jurisdiction of court martial.

Essex's anger cooled as he saw that he had no reply to Ralegh's defense. Furthermore, Ralegh was courteous and reasonably humble; he affirmed repeatedly that he had neither intended

nor given offence to the Earl's honour. The Earl agreed to let
the matter rest; he came ashore to view the situation and then
rested at Ralegh's quarters. Ralegh invited him to dine and with
his usual good nature Essex would have accepted, but his
angry subordinates were busy at his ear. They told him that
unless he took some action his reputation as a commander was
gone. So Essex cashiered all the courageous military officers who
had followed Ralegh up that hot and dangerous road to the
High Fort. Ralegh thereupon took alarm and gathered around
him his captains and kinsmen who agreed to fight rather than
see him submit and be hanged. It could have come to a point
where English warships were firing on one another had not Lord
Thomas Howard arrived to mediate. He persuaded Essex to
accept an apology; then he undertook the difficult task of getting
Ralegh to make one, telling him that while an apology might not
be deserved, he must make it for the good of the service and the
nation. He further promised him that if he would go aboard the
Repulse, Howard himself would personally be responsible for
his safety.

It is another sign of Essex's basically generous nature that
he never mentioned the Fayal imbroglio at all in the official
report and Gorges says that before leaving Fayal, Essex was
treating Ralegh very kindly and had restored all the cashiered
officers to their commands.

The High Fort was easily taken, for its garrison had fled. All
the ordnance was removed and the town was plundered and
burned. Now Essex had his base from which he could have
swept the seas for the treasure fleet. But the captain of the *Repulse*
persuaded him to remove to St. Michael's Island, where, he
said, there was a safer anchorage against the autumn storms.
Essex agreed and that decision meant the end of any chance of
success, for St. Michael's was the island farthest east in the main
group. If the Spanish treasure fleet was alarmed, it could run
to the island of Terceira where the very strong Angra Harbour
offered a sanctuary; and it could likely reach that sanctuary before the British fleet, from its new base, could intercept it.

Ralegh was usually contemptuous of harbour defences as he

had learned to be at Cadiz; but in his *History* he later cited Terceira as an exceptional instance where the harbour defences could successfully resist a fleet. Just three hours after the English fleet weighed anchor and sailed eastward, the *Rainbow*, with three other ships, none of which had received Essex's orders, sighted the treasure fleet of twenty-five sail. They were said to be carrying cargo valued at twelve million pounds.

Sir William Monson, captain of the *Rainbow*, discharged his ordnance according to the pre-arranged signal, but there was no response. He then took the *Rainbow* in under the sails of the Spanish galleons, challenging them to grapple with him as they had once with the *Revenge*. He tried every tactic to delay the fleet, but the captains were too well disciplined. Monson, who had now been joined by his other three ships, watched helplessly while the fleet sailed into Angra Harbour in Terceira. There the treasure ships warped close in under the land guns; workmen came out in swarms, unloaded the treasure from the ships and carried it inside the fortress. Once again, as in 1585, when Drake had missed the treasure fleet by a few hours, Philip was barely saved. His luck was not all bad.

Essex ultimately bore all the blame. He had changed his battle plan half a dozen times; he had taken advice indiscriminately. Had he stuck to any plan of general action which kept his squadrons spread out through the area, he could not have missed. Sir Francis Vere wrote,

All is to be attributed to the want of experience in my lord and his flexible nature to be overruled.

Several days later Essex arrived at Terceira. He had captured a carrack, escorted by two frigates, and the three ships proved to be worth 400,000 ducats, enough to pay for the voyage. But the sight of the treasure fleet in Angra Harbour nearly drove him wild. He wanted at any cost to force the harbour, but Ralegh dissuaded him and the other officers supported Ralegh.

By now the English ships were foul, and their water and supplies were exhausted. Essex still wanted to risk everything on a desperate gamble to capture the island stronghold with the thousand troops he had aboard. Howard and Ralegh replied that they could not land troops in water as rough as the wind was then kicking up around the island. A full council was held and the soldiers, forgetting for once their bias against volunteering, offered their lives for the Queen. Not to be outdone, Ralegh and Howard said they would find 1,500 mariners to accompany the soldiers ashore. But finally it was decided, perhaps at the insistence of the captains, that it would be foolhardy to land, and so they returned to St. Michael's Island where they hoped to clean out their ships, find new supply, and wait for better weather. But even that would require the capture of St. Michael's. A plan was therefore devised under which Ralegh would threaten the town while Essex and the main fleet put troops ashore on the other side of the island. Ralegh manoeuvred and cannonaded outside the town, drawing fire and keeping the fortress alarmed for days, but the troops never appeared. Against an unfavourable wind, Essex had not been able to tack into shore and disembark his men. Finally he wearied and listened to the anxieties of his captains and masters. Then he gave orders for the entire fleet to sail for England.

Essex, Ralegh, and Howard had no idea that the Spanish Armada had now cleared port and was also sailing toward England. The two fleets were on a collision course that should bring them together about the mouth of the Channel. Philip of Spain was dying; masses were being said around the clock for his recovery. He could not eat; he had no strength. But, before he died, he wanted the fleet to sail one more time. Once more God was to be given an opportunity to destroy the 'monster of England', that 'impious Jezebel'. With the last ounce of will and energy he possessed, Philip wanted that one victory that would justify everything.

And so again the Spanish seamen had sailed out badly provisioned and unready, but this time with one hope they had never had before. They knew where the English fleet was and believed they could descend on England before it returned. They planned to seize Falmouth unopposed and establish a base which could be supplied from Spanish ports in France and the Low Countries. Philip and his theological advisers still clung to the hopeless dream that once a hold had been secured on English shores the faithful native Catholics would arise and support them. And they were right in thinking that Tyrone was ready to call out the Redshanks and burn Ireland once more. But again there was no firm plan for engaging the English fleet and destroying it before they seized their harbour. The Spanish never really grasped the new principles of naval warfare.

If the fleets had met on the sea, the Spaniards would have had the advantage. The English ships were in bad condition; timbers in the ships in Ralegh's squadron were so badly strained that he had followed his captain's anxious advice and stowed away his big guns in the holds so that the ships could ride easier. He could not have fought an action. Other ships in other squadrons might have been in the same condition.

However, by the unfathomable turn of chance, the two fleets missed one another. Essex sailed into Plymouth harbour on a southwest wind only to learn, as Drake had in 1588, that the Spanish fleet, running with the same wind, was on its way to engage him. He was not alarmed.

Though we eat ropes' ends and drink nothing but rain water we will out, that we may be partly the instruments to make a final end of this proud nation that is destined to destruction. They are already in distress, and if we can get out I hope none of them shall escape.

On October 29, just a year after the previous attempt of a Spanish naval force, Ralegh received word that the fleet had been seen off the coast of Cornwall. As Lord Lieutenant of Cornwall he prepared to leave his naval command and muster land troops for a defence of the landing points. But before he could do so, an English captain arrived at Plymouth with a small boat which he had captured from the Spanish fleet. The prisoners on that boat said that the same storm that had been battering the English on their way home had also scattered the Spanish fleet. Their information proved true: a few Spanish ships were driven into English ports where they were captured. The rest were finally able to return to Spain where the sailors and soldiers were paid off and the Armada was decommissioned. And so the series of Armadas sent against England, each weaker than the last, each more desperate and foolish had now failed completely and finally because of Philip's confusion of theology and logistics, a mistake he never made except in the 'Enterprise of England', in which the heretic Queen with her nimble and biting tongue and the nimble ships her sea-dogs had built goaded him into unreasoning fury. His mind, locked in the stale glories of the Battle of Lepanto, simply could not conceive that the Cross should not triumph on the waves once again. He had the Virgin's favour, his Twelve Apostles, the blessings of the Pope, the consciousness of his own rectitude. His men were as valorous as the English and his resources incomparably greater. But winds and waves were physical forces that cared nothing for all of this; warfare on the high seas was an intricate dance and only the English had mastered its rhythms. There were other rhythms, however; the sounds and motions of the liturgies that meant more to Philip than his empire. These rhythms soothed him now. His death was peaceful.

15

Ralegh as Parliamentarian

Ralegh was first elected to the Parliament of 1584–6. Ten Parliaments were held during Elizabeth's reign, in sessions lasting from one month to three years. Of the six of these in which he was eligible to sit, Ralegh sat in all but the one held in 1588–9 when, being out of favour with the Queen, he had gone to Ireland and had not been a candidate for election. During these sessions he came to the fore as one of the most witty, shrewd, and effective of a group of remarkably cultivated and able parliamentarians.

Members of the House of Commons – 462 in number by the end of the sixteenth century – were voted into office only by voters qualified by being freeholders with an annual income of 40 shillings or more. Thus all of the landed gentry and some of their tenants could vote. But because a candidate did not have to reside in the district he represented, the membership, though not strictly representative, did contain a high proportion of men of intellectual quality and training. Under the rules, each county was to return a senior and a junior knight, men who wore swords in Parliamentary sessions as a badge of distinction. The rest of the House was to have been made up of citizens or burgesses. But in practice few burgesses cared to sit in Parliament, for their businesses kept them away; time was money for eager and industrious merchants, and consequently the more leisured and educated gentry tended to fill up the House seats. When Ralegh first went to Parliament as junior knight for the shire of Devon, the House, by the formula, should have consisted of ninety country gentlemen and 372 burgesses. But there were in fact only fifty-three burgesses, thirteen members who cannot be classified, and all the rest were country gentlemen and lawyers. This fact helps explain the growth of the power and privilege of the House of Commons, for the gentry were much less easily overawed by the Lords and Crown than were the burgesses. It was men like the Westcountry gentry, Ralegh, Drake, Grenville, Hawkins, Sir Philip Sidney and Peter Wentworth, who made the House of Commons a formidable body virtually independent of the House of Lords in Ralegh's time; some of the men who saw him executed made it later virtually independent even of the Crown, at least for a time.

Traditionally English monarchs were always somewhat reluctant to call sessions of Parliament, for the members tended to go beyond the agenda and attempt to legislate for the kingdom. Most rulers looked upon such attempts as an encroachment on the royal prerogative. But the Crown always had a pitifully meagre income; if it became embroiled in war or there were troubles in Ireland or famine at home, additional income was a necessity. And only the House of Commons could vote a subsidy and only the subsidies could relieve significant financial pressure.

A full subsidy meant a tax of two-fifteenths on the assessed value of the land; it also included a tax of two-tenths on 'movables', that is, on such things as livestock, household goods and chattels. It was customary to exempt from all taxation those whose annual assessed worth fell below three pounds per year. Thus a man qualified to vote might pay no taxes; if he was a very wealthy landowner, his taxes were relatively nominal because of inequities in assessments. Members of the House knew well enough that the cost of taxation was felt most by their own class, and they were usually careful about assenting to the requests of the government.

Of Ralegh's participation in his first Parliament, there is little record. He was then Elizabeth's newest pastoral playmate, and he was busy with his new offices and honours. He was nevertheless responsible for what might now be considered the most important piece of business to come before that Parliament: his request for Letters Patent to colonize America was the first

283

time that difficult and unruly land was discussed in the House of Commons. Ralegh also was placed on a committee to survey and restrain superfluity in dress, surely one of the most amusing political whimsies of all time.

At the time, however, both these matters must have seemed trivial compared with the principal business of the Parliament, which was concern for the Queen's safety. The Throckmorton Plot had just been discovered, the Bond of Association had been signed and most of the debate centred on bills which would prohibit the activities of seminary priests and Jesuits and increase the penalties for harbouring or aiding them. But primarily Parliament was trying to find a legal way to ensure that if Elizabeth were murdered, no Catholic, including Mary Queen of Scots, could claim the throne.

In two later Parliaments, however, those of 1593 and 1601, Ralegh had a major voice in the debates in the House of Commons. In 1586 he had been elected as senior knight for the County of Devon, an honour in keeping with his new position and services to England. It was an almost invariable rule that once a Parliamentarian had made his way up from burgess to junior knight and then to senior knight of the shire, he was never again returned in one of the lesser social positions. But in 1593 Ralegh, in deepest disgrace at Court and with the Queen, was not returned by the County of Devonshire at all. Being still Lord Lieutenant of Cornwall, he stood for the little borough of St. Michael's and was returned as a burgess. Whatever humiliation he had suffered as a result of his imprisonment and the cruel jesting and satire of those who envied and despised him, he certainly showed none of it in Parliament. Rather he spoke with a new independence and even, surprisingly enough, with a little less touchiness and self-consciousness than usual.

In this Parliament he spoke on three main themes. First, and by far most important, he vigorously pushed for subsidies to be voted for the war against Spain; at the same time he tried, perhaps more than any other man in Parliament, to protect the poor from the excessive burden of the taxation, although the poor never thanked him for it. And finally, he consistently

284

opposed governmental encroachment upon the lives and conscience of the citizens.

When Parliament met in 1593, Elizabeth was desperate for money. The previous Parliament had granted her a double subsidy which had yielded only 280,000 pounds. At the same time her wars on the Continent, which she considered defensive, had cost her over a million pounds and, as a result, she had been forced once again to sell many of the Crown lands. At that time Henry of Navarre was attempting to win by force of arms his title to the throne of France, and he was being opposed by the Catholic League under the leadership of the Guises and supported by the resources of Spain. Elizabeth considered it absolutely vital to England's interests that Henry of Navarre should win the throne of France. How England could help him was one of the principal matters on the agenda and it was a remarkable group, in the House, who met to consider it: Fulke Greville, Sir Francis Drake, the Bacon brothers, Anthony and Francis, Ralegh himself and Edward Coke, the newly elected Speaker, who was soon to become acknowledged as England's greatest jurist.

When it came to consider the subsidy, William Cecil, now Lord Burleigh, arose in the House of Lords and complained about the manner of assessing taxes. He said that no single holding of land in all of England had been valued at more than eighty pounds, a ridiculous figure; he further said that in London, where most of the wealth was, only eight men had been assessed at a figure above 100 pounds. Burleigh's facts were wrong, for some 200 Londoners had been assessed above that figure, but the drift of his speech was right. Land and property had increased in value; assessments had not changed and every year the subsidies brought less purchasing power to the Crown. Whether this reform was carried out or not, Burleigh said that the Crown had to have three full subsidies and the rest of the Lords agreed with him. This meant that all eligible taxpayers would pay one-tenth and one-fifteenth every six months for three years, a sobering proposal.

When the House got down to full-scale debate, there was

general sympathy for Elizabeth's need, but few were willing to grant more than two subsidies. Furthermore, Sergeant Harris, a Devon lawyer, asked for a formal declaration of war so that the conflict against the Catholic League would be lawful. To fight without such a declaration offended his legal training and his lawyer's mind. Ralegh was heartily in agreement with his fellow Devonian. He was sure, he said, that if war were declared the Queen would have more volunteers than she needed. He knew the difficulty of impressing men, and he had discovered in Ireland the dubious qualities of the man who was fighting against his own will.

When it became clear to all that the Lords and Commons were talking about different subsidy figures, Burleigh demanded a conference with the House. It was a bad move on his part for the Commons were extremely jealous of their privilege of initiating measures concerning taxation and revenue. It appeared to many in the House that the Lords were trying to encroach upon their most ancient and prized prerogative. Francis Bacon arose in the House to approve the granting of subsidies, but opposed a conference with the Lords, a position that angered Elizabeth.

It was at this point in the debate that Ralegh arose; he was becoming worried that the concern about prerogative might divert the attention of the House from the subsidies. Without so much as a blush or a wink, although he had recently been released from the Tower, he assured his colleagues that he spoke in part 'to please the Queen to whom he was infinitely bound above his desert', but also, he said, he spoke 'for the necessity of what he saw and knew'. The King of Spain, at that moment, was attempting to corrupt the Scots nobility and the King of Denmark. Also Philip had, as they all knew, recently seized the best harbour in Brittany and from there he would undoubtedly try to invade England that summer. As far as Ireland was concerned, he knew that in the entire island there were not six gentlemen of the Protestant religion; the entire people were ready and anxious to join with Spain in the enterprise of England. He begged the House to vote the subsidy.

It was a strong speech and a good one, but it was not enough. Emotions were aroused and the talk veered again to the offence offered by the House of Lords. There were more harsh and angry words and more circling debate. Finally Ralegh rose again, his voice calm, his manner smooth and poised. He said that he believed the House was being troubled by a misunderstanding (he knew better but it was the right thing to say). The House of Lords, he went on, had not requested a conference concerning the subsidy; they rather wished for a general conference in which the subsidy, among other things, might be discussed. Edward Coke, who was very bright, saw that Ralegh's soothing explanation offered a way of conferring with the Lords without loss of face. He thereupon put the question immediately and it received a unanimous 'aye'.

But first there was much debate concerning the levying of the tax and especially concerning those eligible to pay. Sir Thomas Cecil proposed that only men whose income exceeded ten pounds should pay. Ralegh thought such a proposal was impractical. He was in favour of the usual procedure of exempting persons who were valued at under three pounds and making up whatever revenue would be lost by increasing the tax proportionately on those valued at over ten pounds. Once the Queen herself had commanded Ralegh to survey the possibility of raising adequate money through subsidies while exempting the thirty-pound men. He had done so and when the reckoning was made, there simply wasn't enough money. But to exempt the three-pound men, he said, seemed to him both reasonable and practical.

Following Ralegh, the Chancellor of the Exchequer arose to say that, in the present crisis and given the present need, even an exemption of the three-pound men was not realistic. At that moment Francis Bacon arose and made the second mistake of his expedient political career. He thought that the three subsidies should be payable in six years rather than three. It was, he said, impossible to require more, for even then farmers and poor men would have to sell their brass pots. It was a good speech. But the Queen, who did not relish taxing the poor any more than Bacon did, was so outraged by this 'pursuing of popular courses' that Bacon had to retire from the Court; he lost not only Elizabeth's favour but also the office of Attorney General which Essex was trying to procure for him.

After Bacon had spoken, Ralegh rose again to say that he believed the present threat to England's safety was greater than in 1588. Like many others he was alarmed, and probably unduly so, at the new navy, including the Twelve Apostles, which Philip was trying to build. And enough members felt as Ralegh did that three subsidies were finally granted.

This Parliament, like all of its predecessors, was much concerned with religious non-conformity and especially with Catholics. But there now had arisen a new Protestant group which was creating some alarm, especially among the Anglican clergy and the bishops in the House of Lords. The Brownists, as they were called, were not only doctrinally unsound; they were also politically revolutionary, a threat to the state some thought. Rejecting the concept of an established Church, they favoured a congregational policy in which each group would choose its own minister and council of elders and ultimately decide its own articles of faith. They wanted no state regulation of religion whatever. The Brownists were the forerunners of the Independents and the Congregationalists who were to assume a leading role, later, in the English Civil War. Those who thought them revolutionary proved to be right. And it was a time when internal security quite justifiably seemed a paramount concern.

However, the new bill for religious conformity showed signs of extremism. Previously Catholic recusants had been fined twenty pounds a month for not attending church and that was a severe penalty. Now, however, the fine was to be varied according to the wealth of the offender and the penalties were tantamount to expropriation. Such recusants were to forfeit all goods and chattels and two-thirds of their lands; recusant wives were to lose their dowers; anyone marrying a recusant heiress would lose two-thirds of the inheritance and all recusants were disabled from purchasing, selling or leasing lands.

It was proposed to bar all Catholics from office and from the learned professions. Catholic children were to be taken from their parents at age seven and brought up under official supervision at their parents' expense. Finally, and worst of all, recusants were to be forbidden to come within five miles of their former residences; they were to be put into a kind of permanent exile.

For many years Parliamentary action against Catholic recusants had been politically popular. There had been no recent attempts on the Queen's life to stimulate repressive measures but the Jesuits and the seminary priests had returned to England, illegally, but in increasing numbers and they were enjoying some rather startling successes. England was full of Catholic families who had never formally abjured the faith or the Church, and who were only nominal members of the Anglican establishment. In such people's hearts old loyalties and old sympathies were easily revived and the growth of Catholicism was worrying the government. The bishops of the Anglican Church, however, were beginning to see another cloud on the horizon, somewhat bigger now than a man's hand – the growth of Puritan nonconformity. There were Puritans in Parliament and they soon began to see that under measures ostensibly aimed at Catholics, the establishment was also moving strongly against the Puritan left-wing. Another provision had been introduced into the 'five-mile' proposal which said that all 'obstinate recusants', not only those who persisted in absenting themselves from Church but also those who frequented conventicles, should conform themselves at once or undergo a series of successively heavier punishments: for the first offense, imprisonment for three months; the second, the loss of an ear; and for the third, permanent banishment from the realm and exile.

Ralegh had been listening with distaste to the increasing acrimony and divisiveness of the debate. He took the floor and began by admitting his own dislike of Brownists; they deserved 'to be rooted out of a commonwealth'. But he also disliked *ad hoc* legislation; it set precedents that might later entrap the innocent. And he very much disliked any legislation aimed at a man's beliefs.

That law is hard that taketh life, or sendeth into banishment where men's intentions shall be judged by a jury and they shall be judges of what another man meant.

Instead of proceeding against intentions, Ralegh said, the law should proceed against deed and fact; where they could be established, let the law be as harsh as necessary and justice would still be done.

That was the theoretical side of his argument, but there was a practical side to the entire proposal that must be faced. By means of a simple statistical analysis, Ralegh confronted the House with realities. He believed, and was sorry for it, that there might be 20,000 Brownists or more in the kingdom. If they were separated from their families, who would maintain their wives and children? And suppose that several thousand Brownists were assembled by the government at the seaports preparatory to their exile. He himself had equipped expeditions of hundreds of men, in one instance of several thousand men, and he knew what such undertakings cost. Who would pay? And where would the exiles be transported to? Perhaps he was wondering if his Virginia colonies had been selected by the Anglican bishops as a dumping ground for the allegedly disloyal.

In this decisive speech, Ralegh's tone was judicious, his reasoning sound. He was unmoved by the hysterical tone that the debate had engendered in the House. And although the bill passed, it was much milder than the original proposal and, what was more important, it was to expire automatically with the next session of Parliament. When one sees Ralegh in situations of this kind, one wonders why he did not become one of the great Parliamentarians of England. He had the intelligence, the analytical mind, and the foresight. But he lacked the despised middle-class virtues of perserverance, stability and caution. He could conciliate but was not really a conciliatory man. He was unpredictable. Even in Parliament, he was over-sensitive to slights against his personal honour; and he played the game of adversary. He enjoyed arising to reply to Bacon and Cecil especially, but also to others of the Queen's men. He did not function well as a party man. But whenever his speeches are reported in the Parliamentary journals, they show that wiry and heightened style through which shone his intellectual brilliance.

The cast of Ralegh's political thought was even more clearly revealed in the Parliament of 1601. A bill had been introduced which would make it mandatory to cultivate hemp on a certain proportion of the farm lands in England in order to make the nation self-sufficient in the production of rope, which was essential to the functioning of the Royal Navy. When Ralegh arose, he first spoke not against the impending bill but more generally on existing laws which regulated farming. Those laws, originally directed against enclosures, required that every farmer must plow one-third of his land or pay a fine. Ralegh pointed out that many farmers were men of poor ability and could not raise suitable crops. They simply did not understand sophisticated farming techniques. Further, some of them were so poor that they could not afford to buy seed corn for the land which they plowed. But to avoid the penalty of the law, they plowed the land and left it fallow; some even used part of the little store of cash they had to have their lands plowed. They raised nothing on that land and so it was a complete economic loss both to themselves and the country. If there were no such law, Ralegh said, many of these little farmers would let all of their land go into pasture and on it they would graze sheep or cattle.

I do not like the constraining of men to manure or use their grounds at our wills, but rather let every man use his ground to that which it is most fit for and therein use his own discretion.

It was a good speech against a bad bill and there was instantaneous reponse. All the House cried 'away with the bill' and that was the end of it.

But the government was uneasy about Ralegh's speech. The next day Francis Bacon returned to the subject. He hoped England would keep the statutes of tillage. He invoked what was already becoming a nostalgic fiction, the yeoman farmer, and said that he must be preserved. Robert Cecil spoke in support, 'Destroy the plough and you destroy the kingdom'. Neither Bacon nor Cecil had ever farmed; neither understood the realities of farm life in England. To their donnish approach to agriculture, Ralegh repeated his former arguments. To cause economic hardships to poor men out of sentimental nostalgia seemed to him unreasonable.

And therefore I think the best course is to set it at liberty and every man free, which is the desire of a true Englishman.

That, apparently, ended the debate.

In the Parliament of 1601, the matter of subsidies was even more pressing than before. Essex's Irish compaign had put the government deeply in debt in Ireland without gaining anything. Tyrone was still in rebellion and a Spanish army of several thousand men had landed at Kinsale on the southeast Irish coast. The Spanish invasion was at last a reality.

The previous Parliament had voted the three full subsidies; now there would have to be four. Sir Francis Hastings, remembering Bacon's striking phrase of some years ago, repeated that poor men would now have to sell their pots and pans in order to pay it. It was therefore proposed to change the form of taxation. Ordinarily the three-pound men would each have to pay four shillings tax or one-fifteenth; it was suggested now that this be reduced to 2s. 8d. on all lands assessed at or under three pounds. The matter was being considered in a committee, but the interest was so great that almost the entire House was present. Ralegh, quite surprisingly, opposed the motion to further relieve the poor men. 'If all pay alike, none will be aggrieved,' he said. 'If any [are] excepted doubtless it will produce much grief.'

Sir Edward Hoby was unable to hear that thin voice and he cried out, 'You should speak standing, not sitting. We cannot hear you'. Ralegh replied with disdain that in a committee it was equally proper to stand or sit. He then repeated his remarks against the motion, but remained seated. Robert Cecil followed him but stood up, saying 'it was an argument of more reverence' and so he would stand. It was a significant contrast between the two men whose lives would soon be so fatally intertwined. One was the individualist; the other, by nature and training, the party man.

In view of what followed, it appears that Ralegh was speaking against his own convictions on this issue for two good reasons. He felt that the life of the nation depended on the voting of the subsidies, and he knew that any change in established custom and procedure in such a sensitive matter as taxation would hurt the chances of the bill. Also, he believed that he stood a good chance of being appointed to the Privy Council; if his support of the small taxpayer hindered the full subsidy from being voted, it would also hurt his chances.

At the next full session of the House, Cecil reported that the committee had decided to recommend against exemption for the three-pound men. He himself was glad of it for when danger was so imminent, 'neither pots nor pans, nor dish nor spoon should be spared'. His remarks likely irritated Ralegh; they were true but tinged with demagoguery.

Francis Bacon could not resist the temptation of the occasion. He arose to commend the committee's decision for, he said, it was 'a sweet course to go in equal yoke'. What he said and his manner of saying it aroused Ralegh, who was willing to go along with the political necessity but was offended by the hypocrisy. Do you call it an equal yoke, he asked, if the poor pay as much as the rich? And then he struck out at the real inequity in the whole system of Elizabethan taxation, the manner of assessment. The poor man's tiny estate was usually quite fairly valued; it was never worth much more than it was said to be worth in the Queen's book; but the large estates, Ralegh said, and he included his own, were usually valued at less than a hundredth part of their worth. Therefore, the system was neither 'sweet' nor 'equal'.

Now that he was aroused, Ralegh also referred to Cecil's remarks. He did not like it, he said, when the Spaniard knew that poor Englishmen must sell their pots and pans in order to support the war. When he sat down, Cecil arose and smoothly replied that as a matter of fact everyone in the House knew that the selling of pots and pans was a figure of speech; no one would really have to do so. And the House was with him. They all cried out, 'No, No, No,' and Ralegh, who was glad enough to see subsidy voted, said no more. The bill was then put to a vote and passed. It is unlikely that his angry outburst hurt his chances of becoming a Privy Councillor; by now all men knew him rather well and Elizabeth, who knew him best of all, would never have assented.

The age of the Queen was nearing its close; no event ever showed it more clearly than her address to the joint sessions of this Parliament. Always before, members would crowd around, eager to see and greet the monarch, to receive a nod, a smile, or a hand to kiss. But now there was embarrassed silence and an uneasy avoidance of her person and her glance. While there were many reasons for this change, one of the principal grievances was the royal prerogative of monopolies whereby favourites of the Crown, for no services rendered, collected small fees on various items of trade. Ralegh once had a monopoly on the export of cloths; he still had his rich monopoly of wines which Essex, too, had enjoyed until he fell out of favour. Ralegh also had a small monopoly on playing cards and had recently established one on tin. The wine and the card monopolies were simply inexcusable interferences with the merchants' trade; it not only cut into their profits, but it also subjected them to the harassment of a steward who collected the monopoly and who, therefore, busied himself in the merchants' affairs.

But the tin monopoly was something else. Before Ralegh had been made Lord Warden of the Stannaries, the Duke of Cornwall traditionally held a monopoly on all tin produced. When it was refined and made into blocks, it was stamped with his seal and he had the first right to buy it. If he did not wish to buy, the tinners were then free to sell to the London merchants. Since 1585 all Cornish tin had been sold in London where it was the chief ingredient in the making of pewter vessels and utensils, a major industry. It was also used in the casting of bells to which it imparted a certain tintinabulation.

The London merchants were far too much for the simple tinners. They would alternately depress and inflate the tin market, buying only at low prices and making it impossible for the tinners to make a profit, scarcely possible for them even to live. At the same time the miners had to go deeper into the earth for tin, and water in the shafts had become a serious problem; it required expensive machinery to keep shafts dry enough for men to work in them. When Ralegh became Lord Warden the miners were often working in water up to their knees, struggling in a marginal industry and receiving for their inhuman toil the figure of three pounds a year for each man. In the year 1599, Ralegh had persuaded Elizabeth to give him the monopoly of tin. After that time, all tin produced in Cornwall and Devon would go to the Crown, and the miners would be given a fixed price for it. Before the monopoly the tinners' wages had gone up from three to five pounds a year, but that was not enough to match the inflation that was then raging out of control on the Continent and affecting English prices. There is, of course, something inconsistent in Ralegh's opposition to governmental interference in agriculture and his support of the regulation of the mining industry. But it was not a capricious inconsistency. The situations were different, and his own motives were about as pure as an Elizabethan's could ever be. If, in this matter, he, like Philip of Spain, was animated by a consciousness of his own rectitude, he had a right to it.

The London merchants had their problems, too; they favoured a free market and Ralegh's policy, which had doubled the wages of the miners, had also doubled the prices of tin. They therefore had urged upon their own representatives and supporters in Parliament a review of the entire policy of granting monopolies. When the debate on the issue began in the House, it was most sharply and bitterly focussed on the monopoly of salt which was an especial burden to the poor; wine after all was a luxury, and there were other monopolies that were 'pestiferous', but the one on salt walked 'in the forerank' of abuses. One of the pestiferous monopolies mentioned was one on cards; here the Parliamentary diarist noted an unusual phenomenon,

'Sir Walter Ralegh blushed'. However Ralegh held his tongue until another speaker rather heatedly mentioned the monopoly on tin as another abuse. Then Ralegh arose.

His reply was both indignant and clever. His own honour had been touched, he said (a rather common remark from him), but more important the Queen's honour had been touched also, for she issued the monopolies. He said that before he had accepted the monopoly on tin, the price had varied in the London market from seventeen to fifty shillings; yet at the higher prices, the miners' wages had remained the same. Since his patent, every miner in Cornwall had been given four shillings a week, 'truly paid'. And he concluded his speech with a remarkable statement which indicates again how independent he was and how unpredictable his positions were.

Notwithstanding, if all others may be repealed, I will give my consent, as freely to the cancelling of this, as any member of the House.

No one wished to push the impassioned Ralegh further. The diarist noted that there was 'a great silence' in the House that continued for some time. Finally Sir Francis Hastings, who had started the whole thing, arose and made a tactful speech in praise of the freedom of speech enjoyed by English Parliamentarians. He prayed that if sometimes things were said amiss, it might rather be borne with than that freedom should be imperilled. It was the right note and no more was said, but any observer in Parliament would have known that Elizabeth's death would also be the death of monopolies. The royal prerogative was giving way to inevitable economic changes.

When Elizabeth heard of the bitter debate on monopolies, she graciously and wisely acceded. She was a very intelligent women. Some monopolies, she said, the one on salt for example, would be discontinued immediately. All others would be reviewed. The unwonted silence when she had spoken in Parliament was not lost on her.

Another matter of business was, once again, religious conformity. This time it was a bill 'against willful absence from divine service upon Sunday'. The Act of Uniformity had imposed a fine of one shilling for such absence, but no one was collecting it. Under the previous act the churchwardens were collectors; in the proposed bill the Justices of the Peace would collect the fine and it would be paid by every man who did not attend; each householder would also be responsible for the attendance of his wife and servants.

This proved to be the most emotional issue in a highly emotional session of Parliament. When Ralegh spoke, he demonstrated again how emotion recedes before understandable statistical analysis. If Justices of the Peace were to collect the fine, he said, someone would have to appear before them and inform them of transgressions. The informers, presumably, would be the churchwardens. If there were, on the average, 120 parishes in a shire, some 240 churchwardens would have to appear at every Quarter Sessions to give information before a grand jury. If there were only two offenders in each parish (and obviously there would be many more) almost 500 people would be appearing before the court each quarter, some to give information, some to be fined. 'What great multitudes this will bring together; what quarrelling and danger may happen, besides giving authority to a mean churchwarden.'

There was a proviso in the bill which required attendance at Church only eight times a year if the householder held divine service twice every Sunday in his own home with his entire family in attendance. Such a proviso, said Ralegh, is simply an invitation to stay away from church. The statistics and logic were convincing; and behind those statistics was Ralegh's conviction that people, insofar as possible, are best left alone in matters of conscience.

When the bill was put to a vote, the voices were so evenly matched that a division of the House was called for. In every division, the Noes sat still and the Ayes walked to the lobby to be counted. The reason for this procedure was that affirmative votes represented those who wished a change in law or procedure; threfore, it was reasoned, the burden was upon them, through overt action, to secure the change. Men in doubt always found it easier to sit still.

The division revealed an extremely close vote, 106 Noes and 105 Ayes. The bill was lost. Then Robert Bowyer arose and charged that one member who had wished to vote Aye had been pulled back and kept in his seat by another. Robert Cecil angrily demanded that the offender be named. Ralegh chose this unfortunate moment to display his casual arrogance, 'Why if it please you, it is small matter to pull one by the sleeve, for so have I done oftentimes'. The House was in no mood for flippancy; the members felt deeply, one way or the other, about the issue. Robert Cecil arose to say that Parliament had been slandered, and he hoped that any man whose voice could be drawn forwards or backwards, like a dog on a string, would never again be returned to Parliament. Cecil had been eager to see the bill passed; but he now gave it as his judgment that the charges of sleeve-tugging altered nothing. The bill was lost and the debate was over.

Ralegh spoke on two other matters of business. He urged that Parliament continue the tax for maintaining Dover Harbour. He pointed out that many once good harbours such as Plymouth, Winchelsea, and Rye were now practically useless. Further, Dover was the chief port for Newfoundland fishermen for whom there was no other suitable haven for the landing and selling of their cargoes.

Another bill was introduced to prohibit transportation of iron ordnance by merchants for sale abroad. English naval ordnance was still eagerly sought after by all naval powers and foreign ships were refusing to carry regular English merchandise unless their ships were ballasted with ordnance, on which they turned a good profit. The bill was complicated by the fact that such ordnance could only be exported under royal licence; it was a monopoly and a bill to prohibit it touched the prerogative. And Elizabeth received some 3,000 pounds a year from this particular monopoly.

A London ironmonger who was also a Member for the City said that if the Queen would forbid such traffic for seven years, the Spaniard would be helpless. A speaker pointed out, on the other hand, that Her Majesty had already been gracious in the matter of monopolies, and she should not be pushed too far. Ralegh arose and said that there was a time when one of Her Majesty's ships could beat twenty Spaniards, but now, with English ordnance, they matched us 'one to one'. Another speaker said that at that very moment a ship lay on the Thames laden with thirty-six pieces of ordnance. He did not have to say where it was bound for. Ultimately, the bill was killed because Parliament received word of Elizabeth's strong objection to it. But still the situation was 'much marvelled and grutched at'.

In Elizabeth's parliaments, no man served more brilliantly than the sharp-minded free-lance she had once loved, though many performed more consistently. Elizabeth had a sharp eye for men; she loved the aristocrats, but she trusted her affairs to the frugal, industrious and sober men of the middle class. If Ralegh was not one of the great Parliamentarians, his political spirit nevertheless embodied to some degree the voice of England's future and that is why such great Parliamentarians as Pym, Eliot and Hampden came, one day, to his execution, not to watch a spectacle but to see a sacrifice and bear witness to it.

16

The End of an Age

Authority forgets dying kings and queens. But their invisible
treasury of power draws men by silken strings. That intangible
wealth concentrated in the single person of an ageing sovereign
is like the lure of Guiana. It drives men slightly mad; they
swarm around it, partly for personal advantage, but also because
they wish to feel and become part of that living force that is now
flowing from old vessels into new ones. For half a century
Elizabeth and her trusted counsellors had wielded that power
firmly. But in 1598 William Cecil had died; Elizabeth herself
had come to his bedside and fed him with a spoon, cradling his
old, tired head in her lap. When he was gone she was devastated;
she wept; she kept her own chambers; and there was no artifice
in her grief, no consolation for her sorrows. For half a century
she had relied on the good sense and moral integrity of the old
Puritan. Back of her own coquetries and indecisions, her storms
and self-doubts, had been the reliable, constant force of Cecil's
personality. Leicester was gone; Walsingham too; Frobisher,
Drake, Hawkins, all of those men she had understood and loved,
Spenser, Grenville and Sidney; men who had repaid her love
and trust by giving her the immortality of art and glory. Only
two were left, Ralegh and Essex. And Elizabeth knew that they
both found her old and ugly and that each was looking beyond
her, not to other women but to other sources of power. There
would be a new anointing soon, and all England was uneasily
waiting.

Ralegh and Essex, both typical of the gifted and flamboyant
men who sought greatness in the spacious and hazardous days of
Elizabeth's glory, were each allied with one of the new men who

would rise to power in the quite different world of the Court of James I, Ralegh with Robert Cecil, Essex with Francis Bacon. The new men seemed a different breed, reserved, clever, shrewd, without physical prowess or any touch of the desperate courage that would impulsively immolate itself in the pursuit of valour. The two older men possessed names that everyone in England knew as well as personal charm and the grand manner. They sought glory in hazardous action and were too impatient to spin quietly the strong web of 'policy'. But the new men possessed other kinds of brilliant gifts, and they understood the emerging age; their ears were attuned to a subtler tone and a new, evasive style. They were acute and rather coldly opportunistic.

Robert Cecil, with whom Ralegh entwined his fate during the last days of Elizabeth, was a toughly armoured man who had struggled all his life against insuperable handicaps. He was a kind of Telemachus, a promising boy who could never quite match his father. For years he had been doing the work of First Secretary without ever receiving a formal appointment. Whatever bitterness he felt, he concealed. He showed no impulsive rashness, he made no complaints either in rhyme or prose about Fortune or the Queen who called him 'little man'. He simply worked harder and his sense of injustice sharpened his faculties. And there was something worse. He had been born a cripple. Scarcely five feet tall, he was physically weak and badly deformed by a hump between his shoulders. What he must have suffered as a boy from the careless savagery of other children we can guess; what it was like to serve in a Court where dwarfs were kept for amusement, we can feel. Forever closed to him were the lists of honour, the tournaments, the battlefields. His foot would never know the deck of a galleon. He would never wear the favour of a lady; when it came time to marry and he had chosen his bride at a distance, he sent privately to her and asked if his courtship would be welcome. Like Alexander Pope whom he resembled physically, he had a fine face, too sharp-featured, but with large intelligent eyes that were wholly without illusion and unmistakably sad. The lips were tightly drawn.

When Cecil died in 1612, before the mound above him had settled, Francis Bacon had written and published his essay *Of Deformity*. There is no malice in it; but neither is there any kindness. Bacon's scintillating mind, which seems never to have been warmed by an impulse of the heart, has pretty well delineated the character of Cecil. Deformed persons, he says, are frequently 'even with nature', for as nature has done badly by them so they become unnatural; they are 'void of natural affection'. Because they have fixed in their person that which induces contempt, their deformity becomes a perpetual spur which seeks to rescue and deliver itself from scorn. Deprived of the usual masculine weapons, the deformed man must forge himself sharper ones. He watches for weaknesses in others; his own so apparent physical weakness disarms emulators and competitors. And so, Bacon concludes, 'in a great wit, deformity is an advantage to rising'. Bacon perceived what would largely have escaped Ralegh and Essex, that Robert Cecil, though physically weak, was a formidable adversary.

When Elizabeth's power began to ebb, tentatively seeking new channels, Ralegh and Cecil were friends. Together they had gone to Plymouth and saved the cargo of the *Madre de Dios*; it is difficult to say which had been more surprised at the effectiveness of the other. Cecil had supported Ralegh in the Guiana venture and lost money in it; but since then Ralegh had made him a partner in his privateering and had done well by both of them. There were some warm passages of personal friendship between them, too. When Lady Cecil died in 1597, Robert Cecil, who so desperately needed the loyal affection she had given him, was left with small children and no inclination to marry again. Ralegh then wrote him one of the most moving consolatory letters in English literature. Death always fired the imagination of that moody Celt, and his consolation to Cecil was without sentimentality but deeply felt.

Because I know not how you dispose of yourself, I forbear to visit you; preferring your pleasing before mine own desire. I had rather be with you now than at any other time, if I could thereby either take off from you the burden of your sorrows, or lay the greater part thereof on mine own heart . . .

It is true that you have lost a good and virtuous wife, and myself an honourable friend and kinswoman. But there was a time when she was unknown to you, for whom you then lamented not. She is now no more yours, nor of your acquaintance, but immortal, and not needing or knowing your love or sorrow. Therefore you shall but grieve for that which now is as then it was, when not yours; only bettered by the difference in this, that she hath past the wearisome journey of this dark world.

The consolation he then offers Cecil is a Christian humanism as pure as ever flowed from the pen of John Milton. The mind of man, says Ralegh, 'is that part of God which is in us'. To the extent that we allow our griefs and passions to overcome our reason we draw farther away from God. The final descant becomes a universal dirge on the theme of resignation.

Sorrows draw not the dead to life, but the living to death. And if I were myself to advise myself in the like, I would never forget my patience till I saw all and the worst of evils, and so grieve for all at once.

When the Raleghs saw that little Will Cecil was not well, they took him to Sherborne where he was happy. Ralegh wrote Cecil that the boy was eating well, digesting his food and thriving under the hearty and motherly affection of Bess. And little Will loved Sir Walter, to whom he wrote a letter suffused with tenderness and affection.

Sir Walter, we must all exclaim and cry out because you will not come down. You being absent we are like soldiers that when their Captain are absent, they know not what to do: you are so busy about idle matters. Sir Walter, I will be plain with you. I pray you leave all idle matters and come down to us.

Ralegh always charmed children; he seems to have excited them in the same way that old Martin Cockram, with his stories about Brazil, had once excited him.

Close though it was, the friendship of the two men was soon subject to erosion. More than anything else, Ralegh wished to be a peer of the realm; so did Cecil. Ralegh also wanted to be a sworn member of the Privy Council; Cecil already was. And although Cecil had inherited from his father a distrust of Spain as deep as Ralegh's, like his father he disliked war and mistrusted the schemes of the party urging war. Besides, Ralegh's game of adversary in Parliament exasperated Cecil, who was trying to get the Crown's business done. And Ralegh never ceased to plague him to procure the councillorship he desired. But Cecil would not have urged it even if he had wished to: it was Elizabeth who made all decisions concerning Essex and Ralegh, and Cecil was not one to endanger his own position or even to court momentary anger by pressing too hard for a friend. Yet Ralegh seems to have thought he would have been appointed if only Cecil had tried hard enough. At any rate, he bitterly blamed Cecil.

For a time Ralegh had been friends with Essex too. In fact, in 1598 both Ralegh and Cecil courted Essex assiduously. The relations of the three men then had a firm pragmatic basis. Essex had persuaded Elizabeth to restore Ralegh as Captain of the Guard; perhaps he could do more. Ralegh and Cecil had offered the impecunious Essex one-third of the profits from their privateering if Essex would support Ralegh for Vice-Chamberlain and Essex agreed. But the friendship did not last long. On November 17, 1598, there was a tournament to celebrate the Queen's birthday. Having learned that Ralegh was going to dress his handful of followers in orange-plumed hats and orange favours, Essex dressed his own 2,000 men in the same colours, a scornful public comment on Ralegh's lack of station. The underlying enmity grew, until after Essex's disastrous failure to pacify the Irish rebellion, it became deadly, involving Ralegh in Essex's destruction.

Just two months before that birthday celebration for the Queen, the English suffered the worst disaster they had ever known in Ireland. The rebellious Irish in Munster had met the English army under Sir Henry Bagenal and destroyed it. Edmund

Spenser fled Kilcolman when his entire estate was burned. Ralegh's 100 settlers in the town of Tallow and others elsewhere all fled without firing a shot, much to Elizabeth's disgust. The entire English plantation scheme was in ruins.

But that was not the worst of it. It was known that the Earl of Tyrone had been promised an expeditionary force from Spain; so an even greater disaster was threatening in the north. All the unhappy work of making Ireland safe had to be done over again. Someone, of course, had to lead the English troops. Quite naturally Ralegh's name was mentioned. Later it was said that he had been offered the position and had turned it down, but it is difficult to believe that Ralegh would have been so wise and even more difficult to believe that Elizabeth would seriously have considered him; he was almost as unsuited as Essex.

Elizabeth, with her acute judgment of men, did propose Sir Charles Blount, Lord Mountjoy, the man who ultimately succeeded in that almost impossible task. But Essex opposed the appointment. Elizabeth then proposed Sir Henry Knollys. Essex countered with the nomination of Sir George Carew who had become one of his followers without ceasing to be friendly to Ralegh. Elizabeth would not hear of it; Essex argued. Elizabeth was firm, whereupon the rash and immature Essex turned his back on her in a gesture of contempt. Elizabeth, in a fury, slapped his face, hard stinging blows, and told him to go and be hanged. Essex shouted that he would not have endured such an outrage even from Henry VIII and, incoherent with anger, started to draw his sword. Lord Admiral Howard rushed up, seized his arms and spoke sharply to him. Then Essex turned and ran from the room. To draw a weapon in the presence of the Queen was treason; even more disgraceful was the fact that the highest peer in the realm should have tried to draw a sword on the old Queen. Essex never apologized; perhaps his humiliation was too great. And in the insecurity of her failing years, Elizabeth did not have the heart to punish him. But a trust was weakened.

Meanwhile Francis Bacon had attached himself to the rising fortunes of Essex. But soon the protégé tried to reverse their roles and make Essex his pupil. It was as though Machiavelli had become the tutor of some impulsive Sir Gawain. He advised Essex above all else to flatter the Queen, to bind her with the bonds of her own infatuation. Essex must especially eschew 'all popular courses' (a lesson Bacon had once learned in Parliament) and he must be vehement in denouncing such courses. Above all, Bacon wished Essex to become a member of the peace party. He should not seek or accept the positions of Earl Marshal or Master of the Ordnance. He must not even appear to be a military man at all, but should rather strive to be bookish. If impossible advice can ever be good advice, then Essex was never more soundly counselled. But he could not change his nature and Bacon's advice went for nothing. He accepted both of the positions Bacon had urged him not to take and was now the leading military officer of the realm. And he had engaged in a vehement quarrel with William Cecil about whether or not the war should again be carried into Spanish waters. Old Cecil, too tired to fight any longer, too near death himself to look upon it as glorious, merely shrugged and opened his Bible to the Fifty-fifth Psalm, 'Bloodthirsty and deceitful men shall not live out half their days'.

It has been said that Essex was manoeuvred into going to Ireland by his clever enemies. It is difficult to see how. He himself wrote the Queen a letter of advice. She should send to Ireland as commander of the new expeditionary force a man 'of the nobility, strong in power, honour and wealth, in favour with military men, who had been before general of an army'. His own description of the ideal general fitted only one man in England: not Clifford, Vere, Norris or Roger Williams; certainly not Ralegh. He had described himself and everyone knew it.

Finally the Queen gave in. On two occasions in her entire reign she allowed her better judgment to be overruled in a matter of the highest importance by the worse judgment of a favourite: when she had sent Leicester to the Low Countries in 1585 and now when she sent Essex to Ireland. But she did everything she could to ensure the success of the expedition. Essex was allowed to choose his own officers; he was given the authority to create knights; and he was given an army of 16,000 men, the greatest force ever sent to that lost land.

But now that he had his way, contrary to all Bacon's shrewd advice, Essex began to have doubts. Although sometimes foolish he was not a fool and he realized that he had taken on something a little worse than the twelve labours of Hercules. So he and his followers, with their usual prescience, prepared excuses for a failure. He wrote the Earl of Southampton saying that he knew his enemies would practise against him while he was away; and before he left he wrote the Privy Council a foolish letter saying that he was wearing a breastplate but not a cuirass; that is, he was armed on the breast but not on the back.

In March 1599, Essex sailed under orders to march north against Tyrone and defeat his armies. Instead, with the consent of the Irish Council, he decided to march south into Munster, put down the more isolated and unorganized revolt there, secure his rear, and then go north. He did so, fighting no major engagements, but reducing a number of strongholds and pacifying Munster. It was being asked in England if so great an army was needed for such a slight campaign. And what was more disturbing to Elizabeth, Essex seemed to be fumbling his way toward a new Irish policy, one of generosity and placation and she didn't expect it to work.

Soon the Queen was raging; the expedition had cost her at least three full subsidies and some more talk in Parliament about selling pots and pans. She was paying Essex 1,000 pounds a day, she said, to go on a progress. Further, Essex had knighted in the field almost 100 of his followers, practically doubling the number of men in England who now held that honour. Why should so many men have been knighted for bravery when no real engagements had been fought? In August of 1599 rumours began to circulate in England that Essex might turn his army around and invade his own homeland. London was barricaded and Ralegh and Lord Howard were ordered to mobilize the fleet, ostensibly against the Spaniard.

By now Essex and his followers were maligning Ralegh as the cause of their failure. In June Essex had written to Elizabeth complaining of those who were working against his success: he singled out especially Ralegh and his new friend, Lord Cobham.

After the Munster 'progress', to Elizabeth's scathing letters Essex's reply was that Ralegh and Cobham were slandering him and wished the expedition to fail. Elizabeth didn't even answer these diversions but again ordered him north against Tyrone. But he could not go; his army had melted out from under him in six months. Only those acquainted with Irish warfare can understand how it was possible for a force of 16,000 men to be reduced to 4,000 with almost no battle casualties. But sickness and desertion had again done their work.

Before he left England, Essex had extracted a promise from Elizabeth that he might return if he thought it necessary. Now she rescinded the promise and ordered him on his allegiance not to return until he met Tyrone, and Essex's awareness of the magnitude of his own disgrace drove him to the edge of paranoia. His enemies, he thought, were not content with slandering him; now they were trying to keep him even from seeing the Queen.

The Irish Council, called together, agreed that since he was not strong enough to meet Tyrone, he had best try to negotiate. And even in that Essex was bested; he and Tyrone agreed to the most disadvantageous truce ever entered into by an English army. There was to be a cessation of fighting for six weeks and for successive periods of six weeks until May 1, 1600; either side could terminate the truce by giving fourteen days' notice. Essex pledged himself in writing; the Earl of Tyrone gave only his pledged word. He had gained time for the Spanish invasion and England's position was worse than when Essex had entered the field.

The now hysterical Essex decided that his only hope was to see the Queen in person and let charm regain what incompetence had lost. At first he considered bringing his entire army with him, but he was finally persuaded to cross to England with only a small body of supporters, some 200 gentlemen. He arrived at Westminster Palace, covered with mud and sweat, entered the Palace and rushed upstairs to the Presence Chamber. It was empty and the Captain of the Guard was not at his post. Otherwise Ralegh and Essex would probably have settled matters between them. Essex went on into the Privy Chamber and finding it empty, entered the Queen's bedchamber where she was sitting *en deshabille*, being dressed and combed by her attendants. He burst in, fell to his knees, seized her hands and kissed them, his head bowed. Endymion was appealing to Cynthia once again.

Whatever Elizabeth felt, she spoke lightly and pleasantly with the Earl and soon dismissed him. But that same afternoon the Privy Council sent for Essex and examined him for three hours on his conduct of the campaign and on the various rumours and alarms they had heard about his intentions. The next day he was taken into custody and put under house arrest in York House, a large dwelling standing next to Essex House in the Strand. It was generally believed that he was not to be charged with treason, but that there might be further enquiry.

Essex, always subject to psychosomatic disorders when things went badly, now fell into melancholia, and it was given out that he was seriously ill; prayers were offered in all the churches for his recovery. Oddly enough his popularity increased as a result of the Irish fiasco; people felt sorry for him. And he laid all the blame to the machinations of Ralegh, Cecil, Cobham, and Lord Grey, son of the man under whom Ralegh had once served in Ireland.

Previously Essex had done nothing worse to Ralegh than make him England's popular villain. But he now took a step that was to link Ralegh's doom with his own. England's throne would soon be vacant; there were at least fourteen candidates, four of whom had some kind of legitimate claim. Perhaps Essex had already decided that James of Scotland was the only logical choice or perhaps of all the candidates James was the only one who, at the moment, could be helpful to him. In either case, he began to intrigue with James. His supporters were urging James to prepare an army and come to enforce his claim to the throne.

Lord Mountjoy, the new Lord Deputy of Ireland, would

assist the Scottish army, consistent with his allegiance to the Queen, whatever such talk meant.

But James, knowing that Elizabeth's government was far too alert not to know that Essex was in touch with him, did not reply. Instead he sent emissaries to London to represent his cause. The suspicion was then sown in his mind that since the Earl of Essex was supporting his claims, the Earl's enemies, especially Ralegh, were likely to prove James's also.

Essex's career, from this time, is painful to follow. His violent tirades, it seemed even to his followers, could not have proceeded from any sane man. Sometime during this period he told Elizabeth that her mind was cankered and 'her conditions as crooked as her carcass'. (One of Elizabeth's shoulders had always been slightly lower than the other.) Later, Ralegh was to say that it was this remark, rather than his treason, that cost the Earl his head.

Not long after Essex returned to London, Tyrone took the field and Charles Blount, Lord Mountjoy, who should have led the English forces in the first place, sailed to meet him. At about the same time a Latin history of Henry IV (who had gained the crown of England by deposing Richard II) was published with a dedication to the Earl of Essex, who was descended from the Plantagenets. Elizabeth noted the implication but said nothing. The following August, Essex was released from custody but forbidden to come to Court. And when he asked Elizabeth to renew his monopoly on sweet wines, which constituted a good part of his income, she refused saying that 'an unruly beast must be stopped of its provender'. It was probably as close as any one ever came to calling Essex an ass.

Before Essex was released, Ralegh wrote Cecil a letter which was a masterpiece of ambiguity, as he no doubt intended it should be. Read quite literally the letter merely recommends that Essex be kept down. 'If Her Majesty's favour fail him, he will decline to a common person.' But the letter bears other implications. Ralegh is concerned that Cecil, for fear of reprisals, might not be sufficiently severe with Essex. He therefore cites three instances in which noblemen were put to death and their heirs took no revenge. 'I could name you a thousand of those,' Ralegh says. And he gives Cecil some cryptic and impassioned advice, 'Lose not your advantage; if you do, I read your destiny'. And finally, in a postscript, Ralegh says that princes (and queens) are preserved by prevention. 'I have seen the last of her good days and all ours after his liberty.' And so, while Ralegh did not advise that the Earl be put to death, he hinted strongly that it was the wise thing to do. He had not forgotten that morning aboard the Earl's ship off Fayal harbour. But he might as well have saved his advice, for the Earl went free; in matters this close to her Crown and person, Elizabeth would not be advised by Cecil or Ralegh or anyone.

The freed but frustrated Essex tried to renew negotiations with Mountjoy and James about their respective armies. Mount-joy, like many another man who has achieved a striking success, was finding the Establishment to his liking and was no longer interested in treason. Whether Essex now became an actual para-noid or whether he was dissimulating is difficult to say. He repeatedly told his followers that Ralegh and Cobham, in a deep conspiracy with Spain, were plotting his murder. He felt that his only recourse was to seize the Court and control the person of the sovereign. Under his control she would dismiss his enemies from the government; then they would be put on trial for their lives. After the trials, he would summon Parliament and 'alter the government'.

Matters came to a head on February 7, 1601, when rumours spread over London that Essex was actually preparing to take up arms against the Crown. Besides, Shakespeare's *Richard II* was revived at the Globe Theatre on that very day without authorization; the implications were not lost on Elizabeth who regarded the performance as a threat. Know you not, she asked, that I am Richard? But the first explicit information that a *coup* was to be attempted appears to have come to Ralegh in a message from his cousin, Sir Ferdinando Gorges, who was also a follower of Essex. As Governor of Plymouth Fort, Gorges was directly under Ralegh's command as Vice–Admiral of Devon; whatever Ralegh heard led him to order Gorges to come to

Durham House to see him. At the same time he reported what he had heard to the Privy Council and they ordered Essex to appear.

Gorges consulted with Essex who reluctantly permitted him to meet Ralegh but said that the meeting should take place on the Thames River in open boats and that Gorges should take two gentlemen with him to secure himself from violence. Christopher Blount, the father-in-law of Essex, took Gorges aside and urged him to kill Ralegh or at least to take him hostage. But Gorges refused to attack his cousin unless Sir Walter were to give him occasion by 'violent deeds or unkind words', for either of which he was both prepared and resolved.

And so out in the middle of the Thames the two cousins conducted their strange interview. Ralegh warned Gorges that there was a warrant out for his arrest and advised him to return to Plymouth Fort immediately. Gorges replied that he was one of 'two thousand gentlemen who had resolved that day to live or die free men'. At about that time Christopher Blount, who had decided that Ralegh must be killed, fired a musket at him from the bank of the river. Fortunately for Ralegh, muskets in those days seldom hit what they were aimed at.

Gorges assured Ralegh that the rebels upheld the Queen but sought to reform the abuse of the Queen's authority by Ralegh and others. Sir Walter calmly replied that no man was ever 'without a colour for his intent'. By this time Blount had reloaded and he sent another musket ball skipping above the water. Neither Ralegh nor Gorges paid any attention.

Ralegh then advised his cousin to remember his duty and his allegiance. Gorges, probably losing heart a little, began to talk like Essex. This, he said, was likely to be the 'bloodiest day's work that ever was'. Meanwhile Blount, who seemed to be rather better at loading and firing than at aiming, managed to get off a third shot and then a fourth as Ralegh rowed away.

When Gorges returned to Essex House, the Earl informed him and others that Ralegh and Cobham had laid an ambuscade of muskets for him on the river. To save his life, he said, they must march through the streets of London, armed only with swords, and arouse the citizens to flock to their support. And so Essex and 300 followers rode through the streets, Essex continually crying out that Ralegh and Cobham were trying to murder him, that they had sold England out to Spain. 'For the Queen! For the Queen!' they all cried out. It was a depressing farce: many people looked at him in wonderment but, as Bacon later said, not a single man offered him assistance in the streets of London. Almost immediately a government herald rode through the same streets proclaiming Essex a traitor, the trained bands mounted barricades in the streets, and Essex finally surrendered and was imprisoned. He and Sir Christopher Blount were promptly tried and condemned for treason.

Sir Christopher behaved admirably both at the trial and on the scaffold. He said that neither he nor Essex believed that Ralegh and Cobham had any murderous intent: 'It was a word cast out to colour other matters.' On the scaffold Blount asked for Ralegh who was present as Captain of the Guard. He came forward.

Sir Walter Ralegh, I thank God that you are present. I had an infinite desire to speak with you, to ask your forgiveness ere I died. Both for the wrong done you, and for my particular ill intent towards you, I beseech you forgive me.

Ralegh, always magnanimous at the right times, forgave Sir Christopher in the grand style. And when the Queen's men tried to cut short Sir Christopher's final speech, Ralegh intervened and Blount was allowed to have his say.

The trial and death of Essex were less admirable. The emotional rhythms of the Earl's behaviour and speech were now too exaggerated to suggest anything but instability. At the trial he made a great show of attempting to be witty. When Ralegh was sworn as a witness to give the minor testimony about his meeting with Gorges, Essex cried out, 'What booteth it to swear the fox?' Anyway, he said, a large folio should be used rather than a small testament. Ralegh, who had a better sense of appropriate conduct under the public eye, ignored the barbs and made his testimony brief and factual.

Before his execution, Essex went to pieces, talking hysterically, implicating everyone, even accusing his own sister of urging him on to treason. On the scaffold he continued in the same manner, acknowledging 'with thankfulness to God, that he was thus justly spewed out of the realm'. Before he died, he tried to make some amends to Ralegh and Cobham. They were, he said, as far as he knew 'true servants of the Queen and State'. Then as Blount had done he asked to speak with Ralegh. Sir Walter had been standing near, but, hearing hisses and murmurs from the hostile crowd, he withdrew to the armoury where he could watch the execution unseen. And his enemies said that he had puffed out tobacco in disdain and called the Earl a great calf.

After the execution, the name and memory of Essex underwent an unofficial canonization, and since everyone knew that Cobham was a nonentity, without influence on events, all the anger at the death of that bright, mercurial spirit was directed towards Ralegh and Cecil, but especially toward Ralegh.

> Ralegh doth time bestride:
> He sits twixt wind and tide:
> Yet uphill he cannot ride,
> For all his bloody pride.
> He seeks taxes on the tin:
> He polls the poor to the skin:
> Yet he swears 'tis no sin.
> Lord, for thy pity!

Thus the people rewarded Ralegh for his efforts on behalf of the impoverished tinners and his continual concern for the poor man's burdens in Parliamentary debates on subsidies. Yet he had shed tears, he said, when Essex died, and undoubtedly he had; there is nothing unusual in an ambivalence that both desires another man's death and weeps to see it. Robert Cecil did not weep, nor did he claim to. But he saw that a man so generally hated and reviled as Ralegh now was could only be a public liability to him, and that his own future therefore necessitated his separating his fortune from Ralegh's. And so Cecil began to say that he, too, was angry about the Essex affair. And while Ralegh continued as flamboyant as ever, Cecil – unobtrusive, quiet, unassuming – further undermined Ralegh's credit. Later, in his *History*, Ralegh said that no matter what Alexander the Great's virtues had been, people would always say of him, 'But he killed Callisthenes'. And for two years in England no matter what anyone said in Ralegh's behalf or about his services to the state, someone was likely to say, or at least to think, 'But he killed Essex'. And James of Scotland, at one with the popular mind, spoke of Essex as 'my martyr'. It followed that Ralegh was his enemy.

In 1587 it had been said that Ralegh was the most hated man, in court, in the city, and the country. In 1601, he should have been at the height of his career; his only rival with the Queen was dead; his presumed friend Cecil was First Secretary. But the Queen, in her own phrase, had begun to feel time creeping at her gate and had no more time for old lovers and other vanities; and Cecil would not risk his own position to support Ralegh in his unpopularity. Ralegh was left with only one close political friend, Henry Brooke, Lord Cobham, whom Cecil had once described as 'a most silly lord, but one degree from a fool'. Cecil should have known: Cobham was his brother-in-law. Cobham and Ralegh: it was a strange, unpredictable, and volatile combination especially in the unstable times when the succession to the throne of the ailing Elizabeth was in doubt.

Essex had informed James of Scotland, the most obvious candidate, that the Cecil-Ralegh party were in a plot to put the Infanta of Spain on the throne of England. It would have been reasonably accurate if he had said that since Cecil and Ralegh were both dubious about James, they were exploring the other possibilities. Of the fourteen avowed candidates, only four had any kind of chance. James himself had the best title to the throne, although his claim could be challenged on two grounds. His mother had been attainted for treason and had lost her title; there was some legal question as to whether or not this attainder also reached to James. However, back in the days of the Bond of Association, Elizabeth herself had seen to it that the legislation was so written as not to exclude James. The other ground on which James's right could be challenged was a legal quibble that no one took seriously. Under feudal law, no alien could inherit English land and the Scottish James was an alien. Arabella Stuart, on the other hand, a member of the younger branch of the royal family of Scotland, had been born in England. The quibble might have proved more persuasive if she had ever shown any ability, but she was an unattractive, empty-headed girl, desperately searching for a husband or a lover and a chance to get out from under the repressive tutelage of Bess of Hardwick who was a good friend of Lady Ralegh's. Allegations that Ralegh supported Arabella never rested on anything more substantial than that friendship; he himself said that of all women he had ever known he liked Arabella least. She had neither intelligence nor strength of character and her accession would have been a national disaster: no one ever doubted it.

A third claimant was Lord Hertford, a son of Catherine Grey. Finally there was the Infanta of Spain who had some kind of shadowy claim through John of Gaunt and whatever legal right she could find in Mary Stuart's will in which James had been specifically disinherited and Mary's right transferred to the King of Spain. It is true that Cecil engaged in some intrigues concerning the Infanta. But when it was known that the Jesuits were also intriguing on her behalf and that Philip III had declared himself in her favour, the chance of effective support in England was lost. Besides, the Pope, seeing danger in the union of England with Burgundy and Flanders, where the Infanta and her husband, the Archduke, were rulers, refused to sanction the Infanta's claim. Thereupon the few sensible men like Robert Cecil who had been tentatively supporting her immediately lost all interest. Within a few weeks after the Pope's decision, Cecil wrote to King James offering his services, naturally without informing either the Queen or Ralegh of what he had done. James referred Cecil to Lord Henry Howard, the nearest of kin to Lord Charles Howard, the Lord Admiral. Soon a three-way secret correspondence was entered into by James, Howard and Cecil. To ensure secrecy, the letters were partly in simple code in which Cecil was designated by the number 10, Howard by 3, the King by 30, Queen Elizabeth by 24, Ralegh by 2 and Cobham by 7. Number 2 received a good deal of attention.

The three correspondents were a remarkable group. Lord Macaulay once said of James that he was the kind of monarch sent into the world by the Almighty for the specific purpose of hastening revolutions. The statement betrays Macaulay's Puritan sentiments, but many in England, then and later, would have agreed. James, like Cecil, was a cripple; his legs were ricketty and he walked with a hitch and a waddle, usually leaning on the arm or shoulder of a favourite. He drank too much; spittle drooled from the corners of his mouth when he talked or ate. He had some obscure fear of water and would not wash or bathe; occasionally he lightly rubbed his fingertips on a wet napkin. He disliked changing his clothes and his uncoordinated movements at table left them in such a condition that one courtier said if he slept for seven years and then waked he could tell what the king had eaten every day.

He was a physical coward, but intelligent enough to remove some of the sting of reproach by simply admitting his cowardice. As a boy he had seen harsh faces by lantern light which also gleamed off armour and shield; there were continual broils to see who would control his person. Like Elizabeth, he soon perceived that he possessed a mystical body which had strange properties and attractions; whatever party of noblemen possessed it, also possessed that invisible treasury of power. Once an assassin had drawn a sword to kill him; James had grappled and screamed, and held the sword point away from his body until help arrived. And now because he was afraid of steel, he wore quilted doublets so thick that an ordinary stiletto could not pierce them. His breeches were stuffed with padding and protected by plates. He looked grotesque and he smelled like a crowded barracks. He hated 'the sight of a soldier or any valiant man'.

But men must have some pleasure: James's physical pleasure

was whisky; his intellectual pleasure was witchcraft. When he was to marry Anne of Denmark, her first attempt to sail to his nervous bed was precluded by a storm. The Danes, knowing that such storms were the work of witches, burned a few of them. James then sailed to Denmark and led the fair Anne back to Scotland. Hearing what had been done in Denmark, on his return he instituted a witch hunt of his own. Ultimately he discovered three covens, thirteen people to a coven, or thirty-nine witches and warlocks in all. On All Hallows night at North Berwick, they had danced in the churchyard (men had once been turned to stone for doing that in Cornwall). Geilie Duncan, a maidservant, had piped for them and after they were caught James asked her to play the same tunes for him. He listened fascinated. The witches had gone through the standard set of spells. They had hanged a toad and extracted its 'venom' by roasting it; they had some of the King's dirty bed linens which they used to make a charm; they had gone in solemn procession to the sea shore where they had flung a black cat alive into the surf for the express purpose of keeping apart the willing Anne and the reluctant James. Finally, they had made a waxen image of James which was to be melted slowly in the flames. All of this came out during their trial, and something more: it was discovered that the Earl of Bothwell had once been the leader of a coven of witches at North Berwick and so treason and witch-craft had gone hand in hand. Indeed, Satan himself had appeared, telling the witches that 'the King is the greatest enemy he hath in the world'. Inasmuch as this coincided with an opinion James had already formed, he was predisposed to accept it.

James deserves both sympathy and understanding. He never knew his father, and he was separated from his mother while he was still a child. His tutor, the stern 'new humanist' Buchanan, seemed more interested in convincing the prince that his mother was a Romish whore than in teaching him anything humane. Deprived of love, the boy had no masculine image on which to model himself except his tutors who, as he said, taught him to speak Latin before he could speak Scots. He naturally developed after the image of his tutors and became himself a pedant and scholar, a good one too, but he never flowered as a man.

When he was thirteen, there came from France his cousin, Esmé Stuart, Seigneur D'Aubigny who 'descended upon that armed and Calvinistic court, an adorned wonder of a brilliant civilization'. His polished manners, his relaxed ways that contrasted so strongly and pleasantly with the Calvinistic moral tension, his sweet and mellifluous tongue, all charmed James, for he had one thing in common with his mother, a love of the French manner. From the first meeting, James would hardly leave young Stuart's side. As they walked together, he nibbled his ear, kissed his cheeks. His hands, even in public, were perpetually busy in the most embarrassingly private places, fondling himself or his favourite. James's sex life is even more complex than that of Elizabeth. It is unthinkable, given the Scottish temper, that he could have been a sodomite and still remained king: he was never accused of active homosexuality. He married; he laboured dutifully, if distastefully, upon the body of his Queen and brought forth progeny; he never took a male favourite without first securing the Queen's consent. But if he was not a homosexual, he was certainly epicene and women repelled him.

By 1601 James had already paid a high personal price to keep his title to the English throne clear. To pacify England and the English party, he had sent Esmé Stuart back to France. And when his mother had been executed, and every nobleman in Scotland seemed to want to march against England to assuage an outraged national pride, James had shown great restraint and had received much abuse for it. In 1588 the messenger from Elizabeth had promised him something; there could be little doubt of what it was.

James may have been a grotesque king, but his ideas were by no means grotesque. He knew that Scotland was a backwater, an impoverished nation that had done little more than serve as a base for intrigue, whereas England was a world power. If the two kingdoms were united and peace with Spain were secured, what was not possible ? He meant to have the throne and to get it he would negotiate with anyone and promise anything. Among Catholics he talked like a Catholic, among Protestants he sounded not like an elder of the kirk, but not unlike an Anglican bishop.

The question naturally arises as to why Cecil and Ralegh opposed James. Distrust of his relations with the Catholic Church and with Spain were reasons enough. James had been baptized as an infant into the Catholic Church by his mother; he had later repudiated that baptism and undertaken one more in keeping with his position in the land of the covenant, but many were still suspicious of him. Spanish and French gold had always been at work in Scotland; and when some northern earls were found guilty of conniving with Spain, James sentenced them to death for treason and then did not execute the sentence. His representatives in Venice, Rome, and Madrid were assuring all who would listen that James was ready to receive instructions in the Catholic faith. Upon hearing of this, Father Parsons had cried out in his Jesuitical zeal, 'May Jesus Christ make him a Catholic for he would be a mirror to all the princes of Christendom'. One could hear further rumours almost any week that James did not even intend to await Elizabeth's death, and his flirtations with his martyr, Essex, were known to everyone.

In May, 1601, when Cecil first offered his services to James, the chief supporter of the King's title in England was Henry Howard, a crypto-Catholic who had been favourably inclined toward Mary Stuart. How subtly and unerringly the hidden affinities in men seek each other out! Howard, like James, was sexually ambivalent; he was also, like James, a pathological coward; like James he was learned in the esoteric mazes of theology. But while it is easy to see good qualities in Cecil and James and to find valid reasons for their conduct, it is impossible to find any excuse for Howard. An intellectual, he was unusually endowed with malice and envy; the poverty he had known as a poor relative of a noble house had soured his nature very early. Perhaps it was his own physical weakness that gave him sadistic pleasure in destroying reputations and spreading

Lady Elizabeth Throckmorton, Ralegh's wife. The queen's wrath descended upon Ralegh when she learned that he had married her secretly and of necessity hastily, for he had not only been unfaithful to his Cynthia, but had dishonoured one of her high-born ladies in waiting. That storm passed, and Ralegh found that he had won a treasure — patient, affectionate, courageous, and utterly loyal to him through all vicissitudes, which only drew them closer together. *(Courtesy of the National Gallery of Ireland)*

Edmund Spenser, friend and fellow poet, who used his gifts to reconcile Ralegh with his royal mistress. *(Radio Times Hulton Picture Library)*

Robert Cecil, Secretary of State, who sacrificed his friendship for Ralegh to his ambition. *(The National Portrait Gallery, London)*

hatred and contempt. It was he who had broadcast the story that William Cecil's daughter, married to that appalling cad, the Earl of Oxford, was with child by some other man. Without the courage to face an enemy, he would take that enemy's name and reputation into a writing closet and treat it the way the witches had treated their wax image. There his malicious and poisonous pen would destroy the image of the man in the hopes of destroying the man himself. That was his forte. Probably no one was ever more superbly and savagely hated than was Ralegh by Howard, who wrote James long, rambling, incoherent letters that even James found tedious: they were, he said, Asiatic and endless. Elizabeth would never have allowed such a man in her Court. But James was linked with Howard by subtle bonds, and he already feared Ralegh. To anyone else the letters would have seemed absurd; but they did not seem so to him.

Henry Howard seldom mentioned Ralegh in these letters without creating an image of hell; in some underground cavern, the demons, with Ralegh as their leader, were concocting new and terrible charms which are to keep James from his throne as he had once been kept from his bride. In one of the letters, Howard conjured up, for his superstitious sovereign, a grand scene in hell. Presiding as Prosperine was, surprisingly, that hearty Westcountry matron Bess Ralegh; serving under her were Ralegh, Cobham, and the Earl of Northumberland, 'a diabolical triplicity, that denies the Trinity, of wicked plotters hatching treason from cocatrice eggs that are daily and nightly sitten upon'. Treason and witchcraft – James could understand that combination. Again Howard reported that hell had never vomited up such a couple as Ralegh and Cobham, and Ralegh, he said, 'is the greatest Lucifer that hath lived in our age'. Thus the great hunter of witches was continually presented an image of Ralegh as an agent of the devil, or as the devil himself.

Having read some of Howard's letters before they were sent on to James, Cecil realized that, in his own interest, he must repudiate his former friend. He is far more restrained than Howard, but he writes James that Cobham and Ralegh talk wildly about the succession; he, Robert Cecil, puts a stop to such talk. Ralegh continually asserts that James has the right of the succession but he is only being clever: he wants to be on the winning side. Further, if King James ever hears Ralegh speak well of Cecil, he must not assume that the two are friends. And finally, knowing James's piety, Cecil self-righteously hints at Ralegh's atheism, a charge he, of all men, knew to be false. He risks offending God, Cecil tells James, in supporting a man who is generally thought to be an atheist, but he does it only out of private affection. It would be interesting to hear Bacon's comment on that. But James was won over by Cecil and he wrote to him, 'Your suspicion and your disgracing shall be mine'. This search for the new source of power at the end of Elizabeth's life was like the first battle of galleons in narrow waters. There were no known rules for it; the cleverest, the toughest, and the most devious would survive.

Shortly after Essex was put to death in 1601, James asked the Earl of Lennox to seek out Ralegh and try to engage his favour. Ralegh, still playing a game that had lost its meaning, responded in the grand but hopelessly outmoded style that he was so indebted to and enamoured of the divine Elizabeth that he could not seek favour elsewhere. James, not understanding the old courtly game, held this as a proof of Ralegh's enmity to him. Ralegh, pleased with himself like a schoolboy, went to Robert Cecil, told him what he had done, and asked him to pass it on to the Queen. Without the quiver of an eyelid, Cecil replied, 'You did well, and as I myself would have made answer, if the like offer had been made to me'. Compared to the cold suavity and the cynical expediency of that reply, Ralegh seems a child indeed. As to letting the Queen know about it, Cecil reminded Ralegh that she was getting old and suspicious; she might think the Scots had discerned a weakness in Sir Walter before they approached him; and even if she did not think that, she would be sure to think that his motive was merely to 'pick a thank'. It would be better to say nothing. And so Ralegh lost all round.

Sir Walter was never deep in any conspiracy to keep James from the throne. The truth is that everyone who ever reported to James said that Ralegh always acknowledged his title, a fact

Ralegh was repeatedly to stress at his own trial. The Earl of Northumberland, one of Howard's 'diabolical triplicity', a long acquaintance but not particularly a friend of Sir Walter, wrote James a letter that judiciously summed up Ralegh's attitude and character.

I needs must affirm Ralegh's ever allowance of your right, and although I know him insolent, extremely heated, a man that desires to seem to be able to sway all men's courses, and a man that out of himself, when your time shall come, shall never be able to do you much good or harm, yet must I needs confess what I know, that there is excellent good parts of nature in him.

Meanwhile, as Cecil drew away, Ralegh became closer to Lord Cobham. Why he should have been attracted to that rash and silly man is one of the puzzles of Ralegh's career. One finds superficial reasons: he was a peer and very wealthy; for some reason Elizabeth favoured him, so he must have had some personal charm; he was Cecil's brother-in-law. Perhaps having no other friends or supporters among the peerage, Ralegh thought Cobham would be useful to him. But the two were behaving foolishly. In a sensitive and delicate time when the transfer of power from a dying sovereign to her successor was being effected, both were rash in their talk and indiscreet in their behaviour. Cecil once said that Ralegh and Cobham showed every man's letter to every man. Obviously none of the new men would have anything to do with such flamboyant indiscretion. Ralegh, as ever, was guilty of proud speech. 'Let us keep the staff in our own hands,' he is reported to have said, 'and set up a commonwealth and not remain subject to a needy, beggarly nation.' What he must have said privately about James's appearance, his love life, his cowardice and superstition, we can only guess.

But in one thing Ralegh was extremely cautious. He would never talk with Cobham about the succession when anyone else was around. He was under the misapprehension that the old statute was still valid that required two witnesses before a conviction for treason could be obtained. It no longer applied, however, and all Ralegh's conduct accomplished was to add one more suspicious circumstance to his association with Cobham. Because the two men were together so much, because there were so many meetings and assemblies at Durham House, and so much indiscreet talk, it was impossible to believe that Ralegh and Cobham were not entirely in one another's confidence. Ralegh almost certainly must have known that Cobham had been talking with Count Aremberg of Spain about a fantastic sum of money which would be used in England to favour Spanish interests. But there is no evidence and none was ever produced at his trial to indicate that Ralegh himself was more involved in Cobham's improbable negotiations than to be aware that they were going on.

At last the devious plotting, the tantalizing uncertainty, came to an end. In March of 1603, Elizabeth began to act strangely; she would sit in silence for hours and would speak with no one except the Archbishop of Canterbury; she would take no medicine and she would not lie down because she had a 'persuasion' that she might never rise again. Hour after hour, day after day, she sat propped on pillows, staring into space. After four days, three members of the Privy Council went to speak with her; they had already made arrangements for James's succession, but Cecil wanted definite approval from Elizabeth. The accounts vary in detail, but all agree that she did nominate James before she died on March 24. Immediately the Privy Council called in many of the leading men of the nation to draw up an address of welcome to James. Ralegh and Cobham, who were present, had the bad judgment to bring up the matter of how many Scots the King might be allowed to bring south with him. All were anxious to please the new king, however, and the matter was dropped. Ralegh signed the address of welcome.

A proclamation was then issued, forbidding persons holding public office to resort to the King while he journeyed to London lest the business of the State suffer. It was generally believed that this proclamation was aimed at Ralegh who, however, ignored it and met the King's retinue at Burleigh House. As an excuse he said that he had come to ask the renewal of his wardenship of the Stannaries and his lieutenancy of Cornwall. James promised letters of continuance and told his clerk to deliver them speedily so that Ralegh could leave at once.

The surviving anecdotes about this first meeting of King and Captain are not inherently improbable. When Ralegh was introduced to him, James said, 'On my soul, mon, I have heard rawly of thee'. Again, the King is said to have boasted that he could have taken England by force if need be. Ralegh replied that he wished it had been put to the trial, for 'you would then have known your friends from your foes'. And – John Aubrey comments – for this Sir Walter was neither 'forgotten nor forgiven'. Indeed, Aubrey says that Ralegh was 'such a person (every way) that . . . a prince would rather be afraid than ashamed of. He had that awfulness and ascendancy in his aspect over other mortals'.

Almost immediately Ralegh was removed from his Captaincy of the Guard and it was given to a Scotsman. James could not be expected to continue in such an office a man whom he feared and it was reported that 'Sir Walter in a very humble manner did submit himself'.

On May 7, all monopolies were called in until they could be examined, again a wholly predictable procedure in no way aimed specifically at Ralegh. But it meant that he lost the income from the farm of his wines until the matter was resolved. As partial compensation, however, Cecil told him that the 300 pounds a year which he paid the Crown for his governorship of the Isle of Jersey would be forgiven. It was a conciliatory gesture.

But there was nothing conciliatory in the matter of Durham House. On May 31, Ralegh was informed that he would have to leave. It is difficult to quarrel with the decision, for the house did not belong to him; the Queen had hectored it out of the Bishop of Durham; now there was a King who preferred bishops to knights. What incensed Ralegh, however, was that he was given only a week in which to move, an impossibly short time. He pointed out that he had spent 2,000 pounds in improving the house and had stored it with food and provender for forty men and twenty horses for a year. He asked for six months or at least a quarter's notice. Finally he was granted three weeks and he moved. He did, therefore, have some cause for annoyance, but he still retained all of his other titles and perquisites. He was Lord Lieutenant of Cornwall, Vice-Admiral of Devon, Governor of Jersey, and he had his various estates, including Sherborne.

But Ralegh still wanted to be counsellor and maker of policy. When James went on his first triumphal progress, he came to Beddington Park, the home of Sir Nicholas Carew, Lady Ralegh's uncle. There, with a flourish, Ralegh handed James a treatise entitled *A Discourse Touching a War with Spain*. It was a well-reasoned discourse wholly oriented to the Elizabethan outlook, but scarcely the thing to give a king dedicated to a Spanish peace. Ralegh's main concern was that James, in his desire for peace, might discontinue aid to the Netherlands. If he did, Ralegh said, the embittered Netherlanders would be powerful enemies, not only in warfare but also in trade. If England continued to support the Low Countries, Ralegh was sure that the King of Spain would not have the resources to resume active warfare against England.

It is hard to believe that Ralegh could have been so naive as to think that this was a way to become the King's counsellor. It probably both frightened and angered James. Next, Ralegh casually told him that he would take the West Indies for him if he liked and would even raise two thousand men at his own charge for the expedition. Ralegh could not have been serious, for he had not the means to equip such a force. One is almost tempted to think that he was enjoying making James uncomfortable, but it is more likely that he was simply trying to impress him in the style of an earlier, and now irrelevant, age.

All of this time, somewhere in the background, treason was actually being plotted. Ralegh was almost certainly unaware of it, but thanks to his unsavory public reputation and his careless association with Cobham, a net was being spun around him. In 1602, two Catholic priests named Watson and Clarke, hearing of James's much advertised interest in Catholicism, had interviewed him and believed they had secured some promise that he would ease the heavy restrictions against Catholics. They were particularly concerned about the fines against recusants and the penalties against Jesuits and seminary priests. But after James was crowned, when someone mentioned the possibility of a further rapprochement with the Catholic party, James had replies, 'Na, na, we'll no need the Papists noo'. The Catholic priests, naturally feeling betrayed, began to organize a conspiracy for which Father Watson recruited two impecunious swordsmen, Sir Griffin Markham and Anthony Copley.

In the meantime, a Protestant plot to procure relaxation of restrictions on the practice of religion was also brewing, this one under the leadership of George Brooke, Lord Cobham's brother, and the young Lord Grey of Wilton. Grey, a malcontent and apparently a *philosophe* on the subject of liberty, thought James should be forced to permit certain latitude of religious worship: it was of Brownists and Puritans he was thinking, but the desire for toleration provided some tenuous common ground with the Catholic plot (though there is no reason to think that either desired tolerance toward the other). The intermediary between these two unlikely conspiratorial allies – and the only connection between them – was George Brooke.

This strange two-headed plot was never very well defined or organized, and the two parties were never in effective communication with one another. In fact, they were carefully kept from knowledge of each other. Grey told Markham that he would not speak his name before the Puritans, and Markham, in turn, was not to mention Grey before the Catholics. Each group believed it could use the other in executing its own plan without bringing the other into partnership or even into confidence about the real purpose.

Though later treated as parts of one plot, each group had its own plan of action. The Catholic plotters, knowing that in Scotland the seizure of the King's person was not technically treasonous, apparently intended to take the King, guard his life and treat him well, but to put the members of the Privy Council in the Tower. Those evil counsellors who had 'misled the King' would ultimately be put to death, but James would remain King and they his loyal subjects. While he was under their control, the Catholic plotters would demand three things from him: their own personal pardons, toleration of religion, and assurances that Catholics would be placed in positions of power. The plotters had privately agreed on how the high offices of England should be divided among themselves. Actually, under English law, the entire plot was treasonable.

Lord Grey had a different plan, to be backed up by military force. He believed that he could take control of a regiment of soldiers who were being mustered for service in the Low Countries. He would come to the King ostensibly to present a petition and then, backed by the troops, enforce his demands. Grey later admitted that he had entered into an initial conspiracy but, when he learned that the true plans had been withheld from him, he withdrew. It may very well have been so. And after he was arrested, he wrote to his Puritan mother and assured her that he had not assisted any Papists. He had listened to them, he said, merely to discover their designs and then execute a purpose of his own, 'good to the King, to the state, and, as I hold, justifiable before God and Man'.

This disorganized double plot, huddled up by talkative incompetents and malcontents, was soon known to the government and the plotters were seized, arrested, and interrogated. Ralegh's name kept recurring in their testimony. Grey, the most reliable man among the plotters, swore that he had never conferred with either Ralegh or Cobham. But George Brooke immediately incriminated his brother, Cobham, Ralegh's closest friend. Under interrogation, the terrified priests, although denying that they had ever talked with Ralegh, said that they had thought of him as one who might be favourable to their cause. And they had spoken of the possibility that he might seize the Royal Navy. They reported further that Lord Cobham had spoken terrible words about killing the king 'and all his cubs'. And George Brooke believed that his brother had been set on to saying such things by Sir Walter Ralegh. Clearly there was no direct evidence against Ralegh, but there were enough indirectly incriminating circumstances that the Privy Council decided to call Ralegh in for questioning. The Council put to Ralegh the principal question first. Did he know of any practices between his friend, Lord Cobham, and Count Aremberg of Spain ? This was a critical moment. For to know of a treason and fail to reveal it was misprision of treason. If Ralegh had made a frank confession of whatever he knew at this point, it is doubtful that the Council would have proceeded further against him. But that would have meant the betrayal of his friend whose negotiations with Spain were so grotesque that they could scarcely be taken seriously. Besides, informing did not become a man from the older and heroic generation. Unwisely, Ralegh decided to deny all knowledge of such negotiations. It was a lie and a mistake and the moment he uttered it he was guilty of misprision of treason.

The next day he had some second thoughts. It was common knowledge that on several previous occasions Count Aremberg had approached Lord Cobham on behalf of the Archduke, and Cobham had sensibly reported the fact to both James and Cecil. The King had been annoyed that Cobham was busying himself with matters that did not concern him, but there was nothing treasonable in these reported activities. Ralegh, therefore, wrote an innocuous letter to Cecil saying that he had, after all, recalled that on one occasion, Cobham had left Durham House to visit La Renzi, one of Aremberg's suite of followers. Ralegh must have assumed that Cobham, if questioned about this visit, could blandly reply that Cecil and the King already knew about his contacts with Aremberg. Ralegh's letter in no way incriminated Cobham; it was merely an attempt to extricate himself from vulnerability to a charge of misprision of treason.

But Ralegh had again failed in his judgment of a man's character. With his usual cleverness, Cecil said nothing to Cobham. He merely handed him Ralegh's letter. The pathetic Cobham, supposing that Ralegh had betrayed him, went to pieces. 'O traitor Ralegh!' he cried. 'O wretch! I will utter it all;

it is you that have procured me to this villainy.' Then, in a most agitated manner, he told Cecil and the Council that he was to go abroad and obtain some 600,000 crowns from the Archduke and the King of Spain. With that money in his possession, he would return to England, stop at the Isle of Jersey and confer with Ralegh about how it could effectively be spent on behalf of Spain.

Cobham had scarcely finished blurting out his self-pitying justification when he changed his story and exculpated Ralegh; and that ambivalence was the one constant feature of his conduct throughout the trial. He would accuse, and then exonerate, and then accuse again until all anyone knew for certain was that Cobham was a fool and a weakling and that Ralegh was a bigger fool for having had anything to do with him.

The Privy Council had not been impressed by Ralegh's denials, and now they had a full confession which implicated him directly in the Cobham negotiations with Spain, known as the Main Plot, and which indirectly and circumstantially linked him to the plot of the priests and Lord Grey to obtain religious toleration, known as the Bye (or secondary) Plot. He was placed under arrest and, for the second time in his life, taken to the Tower of London to await charges.

Elizabeth was dead, as was her beloved betrayer, Essex. Of the great, daring men she had loved and honoured, only Ralegh was still alive, and he was in prison under charges of treason. The new men were taking over the reins of power in the new age, Cecil secure as Privy Councillor, Francis Bacon about to begin his brilliant rise to Lord Chancellor. If one considers the characters and traits of the coming men – James I, Howard, and Bacon, all effeminate, James and Cecil both cripples, unable any of them to pursue virtue in the classical sense, all except James calculating and free from emotional impulse – and set them against the larger molds of Essex and Ralegh with their heroic weaknesses, the conclusion is predictable: Essex and Ralegh would end on the scaffold and the new men, capable enough if not very likeable, would rule England. Given the curcumstances, it was inevitable. Fortune, too, is bound by necessity.

17

The Justice of the Realm

A man accused of treason was allowed no legal assistance nor was he even informed of the specific charges against him until the trial began. Consequently Ralegh had to be his own lawyer and prepare an entirely hypothetical defence. At no time during his life was he so completely vulnerable to a capricious fortune, for, having studied no law at the Inns of Court, he was ignorant of recent developments in the treason laws. Even during the trial he continued to hold doggedly to his mistaken belief that he could not be convicted for treason without the testimony of two witnesses. But he was wrong.

His mistake involved him in a cruel irony, for the treason law he was relying on had been repealed as the result of the actions of his father-in-law. Sir Nicholas Throckmorton had been an intimate friend of Sir Peter Courtenay, one of the plotters in Wyatt's rebellion whom the elder Ralegh had carried to France. But worse, he had appended his signature to the Letters Patent which, on the death of Edward VI, would have limited the succession of the Crown to Lady Jane Grey and her descendants. These and other suspicious actions in the time of Mary had brought Sir Nicholas to the edge of the block where he was saved by a trick of the law.

Back in the days of Edward III the statutes governing treason demanded the life of any subject who plotted the death of the king or who engaged in an overt act that was intended to depose him. Conspiracy without an overt act was not a capital offence. But, under Henry VIII, a series of new laws had been enacted to secure from danger the caprices of that capricious monarch. Under law, it became treason to slander the king's marriage or

331

any future marriage he might make. It was treason to say that any of his former marriages had been valid, or to call him a heretic, or to uphold the authority of the Pope in religion. Such laws, once Henry was gone, were an embarrassment. Most of them had been repealed under Edward VI although when Mary came to the throne it was still treason to uphold the Pope's authority in religion; she repealed that law hastily, and then only the statutes of Edward III were left in force. By those statutes Sir Nicholas was tried.

It was perfectly clear, in the course of the trial, that he had not engaged in any overt act to depose Mary, whatever preferences he may have shown for the Protestant party. Under the laws in force he was not guilty of treason; an English jury stoutly so held to the distress of Mary's government, which imprisoned the jury and the defendant.

As a result of Throckmorton's escape, new and stringent treason laws were enacted; with these laws Ralegh was unfamiliar. And so it was Sir Nicholas who had inadvertently fashioned a cleaver for the head of his son-in-law.

When Ralegh found himself in the Tower again, he was at first too distraught to make any efforts for his own defence. His keeper, Sir John Peyton, said that he had never seen a man with so strangely dejected a mind. Ralegh would send for him five or six times a day, but his speech was agonized and incoherent; Peyton concluded that Sir Walter's fortitude would not be sufficient to 'support his grief'. Peyton appeared to be right, for one day at dinner, Ralegh seized a knife from the table and stabbed himself. He knew that if he died before he was attainted of treason his lands and goods would not be forfeit to the Crown. Suicide seemed the only way to protect the future of his wife and son. The attempt, however, was more ritualistic than real; Cecil came immediately to see the wound and said it was really a cut under the left pap rather than a stab. However, it effected a kind of psychological release, for within a few days the keeper was assuring the Lords of the Privy Council that Ralegh seemed to be healed both in body and mind. And now his mind began to work.

His first strategem was to send Lawrence Keymis to see Cobham and try to convince him that Ralegh had never accused him, but, in fact, in his most recent appearance before the Council, had tried to clear Cobham of treason. Keymis was also to inform Cobham that under the law 'one witness could not condemn a man for treason'. Keymis carried out his errand, but the unstable Cobham revealed the details of the interview to the Privy Council whose suspicions about Ralegh were further confirmed. They had Keymis arrested and threatened with torture; and he, too, confessed the collusion. It was customary in that time to hold incommunicado prisoners who were indicted for treason: whatever Ralegh was to do, he must do covertly and illegally.

Undeterred by the failure of Keymis, Ralegh soon won the friendship of young John Peyton, the son of the keeper, who was charmed by Ralegh as a man and as a symbol of the glamorous past which he had unfortunately missed being born into. Cobham complained to this young man that Ralegh had injured him while he had never done Ralegh any ill. Peyton answered in some surprise that Ralegh had said precisely the opposite. Obviously the two men needed a better understanding and John Peyton served as their mediator. How much communication went on between the two prisoners is not known, but Ralegh later was to say in his casual way of dropping bombshells that while in the Tower he had been in touch with Cobham every day. Once again the Privy Council discovered the intrigue and Sir John Peyton was relieved of his duties; the sins of the son were visited upon the head of the father. To soothe Peyton's injured feelings, the Council bestowed upon him Ralegh's governorship of the Isle of Jersey; at the same time, they released Ralegh as Lord Lieutenant of Cornwall. It is apparent that the Privy Council was not awaiting a jury's verdict before making up its mind concerning Ralegh's guilt.

The new keeper was Sir George Harvey and soon his young son also became attracted to Ralegh; he, too, began to serve as mediator between the two prisoners. Ralegh wrote a moving letter to Cobham, reminding him again that the life and the fortunes of his family rested solely on Cobham's word; he begged for a letter which would exculpate him. He pinned the letter to an apple and had it thrown in to Cobham's window. He heard nothing in reply. Through young Harvey and a Tower servant, Edward Cottrell, Ralegh continued his appeals until the vacillating Cobham finally sent him such a letter. But Ralegh was not entirely satisfied with it; through his mediators, therefore, he again asked Cobham for a letter that would unequivocally assert his innocence. Finally Cobham sent him another letter; Ralegh read it, was satisfied, folded it and put it in his bosom. It was to be his secret evidence; he believed that he would find a dramatic moment at the trial in which to produce it and that its effect on the jury would be decisive. After that he rested easier.

Cobham's conscience was still not at rest and so he wrote a letter to Sir George Harvey saying that as God was his witness, his conscience was troubled for having accused Sir Walter. This was evidence that should have been turned over to the Privy Council immediately. But Sir George had learned that his son had served as mediator for Sir Walter; he realized that Peyton had lost his job under similar circumstances, and so he suppressed the letter; its contents were not revealed until the trial was over and Ralegh had been reprieved from the scaffold.

What Harvey did not know, nor did Ralegh, was that the pathetic fool, Cobham, had revealed everything to the examiners who, as soon as they had secured all the information, imprisoned young Harvey and extracted from Cobham still another letter which post-dated the one given to Ralegh. The new letter declared that as Cobham hoped to be saved, Ralegh was guilty as he had originally declared. The Attorney-General carefully filed this letter; it was to be his conclusive evidence against Ralegh and he expected its effect on the jury to be decisive. Knowing nothing of this letter, Ralegh was entirely unprepared for it.

In the many weeks of questioning, not much new evidence had been developed; even so, the Privy Council found the case against Ralegh convincing. George Brooke and the priests had both indicated that they had considered him a likely conspirator.

On the other hand both Lord Grey and Sir Griffin Markham, an eccentric but honourable knight, had denied that Ralegh was a conspirator. Both said emphatically that they would have had nothing to do with any project Ralegh was mixed up in on grounds of intense personal dislike. Thus there seemed little chance of convicting Ralegh for implication in the Bye Plot.

The Main Plot was another matter. Cobham had admitted that he had asked Count Aremberg for some 600,000 crowns to be given to disaffected persons. Cobham also had told La Renzi that if he could secure such a sum 'he could show him a better way to prosper than by peace'. Because the Archduke Albert, Aremberg's master, did not have money enough to pay his troops, a fact well-known to everyone, the incredible sum Cobham was dickering for could only be obtained in Spain. He, therefore, was to go to Spain, receive the money and stop at the Isle of Jersey where he would confer with Sir Walter Ralegh. In support of this one unstable witness, the state had a written deposition from La Renzi which said that Ralegh had been in company with Cobham when the latter had received letters from Aremberg. But, what was more convincing to everyone, it was common knowledge that Ralegh and Cobham had been inseparable companions for a long time, that much vaunting speech had come from both of them, and therefore a strong preconception existed that Ralegh, if not a plotter, at least had knowledge of a plot and therefore was guilty of misprision of treason. That was the general opinion before the trial began.

That summer the plague was running a virulent course; from the docks at Southampton, Gravesend, Sheerness or Margate, wherever ships touched and rats ran ashore, it burned its way toward the centre of London. In the poorer, crowded sections it burned with a terrible intensity and soon 2,000 people a week were dying from it. The fever found its way into the Tower where it moved from cell to cell until the Privy Council feared it more than the treason they were investigating. They therefore ordered that the fall term of the Court should be held not in London, but rather in Winchester, some sixty-five miles to the southeast on the edge of Salisbury Plain. The prisoners of the

335

Bye Plot were sent down under the guard of fifty light horse. On November 10, Sir Walter, with Cobham's letter still secure in an inner pocket, was put in a coach under the charge of Sir William Waad and another gentleman.

His keepers had been uneasy about the possible reaction of the populace, whose hatred of Ralegh had become a national mania. They had therefore stationed trained bands along the route they were to take through the city and even well into the suburbs. Even so, their precautions were not enough. It was unbelievable that in a time of such deadly plague, crowds would assemble for any reason, but the people were there to cry out their hatred of the man who had betrayed the canonized Essex and who had now himself been caught in a treason. The mob howled; they threw tobacco pipes, stones, and mud. They pressed around the carriage screaming, shaking their fists, shouting obscenities and threats. It was, Sir William Waad said later, 'hob or nob'. If one 'hare-brain fellow' had started an attack, Ralegh would have been torn to pieces; nothing could have prevented it. The prisoner, however, was unperturbed; he gave no sign that he even saw the angry multitude. Later he wrote, 'Dogs do always bark at those they know not, and it is in their nature to accompany one another in those clamours. So it is with the inconsiderate multitude'.

This was the nadir of Ralegh's life and fortune. Accused of a treason he had not committed, loathed by his countrymen for an execution he had not been responsible for, he was also, as he himself said, almost without a friend left in England. Sir John Harington believed that he was already a dead man. 'I doubt the dice be not fairly thrown, if Ralegh's life be the losing stake.'

The trial was to be held at Wolvesey Castle, the palace of the former Bishops of Winchester; there a jury of twelve citizens was impanelled. Three names on the list of the original jurors were erased and written over. It was said later that they were the names of three men not considered entirely safe and they were, therefore, 'changed overnight'. In addition to the jury, Ralegh was to be heard by a special commission consisting of four judges and seven laymen. The judges were the Lord Chief

336

King James I, painted by Paul Van Somers *(Uffizi)*. Physically weak, cowardly, brilliant, superstitious, scholarly and devious, James disliked and feared the brashly forthright, masculine Ralegh, and made no place for him in the new court. Suspicious of Ralegh's loyalty, he sought a way to get him permanently out of the way. Eventually he found it, and Ralegh went to the scaffold. *(Radio Times Hulton Picture Library)*

The great jurist Sir Edward Coke, as the Crown's Attorney General, prosecuted Ralegh with savage and rough-shod insistence on a flimsy and perhaps rigged charge of treason. Later, when he became Chief Justice of the Common Pleas, he courageously and stubbornly championed the integrity of law and due procedure even against the king himself. Here he is seen in his judge's regalia, with the black four-cornered cap almost covering the white coif, and his chain of office resting on his judicial robes. *(Radio Times Hulton Picture Library)*

Justice of England, Sir John Popham; Sir Edward Anderson and Justices Gaudy and Warburton. Of the seven laymen, five, under modern procedures, undoubtedly should have disqualified themselves. The most shocking presence there was that of Lord Henry Howard, who had so savagely poisoned James's mind against Ralegh; and there was Robert Cecil, already prejudiced but, as it turned out, the fairest of all the panel. Charles Blount, Lord Mountjoy, was there, a kinsman of the Blount who had tried to kill Ralegh, and formerly one of Essex's closest friends; Sir William Waad, Ralegh's keeper, a man who personally detested him; Sir John Stanhope, newly appointed Vice-Chamberlain, a man too weak in such a situation to do other than read the King's mind. That left two members who by a fair procedure could be considered impartial: Lord Wotton and Lord Thomas Howard, who had sailed with Ralegh at Cadiz and in the Islands Voyage.

The chief prosecutor was the Attorney-General, Sir Edward Coke. He was as tall as Ralegh, gaunt, red-faced, with a hawk nose and piercing blue eyes. Both he and Chief Justice Popham had at one time been Speaker of the House of Commons, a very great distinction, and Coke was, even at this time, England's greatest legal scholar. He had the kind of temperament not uncommonly found in scholars where immense learning is combined with a fanaticism which identifies its own interests and beliefs with the universal rule of right. His chief duty as Attorney-General was to uphold the King's prerogative. Later, when he was made Chief Justice of the Common Pleas, he was, by virtue of his office, the principal defender of the Common Law and within three months he was attacking prerogatives that he had formerly so zealously upheld. As late as 1648 men were still remarking the wonderful change that had occurred in him.

It is a wonder that Sir Edward Coke, Lord Chief Justice, should differ from Mr. Attorney Coke, for we know his thoughts in Sir Walter Ralegh's time and his speeches in Charles I's time; they are as different from each other as the times were.

Zealots of real ability are always capable of exerting immense

337

influence on behalf of the cause which finally comes to absorb their complete energies and to which they give their entire devotion. Coke was no exception. He ultimately did more to advance the idea of freedom under the rule of law and due procedures than any man in English history, including Ralegh himself. It is unfortunate for his memory that we must see him when his zeal was more dubiously engaged.

The trial began. The Clerk read the names of the Commissioners and asked the prisoner to raise his hand in order that he might be identified. Then the Clerk read the indictment; it was long and loosely worded, but it was clear that Ralegh was not being accused of misprision of treason as might have been expected. He was being charged with high treason. The indictment alleged that Ralegh had conspired to deprive the King of his government and raise up sedition; to alter religion by bringing in the 'Roman superstition'; to procure foreign enemies to invade the kingdom. It further alleged that he had conspired to bring Arabella Stuart to the throne; he had agreed that Cobham should seek 600,000 crowns in the furtherance of sedition. As part of the plot in which he was to be engaged, Arabella Stuart was to be persuaded to write three letters, one to the King of Spain, another to the Archduke Albert, and a third to the Duke of Savoy. In the letters she was to ask support of her claims to the throne and promise in return to establish peace between England and Spain, to tolerate the 'Roman superstition', and to be ruled by the three monarchs in the matter of her marriage.

There was more. Ralegh had caused a book to be published which was against the 'just title of the King'; he had given this book to Cobham. Further Cobham had promised Ralegh 8,000 crowns of Spanish money and Ralegh had consented to accept it.

When the indictment was finished, Ralegh knew the charges at last, and he was asked if he took exception to any of the jury.

Ralegh: I know none of them; they are all Christians and honest gentlemen; I except against none.

He was given no opportunity to challenge any of the commissioners, who were all noblemen or men of state. Compared

338

with them, the jury were insignificant pawns. Although he took no exception to the jury, Ralegh did make a request. He said that his memory was weak, that he had recently been ill, and he prayed therefore that he might answer each point in the indictment as the Attorney presented it, rather than being required to answer a long, general charge. The Lord Chief Justice denied the request; the King's Counsel, he said, must present all of his evidence first; then Sir Walter, if he wished, might address himself to each particular.

The opening address to the jury was made by King's Sergeant Heale. It was a strange mixture of innuendo and pomposity. The jury, he said, had heard of Ralegh's 'bloody attempts' to kill the king and his royal seed. The indictment, of course, had not alleged any attempt or any overt act, merely a threat reported at second hand.

Next Heale pointed out that on June 9, Cobham, who looked upon Ralegh as a god or an idol, had conspired with him to procure an invasion of England which was intended to dethrone James. As Heale thought of England without James, he was overcome. 'In our king,' he said, 'consists all our happiness and the true use of the Gospel,' whatever that meant. 'As for the Lady Arabella,' he continued, 'she, upon my conscience, hath no more title to the Crown than I have, which before God I utterly renounce.' Heale's renunciation of his own claim to the throne caused Ralegh to smile, and he was not alone. But Heale was oblivious to smiles; he was thinking only of how fine his rhetoric would sound when it finally reached the royal ear. And so he went on. Cobham, as everyone knew, was an insular man; he had no experience abroad; he was incapable of executing a plot. But Ralegh was something else. He was a man of great wit, a swordsman, one who understood military tactics; he was the very man needed to make the plot effective. And so these matters in the indictment, were they bred in a hollow tree? With that last irrelevant rhetorical flourish, Heale announced that there was one who could speak better than he on these matters. It is doubtful that he expected the jury to believe him, but the man to whom he had referred was Sir Edward Coke.

The Attorney began well; both lawyers and laymen would have found his statement of intent admirable and convincing. We have no preconceptions at this trial, he said; we will condemn no man but upon 'plain evidence'. Then he launched into a long, highly discursive account of the Bye Plot. At the end of his narration he tried to make his speech relevant by saying that the two treasons 'were like Sampson's foxes, which were joined in their tails, though their heads were severed'.

According to Popham's ruling, Ralegh should have remained silent until all the evidence was presented, but he did not. He spoke out indignantly, 'You gentlemen of the jury, I pray remember, I am not charged with the Bye, being the treason of the priests'.

In response, Coke entered into a long and pedantic historical discussion, rambling through generations of English history to show that treasonable men, in the past, had frequently and cunningly made use of priests to effect their purposes. It was irrelevant and, worse, it was tedious. At the conclusion, he said that treason was to be determined by two things: the end at which it aimed and the means used. The end of Ralegh's treason, he said, was to kill the King, and here Coke paused in order that he, like Sergeant Heale, might say a few gracious words concerning James whose nature was sweet and bounteous, 'whose thoughts are innocent, whose words are full of wisdom and learning, and whose works are full of honour'. And certainly he had depicted James as James might have wished himself to be. Then Coke turned to Ralegh and, for the first time, brought in the note of personal malice and contempt, 'But to whom do you bear malice ? To the children ?'

Ralegh was stunned, 'To whom speak you this ? You tell me news I never heard of'.

Coke: Oh sir, do I ? I will prove you the notoriest traitor that ever came to the bar. After you have taken away the King you would alter religion, as you Sir Walter Ralegh have followed them of the Bye in imitation, for I will charge you with the words.

Ralegh: Your words cannot condemn me; my innocency is my

defence. Prove one of those things wherewith you have charged me and I will confess the whole indictment.

There was a striking contrast in the tone and manner of the two men. Coke's voice boomed throughout the chamber; he assaulted the ears of his auditory as he was assaulting Ralegh. Sir Walter, on the other hand, had always had a thin voice that did not carry. The listeners were inwardly retreating from Coke's shouting and then leaning forward to hear Sir Walter. Psychologically the advantage, as far as the listeners were concerned, was with the prisoner. Men in the audience were straining to catch his words. He was briefer than Coke and pithier, and he remained poised and courteous. But when he had replied to that first wild insult, he had put all the force of his voice on one word, *Prove*. The Attorney had said that was what the Crown intended to do, bring plain evidence. But none had been brought forward yet.

It is difficult to know what there was in Sir Walter's reply or demeanour that so outraged Coke. It is possible that being the brilliant lawyer he was, he knew that he had a shaky case and that his future might hinge on the King's opinion of how forcefully he was able to present it. Whatever it was, he lost all restraint. 'Nay, I will prove all: thou art a monster; thou hast an English face, but a Spanish heart.'

Sir Edward could shout with a voice of doom until the day of doom, but that was simply one charge no Englishman, however much he hated Ralegh, would ever believe. Nor would he believe the foolish allegation that Ralegh intended to bring in the Catholic religion. Human credibility stretches very far, but it has its outer limits.

Ralegh: Let me answer for myself.
Coke: Thou shalt not.

Coke did not mean that Ralegh should not be given a chance to reply. He meant rather that the Chief Justice had ruled that he must not interrupt. But it was a bad reply and it caused an uneasy stirring in the courtroom.

Ralegh: It concerneth my life.

The Chief Justice interrupted to assure Ralegh that he would have his chance to reply but that properly he must allow the King's Attorney to finish. Coke was pleased. He gloated, 'Oh, do I touch you?' It was another invitation to Ralegh to reply, but he remained silent. The Attorney-General then weakened his case somewhat by acknowledging that the money from Spain was to be used to procure a peace. If that was so, it might be shameful for an Englishman to take it, but scarcely treasonable. Coke, however, said that any peace procured by money was dishonourable.

Then he launched into another long harangue to the effect that Ralegh had wished to make Arabella Stuart a titular Queen who would actually be his 'stale', that is, servant to his wishes. But that word with its ugly overtones was unfortunately chosen inasmuch as Arabella herself was in court under the protection of the Lord High Admiral, Charles Howard. Again Ralegh was surprised, as most of the court must have been, by the violence and brutality, by the coarseness of Coke's prosecution.

Ralegh: You tell me news, Mr. Attorney.
Coke: Oh sir! I am the more large, because I know with whom we have to deal; for we have to deal today with a man of wit.
Ralegh: Did I ever speak with this Lady?
Coke: I will track you out before I have done.

Then, with a heavy-footed transition to a new charge, Coke, apparently intending to be clever, said that Englishmen would never be persuaded by Ralegh's words; so he had used books to persuade them. This rather obscure reference was meant to lead into the matter of the treasonable book which Ralegh had allegedly given to Cobham. Ralegh caught the meaning and replied that the book had not been written by himself, but rather by one of Mr. Coke's profession, that is, a lawyer.

Coke: I would not have you impatient.
Ralegh: Me thinks you fall out with yourself. I say nothing.

342

Coke knew that Ralegh's possession of the book was perfectly legal. To possess a book written against the title of a claimant to the throne was certainly anyone's right, and the book had been written many years before Elizabeth had died. But Coke intended to use the alleged gift of the book to Cobham as proof of the fact that Ralegh was the leader of the plot. Cobham, he said, was a nobleman with a fine reputation. Ralegh, on the other hand, was a Machiavelli, a politician, a swordsman who thought that he had created a sanctuary for treason. This was Coke's first good phrase and his first telling point. Ralegh, he pointed out, would never talk about the succession with anyone except Cobham alone. Furthermore, the prisoner had sent Lawrence Keymis to Cobham in the Tower to say that one witness could not condemn him. Obviously there had been collusion between the two men while they were in prison, but Coke, typically, strained a valid point by calling that collusion one of the most horrible practices 'that ever came out of the bottomless pit of the lowest hell'.

Coke then turned to the verbal retraction that Cobham had once made of the charges against Ralegh. He could explain to the jury, he said, why Cobham had made that retraction. Sir Walter Ralegh was so odious a person that Cobham was afraid to confess any association with him for fear that it would worsen his position. Further Cobham knew that if Ralegh were freed, he himself might be cleared. There was more abuse until finally Ralegh broke in passionately, 'I will wash my hands of the indictment and die a true man to the King'.

Coke: You are the absolutest traitor that ever was.
Ralegh: Your phrases will not prove it.

And as the audience leaned forward to hear Ralegh, again they caught that emphasis on the word *prove*.

Coke now went off on another tangent. Cobham, he said, had written a letter to Robert Cecil and asked a servant to put it in a Spanish Bible in order that it might appear to be found by chance. The point he was making was that Cobham was not clever enough to have thought of such a thing and therefore had

343

done it at the instigation of 'this viper'. Cecil was immediately interested. He had never seen Cobham's letter, he said.

Coke: No, my lord, you had it not. You, my masters of the jury, respect not the wickedness and hatred of the man, respect his cause: if he be guilty, I know you will have care of it, for the preservation of the king, the continuance of the Gospel authorized, and the good of us all.

It was all so irrelevant, so circling and confused. The mind couldn't get hold of just what the Attorney was charging the prisoner with.

Ralegh: I do not hear yet, that you have spoken one word against me; here is no treason of mine done. If my lord Cobham be a traitor, what is that to me.
Coke: All that he did was by thy instigation, thou viper; for I thou thee, thou traitor.

We would give much to know if Will Shakespeare had made the journey down to Winchester and heard that famous piece of pomposity in person. Whether he did or whether he only heard of it later, he could not resist poking fun at it. *Thou* was the familiar form, suitable only for servants and inferiors. Coke's use of it implied that Ralegh was his inferior which a good many people might be inclined to doubt. In any case, this bit of silliness appears again when Sir Toby Belch urges the foolish knight, Sir Andrew Aguecheek, to send a mortal challenge in writing to his rival. 'If thou *thou'st* him some thrice it will not be amiss.' Coke, in plain fact, was making a fool of himself and Ralegh's reply was effective.

It becometh not a man of quality and virtue to call me so. But I take comfort in it, it is all you can do.

In other words, if Coke had any evidence, he would have produced it; lacking evidence, he had resorted to invective.

Coke: Have I angered you?
Ralegh: I am in no case to be angry.

344

Lord Chief Justice: Sir Walter Ralegh, Mr. Attorney speaketh out
of the zeal of his duty for the service of the King, and you
for your life; be patient on both sides.

After this exchange, the Clerk read Cobham's first examination in which he confessed that he would go to Spain, get
600,000 crowns and return to Jersey. In this confession,
Cobham said that Ralegh would never leave him alone concerning the matter. Here Coke stopped the Clerk and asked him
to read that sentence again. But this particular examination
also concluded with a statement which was in Ralegh's favour.
Cobham deposed that he was never sure that he would go to
Jersey because he feared that Ralegh might deliver both him
and the money to the King. When the Clerk had finished reading
Cobham's examination, Ralegh again broke in.

Let me see the accusation: This is absolutely all the evidence [that]
can be brought against me; poor shifts. You gentlemen of the jury,
I pray you understand this. This is that which must either condemn
me or give me life; which must free me, or send my wife and children
to beg their bread about the streets. This [it] is that must prove me a
notorious traitor, or a true subject to the King.

Then Ralegh made his first lengthy reply to the charges.
He repeated that he knew nothing of Cobham's dealings with
Count Aremberg. (The Privy Council had not believed him
when he made this denial first, and no one else ever has except
his sentimental biographers.) As for Arabella Stuart, he knew
nothing of any plot concerning her. He then spoke of Cobham.
Much of the prosecution's case rested on the assumption that
Cobham was a simple man and therefore must have been ruled
by Ralegh who was chief conspirator.

Is he so simple? No, he hath a disposition of his own; he will not
easily be guided by others; but when he has once taken head in a
matter, he is not easily drawn from it; he is no babe.

The whole idea of his engaging in a plot, said Ralegh, was
unreasonable.

345

Is it not strange for me to make myself Robin Hood or a Kett or Cade? I knowing England to be in better estate to defend itself than ever it was. I knew Scotland united; Ireland quieted wherein of late our forces were dispersed; Denmark assured, which before was suspected. I knew that having lost a lady whom time had surprised, we had now an active king, a lawful successor, who would himself be present in all his affairs.

A lady whom time had surprised. He was worth leaning forward to listen to, this man. It was a rich phrase, neither malicious nor sentimental, but charged with implications coming from the man who had written so well about the late Queen and her imperviousness to mutability. Even now it is difficult to think about the last two or three years of Elizabeth's reign without remembering Ralegh's phrase.

Then Ralegh began to speak of Spain, of the long struggle of England against Philip and of his own part in it. Just recently, he said, he had written a discourse against peace with Spain and had presented it to His Majesty. Spain, if anyone had forgotten, had suffered six repulses, three in Ireland and three on the high seas. He did not need to mention that he had participated in one of those in Ireland and in all of those on the high seas. Nor did he even mention Cadiz; he didn't have to. The victory there was his if it was any man's as everyone knew well enough.

I knew the King of Spain to be the proudest prince in Christendom; but now he cometh creeping to the king my master for peace. I knew whereas before he had in his port six or seven score sail of ships, he hath now but six or seven. I know of 25,000,000 he had from his Indies, he scarce hath one left.

All of these things Ralegh had said in the *Discourse* which he had once pressed into the hand of the dismayed James.

Then Ralegh made the most convincing argument in the entire trial. Everything, he said, hinged on whether he had in fact conspired with Cobham to receive 600,000 crowns from the King of Spain, a fantastic sum of money. (It was common knowledge that Spain had recently declared bankruptcy once again. Her credit was worthless; the treasure heaps from the New World were diminishing.) Was it rational, Ralegh asked,

346

to believe that a king would hand over to a man like Cobham that kind of money when there were no firm plans, no pledges for security?

Was it ever read or heard that any prince should disburse so much money without a sufficient pawn? I knew her own subjects, the citizens of London, would not lend Her Majesty money without lands in mortgage.

And Queen Elizabeth had loaned money to the French or Dutch only when jewels were pledged or cautionary towns delivered up.

Up to this point everything Ralegh said was so sensible that few could have doubted it. He was clear and convincing. But then he swore again that he had never dealt with Cobham in anything except matters of business such as purchasing land and buying books. Here he was not candid; common knowledge would override his testimony. If Cobham had openly confessed so much, Ralegh must have known something. That the plot was quixotic, everyone was prepared to believe; but that Ralegh knew nothing of what Cobham was doing was simply too much to accept.

The crucial point in the trial had been reached. There was one witness; his testimony flatly contradicted that of the accused. Which was to be believed? Ralegh again invoked the protection of the law. He asked first that he not be condemned without two witnesses, and he further asked that his accuser be brought into court to face him. Ralegh was certainly wrong on the first point of law; all the judges were agreed on that point and later English courts of law subsequently upheld their position. Ralegh's casual assurance on this point had simply betrayed him. On the second point, however, the right to face his accuser, there is some doubt. Later, when Coke came to write his *Institutes*, one of the great works of English legal history, he said that the statute requiring an accuser to appear and avow openly the truth of his testimony concerning treason was still valid. In other words, on this point, Coke changed his mind a quarter of a century after Ralegh's trial, but during the trial itself he would not hear of it.

347

Ralegh: You try me by the Spanish Inquisition, if you proceed only
by the circumstances without two witnesses.
Coke: This is a treasonable speech.

A modern legal historian has said that Ralegh was in error
here also; he would have been allowed much better judicial
procedures in a court of the Spanish Inquisition.

Ralegh could see that he was being hedged in by 'tricks 'of
the law, and so he began to enunciate a metaphysical and
theological concept of law that he would continue to develop
throughout the trial.

Good my lords, let it be proved, either by the laws of the land, or the
laws of God that there ought not to be two witnesses appointed . . .
If Christ requireth it, as it appeareth by Matthew XVIII, if by the
canon, civil law and God's word it be required, that there must be
two witnesses at the least, bear with me, if I desire one. I would not
desire to live if I were privy to Cobham's proceedings. I have been a
slave, a villain, a fool, if I had endeavoured to set up Arabella . . .
But urge your proofs.

It was that uncomfortable word again that the Attorney was
having such a difficult time with. And the Puritans in the
audience were fidgeting uneasily about that Biblical injunction
which says that truth is to be established in the mouths of two
or three witnesses.

The Lord Chief Justice informed Ralegh that his understanding of the law was erroneous; the laws and statutes he had
cited requiring two witnesses had been repealed.

Ralegh: It may be an error in me; and if those laws be repealed, yet
I hope the equity of them remains still; but if you affirm it,
it must be a law to posterity. The proof of the common law
is my witness and jury; let Cobham be here, let him speak
it. Call my accuser before my face and I have done.

Coke ignored the second part of Ralegh's plea, that uncomfortable and moving cry to face the man who had accused him. He
returned, rather, to the demand for two witnesses and he began

in Latin: *Scientia sceleris est mera ignorantia.* The knowledge of the wicked is ignorance. Ralegh, he said, had trusted in the fact that he could not be condemned without two witnesses. It was the 'sanctuary of treason' theme again and it was forceful. In reply, Ralegh dropped the request for the witnesses but urged his right to face Cobham.

Ralegh: I beseech you my lords, let Cobham be sent for, charge him on his soul, on his allegiance to the king; if he affirm it, I am guilty . . . The king at his coronation is sworn, *In omnibus judiciis suis aequitatem, non rigorem legis, observare* [to observe all the equity of the laws and not merely their rigour.]

Lord Chief Justice: [It is] the justice of the law; else when a man has made a plain accusation, by practise he might be brought to retract it again.

Ralegh: O my lord, you may use equity.

Lord Chief Justice: That is from the King; you are to have justice from us.

Now, Lord Cecil realized that the trial had again fallen into wrangling and debate; Ralegh was not remaining silent as he should. Cecil suggested that Sir Walter be given a tablet and pen and ink to assist his memory. He could note down the points he wished to refute and allow the trial to proceed properly.

The Clerk of the Court then read Ralegh's examination. In it he had confessed that Cobham had once offered him 8,000 crowns for the furtherance of peace between England and Spain and that he was to have the money in three days. But Ralegh said that he had not consented; rather he had said 'When I see the money, I will tell you more.' He further said that he thought this had been one of Cobham's 'idle conceits' and, therefore, he had taken no account of it. The Clerk finished his reading and Lord Henry Howard then asked a difficult and damaging question. Why, he said, should you have given any ear to Cobham about receiving pensions in matters whereof you are not concerned?

Ralegh: Could I stop my Lord Cobham's mouth?

349

It was not a good answer. It was an evasion of the only important matter the trial had yet developed. Ralegh, realizing that the trial hinged on the conflict of testimony, again begged that his accuser be brought to face him and that he be not condemned by circumstantial evidence without witnesses. Cecil was plainly uneasy. He did not know the law personally, he said, and would like to hear all four judges speak to Ralegh's point. They all agreed and Justice Warburton gave the most convincing reply. Supposing, he says, that a king is murdered, and someone is seen coming out of his chamber with a bloody sword; there are no witnesses, but circumstances will condemn him. 'I marvel, Sir Walter, that you being of such experience and wit, should stand on this point.'

This gave Ralegh an opening to speak about the conception and meaning of law in the broader sense, a conception that was being ignored that day in Winchester. He began, 'I know not how you conceive the law'.

Lord Chief Justice: Nay, we do not conceive the law, but we know the law.

He did not know the law Ralegh was talking about and his slightly pompous rebuke did not deter Ralegh.

The wisdom of the Law of God is absolute and perfect . . . But now, by the wisdom of the state, the wisdom of the Law is uncertain.

Now, at least some of his auditors knew what he was driving at. A brilliant thinker, Richard Hooker, had not invented this concept of the law, but he had made it known to every literate man in the nation. Against the Puritan assertion that the mind of God can only be known from the Bible, Hooker had developed a concept of *logos* theology. In this concept, God is the great mind coiled in upon itself which, out of love and not necessity, decided to impart its goodness to the unstructured chaos of material things. In his mind, therefore, God conceived the pure forms, the structure of all things. In their totality these forms were a harmonious whole, a vision of rationality, a pure manifestation of a Pure Mind.

It was these thoughts, pure as crystal in the Mind of God, that formed the basis for all law, and they had a three-fold reflection. First, they were reflected in the laws of nature, by which the stars wheel and the seasons change; they were also reflected in the mind of man where the faculty of reason is the indwelling *logos*. Most dimly and most uncertainly the Mind of God was also reflected in the positive law, the laws of states, which are only valid as they reflect that ultimate Law which is their source. This is a Law far above courts and statutes and sovereigns; it is a living entity always receiving fresh access of power from the Mind of God which ultimately must validate or reject all positive law. The only real test man ever had for the validity of the positive law was to measure it against his own reason and also against the Word of God for the higher law was reflected in one and revealed in the other.

This was the mystique of Law to which Ralegh was appealing. What the court was doing to him that day was irrational; it also was contrary to Biblical injunction. By both known tests, the 'wisdom of the state' there displayed failed to conform to the Divine Wisdom. And nothing was more unreasonable than the failure of the court to allow him to confront the man whose accusation imperilled his life.

Indeed, where the accuser is not to be had conveniently, I agree with you; but here my accuser may; he is alive and in the house. Susanna had been condemned if Daniel had not cried out, "Will you condemn an innocent Israelite, without examination or knowledge of the truth?"

Ralegh's eloquence is manifest, but it is easy to underestimate the power of a metaphysical argument. Whatever points of law he lost that day, he nevertheless carried his auditory and posterity with him. A condemned man, they thought, was entitled to something more than precise legalities; he was also entitled to rational and just procedures.

Lord Chief Justice: You plead hard for yourself, but the laws plead as hard for the King. I did never hear that course to be taken in a case of treason as to write one to another or to

speak one to another during the time of their imprisonment.
There hath been intelligence between you; and what under-
hand practise there my be, I know not. If the circumstances agree not with the evidence, we will not condemn
you.

Ralegh: The King desires nothing but the knowledge of the truth,
and would have no advantage taken by severity of the law.
If ever we had a gracious king, now we have; I hope as he is,
such are his ministers. If there be but a trial of five marks at
common law, a witness must be deposed. Good my lords,
let my accuser come face to face and be deposed.

But again Ralegh's plea was rejected by the court. Coke then
made the rather artificial point that the law presumes a man will
not accuse himself in order to accuse another. In fact, he said,
when a man accuses someone else and himself at the same time,
that accusation has the force of many witnesses. Coke then
continued with his presentation of the evidence and began to
read Copley's examination. 'Now,' he said, 'let us come to those
words "of destroying the king and his cubs" '.

Ralegh: O barbarous! If they, like unnatural villains, should use
those words, shall I be charged with them? I will not hear
it; I was never any plotter with them against my country;
I was never false to the crown of England. I have spent
4,000 pounds of my own against the Spanish faction, for the
good of my country. Do you bring the words of these hellish
spiders, Clark, Watson and others against me?

Coke: Thou hast a Spanish heart and thyself art a spider of hell.

Coke then read testimony by George Brooke in which he
admitted that his brother had talked of killing the King and his
progeny. But Brooke believed all this had been infused into his
head by Ralegh. At this point Ralegh protested vigorously. This
was the wildest hearsay and opinion without a hint of evidence
to support it. But again he was over-ruled; two of the commissioners cited precedents for admitting such evidence. When
Ralegh replied, his voice was firm and everyone in the hall
heard him this time, 'If this may be, you will have any man's
life in a week'. And some men, suddenly, began to put them-

selves in Ralegh's place. What if they were on the stand, their life at hazard, and the unsupported opinion of a hostile witness was allowed in evidence against them. Later, a viewer of the trial said that at one point, which he did not specify, the auditory began to hiss Edward Coke who was greatly shaken by it. Certainly by now sentiment had begun to shift to Ralegh.

Coke returned to Cobham's examination and to the allegation that Ralegh had given him a book against the King's title; at the same time Cobham admitted that Ralegh had told him the book was foolishly written. Ralegh again interrupted Coke to insist, and truthfully one feels, that he did not offer the book to Cobham; rather, he said, Cobham saw it on his table and picked it up. Lord Henry Howard asked where Ralegh got the book and Sir Walter replied that he had it from the library of William Cecil. Robert Cecil immediately took alarm, for James would certainly hear of this bit of evidence. He said Ralegh must have taken the book without his father's knowledge; furthermore, as First Secretary, his father had a duty to read all libellous things, including the many libels written against the late Queen. Ralegh equably replied that he, too, had read all of the libels printed against her. Reading of a libel did not imply concurrence in it and by Cobham's own testimony Ralegh had not concurred in the book against the King's title.

Ralegh: Here is a book supposed to be treasonable; I never read it, commended it, or delivered it, nor urged it.
Coke: Why this is cunning.
Ralegh: Everything that doth make for me is cunning and everything that maketh against me is probable.

Coke dropped the subject of the book and shifted to the serious charge that Ralegh had sent Keymis to Cobham to urge him to retract. Ralegh still had Cobham's written retraction in his pocket, but its effect, when produced, would be diminished if it could be established that he had 'practised' with Cobham. And so instead of answering the charge, he created a momentarily successful diversion by charging that Keymis had confessed only because he had been threatened with torture.

353

In England, at this time, there was much pride in the fact that, unlike France and Spain, torture was not a common or even a usual practice; it could only be applied with the consent of the sovereign. To the assembly it therefore appeared, if Ralegh was right, that James had ordered torture. Henry Howard was immediately outraged. Keymis, he shouted, was never on the rack. It was a shifty reply for Ralegh did not say he had been racked, merely that he had been threatened. 'The King,' Howard continued, 'gave charge that no rigour should be used.'

The Commissioners: We protest before God, there was no such matter intended to our knowledge.

Ralegh: Was not the Keeper of the Rack sent for, and he threatened with it?

Sir W. Waad: When Mr. Solicitor and myself examined Keymis, we told him he deserved the rack, but did not threaten him with it.

This was a sad business, and no one was going to believe Waad's fine distinction. If the Keeper of the Rack had been sent for, and Waad did not deny it, it is obvious that there was a threat.

The Commissioners: It was more than we knew.

Lord Cecil then spoke. Cobham, he said, had confessed to hearing from Ralegh every day. Ralegh replied that he had indeed sent Keymis to Cobham but only on private business and he had never bidden him speak the words about one witness. Keymis, Ralegh said, had added those words himself. It was an obvious lie. Keymis was a loyal and brave man, faithful to Ralegh, although likely to become confused in times of stress. He likely had blurted out the truth; he had no reason to do otherwise. And it is doubtful that the threat of the rack disturbed him as much as Ralegh wished to have it thought.

While Ralegh was speaking, Coke tried to interrupt, but Lord Cecil intervened. 'It is his last discourse; give him leave, Mr. Attorney.'

354

Ralegh: My lords, vouchsafe me this grace: let [Cobham] be brought, being alive, and in the house; let him avouch any of these things, I will confess the whole indictment and renounce the King's mercy.

It was a strong plea and a desperate gamble. But Ralegh had Cobham's retraction and he did not think Cobham could very well deny in public such a strongly worded document. Coke said again that the law was against Ralegh.

Ralegh: It is a toy to tell me of law; I defy such law; I stand on the fact.

Cecil spoke again. He wished to make it clear that Arabella Stuart was not being charged. She was as innocent, he said, of all these things as he himself or any man here. Her only part in the plot was that she had received a letter from Lord Cobham which she had immediately delivered to the King. Then grizzled old Charles Howard arose and addressed the court. Arabella Stuart, he said, whom he had himself brought into the court, 'doth here protest upon her salvation, that she never dealt in any of these things; and so she willed me to tell the court'. What a flimsy charge it was! The Main Plot, after all, was the supplantation of James by Arabella and she had never known of it, never even exchanged a word with Ralegh. Again it all went back to intent, and Ralegh's treasonable intent was alleged by one witness, who was even then almost within hearing, and whom the prosecution would not produce.

This distraction concluded, Cecil wished to pursue Ralegh's offer concerning Cobham.

Cecil: If my lord Cobham will say you were the only instigator of him to proceed in the treasons, dare you put yourself on this?

Ralegh: If he will speak it before God and the King, that ever I knew of Arabella's matter or the money out of Spain or the surprising [Bye] treason, I put myself on it, God's will and the King's will be done with me.

Cecil: If he say you have been the instigator of him to deal with

355

the Spanish king, had not the Council cause to draw you hither?

Ralegh: I put myself on it.

Cecil: Then Sir Walter call upon God and prepare yourself; for I do verily believe my lords will prove this.

But Coke was not ready to prove it yet. He had some more shabby evidence to present first. A man named Dyer, who had been a pilot in Lisbon, had met there a Portuguese gentleman who had told him that Don Ralegh and Don Cobham were going to cut the King's throat.

Ralegh: What infer you upon this?

Coke: That your treason hath wings.

It was inconceivable that the judges should have allowed in evidence such prejudicial and unsupported hearsay. And Ralegh's reply was firm and convincing.

Consider you, gentlemen of the jury, there is no cause so doubtful which the King's counsel cannot make good against the law. Consider my disability and their ability; they prove nothing against me, only they bring the accusation of my Lord Cobham, which he hath lamented and repented as heartily as if it had been for an horrible murder . . . Presumptions must proceed from precedent or subsequent facts. I have spent 40,000 crowns against the Spaniard. . . . If I had died in Guiana, I had not left 300 marks a year to my wife and son. I that have always condemned the Spanish faction, methinks it is a strange thing that now I should affect it. . . . If you would be contented on presumptions to be delivered up to be slaughtered. . . . If you would be contented to be so judged, judge so of me.

Sergeant Philips said that it was now a matter of who was the more credible witness. Philips thought he knew. Ralegh, he said, had as much wit as any man could have and yet he had been able to do nothing except assert his innocence. The bare denial of the defendant, he said, must not move the jury. If Ralegh's appeal to the concept of Law as an embodiment of the Divine Rationality had reached any hearts at all, this must have been a shocker. Ralegh was there alone, without counsel or friends, with a packed jury and a hostile commission. His only conceivable hope of proving his innocence lay in facing his accuser and cross-examining him; yet under the law that was denied him. What could he do other than assert his innocence? But, according to Philips, the accused must prove his innocence.

Ralegh: If truth be constant, and constancy be in truth, why hath [Cobham] forsworn that he hath said? You have not proved any one thing against me by direct proof, but all by circumstances.

Coke: Have you done? The King must have the last.

Ralegh: Nay, Mr. Attorney, he which speaketh for his life must speak last. False repetitions and mistaking must not mar my cause. . . . I appeal to God and the King whether Cobham's accusation be sufficient to condemn me.

Coke: The King's safety and your clearing cannot agree. I protest before God I never knew a clearer treason.

Again Coke had spoken to excess. The treason was anything but clear. But Ralegh, driven to desperation, also went too far. 'I never,' he said, 'had intelligence with Cobham since I came to the Tower.' It is difficult to know why he persisted in this lie, but it was probably to uphold the validity of the document he still intended to produce. But everyone, by now, knew that Ralegh had communicated with Cobham and most of them probably did not blame him. It was a matter of his life.

Coke: Go to, I will lay thee upon thy back for the confidentest traitor that ever came at a bar. Why should you take 8,000 crowns for a peace.

It was not alleged that Ralegh had taken the money and Cecil spoke, 'Be not so impatient, good Mr. Attorney, give him leave to speak'.

Coke had been hissed by the people and now he was being chided by the Commission. He was a sensitive man and rather easily upset; now he sat down 'in a chafe' and refused to continue the case. Several of the commissioners pleaded with him, but he would not. It was a tense moment. If Coke had continued to refuse, one of the Sergeants could have gone ahead with the prosecution but it would have looked very bad. 'After much ado,' as the Court reporter has it, Coke made a 'long repetition' of all the evidence. When he came to repeat 'some things' the prisoner, who still refused to be coerced or intimidated, interrupted him again and Coke became livid. He raged and shrieked.

Coke: Thou art the most vile and execrable traitor that ever lived.
Ralegh: You speak indiscreetly, barbarously and uncivilly.
Coke: I want words sufficient to express thy viperous treasons.
Ralegh: I think you want words indeed, for you have spoken one thing half a dozen times.
Coke: Thou art an odious fellow, thy name is hateful to all the realm of England for thy pride.
Ralegh: It will go near to prove a measuring cast between you and me, Mr. Attorney.

At this there must have been laughter in the court. Coke was behaving like a fishwife and Ralegh like a gentleman. And the gentleman was winning.

Then Coke decided to play his trump. He drew from his pocket Cobham's latest retraction. The Lord Cobham, he said, 'who of his own nature was a good and honourable gentleman, till overtaken by this wretch'; that good and sweet lord, to disburden his conscience before God and out of duty to the King, 'upon his salvation that he wrote nothing but the truth', had deposed that Ralegh had wanted a pension from Spain of 1,500 pounds a year. He further affirmed that Ralegh had affixed a letter to an apple and thrown it into his window. Also Ralegh had sent him word not to be like the Earl of Essex who had revealed everything, at the end, to a preacher. Coke now wished to be memorable. That apple, he said dramatically, was like Adam's apple whereby the Devil did deceive. His tone grew elevated. The Son of God, he said, would be glorified this day by the unmasking of this traitor. You have conquered O Galilean, he thundered in Latin (*Vicisti Galilaee*), the phrase attributed to Julian the Apostate whose resemblance to Ralegh he was now suggesting.

He went on. 'Oh, damnable atheist,' he cried. Essex, he said, had died the child of God. Coke, of course, had bullied Essex at his trial just as he was bullying Ralegh now, not as savagely perhaps, but it was only a matter of degree. Atheism, betrayal of Essex, highly emotional charges not even mentioned in the indictment were surreptitiously brought in to support and give credence to the charge of treason.

Cobham's letter was entered as evidence. Ralegh sat stunned. He seemed entirely dejected and could not rally his spirits from this last blow. Some observers thought he might not speak again. After a little, he confessed in a weak and tired voice, that he had given a servant a letter to deliver to Cobham. All the letter contained, he said, was one line: 'You know you have undone me, now write three lines to justify me.' The Lord Chief Justice broke in to ask about the matter of the pension from Spain. Ralegh did not reply directly. He merely said that Cobham was a 'base, dishonourable, poor soul'. The Lord Chief Justice then said, 'I perceive you are not so clear a man as you have protested all this while; for you should have discovered these matters to the King'. His words were serious; very serious. But they indicated misprision of treason rather than high treason.

Now, it was life or death. Ralegh reached into his pocket and brought forth the letter Cobham had written to him. He begged Lord Cecil to read it aloud; Lord Cecil was Cobham's brother-in-law; he could certify that the handwriting was Cobham's and the letter genuine. However distasteful it must have been for Cecil, he could not refuse. He took the letter and read:

Seeing myself so near my end, for the discharge of my own conscience, and freeing myself from your blood, which else will cry vengeance against me, I protest upon my salvation I never practised with Spain by your procurement; God so comfort me in this my affliction, as you are a true subject for anything that I know. I will say as Daniel, *Purus sum a sanguine hujus* [I am now free of your blood]. So God have mercy upon my soul, as I know no treason by you.

Ralegh was the first to break the silence that ensued. 'Now I

359

wonder how many souls this man hath.' Poor Cobham, sworn and forsworn, a coward and a fool, apparently at the mercy of whatever man was most recently with him. The courtroom was buzzing now; the commissioners were talking among themselves; the court reporter simply gave up and fell back on his familiar formula, 'Here was much ado'. Coke shouted that Ralegh's letter had been cunningly extracted whereas the prosecution's letter 'was simply the truth'. It was a transparent lawyer's trick, but the Lord Chief Justice supported him and the Earl of Devonshire assured the jury that Cobham had not been given any hopes of pardon. That was almost certainly a falsehood.

But Ralegh had had the last say as he intended to all along. There was no more evidence. The jury retired and began to deliberate. While they were out the thoughts of an intelligent observer would likely have ranged themselves in this fashion: Ralegh, despite his earlier denials, had obviously had intelligence in the Tower with Cobham and that fact impugned, to some degree, the validity of his letter. Also, despite his denials, Ralegh must have known of Cobham's fantastic plans to secure 600,000 crowns from the King of Spain. At worst, therefore, Ralegh was guilty of misprision of treason. On the other hand, if the money Cobham was to secure was for peace and not for sedition, Ralegh was guilty of nothing more than bad judgment. The charges of his desiring to alter religion were absurd; the alleged plot to put Arabella on the throne was too flimsy to need denial; no connection with the plotters of the Bye had been established. On the testimony of an obviously perjured witness, he still stood accused. He had been outrageously bullied by the prosecution; he had been denied the most elementary forms of fair play. And yet everyone knew what the verdict would be.

It took the jury just fifteen minutes to reach that verdict. Guilty of treason. When the news was carried to Coke, who was outside in the garden, he is reported to have expressed surprise, saying that he had only accused Ralegh of misprision. Coke could not have said that, for it was obviously not true, but he may have said that misprision was the verdict he expected.

The Court asked Ralegh if he had anything to say.

Ralegh: I submit myself to the King's mercy; I know his mercy is
greater than my offence. I recommend my wife and son of
tender years, unbrought up, to his compassion.

Now the Lord Chief Justice had to pass sentence. He had some
words prepared that came rather easily to those trained in the
classics. It was best, he said, for man not to climb too high nor
yet aim too low. Two vices had lodged themselves in Ralegh,
ambition and covetousness. Further, the world believed that
Ralegh held 'heathenish and blasphemous opinions', such
opinions as the Chief Justice could not repeat because Christian
ears could not endure to hear them; in fact, anyone who held
such opinions could not be permitted to live in a Commonwealth. All of this sermonizing to a beaten man was irrelevant
to the matters which the Court had heard.

Then the Chief Justice intoned those terrible words that
terminated Ralegh's legal existence and were intended to terminate his life.

Since you have been found guilty of these horrible treasons, the
judgment of the Court is that you shall be had from hence to the
[Tower of London], there to remain until the day of execution; and
from thence you shall be drawn upon a hurdle, through the open
streets, to the place of execution, there to be hanged and cut down
alive, and your body shall be opened, your heart and bowels plucked
out, and your privy members cut off and thrown into the fire before
your eyes; then your head to be stricken off from your body and your
body shall be divided into four quarters to be disposed of at the
King's pleasure: and God have mercy on your soul.

'Mercy' was a lonely word in that savage ritual which had been
designed to keep ambitious men from thinking deep thoughts
about the head which wore the bright circlet.

Soon there were reactions from the auditors. Sir Dudley
Carelton, who was at the trial, said that Sir Walter had 'answered
with that temper, wit, learning, courage and judgment, that
save it went with the hazard of his life, it was the happiest day
that ever he spent'. Carleton was sure Ralegh would have been
acquitted if he had not already had such a bad name, and

Popham's gratuitous remarks about atheism and ambition would lead one to think that Carleton was right.

Two men rode immediately to Windsor to convey the news to the King. He was pleased with the verdict, but uneasy about the rest of what he heard. Sir Roger Ashton, the first man to reach him, told him 'that never any man spoke so well in times past, nor would do in the world to come'. One of James's own Scottish knights was the second man there and he informed his perplexed sovereign that he himself had been so inflamed with the common hatred of Ralegh that he would have ridden a hundred miles to see him hanged. Now, having seen and heard the man, he would ride a thousand miles to save his life.

Carleton recorded that remarkable contrast in the public attitude toward Ralegh at the beginning and the end of the trial. 'In one word, never was a man so hated and so popular in so short a time.'

Unlike Lord Grey, who had also been condemned, Ralegh begged for his life. Letters he must have written to other lords of the Council have been lost; those to Cecil and the King survive. To Cecil he wrote that it was a heavy burden to be executed for allegedly serving the King of Spain whom he had despised so long.

If ought remain of good, of love, of compassion toward me, your Lordship will now show it when I am now most unworthy of your love and most unable to deserve it. For even then is love, true honour, and true virtue expressed. And what I shall leave to pay of so great a debt, God will perform to your Lordship and yours.

To James he wrote that it was part of the duty of a just prince to hear the complaints of his vassals, even those in the greatest misery.

Save me, therefore, most merciful prince, that I may owe Your Majesty my life itself than which there cannot be a greater debt. Lend it me at least, my sovereign Lord, that I may pay it again for your service when Your Majesty shall please. If the law destroy me, Your Majesty shall put me out of your power; and I shall have then none to fear, none to reverence, but the King of kings.

362

It was after he had written these letters that Ralegh heard of the proud words of Lord Grey:

The House of the Wiltons have spent many lives in their Prince's service. Grey cannot beg his. God send the King a long and prosperous reign and your lordships all honour.

Then, the night before he was to be executed, Ralegh wrote a letter to his wife and a poem.

First, I send you all the thanks my heart can conceive or my pen express, for your many troubles and cares taken for me, which–though they have not taken effect as you wished–yet my debt is to you nevertheless; but pay it I never shall in this world.

He then told Bess that his lands have been conveyed to his son; they no longer belonged to him, and therefore could not be escheated to the Crown. He had intended to leave her the income from his monopoly of wines, half of his goods and jewels, but 'God hath prevented all my determinations'.

If you can live free from want, care for no more; for the rest is but vanity. Love God, and begin betimes to repose yourself on Him; therein shall you find true and lasting riches and endless comfort. For the rest, when you have travelled and wearied your thoughts on all sorts of worldly cogitations, you shall sit down by sorrow in the end.

He urges Bess to marry after he is gone, but to avoid fortune hunters and to find an honest, worthy man. 'Remember your poor child for his father's sake that chose you and loved you in his happiest times.' He then asked her to try to recover the letters which he wrote begging for his life. He had done it only for her and his son, but he now disdained himself for it. 'And know it (dear wife) that your son is the child of a true man, and who, in his own respect, despiseth Death and all his misshapen and ugly forms.'

I cannot write much, God knows how hardly I stole this time when

363

all sleep; and it is time to separate my thoughts from the world. Beg my dead body, which living was denied you . . . I can write no more. Time and Death call me away.

The poem he wrote that night is one of his best.

> Give me my scallop shell of quiet,
> My staff of Faith to walk upon.
> My scrip of joy, immortal diet,
> My bottle of salvation;
> My gown of glory, hope's true gage,
> And thus I'll take my pilgrimage . . .
>
> And this is my eternal plea,
> To him that made heaven, earth and sea,
> Seeing my flesh must die so soon,
> And want a head to dine next noon,
> Just at the stroke when my veins start and spread,
> Set on my soul an everlasting head.
> Then am I ready like a palmer fit,
> To tread those blest paths which before I writ.

Thus the 'damnable atheist' prepared for his death.

Early in December the two Catholic priests, Clarke and Watson, were brought to the scaffold where they were 'bloodily handled'. Both were cut down alive to be drawn and quartered. Clarke spoke after he had been hanged and fought with the sheriff; he had to be subdued and held while the horrible penalties were carried out. George Brooke was beheaded in the castle yard.

Since James was still distressed by the unresolved discrepancies in the testimonies of Ralegh and Cobham, he sent the Bishop of Chichester to Cobham, the Bishop of Winchester to Ralegh with instructions to bring both men to liberal confessions that would reconcile their stories and vindicate the justice of the realm. Ralegh wished to die bravely and a Christian; he submitted himself to God and to the Bishop's instructions; but he would admit nothing. A Spanish pension had been mentioned to him once, he said, but he had only listened and never concurred.

364

Sir Griffin Markham had secretly received word that he would not be executed. But at ten in the morning on December 10, he was led to the scaffold, his face dejected and despairing. He complained that he had been falsely deluded with hope, but refused the napkin saying that he could look upon death without blushing. As he knelt to the axe, a messenger from James tried to push his way through the crowd. The apprentices were not going to allow anyone in front of them and they rudely shoved him back. He cried out to the sheriff that he had a warrant. The sheriff read the warrant and then told Markham that because he was ill-prepared for death he would be given two hours more. In the meantime, Lord Grey would be executed. Grey, like the good Puritan he was, kept the people standing in the freezing rain for more than half an hour while he prayed. As he prepared to kneel, the sheriff told him that his execution would also be stayed for a while. Lord Cobham would be executed first.

When Cobham came to the scaffold, it was clear that something was afoot. During his trial he had been witless and craven; his conduct was downright embarrassing. Now he was assured and confident; for the first time since his arrest, he was acting like a nobleman. He repeated some prayers with his ministers and many of the spectators joined in. Cobham was in very good voice; he could be heard above everyone as he 'outprayed the company'. After the prayers he made a good speech. He sorrowed for his offense to the King and craved his royal pardon. And, 'upon the hope of his soul's resurrection' he affirmed that all of his charges against Ralegh were true. Then Grey and Markham were brought back to the scaffold. Ralegh was now looking out a window at these strange proceedings, 'hammers working in his head to beat out the meaning of the stratagem'. Some of the spectators were beginning to realize by now that they had seen a little comedy written by the King in which the sheriff was to speak the epilogue. The theme of that epilogue was the mercy of the prince who had decided that all remaining lives were to be spared. The audience roared and clapped and cried out its approval. In the relief occasioned by the amnesty, the cruelty of the affair was forgotten. Markham and Copley were to be banished from the realm. Sir Walter Ralegh, along with Lords Cobham and Grey, would be held in the Tower of London.

There is another epilogue to be written. Within a year, four of the commissioners who judged Ralegh had accepted pensions from Spain. Robert Cecil at first received 1,000 pounds a year; later it was raised to 1,500.

And an interesting evidence of the influence of the trial has survived the general decay of the centuries. Coke, in his *Third Institute*, has a section on high treason. In that section he refers to the trials of Cobham, Grey, and the priests, Watson and Clarke. Neither Ralegh's name nor his trial is mentioned. It is as though the whole proceeding had never occurred. And fifteen years after the trial, when James finally decided to send Ralegh to the block, he would not again risk a public trial. The kind of procedure Ralegh had been subjected to would not be seen again in England. His trial had dramatically shown that the common law must be brought closer to man's concept of justice. The two would never coincide but after Ralegh's trial, they would never again be so far apart.

18

The King's Prisoner

Ralegh believed that everyone in England must feel as he did, that he was innocent of everything except foolish talk and association. If he had known that he was to spend thirteen years in the Tower he might have been unable to endure it. At first, however, he thought that as soon as the legal formalities had been complied with, he would be released if some face-saving device could be found. Eager to help, he offered to be put into the custody of some bishop or nobleman; he was willing to give his word to stay within the hundred of Sherborne; when these offers were flatly rejected, he resignedly offered to go to Holland and live there. He could not imagine that anything would be gained by keeping him in the Tower. He was never quite able to understand those deep irrational fears, that instinctive mistrust and dislike James had for him.

But as Ralegh finally accepted the fact that he might stay many years in the Tower, he began to cast around for significant activities, not merely to pass time and keep himself sane, but also because he was still urged by that powerful sense of a destiny unfulfilled. Soon Sir George Harvey, the Keeper, came to see why his son had been attracted to the old Elizabethan. Ralegh was full of stories, anecdotes, and reminiscences; there was a strange magnetism in the man and he was charming as survivors from an older time often are with that picturesqueness of manner, that quality of strangeness. Sir George asked Sir Walter to dine with him, and soon the two sat down to supper together every night. Sir Walter explained that the Indians he had brought to England from Guiana needed to spend some time with him, in order that he might instruct them in language, religion, and English law, and in order that he, in turn, might be instructed by them in religion and manners and also in the use of the herbs he had brought from their country.

Ralegh explained to Sir George about a book which had been written by a Spanish doctor and herbalist and translated into English under the title, *Joyful News out of the New Found World*. The Spaniard had talked of these herbs as modern doctors speak of wonder drugs. Never, he said, had there been such a success in medicine: the American herbs made it possible to cure hitherto incurable diseases. In a curious piece of illogic, he said that it was a providential miracle that syphilis and the cure for syphilis came from the same country. Ralegh's cure, a potion made from the bark of a South American tree, was like his antidote for *curare*, more to be admired than relied upon.

There has been speculation that Ralegh may have stumbled upon quinine, which is effective in relieving fevers, but that seems unlikely. Presumably his medical knowledge was in no way ahead of his time. Many medicines were effective then because they were exotic, psychically potent; and that potency could be enhanced by the personality of the man who administered them. Common remedies were dust from Egyptian mummies; powder from the horn of a unicorn; the eyes of toads; the wings of bats; or ground-up pearls and rubies. But for a time American herbs were more potent than any of them. Ralegh convinced Sir George that he could do a great service if he were allowed to grow these herbs in the garden of the Tower; and soon tobacco, sassafras, and other new world plants were sprouting inside the walls of the ancient prison.

These herbs, Ralegh explained, must be dried and then 'concocted' into a medicine. He could make, he said, an elixir which he called the Balsam of Guiana which would prolong life, restore virility, even rescue those who were in the harsh and certain grip of death's embrace. As Harvey, like most bewildered laymen, had no desire to impede the progress of science, he assigned to Sir Walter a little shed where Bishop Latimer had once been imprisoned by Mary. He allowed him to bring in the necessary retorts and copper tubing and soon Ralegh had a little chemist's shop working; soon, also, word began to spread around London that Ralegh had made a medicine of rare and potent power. In 1605 the wife of the French ambassador was brought to the Tower to see the lions that were kept there. When she saw Ralegh she lost interest in the beasts and engaged him in a long conversation. In the course of it she asked him for some Balsam of Guiana; he replied that he would have to concoct it, but would send it around to her. By ill chance, he chose to send it by Captain Whitelocke, a retainer of the Earl of Northumberland. Within two months, the Earl himself was in the Tower charged with complicity in the Gunpowder Plot and Ralegh's connection with him resulted in the Privy Council's sending for Ralegh to question him about his suspicious friend. Ralegh was excessively annoyed.

But suspicion of him increased when, about the same time, Lady Ralegh, for no reason other than housewifery, decided to have the armour in the castle of Sherborne scoured. This gave rise to rumours that there was to be an uprising to free Ralegh by force of arms.

Northumberland, the 'wizard Earl', brought his three magi into the Tower to work with him almost daily. They were the fine mathematicians, Thomas Hariot, Robert Hughes, and Walter Warner. Ralegh presumably worked with them too, especially with Hariot, on the chronologies of early civilizations, trying to set the exact times of the Egyptian dynasties and the Trojan war, deciding when the flood occurred and how long after it Abraham actually lived. But mostly these five men were interested in the new science and they probably carried on more significant intellectual activity in the Tower of London than was then being carried on in either of England's major universities.

With his retorts and tubings, Ralegh had the material to work on a problem that had plagued every English naval commander. One of the chief causes of low morale and illness on naval expeditions was bad water. After ships had been out for a while, green scum settled on the top of the water casks; sailors could scarcely drink the water because it stank so badly.

What was needed was an apparatus which could take salt water from the ocean and turn it into sweet drinking water. The nation that had such a device would greatly extend its capabilities for long voyages and large naval expeditions. Ralegh developed an apparatus which worked to his own satisfaction, but it was never used by the Royal Navy, either because of the limitations in the device itself or because of bureaucratic inertia.

Ralegh told Sir George Harvey that it was in the national interest to give him freer access to his friends and other citizens who wished to consult him about Guiana, Newfoundland, Ireland or Virginia. Many noblemen wished to purchase his medicines; some wished to speak with him about political matters, the most pressing of which was the King's continued refusal to call Parliament into session. Soon Harvey began leaving Ralegh's door unlocked so that he could conduct his affairs without restraint. Ralegh had warrants for two servants to attend him personally and one to run errands outside the Tower for him; soon, without warrant, he had taken in a preacher and three additional servants. And Lady Ralegh, who drove grandly into the courtyard of the Tower each day in her coach, was pregnant.

On a certain hour of each day, crowds would gather at the wharves on the Thames. And punctually there would appear on the terrace of the Tower above them the tall, wiry figure wearing a black velvet cloak with a cut lace cap on his head, his doublet covered with gold buttons set in diamond sparkles, his fingers covered with rare jewels. It was one of the sights of London.

And then Queen Anne heard about the Balsam of Guiana. Perhaps it had been an effective cordial for the wife of the French ambassador. She herself called on Ralegh and was fascinated by him. She is not the first unloved matron to place her body in the care of a physician, to feel strange sympathies as he examined it, cared for it, prescribed for it, and healed it. Ralegh, she was convinced, had given her her life. And soon she took her young son, Prince Henry, to see the prisoner. He was

370

then twelve or thirteen years of age, highly impressionable and in search of a father, as his own father had once been, of some image of manhood on which he could model himself. His effeminate and royal beggetter disgusted the Prince. Ralegh soon exercised the same fascination on this boy as he had on young Cecil and the Peyton and Harvey boys; and soon Henry was turning to Ralegh for advice, saying precociously that only his father would keep such a bird in a cage.

The King of Denmark, Anne's brother, visited England and possibly at her instigation asked James to release Ralegh in order that he might serve him as admiral. James refused. The French Huguenots still remembered with nostalgia that the seventeen-year-old Ralegh had voyaged with their Princes; they, too, asked for his services, and James again refused. Later Ralegh was to say that there was no parallel in history to the fact that the brother-in-law, the wife, and the son of a king all urged the release of a man convicted of treason.

But all of this attention to Ralegh was too much. It was decided again to change the Keeper and Harvey was replaced by Sir William Waad, who had been one of his judges. Waad was apprehensive about the crowds who gathered to gaze at Ralegh; he thought it should be forbidden; he issued an order forbidding Lady Ralegh to drive her coach into the courtyard. She would have to halt it in the street and walk in; all prisoners would have to remain in their quarters after five in the afternoon; and, finally, Waad erected a brick wall between Ralegh's quarters and his own office. The Tower, after all, was supposed to be a prison.

But Ralegh had too much popular support and too many powerful friends to be deprived of the privileges that he had now come to think of as essential, especially the company of visiting scholars, the use of many books, and the continued use of the chemical shop and the herb garden.

In the Tower Ralegh had his troubles and problems, but he had been treated better than the other prisoners. Cobham and Grey simply lost everything. But the Crown appointed trustees for Ralegh's estate, to dispose of his goods, pay his debts and maintain his wife and child. And Sherborne, he thought, was secure. For in 1602 he had been challenged to a duel by a member of the Essex faction and, as a part of putting his affairs in order, he had deeded Sherborne to his son; now only his own life interest in it could be forfeited. As soon as he was legally dead, therefore, the estate passed to young Walter. His debtors and the agents of the Crown, who either did not understand the legal situation or else didn't care, were at Sherborne selling the livestock, felling timber and even dismantling the castle. Ralegh appealed to Cecil to stop the spoilage and Cecil responded immediately.

But a year after Ralegh entered the Tower, as his various titles were being reviewed, it was found to his dismay and shock that the legal conveyance of Sherborne to his son was invalid. In a warm room, some copy clerk had made a sound deed worthless by nodding long enough to skip over ten words; and the omission invalidated the deed. The land had therefore not been conveyed; it still belonged to Sir Walter and was therefore forfeit to the Crown. Lady Ralegh, even more distraught than her husband, immediately sought an audience with James and begged him not to take advantage of this legal technicality. James agreed that he would not. He then directed Cecil to have a grant prepared which would deed the estate to Lady Ralegh and her children. But for some reason Cecil never did so; perhaps the press of business simply led him to forget it, but that is improbable. Certainly both Ralegh and Lady Ralegh reminded him often enough. One of Ralegh's letters is graphic.

I shall be made more than weary of my life by her crying and bewailing who will return in post when she hears of your Lordship's departure and nothing done. She hath already brought her eldest son in one hand and her sucking child in another, crying out of her and their destruction; charging me with unnatural negligence, and that having provided for mine own life, I am without sense and compassion of theirs.

But Robert Cecil still did nothing; it was unlike him. Most likely James had given him a private word that countermanded the public order.

When it appeared that Ralegh might lose Sherborne, the people of England remembered Bishop Osmund's curse and in 1608 Sir Dudley Carleton wrote, 'The error or oversight is said to be so gross that men do merely ascribe it to God's own hand that blinded him and his counsel.'

Early in 1607, young Robert Kerr (or Carr) had broken his leg while tilting before the King. James had shambled over to the side of the young man whose handsome, suffering face made a deep impression on him. Soon he had asked Queen Anne to pass judgment on the young man as a new favourite; the Queen dutifully did so and Kerr was knighted. Now he needed an estate; James told Cecil to find one and Cecil immediately suggested Sherborne. It was the shabbiest thing he ever did, but James was entirely delighted. Their intention was not simply to confiscate the estate but to offer Lady Ralegh a price for it and leave her no option about accepting. The price finally offered was 8,000 pounds and a 400 pound annuity for the life of herself and her son. Much has been said about how grossly unfair the price was; but, although the transaction was unfair, the price was not. A year later the estate was valued at 20,000 pounds. Lady Ralegh lived for another forty years. If the annuity had been paid regularly and fully, she would have received approximately 24,000 pounds for Sherborne. The figure offered, although ungenerous, was not cruelly so.

Lady Ralegh could not endure the loss of Sherborne. She sought audience with James at Hampton Court where he refused to see her. Being a resolute woman, she stationed herself at a likely place and waited for him to pass. Soon he came and she threw herself on her knees, pleading wildly that she might be allowed her estate as James had promised. The guilty monarch shambled on, muttering as he passed, 'I mun have the land, I mun have it for Kerr,' whereupon, as one observer recorded,

she, being a woman of a very high spirit and noble birth and breeding, fell down upon her knees, with her hands heaved up to heaven, and in the bitterness of her spirit, beseeched God Almighty to look upon the justness of her cause and punish those who had so wrongfully exposed her and her poor children to ruin and beggary.

Now to Bishop Osmund's curse was added Lady Ralegh's. Kerr might have done well to ponder awhile.

While the issue was still in doubt, Ralegh wrote Kerr a dignified and powerful letter in which he pleaded with him not to take Sherborne.

After many great losses and many years' sorrows, of both which I have cause to fear I was mistaken in their ends, it is come to my knowledge that yourself (whom I know not but by an honourable fame) have been persuaded to give me and mine our last fatal blow by obtaining from His Majesty the inheritance of my children and nephews, lost in law for want of words . . .

And for yourself, Sir, seeing your day is but now in the dawn and mine coming to the evening (your own virtues and the King's grace assuring you of many good fortunes and much honour) I beseech you not to begin your first building upon the ruins of the innocent; and that their griefs and sorrows do not attend your first plantation . . .

I therefore trust, sir, that you will not be the first that will kill us outright, cut down the tree with the fruit, and undergo the curse of them that enter into the fields of the fatherless.

But Kerr was the King's favourite; he believed himself invulnerable to curses and he could not be touched by pleas. He had a certain marriage in mind; it was too early to reveal it yet, for there were certain uncomfortable details to be worked out, but they would be worked out and he would need an estate. To Ralegh's letter he never made a reply.

Before Sherborne could be deeded to Kerr young Prince Henry interposed. He angrily informed his father that such a valuable estate could not be handed over to a favourite and James, who was never at ease with his strong-willed, masculine son, retreated. He placated Kerr by paying him 20,000 pounds, or perhaps even more, and Sherborne reverted from Ralegh to the Crown. But Sir Walter believed that the Prince intended eventually to restore it to him. And most likely that was the Prince's intention; but there is always Destiny to be reckoned with.

There were other strokes of ill-fortune which now beat upon

Sir Walter. About two years after he entered the Tower, he suffered a severe cerebral haemorrhage. His left side was paralyzed; for a time he lost completely the motion of his left hand and arm; his speech became thick, his mind somewhat erratic. But his speech returned, and soon he could use his arm; there always remained, however, some deterioration in the left side.

Ralegh's attitude must have been exasperating to the King and Council; he refused to consider himself a criminal and he believed that he could advise the King much better than his counsellors were doing. Consequently he turned out a stream of writings filled with advice, plans, warnings and solemn adjurations as though he were himself the First Secretary. James had always favoured a French or Spanish marriage for his children in order to cement alliances which would give him the peace he sought. A number of proposals had been made and one, upon which he was inclined to look favourably, would have resulted in a double marriage in which Prince Henry would marry the eldest daughter of the Duke of Savoy, while Princess Elizabeth, his sister and James's only surviving daughter, would marry the Duke's son, the Prince of Piedmont. At young Prince Henry's request, Ralegh produced a treatise on the matter; in fact, he produced two, one on each proposal, in which he strongly advised against both matches. He wrote without apology or defensiveness, expressing himself as openly and freely as if he had been a member of Parliament under special immunity, knowing full well that he was advising against a course that the King seemed to favour. And his arguments were sound and persuasive. The royal children of England, he said, were the best match in Europe; Savoy was small and of no consequence. All France lay interjacent between England and Savoy, which had always been in the Spanish-French sphere of influence. It was foolish to think that Savoy, in any conflict, could help England. Further, if there were conflicts, the King would have to abandon his daughter or engage in a costly war far from home and at too great a charge. And Ralegh considers the plight of a young girl married to this 'poor popish prince of

375

Savoy'. She will be removed into a strange country where the difference in faith is a crucial matter; for either she will live with a perpetually wounded conscience or she will 'undergo the scorns and dangers which shall be daily cast upon her and her family for the exercise of their religion'. Although his opinion had not been further solicited, he gave it anyway. The best match for Princess Elizabeth would be the Protestant Prince Palatine (whom Elizabeth ultimately did marry to become the sentimental 'Winter Queen of Bohemia' of the German novella).

His advice on the proposed Prince's match was about the same. What would Henry get from the marriage? A beautiful lady, no doubt, but beauty 'is ever better loved in the hope than when it is had'. And he would get a million crowns dowry. But when all of the expenses were subtracted, it would make but two of the English subsidies, a small matter. (But of course it was not a small matter: it was gall and wormwood to James who could not agree with his Parliaments. He rejected their demands for reform and they steadfastly refused to vote him a subsidy. He needed that million crowns.)

Ralegh took the occasion to remind the Prince that 4,000 Englishmen could chase the Spaniard out of the New World; that his marriage with a Catholic would break Protestant hearts in Europe and that it would in fact be best if the Prince should remain unmarried.

All of this advice no doubt infuriated James and his ministers; but it persuaded the Prince who said sensibly that two religions should never lie in his bed. And so Ralegh remained the proud genius of the Tower whose reputation grew with every year, the adversary who could not be quelled.

Prince Henry became interested in sea-power, and he sought Ralegh's advice and assistance in building a model ship. Ralegh wrote him a letter full of the standard theories of Elizabethan naval construction and then set to work writing a *Discourse on the Art of War by Sea* which included a section on shipbuilding.

Ralegh began to perceive that he had become unofficially what he had always wanted to be: the adviser to the Prince. And slowly there took shape in his mind one of his most ambitious designs. Aristotle had taught Alexander the Great whose vices had so unfortunately overcome his good education. Plato had tried to bring rational government into the kingdom of the tyrant Dionysus. Now Sir Walter had a similar opportunity to be the teacher of a Prince, to instill into him the traditional humane values of Western civilization. And so he began to be less concerned in the great *History* he was planning with the dates and boundaries of empires and more with depicting the characters and events in such a way that they would contribute to the shaping of the mind of a just and virtuous prince.

On May 12, 1612, Robert Cecil died; the responsibilities and the labour had been too much for his frail body. He was thoroughly detested in England, and men said he had died of syphilis, a common enough slander. It was said that after his death the Prince received a promise from his father that Ralegh would be freed in the Christmas season of that year. Then the Prince went swimming in the garbage infested Thames and soon lay ill of a raging fever, typhoid or diphtheria most likely. The physicians despaired of his life and Queen Anne insisted that Ralegh's elixir be administered. The Privy Council met to discuss the matter; the physicians were in disagreement among themselves. The boy's condition worsened so rapidly that obviously he would soon be dead. Therefore, they sent for Ralegh's Balsam as if it were a *viaticum*; Ralegh hastily prepared it but couldn't resist adding his own touch. He said the Balsam would infallibly heal any fever, including the Prince's unless, he added darkly, poison had previously been administered.

The elixir was poured down the throat of the dying Prince. He aroused himself; he spoke; it appeared to be the miracle the Queen had hoped for. But it was only a 'lightening before death'. The distraught Queen, with her touching faith in Ralegh's medicines, believed that her son had been poisoned, and she did not scruple to say so, many times and publicly, too. Perhaps in a way she had not intended, she was right. James with his un-loving ways had poisoned her, certainly, and perhaps her son too.

The tragedy for Ralegh was almost as great as for the Queen. He had spent years on the *History* in which he had embodied the spirit which was to animate England's new age and the heart of next her king. All that work now seemed wasted, and disconsolately he broke off and left it unfinished. He had been within weeks of his freedom and once more he was a hopeless prisoner. Sherborne, immediately after the Prince's death, was given to Robert Kerr after all. Fortune's tennis ball, men began to call Ralegh, her shuttlecock and sport.

But Fortune's game was slightly more complicated than men realized. Sherborne after all had been thrice-cursed and for many years a design of savagery and lust had been working itself out around that ancient manor. Back in 1606 the children of two of Ralegh's old acquaintances had married. The young Earl of Essex, a boy of fourteen, had married Lady Frances Howard, daughter of Lord Thomas Howard who had sailed with Ralegh at Cadiz and Fayal and who had been on the commission that convicted him and sentenced him to death for treason. Lady Howard was also the niece of Lord Henry Howard, the artist of the poison pen. Because the principals were so young, the marriage was not consummated; instead, the bride and groom were separated for four years. In that time, Frances Howard became one of the most beautiful women of the Court and, being ambitious, she began to look wantonly at Robert Kerr who was so close to the throne and so obviously the principal recipient of the royal bounty.

She was a completely unscrupulous woman with a will of tempered steel; she could have been a lamia. She determined that when she was reunited with her childhood husband, he would never enjoy her. She therefore went to an astrological quack who, among other things, provided women with love and hate philtres. From him she received medicines designed to keep the Earl of Essex impotent. Associated with this doctor was a Mistress Anne Turner whose speciality was witchcraft. She made a statue of the Earl which was anatomically so complete that she was able to run a large pin through the testicles. When this image was later exhibited in court, the pin still in place, it sent a shudder and a pang through the male loins of England.

But more effective than witchcraft was Lady Howard's savage hatred, which she employed with cunning and malice. For three years she and the Earl slept in the same bed. Servants who made that bed later testified in court that there were always two plain indentations in the mattress, made by the bodies of the principals with a ridge between. That ridge was like Arthur's naked sword; it was never crossed. Lady Howard maintained that she had preserved her virginity through three years of marriage and Essex did not deny it. She requested a divorce on the grounds of his general impotence. He admitted that he was impotent as far as she was concerned, but not with others; he declined to be publicly certified of general incompetence and this created a difficulty which the pedantic James decided to settle by appointing a committee of bishops to consider the evidence and make a recommendation. James was very much interested in the case for several reasons: his favourite Kerr wished to marry the lady if she could get a divorce; he loved theological tangles, and he strongly suspected that someone had practised witchcraft.

While all of this domestic difficulty was being aired, Thomas Overbury, a writer and a close friend of Kerr, was trying to persuade his friend not to marry the lady who, he said, was a common whore. It was a dangerous thing to say about such a powerful woman; she complained of Overbury to her uncle, Henry Howard, and he and Kerr, in turn, complained to James. It was resolved, sensibly enough, that the simplest course was to send Overbury abroad until the bishops had completed their weighty assignment. He was offered the post of ambassador; naturally, he saw the reason for the offer, and some stubbornness of character or some fatal touch of the hand of Destiny led him to refuse. As a result of his impertinences, he was sent to the Tower on April 21, 1613. Less than a month later, Sir William Waad quietly pocketed 2,000 pounds and turned the position of Keeper of the Tower over to Sir Gervase Elwys. After Elwys had held the position for a few weeks, he learned by accident, he said, that Overbury was being poisoned by food sent to him from Frances Howard.

Also in May of that year, the seven 'reverend bawdy bishops' voted four to three that the divorce could properly be granted provided that the marriage had never been consummated. This was a ticklish point but they were ingenious in resolving it. They appointed a jury 'of grave matrons, fearing God, and the mothers of children' who were given the solemn duty of inspecting Lady Howard. Out of deference to her high birth, this delicate matron appeared before them heavily veiled. Whoever was examined was pronounced *virgo intacta*. Lady Howard, who had a well-established reputation as a worn glove, became the object of some blasphemous humour in which this new miracle was compared to that of the Virgin Mary.

In September Overbury suddenly died and Henry Howard wrote a letter to the Keeper urging him to dispose of the body immediately. It was done, but Overbury refused to remain buried; too many people knew too many things and soon rumours were all over the Court and all over London, bitter rumours about James's favourites and advisers and their concerted implication in a murder. Lord Henry Howard died; James was tiring of Kerr. The scandal was so great that it simply could not be stilled especially after the alarmed Elwys confessed all he knew in a hopeless attempt to exculpate himself. So James finally gave to Edward Coke the task of sifting to the bottom of it all and that legal bloodhound was off on the scent, indignant and free with innuendo as ever but careful in his legal procedures.

It was likely the most sensational trial ever held in England. Elwys and Mistress Turner were hanged; Dr. Forman and Howard had died. Kerr was attainted and lost Sherborne which James promptly offered to his newest favourite, Robert Villiers, who politely declined that haunted estate. Robert Kerr and his countess were soon to be lodged in the Tower. Coke, with great zeal, had turned up the fact that the dead Cecil and Howard, along with two other commissioners from the Ralegh trial, were in the pay of Spain, guilty of that which they had convicted

Ralegh not of doing but merely of wishing to do. And so Coke, indirectly, was one of the instruments of Ralegh's release from prison, for public opinion was outraged at this sensational and intricate combination of murder and near-treason among those who had convicted the old Elizabethan. Among his other unproved insinuations, Coke thundered out that Overbury had probably been poisoned because he knew that poison had been administered to 'a sweet prince'. This, along with the Queen's assertions, convinced many that James's Court was morally foul, although no one implied that the King was touched in any way, except by association.

Ralegh watched all of this with awe; he believed that the lessons of centuries of history had been suddenly epitomized for all men, but especially for himself to see. Destiny had chosen him to play a role that would illustrate a moral truth for all time, the same truth his *History* had been written to convey, that good and evil are entities with lives of their own, instruments through which moral laws operate in the lives of men and nations. And there were other events that supported the lesson from the Overbury case. In 1594 he had written a letter urging Elizabeth to keep in the Tower the dangerous Irish traitor, Florence McCarthy. Now that gentleman, a near-sighted, unwarlike scholar, was in an adjoining cell and, like Ralegh, writing a history, only his was a history of Ireland. Lady Desmond had made her moan to Burleigh about the loss of her lands to Ralegh, and Bess in turn had lamented before James the loss of Sherborne to Kerr. Two of the Howards and William Waad, who had been on the Commission that unjustly convicted him, had all been found out by the secret workings of justice. 'The whole history of the world.' Ralegh said, 'hath not the like precedent of a King's prisoner to purchase his freedom, and his bosom favourite to have the halter, but in the Scripture in the case of Mordecai and Haman.'

With his enlarged insight, Ralegh considered it more than ever his duty to advise the King whose course he now believed to be perilous. In ten years Parliament had met only once, and then for only two months of bitter debate in 1514. The House of Commons refused to vote the needed subsidies unless they were first given assurance of reforms some of which touched James closely, too closely, such as the extravagances of his Court and his dependence on handsome but injudicious favourites. And so James had set out to show that he could govern England without the House of Commons. Robert Cecil had proposed the device of creating a new honour, the baronetcy, and selling it for some 1,000 pounds. By this device James made 90,000 pounds, but that was not nearly enough. He then began to sell peerages. He also resorted to forced loans from the London merchants, which were really an illegal form of taxation. Elizabeth had levied such loans but only in times of national distress and she had always repaid them. James did not repay and the merchants, to recoup, were charging exorbitant prices for every commodity sold to the government; they also raised their rates of interest. Though James was 700,000 pounds in debt, he would not call Parliament. His only hope was to marry his remaining son, Baby Charles, as he called him, to the Infanta of Spain. He fondly thought that such a marriage might bring him a million pounds in dowry and make him a free monarch again. About the only other possibility he had was that traitor in the Tower who kept talking about the golden empire of Guiana. But that was fanciful and dangerous.

Ralegh thought James's course was one of deadliest peril, and again, without consent or approval, he wrote him an advisory treatise, one of the soundest he ever produced, *The Prerogative of Parliaments*. His arguments were irrefutable and his prescriptions might have saved the Stuart monarchy. He begins by saying that he himself has been the victim of an injustice; he has been struck by a stone and that stone was 'the borrowed authority of his sovereign misinformed'. The arms that had flung that stone (and he means Cecil and Howard) were now rotten. Because he had been immured for so long, he had not been able to serve his sovereign as he wished. All he could offer him were thoughts and he does so on the altar of love.

The treatise is in the form of a dialogue between a counsellor of state (a man who, like Cecil or Howard, is out of touch with

the citizens and blindly committed to the royal prerogative) and
a justice of the peace, a man who must constantly work directly
with the King's subjects and who, therefore, knows them well.
The former argues that Parliament should not be called and the
latter that it should. In this age of analogies and analogical
arguments, it was common to say that the King was like the
head and the subjects were like the feet. To the question of the
counsellor, Shall the head yield to the feet, the Justice of the
Peace replied, 'Certainly it ought, when they are grieved . . . If
the feet lie in fetters, the head cannot be freed.'

Ralegh says that nothing could conceivably be more unfortunate than for the King to meet his Commons with ill
success. 'It is only love (most renowned sovereign) must prepare
the way for Your Majesty's following desires. It is love which
obeys, which suffers, which gives, which sticks at nothing.'

The King's counsellor is equipped with every argument that
James himself had used for not calling Parliament. In the past,
he says, the Parliaments have whittled away at the royal
prerogative and James considered himself divinely commissioned to restore what had been lost. In France, the counsellor
argues, a Parliament is almost never assembled. Ralegh has
carefully prepared this opening for his wise Justice of the Peace.
He knows all about France which is never free from civil wars
and which is a weaker nation than England, where the national
strength lies in the people and the yeomanry and in their belief
and satisfaction that they live under a just law and a just ruler.
The only strength of any monarch is ultimately the love of his
people; Ralegh continually returns to this theme like some
Elizabethan Saint Paul. A king will lose more by one rebellion
than by a hundred years of following *Magna Charta*. Ralegh
then tries to maintain the rather difficult thesis that no wise
king of England has ever lost any prerogatives through amicable
relations with Parliament. And he saves face for James through
the usual device that he has been badly advised by his counsellors who know that the King never believes anyone who speaks
against them. This is a bitter truth, says Ralegh, which he tells
the King only out of love.

The Justice of the Peace then makes a bitter attack on 'insolent and avaricious favourites'. By discharging these Lucifers a king shows that his reason is stronger than his passion and thereby offers an acceptable sacrifice to all of his people. Why do those about the King fear the calling of a Parliament? Because there will be plain speaking and the King will learn how his subjects feel about his evil counsellors. Ralegh, perhaps unwisely, then refers to the late Queen who, he said, 'would set the reason of a mean man before the authority of the greatest counsellor she had'.

Through the voice of the Justice, Ralegh informs the King that the farming of customs, a privilege he himself had enjoyed for almost twenty years, was an abuse. It was as if a subject was taxed by another subject rather than by the Crown. But an even greater abuse, he says, has been the King's sale of Crown lands, many of which have passed to favourites. Elizabeth, too, sold such lands but only for defence, but now the eyes of the kingdom weep, the heart of the kingdom mourns for the loss of the land. The greatest of all such abuses was the estate Robert Cecil amassed for himself, a shocking misuse of position and power.

It is an astounding document, absolutely without fear and yet, except for the veiled references to Cecil and Howard, without insolence. Solidly argued, moderate in tone, and wise in conception, it was brilliant advice but, given the character of James, it was also impossible advice, like that which Bacon had once given Essex. In a few years the Stuarts would have to settle their grievances with Parliament on the battlefield.

Ralegh concludes by saying that the wrongs of a king are 'written in marble'. He remembers that the Duc de Biron once taxed a king of France with sloth and cowardice. That, said Ralegh, was wrong; one must always treat a king with respect. And, in his treatise, he had; but under the slight fiction of a dialogue he had given James tough-minded and fearless advice.

In the Tower, Ralegh wrote many other things. One work, *The Sceptic*, has been much over-rated and too many unwarrantable conclusions have been drawn from it. It is simply a loose translation of parts of Sextus Empiricus. His *Instructions to his Son* was much admired in his own time and much decried by Victorian biographers who seem to feel that in it Ralegh insulted his wife. What he really did was to inform his son, in humanistic fashion, that men are more likely to be betrayed by beauty than by any other thing and that affections inspired by mere beauty do not last. Therefore, he says, it is better to choose a mistress for her beauty than a wife, for a mistress can be conveniently dropped when transient affection is gone. But one must be prepared for the inevitable fact that every mistress will some day become an enemy.

He counsels marriage with a comely woman of sound character and gives two ways a man may know whether his wife truly loves him: if she takes care of his estate and is sweet in conversation without being instructed, for love needs no precept. He advises his son to beware of flatterers and to avoid quarrels. Bravery of apparel, he says with no apology, is esteemed only by women and fools. And the vice Ralegh despises above all others is drunkenness. It was, of course, James's vice. If it all sounds too coldly practical and disillusioned it is also unexceptionable.

He wrote other things, jottings in notebooks, a treatise on the West Indies, now lost; on war; on the soul, and many others, but all of these were ancillary to the great work which, during the long years of his imprisonment, had come to absorb his energies and to which he was devoting all the shaping powers of his imagination, that treatise intended for the humanistic education of the wise and gifted young Prince Henry, *The History of the World*.

His conception was vast – a compendium of the stories of the rise and fall of the great civilizations from the creation of the world. But of this great panorama, planned in three parts, only one was completed: cut short by the death of the prince for whose sake it was undertaken, the history abruptly terminates with the rise of Rome. But nevertheless the unifying themes of mankind's history, the universal and eternal truths of God's providence and man's vice and virtue, the truths that the story of the past can make clear to the present, have been lined out and illustrated.

In the eloquent preface Ralegh introduces these themes in the tone of the sad Wisdom literature of the Bible, of Job, Ecclesiastes, and Proverbs. In flowing, melancholy phrases he invokes the mysteries of fortune, ambition, vanity, cruelty, time and death. He knows that, like the late, great Queen, he too has been surprised by time; he is too old to start such a monumental task. Why then does he undertake it? Partly because he feels 'inmost and soul-piercing wounds which are ever aching', wounds which the writing of this *History* may recure. Besides, there are a few old friends who have remained faithful to him; he would like to satisfy them, now that he can speak without ambitions, hopes, or fears. For as he writes of the ancient world, he reviews and judges the recent history he knew, and even more poignantly, his own part in it. He comes to terms with himself in level judgment.

Most of those who have come to know Ralegh's work well feel an affection for him, a deep, personal affection. It does not come from his poetry, certainly not from the incessant complaints of his letters nor from contemplation of the impermanence and imperfections of his designs and deeds. It comes mainly from the *History*, his *apologia;* there his heart is found, in Plutarch's phrase, at the end of his tongue. There he is saying, movingly though often indirectly, many of these things that happened so long ago happened also to me. I have seen them all, done them all, known them all, the lust and ambition, the cruelty and greed. I have played the beast and used my reason to justify it; I have praised humility while acting the demi-god; I have pretended the wise man and played the fool. And although he never says outright, 'Forgive me', the cry of his heart that rings through every chapter is eloquent enough. To himself as to the young Prince he is asking, Cannot man ever learn?

He makes clear again and again that the intent of his work is moral. 'The end and scope of all history.' he says, is 'to teach by examples of times past such wisdom as may guide our desires and actions'. That is why Ralegh devoted himself to history rather than to philosophy or some other intellectual discipline; except for Eternity itself, he says, only history has conquered 'the consuming disease of Time'. History 'hath carried our knowledge over the vast and devouring space of so many thousands of years and given so fair and piercing eyes to our mind, that we plainly behold living now, as if we had lived then, that great world'. And as we view that solemn pageant of fools and madmen, heroes and saints, we see why kings have flourished and why they have fallen; we see that prosperity is linked with virtue, wretchedness with vice and deformity. As we view history, we gather 'a policy no less wise than eternal'.

For who hath not observed what labour, practice, peril, bloodshed, and cruelty the kings and princes of the world have undergone, exercised, taken on them, and committed to make themselves and their issues masters of the world? And yet hath Babylon, Persia, Egypt, Syria, Macedon, Carthage, Rome, and the rest, no fruit, no flower, grass nor leaf, springing upon the face of the earth of those seeds.

History is able to provide moral lessons for two reasons, one of them supernatural: it is God who created the world and governs its course; his judgments, being unchanging, operate the same in all kingdoms and ages; they apply equally to Alexander, to Coligny or to Robert Kerr. Ill-doing, now as then, is finally attended with ill-success; it remains only to analyse the nature of the ill-doing and avoid it. The other reason is secular and natural. Because nature is finite and matter is limited, nature's works will frequently resemble one another: in human events as in inanimate nature there will be patterns and similitudes. Most important, since human nature remains the same, the most common patterns will be repeated: man's reason will again and again be over-ruled by his affections as he attempts to manage the difficult affairs of his life. So success or failure in statecraft may be measured by the degree of rationality and charity any prince brings to the managing of his kingdom. That is the central message, repeated for the benefit of the Prince a dozen times, illustrated a hundred times.

Before turning to the history proper, Ralegh illustrates this message by briefly reviewing the lives and actions of recent kings and showing how the judgments of God have been manifested through them. Among the English kings he finds few to praise, though he does honour Henry VII for his justice and strength. But of Henry VIII he writes, 'If all the pictures and patterns of a merciless prince were lost in the world, they might all again be painted to the life out of the story of this king.' And then, without sparing anything, he enumerates the crimes and cruelties of Elizabeth's father. Later, when James tried to suppress the *History*, he alleged as one of his reasons that Ralegh was 'too saucy in censuring Princes', and especially, he said, he resented his treatment of Henry VIII. James was hypersensitive: he himself never tired of railing at Henry, but in the *History* there were tacit lessons for him too.

After the kings of England, Ralegh reviews the kings of France and Spain. He finds that most of them have followed a Machiavellian policy of *Raggione del Stato* that has consistently failed and drawn down God's wrath.

Oh by what plots, by what forswearings, betrayings, oppressions, imprisonments, tortures, poisonings, and under what reasons of state have these forenamed kings, both strangers and of our own nation, pulled the vengeance of God upon themselves, upon theirs and upon their prudent ministers!

And out of all this outcry against oppression and injustice, one word emerges again and again. It is the theme and key of all human evil: cruelty.

When we once come in sight of the port of death to which all winds drive us; and when by letting fall that fatal anchor which can never be weighed again, the navigation of this life takes end . . . it is then that we cry out to God for mercy; then, when ourselves can no longer exercise cruelty towards others.

In contrast to cruelty is charity, the most lasting of human virtues. When darkness covers men or nations, the only comfort that remains to them is the charity which they exercised while living.

Before closing his preface, Ralegh explains the simplifying order he has imposed on the past in order to write about it. Perhaps by analogy with the familiar patters of fours, like the four elements, the four humours, the four ages of man, he plans to treat only four great peoples or empires and to correlate, as subsidiary to them, the stories of contemporary kingdoms that they fought with or conquered or survived. The early history of the Hebrews and the Assyrian-Babylonian empires he treats together, because they were interrelated, but lays emphasis on the Hebraic history because it is the more fully recorded. The story next centres on the Mede-Persian empire, which produced 'actions of more importance than were elsewhere to be found'. Next the Greeks extended their power, and finally they were supplanted by the Romans. In each the pattern of early strength, moral deterioration, and collapse can be perceived and throughout shine the ever consistent judgments of God. That was the framework.

But since it is a history of the world, Ralegh begins at the very beginning – with the nature of the Deity who created it. Having defined God after the negative way of the mystics, he investigates His relations to Nature, which Ralegh conceives as having no autonomous force of its own, but as simply the mechanism whereby God's will works its way in the world. At this point he must re-examine the concept of Fate or Destiny, which he had in his youth found so compelling. He had once written, 'The success of all human actions seems rather to proceed from fortune than from virtue.' But the whole impact of the *History* denies such a position, to affirm that nations and men rise by virtuous thoughts and deeds.

Destiny, he says in the *History*, is a valid concept, provided it is not joined with 'an inevitable necessity', as in Stoic thought. The ancients, says Ralegh, have tended to make it 'more general and universally powerful than it is, by giving it dominion over the mind of man and his will'. And so he plots a middle course. We must not bind God to his creatures by necessity; but neither should we rob the stars, the planets and the heavens, 'those beautiful creatures', of all influence. As second causes, they incline the will; they may even wholly direct the actions of 'reasonless minds' (a good explanation for Cobham no doubt). Over the appetitive natures of man and beast, celestial bodies may have 'absolute dominion'. But to the extent that men and societies are rational, to that extent they are also free. Apart from God's will, education is the most powerful force in turning away Destiny. Even if the constellations are unfavourable, a good education may reform wicked inclinations; but with favourable constellations and a virtuous education, a man may achieve exceptional virtue. Later, Ralegh comes close to ridiculing the whole notion of Destiny. In a tough, analytic passage, he says that it is nothing else but an 'imaginary power' to which we ascribe success or failure of human actions when we do not know the real causes. That, at least, was what his mind told him; but his heart never seems to have been convinced, for later when he left the Tower to sail to Guiana on his last, sad voyage, he named his ship *The Destiny*.

His discussion of the processes of the creation makes evident – as the whole ensuing history verifies – that the mature and disillusioned Ralegh in the Tower was in no way a sceptical atheist 'corrupted' by the new science, but a profoundly religious man, and a surprisingly orthodox one. He was, indeed, far more orthodox than the intense Puritan John Milton was a quarter of a century later, both in his account of the beginnings of the world and of the historical validity of the Old Testament. In defense of Genesis, he attacks head on Aristotle's thesis that matter is uncreated and eternally existent; he holds rather 'by faith' to the doctrine of creation *ex nihilo* and in time. He rejects the pantheistic excesses of the Neo-Platonists, for it is a 'monstrous impiety' to confound God and nature. He does, to be sure, take account of the views of scientists like Thomas Hariot when he speaks of the 'supposed' element of fire which most thoughtful men had long since discarded. And when he comes to the scriptural account of waters above the earth, he explains them in naturalistic terms as clouds and vapours engendered in the upper air.

But he is not often the scientific rationalizer. He knows the theory that Noah's flood was local, but tries to demonstrate that it was in fact universal and that the ark could contain all the animals; he rejects the theories that other accounts of great floods, like that of Deucalion's, refer to the same catastrophe. Perhaps the hardest problem for him as a man of faith is the traditional chronology of the Old Testament. Ralegh was aware (as Hariot was said to have maintained) that some had believed that men existed before Adam, and he knows of good arguments for such a position. Egyptian chronologies were extant, for example, that added up to 13,000 years. Ralegh makes strenuous efforts to explain away the inconsistencies with scripture by maintaining that these are only lunar years, each equivalent to one month. The names of all the Pharaohs, and the number of years they ruled, stretch out a long time which he telescopes by arguing that the names include regents and others who ruled simultaneously. As for all those Egyptian antiquities and artifacts which argue for a long period of settlement and civilization, he says that some of them may have been made or built before the Flood. But most puzzling to him is the millions of people known to exist so shortly after the time of the Flood. 'True chronology' cannot allow much more than 360 years from the Flood to Semiramis, who had an army of three million men. Nevertheless Ralegh never wavers in the face of these problems. He is concerned (as Isaac Newton was to be later) to preserve the integrity of Biblical chronology.

He is so concerned to defend the Bible as authoritative history that he enters into some intolerably long and arid discussions of 'rabbinical curiosities'. From the Bible he must establish the geographical and chronological boundaries of nations and empires. And he devotes a long chapter to discovering the place of Paradise, the navel of the earth. The Greeks had located the earth's omphalos at Delphi and the mystical Hebrews had placed it at Mount Moriah where Solomon's Temple stood. But for Ralegh, Eden is the navel, the centre from which all peoples were dispersed or planted. Only if we know where it is can we understand the 'beginning of nations and the world's inhabitations'. He finally locates Eden between the Tigris and Euphrates rivers in lower Mesopotamia.

In his leisurely story of universal history Ralegh inserts many digressions. Some of these are not, as he explains in his preface, really digressions at all; they are explorations of important activities and principles at those junctures in the story where they arise, or are clearly relevant. Nor do the others require apology, for as he says, not only is man's life full of digressions – it is itself a great digression. One of the most important digressions in the *History* is an essay on the nature of law which arises naturally from that crucial point in Hebrew history when God transmitted the laws to Moses. In his trial, when Ralegh had said to Popham and Coke, 'I know not how you conceive the law', Popham had answered him pointlessly. Now he intended to leave England his own conception of law, which in its brilliant acuity deserves to stand with those of Hooker and Aquinas, both of whom he cites, as one of the great humanistic treatises on the mystique of law.

He begins with Aquinas's definition of eternal law as 'the high and eternal reason of divine sapience'. A pattern and design in the mind of God is the basis of all law. It is eternal and uncreated and is mirrored in creation, both in nature and in human society. But all laws derive validity from the eternal law. Human law is good if based upon right reason; if not, it is a 'wicked imposition' with only the name but not the substance of law. Ralegh, having provided this context, defines law as 'a righteous decree, agreeing with the law natural and eternal; made by the rational discourse of those who exercise public authority; prescribing necessary observances to the subject'.

On the touchy but essential matter of the relation of the prince to the law, he is somewhat equivocal. In a decade or so, and not without peril to himself, Edward Coke would establish firmly that the prince was under the law. Ralegh begins deferentially by affirming that the prince is above the law. But then he quotes Bracton out of Justinian, 'Rightfully ought the king to attribute to the law, which the law first attributeth to the king; for it is the law that doth make kings'. Somewhat apprehensively Ralegh then says that Bracton is wrong in saying that human law makes kings; it is rather divine law, and princes must give account of their actions to God only. He concludes the section by saying that subjects are bound to fulfill the law by the necessity of compulsion, but the prince only by his own will and by his regard for the common good.

In some of the digressions, Ralegh illuminates the motives or tactics of ancient heroes by his memories of Coligny in France or Drake on the high seas; again and again he illustrates the continuity of cruelty by comparing ancient and modern instances, as when he moves from ancient Damascus to the more recent destroyer of the city, Tamburlane, who by 1400 had conquered India and Asia 'with a storm-like and terrible success; but to prevalent fury God hath adjoined a short life, and whatsoever things nature herself worketh in haste, she taketh the least care of their continuance. The fruit of his victories perished with him, if not before .'

Frequently, events move him to recall his personal experiences, or to insert his personal opinions, or to dwell lyrically on one of the themes that move him. So the demise of the heathen gods evokes prose of poignant beauty about the haunting sense of Time's erosion of all man's works.

But all these are again vanished; for the inventions of mortal men are no less mortal than themselves. The fire, which the Chaldeans worshipped for a god, is crept into every man's chimney, which the lack of fuel starveth, water quencheth, and want of air suffocateth. Jupiter is no more vexed with Juno's jealousies; death hath persuaded him to chastity and her to patience; and that time, which hath devoured itself, hath also eaten up both the bodies and images of him and his, yea, their stately temples of stone and dureful marble.

These ancient gods, he says, as Milton said later, were merely devils seeking to be worshipped by credulous men; but now the Devil is subtler; knowing that men will not worship the old idols, he sets up the 'high and shining idol of glory, the all-commanding image of bright gold'. One gets the feeling at times that Ralegh is addressing the *History* more to himself than to the young Prince.

In similar mood, contemplation of life in Eden, where man was healthy and sound of body, leads him to soliloquize mournfully about how

Time itself (under the deathful shade of whose wings all things decay and wither) hath wasted and worn out that lively virtue of nature in man, and beasts and plants, yea the heavens themselves, being of a most pure and cleansed matter, shall wax old as a garment.

Indeed, all the great kingdoms of the earth have deteriorated and passed away, and Ralegh accounts for this decay throughout his *History* not only by the gnawing of Time, but also by man's insistent pride, ambition, and intemperance. It is an archetypal pattern he learned from Greco-Roman writings about the Golden Age. Though in every civilization, it seems, the first men lived simply and hardily, later generations always became increasingly luxurious and effete. Ancient and modern man alike wears out the virtue of nature by his own excesses.

Intertwining the stories of the Hebrews and the concurrent Syrian-Babylonian empires, Ralegh continues to illuminate one age by analogies with others, reminding the reader of the consistent texture of man's actions in God's world through time. The child Moses is seen as a Vergilian golden-age shepherd:

Where the glory of the world shined least, amidst mountainous deserts, there the glory of God, which shineth most, covered him over, and appeared unto him, not finding him as a king's son or an adopted child of great Pharaoh's daughter, but as a meek and humble shepherd, sitting at a mountain's foot, a keeper and commander of those poor beasts only.

And the effete son of the heroic Semiramis, Ninias, is described in terms that James I found uncomfortably suitable to him as Elizabeth's successor. Semiramis was as worthy of fame, Ralegh said, as any prince or princess that ever lived. But Ninias was 'no man of war at all, but altogether feminine and subjected to ease and delicacy'.

Some thought that James might well have taken umbrage also at the story of Cambises, who 'took more than usual delight in the taste of wine', and sought ways to adjust the laws to his own wishes. For though Ralegh had theoretically placed the king above the law, whenever he discussed incidents in which the principle was at issue, he clearly did not think the king ought to be free of law, Cambises, desiring to marry his own sister, asked his judges if there was any law among the Persians which permitted such marriages. But, said Ralegh, the judges 'had always either laws or distinctions in store to satisfy kings and times'; they answered that while justification could not be found in the written laws, the action could be justified out of precedent and unwritten custom. It sounds like an oblique and bitter commentary on the legal procedures of his own trial.

Even though the idea that history has been a demonstration of God's judgments was congenial to Ralegh, his independence of mind was somewhat constricted when he treated Hebrew history because his sources were to him sacred and authoritative, and the Hebrew people was the true protagonist in the ancient world theatre. And to the Puritans and their descendents it has seemed proper that the history and legends of the rest of the world should be coordinated with Biblical events. At about the time of Moses, Ralegh says, Prometheus lived, as did Atlas, Deucalion, and Phaeton (fabulous characters but not without background of dim historical truth). In the eleventh year of Gideon, Jason and the Argonauts sailed for the Golden Fleece. And after a discussion of the Minotaur, Theseus, Oedipus, and the wars of Thebes and Troy, Ralegh returns to Palestine to tell of the contemporary Samuel, Eli and Samson.

Despite their nearness to God's word, the kings of Israel worked out the same central lessons of history that Ralegh finds everywhere: the primitive virtues of an Age of Gold are swallowed up in the vices inherent in luxury and power. Gideon was cruel and merciless, and after his death his children suffered in consequence: 'the debts of cruelty and mercy are never left unsatisfied.' Because he was a man of war and treachery, even David was not allowed to build a temple. Princes would do well, Ralegh insisted, to imitate God's mercy, but they imitate instead his might, as did Lucifer; this is 'damnable pride', with which Ralegh was very familiar. In the roll-call of early history's cruel, sensual and ambitious princes, their end is all the same: 'silence and oblivion hath oppressed them.'

When Ralegh moves into purely secular history in the beginning of Book III, the narrative becomes more animated as Ralegh himself is more immediately engaged.

The depiction of men and events is full-blooded, and the moral judgments are fresh and independent, nor having already been made by inspired and infallible writers. His persuasive authority comes, as did that of Thucydides, from Ralegh's having been a man of action as well as letters. He had been a general, an admiral, an explorer; he had served in the courts and in the wars of his own age; he had been a confidant of princes, and a victim of the scramble for high place and of the rigour of the law. He had seen the overt and the hidden motives that move men to action. He moves easily and confidently in the battles and political struggles he writes about. When it depicts events like those in which he had himself been a participant, his *History* is energetic and unpedantic.

Following the now familiar pattern of moral judgment, Cyrus and his followers are seen as living in the simplicity of the Golden Age, wearing skins, drinking water, a nation of hardy and valiant men. And Cyrus himself was a prince 'who remembered the changes of fortune and his own mortality'. On the other hand, Croesus and his nation are luxurious sensualists, drinkers of wine, wearers of silk. And Croesus himself was filled with a strong sense of kingly prerogative – like someone else Ralegh could have named.

Like Cambises, Xerxes was an irrational prince who could not govern himself, which is a prince's first duty; he was both foolish and a coward, and because he was a coward he was merciless. Indeed, the Persian empire, founded on the virtue of Cyrus, was broken by a lack of *virtu* in his successors. As a man of his time, Ralegh is unaware of economic forces, of trends in public sentiment, or the gradual changes of custom that slowly alter the nature of states. States to him are conditioned by their kings, and kings and nations alike are made great by simplicity of life, rational conduct, by the courage of captains, the chastity of women, and by gentleness and mercy, especially in the powerful. The causes and signs of degeneracy are equally clear and unmistakable: drunkenness, cowardice, sensuality, effeminacy, and above all cruelty.

It was the sensuality of the Persians and the irrationality of their kings after Cyrus that made inevitable the Greek victories at Thermopylae, Salamis, and Platea. And the Greek rulers, in turn, 'by their great ambition' sought dominion over one another and plunged their countries into the endless fratricide of the Peloponnesian War. Initially Ralegh sympathizes with the Spartans, who lived 'Utopian-like', but they were at fault in placing 'all their felicity in the glory of their valour'. Athens was even worse. With sudden prosperity the Athenians grew insolent; they became ungrateful to their own best and wisest men and were swayed instead by a 'rascal multitude'. And Divine Justice, which never sleeps, saw all these things, including their shameful treatment of 'the wise and virtuous philosopher' Socrates.

But to a historian who cherished action as much as thought, Epaminondas of Thebes seemed even more admirable than Socrates, and his death is the occasion of Ralegh's highest tribute. The surgeons had told the Theban general that when the head of the dart – left in his body from a broken Spartan shaft – should be drawn out, he must die. Epaminondas thereupon called for his shield, symbol that he had fought with courage, advised the Thebans to make peace, and then willed the weapon to be withdrawn.

So died Epaminondas, the worthiest man that ever was bred in that nation of Greece and hardly to be matched in any age or country; for he equalled all others in the several virtues which in each of them were singular. His justice and sincerity, his temperance, wisdom and high magnanimity were in no way inferior to his military virtue . . . Neither was his private conversation unanswerable to those high parts which gave him praise abroad. For he was grave, and yet very affable and courteous; resolute in public business, but in his own particular easy, and of much mildness; a lover of his people, bearing with men's infirmities, witty and pleasant in speech, far from insolence, master of his own affections, and furnished with all qualities that might win and keep love. To these graces were added great ability of body, much eloquence, and very deep knowledge in all parts of philosophy and learning, wherewith his mind being enlightened, rested not in the sweetness of contemplation, but brake forth into such effects as gave unto Thebes, which had evermore been an underling, a dreadful reputation among all people adjoining and highest command in Greece.

Of all the ancients, Alexander the Great might perhaps be the most instructive to Ralegh's own young prince, for Alexander had been nurtured by no less a teacher than the humanistic Aristotle, who had taught him in his youth to be temperate, just, and prudent. But something in that journey he made into Asia altered his nature so that he refused to moderate his overweening ambition, as Aristotle had taught him; he became a lover of wine, of flattery, and of 'extreme cruelty'. Those who came for an audience with him in Persia were required to prostrate themselves and adore him. He brought into his Court whores and sodomitical eunuchs; he came to imitate the sensual, proud, and detestable manners of the Persians. And, without trial, he ordered the killing of his friend and follower Callisthenes. Ralegh quotes with approval Seneca's remark that no matter what great deeds Alexander did or had done, men would always say, 'But he killed Callisthenes'. Thus cruelty always poisons fame. Finally, Ralegh finds Alexander's life as instructive as that of Epaminondas, but in a different way: he shows that even courage and valour are nothing, unless they are directed to good ends. Were it not so, we would value most highly thieves and mastiff dogs. Inferior to Julius Caesar and others as ruler and general, in Ralegh's final judgment Alexander was simply a troubler of the world, a man who wished to buy glory with blood.

Concluding his history of the Macedonian kingdom, Ralegh paused to portray one of Alexander's surviving captains named Demetrius in terms that suggest an oblique self-portrait.

There was in this prince a strange medley of conditions . . . He was of a most amiable countenance, a gentle nature and a good wit;

excellent in devising engines of war and curious in working them with his own hands. He knew better how to reform his bad fortune, than how to rule his good. For adversity made his valour more active; prosperity puffed him with an overweening, wherein he thought he might do as he listed. His fortune was as changeable as were his qualities: turning often round, like the picture of her wheel, till she had wound up the thread of his life.

Many readers of the *History*, upon reading this passage, were reminded of its author.

As Ralegh turns at last to the rise of the final kingdom, Rome, he thinks of the infancy of that kingdom as a golden age, and take opportunity to contrast his own times.

For cottages and houses of clay and timber, we have raised palaces of stone; we carve them, we paint them, and adorn them with gold; insomuch as men are rather known by their houses than their houses by them; we are fallen from two dishes to two hundred; from water to wine and drunkenness; from the covering of our bodies with the skins of beasts, not only to silk and gold, but to the very skins of men . . . Time will also take revenge of the excess which it hath brought forth.

But in the Roman world, too, evil cropped up: Syracuse developed the vicious practise of ostracizing its strongest and wisest men: 'There is nothing,' Ralegh said in one of his most quoted phrases, 'so terrible in any state as a powerful and authorized ignorance.' As might be expected, tyranny developed in the Greek state of Sicily: there too men seemed unable to learn that the 'moderate use of sovereign power' is the most effective means of getting and retaining the love of subjects. Man is indeed a political animal: he has an innate desire to rule or to be ruled, but tyranny is the common corruption of that desire.

Though the Punic Wars demonstrate the virtues of Scipio, the courage and loyalty of Hannibal and Hanno, we know what to expect once more. After Carthage is defeated, the 'seeds of luxury' will soon overgrow and choke the Roman valour, and that state will be vulnerable to destruction by a hardier race who live more simply and are more valiant.

And there the *History* abruptly stops. That 'glorious prince' to whom it had been directed God had been pleased to take out of the world, and Ralegh can only say with Job that his harp has been turned into mourning and his organ into the voice of them that weep.

But then the grandeur and inevitability of Death took hold of his mind once more, and there was one final flood of song as that great haunting theme brooded over all he had thought, over all that had been done and said in the world since mankind began. The four great monarchies had all thought themselves imperishable, but the storms of ambition had beaten them all down. The mighty princes and tragical poets who had written of them complained of time, destiny, and the instability of fortune, but these should not be blamed. Most of the great princes had been stirred up by a desire for fame which was like plowing the air or sowing the wind. It would have been better for such princes to die quietly, to steal silently from the world, than to purchase remembrance by rapine, oppression, and cruelty, by spoiling the innocent, by emptying cities of their ancient inhabitants and filling them again with sorrow.

I have considered, saith Solomon, *all the works that are Under the sun, and behold all is vanity and vexation of spirit;* but who believes it till Death tells it us? . . . It is therefore Death alone that can suddenly make man to know himself. He tells the proud and insolent that they are but abjects and humbles them at the instant; makes them cry, complain, and repent, yea, even to hate their forepast happiness. He takes the account of the rich and proves him a beggar, a naked beggar, which hath interest in nothing but in the gravel that fills his mouth. He holds a glass before the eyes of the most beautiful and makes them see therein their deformity and rottenness; and they acknowledge it.

O eloquent, just, and mighty Death! whom none could advise, thou hast persuaded; what none hath dared, thou hast done; and whom all the world hath flattered, thou only hast cast out of the world and despised; thou hast drawn together all the far-stretched greatness, all the pride, cruelty, and ambition of man and covered it all over with these two narrow words, *Hic jacet.*

Prince Henry was dead; Ralegh himself was legally dead;

the future was oppressively dark, and his *History* would never be finished. Another of his great designs lay shattered and incomplete. There was nothing left for Ralegh himself now except that death of which he had written so movingly.

Or was there? What of Destiny which inclines the will of living men? Was it Destiny that kept inclining him toward Guiana, that land so outwardly savage, so filled with concealed riches? Why could he never forget that journey he had made so many years ago? Why did he still have that haunting sense of an uncompleted life, of a Destiny waiting to be fulfilled?

19

The Final Voyage

Ralegh's *History* is one of the great pieces of Wisdom literature. In it he has viewed the pageant of man without bitterness or rancour but with philosophic melancholy, as he sees the divine faculty in man, his reason, continually overcome by ambition, greed, or more venial follies. When reading the *History* one feels that its author, of all mortals, must be safest, best armed, most likely to see and recognize the subversions of the irrational. But it was not so. Ralegh proved to be the best illustration of the central truth of his *History*: our desires and passions are generally too strong and too clever to be fully understood or controlled by reason.

The last chapter of Ralegh's life was a long exercise in irrational conduct. In spite of opposition and ill-health, he persisted in seeking permission to search half way around the earth for a gold mine that never existed. By the time he was allowed to leave prison and go, he was an old man of sixty-five who had never entirely recovered from a severe stroke, which had left one side alternately swollen and numb. The return to Guiana was a task that would have challenged all of his youthful powers when they were at their best in the days of the French or Irish campaigns. But now he was ill, ageing, and something of a hypochondriac, continually dosing himself with his own exotic potions. He had become indecisive, his mind veering from one project and set of plans to another. And while his name still had some residue of power in the Westcountry, for the most part the men who were associated with him in his last journey lacked confidence in him and were suspicious and uneasy. From the first all sensed that there was something strange and unreal about the venture. They were, therefore, disinclined to submit to naval discipline and Ralegh seems never to have been firmly in control.

Many modern accounts of this last journey are the accounts of rational men who have believed that if the evidence were combed once more, a consistent explanation might emerge which would somehow make sense of that tangled skein of charges, denials, lies, allegations and distortions found in the various documents. But making sense of this journey is not a work for lawyers or judges or logicians; it falls rather in the province of the psychiatrist and folk-lorist. It becomes intelligible only if we realize that Ralegh and Keymis were both men obsessed by powerful delusions; then everything that happened is about what we would expect.

To pick up the subtle strands of the web that finally caught this elusive opponent of Fortune, we need to go back to the year of his greatest success: the fight at Cadiz in 1596. In that year he had sent Lawrence Keymis with two ships out to Guiana to see if he could find a better way to Manoa. Ralegh himself had been balked by the Caroni Falls and the great scarp; he now wondered if one of the tributaries of the Amazon River might not provide a way to the inland lake that would avoid those impassable headlands. Keymis sailed to the mouth of the Amazon River where he turned north and explored some of the major tributaries; he was told that the Essequibo, the most northerly of the large tributaries, was navigable to within one day's overland journey of the Lake of Parima.

Having secured this information, Keymis sailed on to the Orinoco where he found a much better way through the Delta than the one Ralegh had taken, a new channel that would carry ships of one or two hundred tons. Keymis sailed up the Orinoco once more to the Port of Morequito. There he found that Death had made his final call on the old cacique, Topiawari. He tried to trade for gold, but could find none – a fact that should have meant something to him and Ralegh. He spoke to the natives along the river, reminded them of Ralegh's promise to liberate them, assuring them that Sir Walter would return when he had finished raiding the Spanish under the orders of Cassipuna Ezrabeta who loved the people of Guiana and desired to protect them.

But finally Keymis brought dismaying news back to England. At the confluence of the Caroni and Orinoco there was a large rocky island that, effectively fortified, would bar further access upstream on either river. Ralegh had wanted to make a fortified settlement there, but the Spaniard had beaten him to it, and on the south bank of the Orinoco, just two or three miles from the Caroni, there was a new Spanish town called San Thomé. The Spaniards intended to block permanently the entrance to the golden halls of Manoa. In all of this disastrous news there was one comfort. Spain had been readying an expedition of 600 men for Guiana, but Ralegh and Essex had burned the ships they were to sail in at Cadiz harbour.

The next year Ralegh sent Captain Leonard Berry out with the specific task of exploring the Essequibo River, which he did. He also entered the Wiapoco, the Marawyne, and Corentyne, all arms of the Amazon. Berry again assured the natives that Ralegh would return with healing wings under which the Guianans would find freedom and peace. The legend of Ralegh was becoming as great a myth in Guiana as Guiana had become in the mind of Ralegh.

By now Keymis had readied for publication an account of his trip which is an essential document in understanding what followed. First, he renamed Guiana *Raleana* and never called it anything else. He also named the cape north of the Amazon River Cape Cecil, a name which did not endure. As he had sailed down the Orinoco on his return from San Thomé, he looked for the old cacique, Putijma, who had told him of the gold mine on Mt. Iconuri. Apparently he wished to rectify his mistake of a year earlier, visit the mine, and verify its riches. He could not find Putijma, but his own interpreter offered to bring him to a mine which contained precious stones and gold. The mine, distantly and vaguely pointed out to him, was in the vicinity of the mountain Putijma had showed him; he listened attentively to the story which accompanied it. It was the richest mine in Guiana, the interpreter said. In fact, when Berreo had seized Morequito, the Guianans had thought of offering him the mine as a ransom for their chief's life, but they did not. And to this day the mine remained hidden from the Spaniards. Actually, every Indian in Guiana probably had a story similar to this but by now Keymis was outside the pale of reason. When the cacique told him that a dragon guarded the treasure, Keymis showed his only sceptical moment; that was obviously a fable, he said, to keep the superstitious away. But the greater fable went unchallenged.

The Indians further said that because the news of gold in Guiana had become generally known, they could not hope to hold the land by themselves, and it was better to have the English there than the Spaniards for, if they came, the Spanish would make Indians run and row and carry burdens like asses and their women would become the victims of Spanish lust. Keymis was so fully convinced that he concluded his account:

Myself and the remains of my few years, I have bequeathed wholly to *Raleana* and all my thoughts live only in that action.

Ralegh promptly made plans to settle a colony of 5,000 men in Guiana. He intended to drive out the Spaniards, civilize and educate the unapparelled people, and find and join fortunes with the civilized men of Manoa. But then Tyrone rebelled in the north of Ireland and a savage empire nearer home must be subdued; Elizabeth forbade Ralegh to take any men or vessels for his proposed enterprise in Guiana.

After Ralegh went to the Tower, there were abortive attempts, under James and his ministers, to colonize overseas. In 1604, Captain Charles Leigh had founded a small trading company on the Wiapoco River. He was naturally looking for gold, but sustained himself and his colony by raising flax, cotton, and sugar cane. The farming went badly, as it always seemed to in the New World, and soon his men were living off the Indians. The colony failed and Leigh himself died in 1605.

Two years later, in 1607, Ralegh approached Robert Cecil

about Guiana. He said that by chance a refiner had come to him and he had allowed the man to take a sample of the ore he had brought back from Guiana twelve years earlier. The refiner had returned an assay that showed the ore to be fabulously rich. Ralegh admitted that he had offered to pay the refiner twenty pounds if he found gold in the ore (a strangely irrational procedure), but the man was skillful and his judgment had not been influenced by the bribe; in fact the refiner offered to go to Guiana himself and be hanged there if his assay proved false. Ralegh even offered to let Cecil take a little of the ore and have it tested by any assayer Cecil should name. He pointed out that an expedition would be feasible: of the 5,000 pounds the journey to the mines would cost, Queen Anne, Ralegh believed, would bear a third; if Cecil himself would bear a similar amount, Ralegh would find the rest.

In this letter to Cecil a strange medley of fact and fancy, deceit and reality begins to be evident. Ralegh tells Cecil that the assayed ore was the metal he himself had gathered in Guiana. If so, he was referring to the mine up near the Caroni falls where, with his dagger, he had hacked some metal out of a ledge of quartz. But this is not what he leads Cecil to believe. He says rather that the mine is on a mountain near a river side and the ore is 'of easy carriage thither'. This last description refers to the mine Putijma had told Keymis about. Neither Keymis nor Ralegh had ever been to this latter mine or in any way confirmed its existence. The gold ore from one place was being used to prove the existence of a mine in another.

Ralegh proposed an ingenious plan for recovering the gold. A ship was to be fitted up with six pairs of great bellows and brick furnaces. The ore would be carried from the mine to the ship and there refined and made into ingots. And it could be done, Ralegh was sure, without endangering the Spanish peace. 'We will break no peace; invade none of the Spanish towns. We will only trade with the Indians and see [no Spaniards] except they assail us.'

Everyone in England who had any interest in the matter knew that the Spaniards were planted at San Thomé. If Ralegh had ever revealed the exact location of the mine he had himself discovered, it would have been immediately apparent that he could not reach it or work it without first taking San Thomé or else immobilizing the garrison and the guns. Therefore, without giving up in his own mind the possibility of falling back on the Caroni mine as a second choice, he always talked of the Keymis-Putijma mine on Mt. Iconuri, twenty miles south of San Thomé and fifteen miles inland. If the English worked this site there was no reason why they should clash with the Spaniards unless the Spaniards attacked them first. The proved ore, if it was proved, came from one location and the mine that it was politically and militarily feasible to work was in another site twenty-five miles away. That was the essence of Ralegh's dilemma, and it explains much of what followed.

In 1609, Ralegh wrote from the Tower to Viscount Haddington, 'When God shall permit us to arrive, if I bring them not to a mountain (near a navigable river) covered with gold and silver ore, let the commander have a commission to cut off my head there.' By then he had been a prisoner for over five years and in his mind dubieties were beginning to become certainties if only they held the promise of freedom.

In the same year the King of Spain received word from one of his agents that 'Watawales' would soon be 'banished to Guiana' in two small vessels to look for gold and silver. And apparently in this year the Privy Council did make Ralegh an offer which he refused. They had proposed that a small ship be sent to Guiana to bring home ore from the mine. If it returned successfully, Cecil would assist Ralegh to regain his lost liberty and his lost estate. Ralegh's reasons for refusing the offer were not altogether compelling. It was sixteen years, he said, since he and Keymis had been to Guiana. To locate an acre of ground in a desolate and overgrown country would be difficult for two men and impossible for one. A second reason was that if Keymis died or perished by shipwreck, the charge of the voyage would be lost and the entire enterprise finished, for he dared not trust his own memory or landmarks for the finding of the mine. Finally, the Spaniards knew there was a mine but did not know its whereabouts; they had already tormented a hundred natives to death to find it. If Keymis went with a small force, discovered the location of the mine and then sailed home, the Spaniards would immediately move in and possess it. This last reason most Englishmen would find valid.

But Ralegh was not being entirely candid. He was deceiving the Council to some degree, and undoubtedly he was partly self-deceived. When he says that the mine is located on a single acre in a tangled jungle, he can only be imaging the quartz ledge he had found up on the Caroni; finding that again would indeed be an impossible task. But earlier he had talked of a mountain covered with precious ore and stones and near a navigable river: that was the Keymis mine which even a blind man could find. He also says that the gold in this mine, whichever one he had in mind, lay 'at the root of the grass in a broad and flat slate'. It was so accessible that whoever found it first could simply carry it away and that was why the Spaniards must not be allowed to find it. Inasmuch as he had no idea of what Putijma's mine was really like, it is clear that once again he was extrapolating from something he had heard on a previous voyage. Topiawari had told the Spaniards how the Manoans got their gold: they went into a plain and pulled out grass by the roots, and there the gold lay. So Ralegh had taken a third element from the legends of Guianan gold and visualized that problematical mine on Mt. Iconuri as being like the one Topiawari said existed in Manoa.

In the meantime colonizing efforts were continuing. In 1609, under Letters Patent from James, Robert Harcourt took sixty settlers to the Wiapoco River. There his first action was to call the caciques together and remind them that Ralegh had delivered them from Spanish tyranny. He sent out exploring parties, one of which found a chief named Leonard who had been in England with Ralegh, who had visited him in the Tower; he had come a hundred miles to see the Englishmen. Harcourt lifted up turf and twig, as Ralegh had not done, and formally took possession of all the land between the Amazon and Orinoco for King James. The Spaniard had performed this ritual earlier, but according to English custom, now more than half a century old, the Spanish claim was invalid because they had not settled the land and did not control it. Later Ralegh, in defence of his life, maintained that Guiana was English territory and that the Spanish were intruders there.

In 1610, Ralegh turned to his one sure benefactor, Queen Anne, and renewed an offer he had once made her to plant a new colony in Virginia. He knew it was being said that all he wanted was liberty; that if released, he would never sail at all, or that if he did he would flee to some other country. But Ralegh assured the Queen that he was willing to forfeit his life and estate if he did not leave England on the scheduled date, a most dangerous promise in an age when no man could command wind and plague. He also told the Queen that his wife had agreed to 'yield herself unto death' if he did not perform his duties to the King. And, if he should try to sail to a foreign port other than Guiana, the mariners and masters could be given orders from the King to throw him into the sea. In all of this there is a suggestion of excess, of near-hysteria, very unlike the calm and rational tone of his *History*.

But he knew how to win the affection and trust of women. He concluded the letter with a marvellous paragraph.

But were there nothing else, let Your Majesty, I beseech you, be resolved that it shall never be said of me that the Queen of England gave her word for this man; that the Queen took him out of the hands of Death; that he, like a villain and perjured slave, hath betrayed so worthy a princess and broken his faith. No, Madam, as God liveth there is no bond, no not the loss of twenty sons can tie me so fast as the memory of your goodness, and there is neither death nor life that can allure me or fear me from the performance of my duty to so worthy and charitable a lady.

It was the old grand manner, the Elizabethan style, and the romantic Anne, trapped in a newer and meaner age, found it irresistible.

Ralegh had aroused such interest in Guiana that an expedition was fitted out in 1610 and sailed under the direction of Sir

Thomas Roe, a merchant adventurer of great ability and notable veracity. Whatever he reported would command credence from Cecil and the Council. To this expedition, Ralegh the prisoner contributed 600 pounds, which may have made him the largest single investor. Roe sailed for 200 miles up the Amazon itself and explored a number of its tributaries. In this report to Cecil, he said that he had seen more of Guiana than had any living Englishman. He discounted the whole business of El Dorado, but did say that, though the Spanish were intending to colonize along the Orinoco, at present they were weak and could easily be displaced. The town of San Thomé itself, he said, was 'infinite rich and weak'. And Roe did believe there was gold to be found in Guiana. It was this, of course, that now kept the English government interested in that land, as Ralegh well knew, and after Roe's report he said nothing more of an Indian empire or the search for Manoa. He talked only of a rich gold mine, for Roe's report had at least given the existence of such a mine a kind of indirect credibility.

In 1611, Ralegh wrote to the Queen again, this time about Guiana. He told her that he was now old and weak, his shortness of breath growing upon him so that he could scarcely walk up Tower Hill. But he wished before he died to perform some work that would show the King his true faith and demonstrate his innocence, 'such service as hath seldom been performed for any king.'

At the same time he wrote to the King. Guiana, he said, was not a project he had devised to gain his liberty; the imprisonment of a long sea voyage was worse than the Tower. And he himself would be the only one to hazard anything. If he failed, he would make himself 'a ridiculous liar and a beggar' and would leave his children nothing except shame.

Finally he wrote to the Lords of the Council, returning to their old offer which he had once refused. Now he was willing that Keymis should go to Guiana if they would allow him sufficient force to protect himself against the Spanish. And Ralegh offered generous terms. If Keymis did not bring back half a ton of that 'slate gold ore', Ralegh would be willing to pay the total cost of the expedition. The Lords, in turn, were to promise that half a ton of ore safely delivered would give Ralegh his liberty and a pardon under the Great Seal. Again Ralegh was willing to hazard all that was left of his estate on the desperate and even hopeless gamble that Keymis could find a fabled mine. But for some reason the expedition never sailed; perhaps the Council simply refused the offer.

In 1614 Ralegh's hopes were encouraged. The Puritan Sir Ralph Winwood became First Secretary; being anti-Spanish he was inclined to listen to Ralegh. In the same year, Parliament having refused to vote a subsidy, the government was desperate for money. James was 700,000 pounds in debt and seemed to have no hope of being relieved of this burden by Parliament. His hope all along had been a Spanish marriage for Charles, from which he hoped to get a million pounds; privately he told his ambassador that he would settle for 500,000. Theologians in Madrid were trying hopelessly to work out a solution that would be acceptable to God, the Pope, Philip III and England. When Sir John Digby returned from Madrid in 1614 and at last brought James the proposed terms in writing, he saw how hopeless it was. The proposal that all children of the marriage should be baptized into the Catholic faith would itself arouse England beyond anything James dared to risk. But other terms were worse. Though they were ultimately to be given the right to choose their own religion, the children were to be educated entirely by Catholics. The succession was not to be affected if they decided, after being reared by a devout Catholic mother and educated by priests, to remain Catholic. In London there was to be a chapel open to everyone in which Catholic rites would be administered by priests in robes and vestments. And finally all civil laws against Catholics were to be abrogated. James was not only disillusioned by these proposals; he was also angered. The Spanish marriage had been for him what Guiana was for Ralegh, the visionary key to wealth and peace secured with honour. Now he saw it all for the mirage it was and so he began to listen favourably to Ralegh's proposals transmitted through George Villiers, his newest favourite, whose brother had recently received a remembrance of 750 pounds from Ralegh and Winwood. On March 19, 1616, a royal warrant was issued which permitted Sir Walter Ralegh to go abroad in the custody of a keeper in order to make preparations for his voyage.

The day Ralegh moved out of the Tower, Robert Kerr and his noble bride moved into his vacated quarters. Lord Grey had died in 1614; Arabella Stuart in 1615 – both in the Tower. Soon Cobham too would be dead. The wizard Earl of Northumberland was still in prison, patiently working out his chemical experiments and mathematical formulae. Florence McCarthy, now 'infinitely adored' in Ireland, was still writing history. Ralegh alone was free.

For a year he lived in his house in London, attended by a keeper and forbidden to go near the Court or into any public assembly. But he soon took a few days to stroll through the streets of London to see the new buildings and visit old friends, and then he turned to work. Eight days after his release he commissioned Phineas Pett, the King's shipwright, to build from his design and under his direction a ship of the *Revenge* class, of about 500 tons, swift, yare and heavily gunned. He called it the *Destiny*; this was to be his last round with that ancient antagonist.

To raise money, Lady Ralegh loyally sold some of her own lands and she called in the money she had been given for Sherborne (it had been loaned at interest to the Countess of Bedford); and Ralegh himself was able to secure some ten or eleven thousand pounds. Again he backed his project with everything he had, an unanswerable reply to those who said he never believed in the venture. With all this and some 20,000 pounds invested by others in Ralegh's hopes, he set about equipping his expedition. About forty gentlemen volunteered to go with him, among whom were Warham St. Leger, son of the man he had served with in Ireland; a nephew, George Ralegh, and his own young son Walter. Walter was a scapegrace, already famous for duels, brawls and jests. Once after fighting a duel he had found it necessary to leave England. Sir Walter had sent him abroad with Ben Jonson as his tutor, a somewhat doubtful choice. Once in a French town the boy had got Ben dead drunk and as he lay sprawled out, Walter had him carried about the streets and exhibited him at every corner as a more lively image of the crucifix than one could see in any Catholic church.

On another occasion Sir Walter was going to dinner 'with some great person' to which the son was also invited. The father specifically asked the boy to behave himself and, for a while, he did. And then he made his father the butt of one of the most outrageous jests of even that permissive age. That very morning, he said, he had gone in to a whore, kissed and embraced her and grown very eager, but she would not have him. When he asked why, the woman replied, 'Your father lay with me but an hour ago'. Ralegh was stunned by the grossness and bad taste, and he hit his son across the mouth, hard. There was a hushed moment, for young Walter was not accustomed to receiving blows even from his father. Finally he turned to the man next to him and struck him across the face. 'Box about,' he said, ''twill come to my father anon.'

Ralegh had once written a poem to the boy which, in a good-natured way, carried undertones of concern.

> Three things there be that prosper up apace
> And flourish whilst they grow asunder far,
> But on a day, they meet all in one place,
> And when they meet, they one another mar;
> And they be these, the wood, the weed, the wag.
> The wood is that which makes the gallow tree,
> The weed is that which strings the hangman's bag,
> The wag my pretty knave betokeneth thee.
> Mark well dear boy whilst these assemble not,
> Green springs the tree, hemp grows, the wag is wild;
> But when they meet, it makes the timber rot,
> It frets the halter and it chokes the child.
>   Then bless thee and beware, and let us pray,
>   We part not with thee at this meeting day.

Bess Ralegh counselled patience; after all, she said, the boy was just like his father. This expedition was to be his first chance to prove himself in a serious undertaking.

Ralegh received his commission in 1616, but it was not given to him under the Great Seal and the adjectives 'trusty and well-beloved' had been written in, probably at Winwood's directions, and then erased. Ralegh also wanted a pardon before he sailed and he believed that he could buy one, probably having in mind the receptivity of the Villiers brothers to hard cash. But Bacon, it is said, persuaded him to save his money and to trust to the implications of his commission. If he was an Admiral he had the power of life and death over his men; if that were so he must have a real legal existence and was no longer civilly dead; therefore, by implication, he had been pardoned. Certainly, this was Ralegh's defence later. The King, on the other hand, contended that he had withheld a grant of pardon for the specific reason that he wished 'the better to contain Sir Walter Ralegh and to hold him unto his good behaviour'. It is not likely that Ralegh would have sailed without a pardon if there had been any chance of getting one. He was much too intelligent for that.

Once the news of Ralegh's expedition was out, James found himself in a dilemma. Gondomar, probably the ablest ambassador Spain had ever sent to England, knew how to manage James, how to flatter his pedantic vanities, how to tempt him with Spanish friendships and marriages and how to threaten him with Spanish anger. He completely outmanoeuvred James who was now like Buridan's ass which had been placed at an equal distance between two piles of hay, both of the same size and quality. Equally torn by his appetite in both directions, unable to move, he died of starvation. So it was with James. Gondomar would hold out the hope of a Spanish marriage under new and better terms; then Winwood would show him the assays of Ralegh's ore. While the issue was still unresolved, Count Gondomar offered Ralegh a safe conduct to the mine. If he would sail with a small, unarmed force, the Spanish King would send an escort with him to the mine; Ralegh was welcome to bring home all the gold he could find. The Spaniards were not worried about the loss of gold; they had become realistic in Madrid, if not in Trinidad, about the legends of Guiana. Ralegh refused the offer, ostensibly because he didn't trust the Spaniard – and every Englishman could sympathize with that. But Ralegh had a deeper motive. He had no firm plan in mind; if one mine didn't work out, he intended to try another. He had to be free to improvise if his journey was to be a success.

James made the best compromise he could. Repeatedly he obtained assurance from Ralegh that he would not engage the Spaniards unless they attacked him first. James required him to explain the details of his scheme in writing and mark his intended route upon a map. According to Ralegh, James promised upon the faith of a king to keep it secret, but a man who had just written a history in which he had told the world what the faith of kings was worth should not have been wholly dismayed when James sent the whole account through Gondomar to Madrid. From there, it was forwarded to San Thomé where Ralegh's men found it and brought it back to England to prove the royal perfidy. To be sure, that perfidy probably did not contribute either to Ralegh's failure or his danger. After all his *Destiny*, while it was being built in a Thames shipyard, was one of the sights of London. Everyone knew where Ralegh was going and the Spaniards had all the information Gondomar ever gave them from a dozen different sources, and they were peculiarly inept in using it or doing anything about it. But it is still sad to think that a king of England would betray the confidence of one of his own captains. It was cowardly and small-minded, unthinkable in the age of Elizabeth and shameful even in the age of James.

James and Ralegh also had a secret understanding which was designed to further obviate difficulties with the Spanish. Ralegh was to secure four French vessels for his expedition; they were to be in the vanguard when he approached the mine, so that if the Spaniards engaged, the French would meet the enemy and hold them off while the English worked the mine.

At the end of January, 1617, James, still torn with indecision, agreed that Ralegh could sail but, through Winwood, promised

Gondomar once more that if he went beyond his commission he would pay with his head. Gondomar, in turn, assured James that the Spanish theologians appeared to be favourable to the marriage. James now believed that he had done everything possible to avoid trouble with Spain. There was danger, of course, in allowing Ralegh to sail, but his departure would direct public attention from the unsavoury murder of Overbury and the Spanish pensions; it would also placate Villiers and Winwood. Conceivably Ralegh's journey might make James independent of his Parliament, although the King was probably not very sanguine about that.

Though Ralegh's commission did not entitle him to subdue or conquer any foreign lands, it did allow him to explore and search for gold, a fifth part of which was to be paid to the Crown. Ralegh believed in the riches of Guiana – that point is beyond dispute – but he did not really know where he could find them. He might rob the rich graves of Guiana's noble dead; or four days up the Orinoco from Morequito he might find those apparelled people who lived at the border of the land of El Dorado. As a last resort he might rob the Spaniards who were working some small mines near San Thomé. But the most likely place to find treasure was in one of the two mines he knew about. If everything failed, Ralegh had a force strong enough to raid Spanish shipping and even to capture the Plate Fleet. When Lord Bacon had asked him what he would do if he missed the mine, Ralegh allegedly had said that he would look for the Plate Fleet. But then you will be pirates, Bacon said, and Ralegh replied, 'Whoever heard of men being pirates for millions?' He seemed to think he was still living in the age of Elizabeth when such things could be safely done. In any case, Ralegh did not intend to return to the Tower. Like the dying Drake, he needed gold before he returned to England.

But by this time Ralegh was no longer really competent to lead such an expedition. In 1615 he had suffered a second stroke which had sapped his energy and seems to have affected his judgment. Certainly bad judgment of men or carelessness of detail in planning jeopardized the French aid he counted on.

To procure the ships promised him, he sent two Frenchmen to carry a letter to France asking for the four ships and also asking for a letter, promised him, he said, by Admiral de Montmorency, allowing him to enter a French port with all his ships and any goods he might acquire through treaty or conquest. This request was later used as evidence that Ralegh was bent on violence from the beginning, but all it really shows is that he was trying to establish a refuge in case everything went bad. Unfortunately the two Frenchmen, instead of carrying the message to Paris, went to Rome where they were picked up and sent on to Madrid. There they confessed all they knew and somewhat more, piously affirming that they had deserted because they did not wish to sail with Huguenots and heretics. They claimed that Ralegh intended to invade both Trinidad and Margarita and annex them to England.

At one point the expedition was nearly diverted from its intended destination. It was difficult for political realists to believe that such a large and expensive force was being assembled merely to hunt for a gold mine. In 1616 Savoy was at war with Spain and the city of Genoa was proving troublesome to Savoy. The port was being used to disembark Spanish troops, and the Genoese bankers were financing the Spanish King who had always been their most frequent if not most reliable customer. So Count Scarnafissi proposed to James that Ralegh's forces should be allowed to attack and capture Genoa. Ralegh knew the defences of the port and said that with some ships from the Royal Navy he would be willing to reduce them. A victory at Genoa would have freed him and redeemed his name; even an honourable defeat could scarcely have done less. But Madrid, seeing the way things were going, teased James again with the marriage, and he backed away from the Savoyan alliance. Ralegh, he said, could not be spared from the Guiana voyage.

Ralegh published his orders to the fleet at Plymouth on May 3, 1617. They were both godly and sensible. They included the usual injunctions against sailor's vices of cards, dice, and swearing. And Ralegh said that no man was to force any woman, Christian or heathen, on pain of death. He devised signals for apprising the fleet of the approach of an enemy and gave a few basic tactical instructions: any ship under the lee of an enemy must strive to recover the wind and so on. In the Indies the sailors must avoid unknown fruits and unsalted flesh; they must avoid swimming in the alligator-infested rivers, and they must not take anything from the Indians by force. Ralegh explained this instruction and most of the others: if they used the Indians kindly, the Indians would give them food. Otherwise they might suffer serious privation.

The Spanish, in the meantime, were never as active or as excited as Ralegh believed. Philip's Council reported to him that it was not practical to send a fleet to intercept Ralegh for no one really knew where he would land. All that could be done, they said, was to send a packet boat with letters warning the governor of each territory and this was done in June, 1617. Had Ralegh known this when he reached Guiana, he and his men would have acted more boldly, but since they daily, almost hourly, expected the arrival of Spanish galleons, everything they did was coloured by the image of the great sails making down on the mouth of the Orinoco to entrap them.

As the expedition prepared to sail, Sir George Carew wrote that Ralegh was 'extremely confident' of the gold mine. 'I am sure,' he continued, 'he will be able to land 500 men which is a competent army to perform any exploit upon the continent of America.' He concluded by praying that Sir Walter might return deep laden with the gold ore of Guiana.

Even before the fleet sailed, discipline was bad; always an aloof commander, Ralegh now kept apart from all except a few of the officers. At Gravesend, there was a riot between sailors and townspeople, and on the ships, as they sailed down the Thames to assemble at Plymouth, there were continual quarrels and fighting among the company 'with many dangerous hurts'. At Plymouth suspicion of the enterprise increased. Fair winds blew and the expedition did not sail, but not as some thought, from deep policy; it was merely lack of money and uncoordinated planning. Captain Pennington of the *Star* was detained at the Isle of Wight because he had no money for provisions. Ralegh sent him riding off to London where Lady Ralegh, that admirable wife, helped him to raise the funds. Then Captain Whitney needed supply, and Ralegh sold his own plate to provision him; all the while fair winds were blowing. Finally on June 12, 1617, seven ships of war and three pinnaces set out to sea. They were joined by more ships until finally the expedition numbered thirteen ships and nearly 1,000 men. But almost immediately the winds scattered the ships, driving some back to to Plymouth and some to Falmouth. There Ralegh reduced his force considerably, saying that he could provision his ships for a year only if he had fewer men. This strategy, if it did nothing else, helped him to get rid of the worst of the potential mutineers among the crew.

The waiting was especially bad for the morale of this disorderly expedition, but finally it set out again and cleared the channel. Off the Scilly Islands the winds were adverse and strong; the ships ran before them and came to the port of Kinsale in Ireland where Lord Boyle lived on Ralegh's former estates, which were now flourishing, bringing in some 12,000 pounds a year to the new owner. Boyle treated Ralegh most generously. He gave the expedition without charge 100 oxen, as well as some biscuit, beer and iron; he also gave Ralegh 350 pounds in cash and a 32-gallon cask of whisky. He kept open house for Sir Walter and his gentlemen for three weeks and Ralegh, in turn, relinquished any lingering past claims on Boyle that might still have been unsatisfied. Everything he had was now staked on the voyage of the *Destiny*.

On August 10, the fleet stood out to sea again, this time with fine, following winds. Off Cape St. Vincent, Captain Bailey boarded four French vessels and helped himself to their cargo and supply. When Ralegh heard of it, he insisted that Bailey pay cash for everything he had taken. Bailey angrily replied that the French ships had taken their cargo in the West Indies by piracy (which was true) and that he was therefore entitled to it. But Ralegh made him pay nevertheless. On September 6, the expedition reached Lancerota in the Grand Canaries, where the natives at first believed them to be Barbary corsairs and would not allow them to land. Later Ralegh was given permission to come ashore, but two or three of his men, while securing supplies, were murdered. The captains wished to retaliate by reducing the island, but Ralegh required his men to re-embark without firing a shot and proceeded on his way. Captain Bailey, however, still resenting the loss of his French prizes, took occasion to desert and returned to London where he gave out that he had left because Ralegh had turned pirate. Bailey's story set the Court in a turmoil. Sir George Carew refused to believe it; the Privy Council was investigating, but James's mind was already made up. Sir Thomas Lake wrote to Gondomar on October 21, 1617, 'I have just received a letter from Viscount Genton, respecting Ralegh's business and his action in Canary. He tells me that His Majesty is very disposed and determined against Ralegh and he will join the King of Spain in ruining him.'

Soon an English merchant who had been at Lancerota returned to England and told the truth about Ralegh's conduct there. As a result, Bailey was imprisoned by the Privy Council and sharply rebuked. Ralegh was entitled to feel that his conduct up to this point had established his good faith. He sailed on to the island of Gomara where he was permitted to water and buy provisions: there too he kept his men in good order. To the governor's wife, who had been born an Englishwoman, he sent a present; she returned the compliment by sending sugar and fruit to Ralegh. Not to be outdone in this Oriental exchange of courtesies, Ralegh sent her ambergris, rosewater, and a picture of Magdalen weeping.

By now his provisions were too old and his ships had been out too long. As contrary winds continued to hold him back, sickness broke out in the fleet. On board the flagship, forty-two men died and Ralegh himself contracted fever. For twenty-eight days as the ships rolled and tossed and manoeuvred for wind, he burned and weakened. He could take no food except the fruit the governor's wife had given him at Gomara: the oranges, lemons, and quinces, which had been preserved in boxes of sand, sustained his life until the ships arrived at Cape Oyapoco on November 11. While he lay ill, dying as it was feared, a deputation of gentlemen waited on him. They begged him to do two things: to appoint a successive commander and to show them on a map the exact location of the mine. Ralegh would do neither, knowing that the success of the venture depended on improvisation and that any final and open commitment to one place might destroy all confidence, for suspicions were already thoroughly aroused.

At the Cayenne River, Ralegh and his men rested for three weeks. Ralegh wrote Bess that their son had suffered no sickness; he himself, however, had suffered as violent a fever as a man could endure and still live. He still had 200 men and his ships were strong. He had already learned, however, that the King had betrayed all of his plans to Spain. Still he could not conceal his pleasure in the fact that the Indians still remembered him. 'To tell you I might be here King of the Indians were a vanity; but my name hath still lived among them. Here they feed me with fresh meat, and all that the country yields; all offer to obey me.'

Keymis also wrote a letter home, not without ominous undertones.

Our General is but lately risen from his bed, having laboured in extremity of sickness and weakness this month, but God be thanked he is now to the great comfort of us all recovered, for without him it may be doubted all had been lost.

Obviously Keymis thought the success of the expedition depended on Ralegh, and Ralegh had staked everything on Keymis, his memory and his good faith.

For Ralegh, still so weak that he had to be carried about in a chair, was obviously in no condition to lead the expedition. And anyway, his men and captains were all looking anxiously to sea where the Spanish galleons might soon appear. Because Ralegh was the only man among them who had ever fought Spanish warships, they would not consent to go up the Orinoco unless he stayed to secure their rear. Since Warham St. Leger was too ill to command the troops, Ralegh put his nephew,

George Ralegh, in charge of them. Keymis was in charge of finding the mine.

In his written instructions to Keymis, Ralegh reminded him that George Ralegh was a young, inexperienced man. 'It is therefore on your judgment that I rely, whom I hope God will direct for the best.' Keymis was to weigh anchor down river from Mt. Aio. From thence, says Ralegh, he should have less than three miles to the mine. Actually the original mine of Putijma was supposed to be some fifteen miles inland. But then neither Ralegh nor Keymis was ever completely sure of just where it was. In any case, Keymis was to land his men twenty miles downstream from San Thomé; there he was to throw up a screen of troops between the town and the mine. If the mine proved to be very rich, the party was to stay and work it. If the Spanish assaulted the party, George Ralegh was to repel them. If the mine proved not very rich, Keymis was to bring out a basket or two of ore to satisfy everyone that Ralegh had been truthful and sincere in asserting the existence of a mine. His conclusion rang with the old assurance. Keymis, he said, would find him when he returned, 'at Puncto Gallo dead or alive, and if you find not the ships there, yet shall you find their ashes, for I will fire with the galleons (and if it come to extremity) but run away I will never.'

Ralegh's written instructions to Keymis were precisely in accord with what he had told James, Cecil and the Council for many years that he would do. But no attempt was made to carry out those instructions, and we can never know why. Either Keymis was incompetent to carry out the orders, or he and Ralegh had a secret understanding which was different from the document which had been written merely for the record, or else Keymis disobeyed deliberately. It is certainly impossible that Keymis could have inadvertently missed Mt. Aio. When they sailed past that most prominent landmark, everyone would have known it. And in an attempt to explain why his instructions had not been obeyed, Ralegh later said that the town of San Thomé had, without anyone's knowledge, been moved some twenty miles downstream. But that was a desperate lie; the

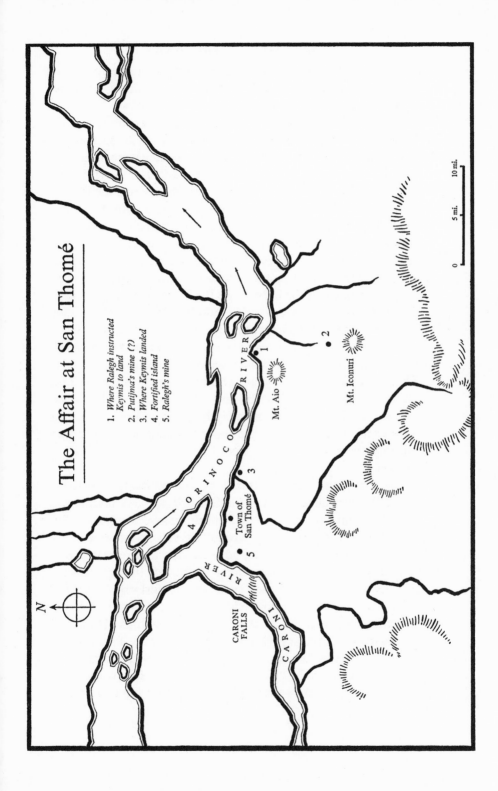

The Affair at San Thomé

1. *Where Ralegh instructed Keymis to land*
2. *Putijma's mine (?)*
3. *Where Keymis landed*
4. *Fortified island*
5. *Ralegh's mine*

ORINOCO RIVER

Mt. Aio

1

2

Mt. Iconuri

3

Town of San Thomé

5

4

CARONI FALLS

CARONI RIVER

N

0   5 mi.   10 mi.

village may have been moved a mile or two downstream from its first location, but not enough to make any significant difference if Keymis had done as his instructions directed.

But he did not. Instead he sailed ten miles beyond Mt. Aio, to within five miles of San Thomé. He sent his larger ships on upstream where they blockaded the town; they were fired upon but did not return the fire. In the darkness, Keymis disembarked his troops and set them marching toward the town in good battle order. Captain Cosmor was in front with the forlorn hope, the lost children, the usual advance guard of musketeers. Behind him came the main body of the muskets and behind them were the pikes led by young Walter Ralegh. The Spanish, in the meantime, had sent an advance guard out into the night to lie in ambush on the hillside. As the English blundered along in the darkness, they were suddenly swept with a volley of shot. This was a critical moment; the English could have withdrawn a short distance and held, or they could have asked for a parley. It was known that there was dissension in the garrison at San Thomé; in fact, one of the soldiers had recently attempted the life of the governor. A calm and experienced English commander might have gotten everything he wanted, even the town itself, without a shot. Certainly he could have withdrawn and thrown up his screen of troops between the town and Mt. Iconuri.

But any plans were shattered by the foolhardy valour of young Walter Ralegh. When the Spanish muskets discharged, there was some disorder in the English ranks. Except for a few gentlemen, they were not a particularly valiant lot, and in the darkness it appeared as if the advance unit had retreated precipitously. It was then that young Walter left his post, rushed past the musketeers and then even past the forlorn hope, a lost child out beyond the lost children, past Captain Cosmor himself who, not to be outdone, rushed after him. These two ran on ahead and, unsupported, they assaulted the Spanish line. Before he made his last charge, young Walter turned and cried out in the night, 'Come on my hearts. Here is the mine you must expect; they that look for any other mine are fools.'

King James and his advisers later cited this speech as evidence of Ralegh's deceit; young Walter, they said, was 'likest to know his father's secret', but the truth is far more obvious and much sadder. A rash boy was trying to equal his famous father's past reputation for heroics, and he had been clear-eyed enough to see that his father was now on a fool's errand. Young Wat thought that by taking a town rich in tobacco, possibly rich in silver and gold, he might redeem the enterprise and his father's name. But he and Captain Cosmor were killed immediately by musket shots as was the Spanish governor. Another man or two were wounded on both sides and that was the extent of it. But blood was up; the pikes had followed young Walter and when they saw him dead, they stormed over the walls of the town and soon possessed it. And then, for no reason anyone can assign, they burned the town; perhaps that was simply what was customarily done when Englishmen found themselves inside Spanish walls. Everyone agreed that young Wat's rashness was responsible for the unplanned assault on the town.

From that moment Keymis was like a man paralysed. For a week he delayed writing Sir Walter about his son. The captains and gentlemen confidently expected that the day after the town was taken, Keymis would give instructions for pushing on to the mine. Instead he delayed. At night he took a few of his own followers and went out exploring. The party was not gone long enough to have been near Mt. Iconuri and it returned with a few rocks that the assayers pronounced worthless. Now the company were all convinced that they had been hoaxed.

Ralegh and those who believed in him, could never understand why Keymis acted as he did, but his motives would not appear too difficult to fathom. His fantasies, his obsession, had suddenly been confronted with reality. It was well enough to say in England that there was gold slate lying around near Mt. Iconuri or Mt. Aio, but all he actually knew was that two Indians had vaguely said so. If Keymis had pushed his men through the jungle and explored both mountains he would not have known what to do next or where to look. He is not the first man who, finding that he must put a lifelong fantasy to the test, suddenly finds excuses for delay, for inaction, anything to conceal from himself a little longer that he has been beguiled by desire. Captain Parker, whom Ralegh thought one of his best men, later wrote that Keymis 'trifled up and down some twenty days, keeping us in hope . . . but at last we found all his delays mere illusions and himself a Machiavel; for he was false to all men.' Poor Keymis. No man was ever less of a Machiavel; but goodness of heart and sincerity of intent could not turn illusion into fact.

Keymis finally sent two launches up the Orinoco. When they came to the fortified island at the mouth of the Caroni they were fired upon; two men were killed and six hurt. The rest returned. In the meantime, English food-gathering parties were ambushed and the captured town of San Thomé was continually fired upon by the Spaniards. Keymis probably believed now that his only hope was to discover the Spanish mines or some gold that had supposedly been taken from them. He seized a priest and an Indian woman and threatened them with torture. He led a Portuguese boy around in ropes, beating him with sticks to make him reveal the hiding place of the treasure. This unusually sensible boy pointed to the poverty of the town and asked if it was plausible that there would be gold in such a place.

George Ralegh made one heroic effort. He remembered that Topiawari had told Ralegh that he would find the border people of the Manoan empire four days upriver; that all the gold traded along the Orinoco came from there. Perhaps he believed that in the villages he would find graves to rob, or chiefs to ransom. Whatever the hope, he and his men fought their way upstream for 300 miles only to find nothing but naked savages. When he returned, it was all over; the dream had collapsed. There was not a man in the company who would have followed either Keymis or Ralegh another mile. The final irony came on the way down river toward the ships. When the expedition came abreast of Mt. Aio, Keymis told Captains Parker and King and Sergeant Major George Ralegh that if they would drop anchor and accompany him, he would take them to the mine at last. They showed not the slightest interest.

426

Ralegh could not understand why everyone had given up so soon. Keymis and the others had with them, as a prisoner, the governor's servant; if they had only 'pinched him' he would have told them of two or three gold mines and a silver mine near the town itself. Ralegh had not been with that servant an hour until he knew 'the precise way to five or six of the richest mines which the Spaniards have'. But no one believed him now; they saw him as a pitiful, deluded, sick old man whose fantasies had been supported by a loyal friend who, without wishing it, had ruined him irretrievably. Keymis had taken from the Spaniards two gold ingots, three Negroes, two Indians and several tons of tobacco. That was the extent of Guiana's riches.

Ralegh's journal ends abruptly on February 14, probably on the day he received news about the death of his son. Some two weeks later the survivors of the expedition joined him at the mouth of the Orinoco. Incredulous and aghast, Ralegh listened to the tale of Keymis's ineptness. That poor man, intellectual turned adventurer, unable to give the real reason for his failure – that he had suddenly discovered the mine to be a mirage – invented a number of other reasons. He said that the water in the river was so low that he couldn't land where he was supposed to. Besides the English were so weak that they could not have stayed long enough to work the mine on Mt. Iconuri; therefore he did not wish to discover it for the benefit of the Spaniards. As he invented one lame, implausible excuse after another, Ralegh rejected them all. When his son was killed, Ralegh said, Keymis might at least have risked a few more men to satisfy the King and save Ralegh's life and honour. Keymis then composed a letter to the Earl of Arundel, one of the chief financial backers of the expedition and one of the men who had stood surety for Ralegh's conduct. Ralegh read the letter and forbade Keymis to send it. He would not allow such a weak and foolish thing to be sent, he said. It would make them all fools in the eyes of the world.

The despairing Keymis replied that in such a case he knew what course he must take. Soon from his cabin there came the sound of a pistol shot. Ralegh sent his cabin boy to find out what it meant. The boy knocked and Keymis answered. He had only been cleaning his pistol, he said, and it had discharged accidentally. Actually he had shot himself, but the ball had been deflected by a rib. As soon as the cabin boy left, Keymis stabbed himself to the heart with his dagger.

After he learned the completeness of the failure, Ralegh wrote two letters home. The first, on March 21, 1618, was to Secretary Winwood. In it he asserted that the Spaniards had begun the attack; he also flatly accused the King of betraying the expedition to the Spaniards and enclosed proof of it. He insisted that the reason for the effective Spanish fighting was their desire to guard the entrance to 'the mine'; they were not greatly concerned for the town itself.

Again Ralegh was self-deluded. The Spanish mines outside San Thomé were of no significance. The Spaniards were, in fact, fearful that the English would stir up the native tribes to a revolt in which the Spanish settlers would be massacred. The entire gallant Spanish effort was aimed at preventing the communication of the English with neighbouring tribes.

Ralegh concluded his letter with a hint that he might not return to England: 'I am unpardoned . . . and my estate consumed; and whether any other Prince or State will give me bread, I know not.'

On the next day, March 22, he wrote a short, heartbroken note to his wife.

I was loath to write because I know not how to comfort you. And God knows I never knew what sorrow meant till now. All that I can say to you is, that you must obey the will and providence of God and remember that the Queen's Majesty bare the loss of Prince Henry with a magnanimous heart and the Lady Harrington of her only son. Comfort your heart (dearest Bess), I shall sorrow for us both; and I shall sorrow the less because I have not long to sorrow, because not long to live . . . My brains are broken, and it is a torment to me to write . . . The Lord bless and comfort you, that you may bear patiently the death of your valiant son.

That was the end of the letter, but Ralegh could not resist justifying himself to the only person in the world who still cared for him enough to sympathize with his failure, and so he started a postscript which soon was several times longer than the letter itself. He remembered that Drake and Hawkins had died failures; he complained bitterly of the King's betrayal of the expedition; his captains, he said, had run away from him, even the ones he had done the most for, sacrificing his own plate and goods to supply their ships. The rest of his men are 'a rabble of idle rascals' who will wound his reputation in England. He has worked harder, slept less, taken more pains than any of them. His friends will believe it; for the rest he cares not. And having unburdened himself, he closed the letter and turned to the task of salvaging something from the expedition.

Throughout his last voyage, Ralegh's mind had vacillated a good deal; now it was worse; he proposed first one thing and then another. The expedition would capture Trinidad; or he himself would lead them back up the Orinoco; they would seek out the Plate Fleet; they would go to Virginia, re-victual and clean their ships and return in the spring to Guiana. But no one listened. Whitney and Wollaston deserted and went off looking for prizes. The captains who stayed held a council of war at which it was decided to sail to Newfoundland.

As the expedition approached Newfoundland, Ralegh was informed that a hundred of his men were going to wait until his flagship had been beached for cleaning; then they would seize the best English ship in St. John's harbour and turn pirate, plundering the French and Portuguese, knowing that Ralegh could not get his ship back into the water in less than ten or twelve days. And even then, with so many defectors, he likely would not have enough men to pursue them.

Although Ralegh's abilities no longer matched his courage, the courage remained. He called the conspirators together and confronted them with their conspiracy. Because of it, he told them, he had decided to return directly to England rather than going to Newfoundland. Immediately there was an uproar and an outcry; the conspirators said they would rather die than return. Already they had seized the ship's magazine and had control of all the weapons. Ralegh had no choice but to sail for

Newfoundland, but on the way he treated with the leaders of the mutiny who finally agreed to return to England if he would first put in at Killibeg in northern Ireland, a pirate base, and if he would try to secure them a pardon for past and present offences. Even now, when he was no longer in control of his own vessel, Ralegh's delusions were strong. He later told Sir George Carew that, at this point, he could have turned pirate and enriched himself by 100,000 in three months, or he could have collected a force which 'would have impeded the traffic to Europe', and so on.

On June 21, the foul and unkempt *Destiny* arrived at Plymouth alone; all the captains had now deserted except Captain King. Lady Ralegh was there; she had come from London to tend her sick husband and share his grief. Ralegh began to bargain for the disposal of his small cargo; whatever he got for the few tons of tobacco would be all he had in the world. However, the new Vice-Admiral of Devon, a distant kinsman, Sir Lewis Stukely, was even then on his way to Plymouth with orders to arrest Ralegh and bring him to London.

Stukely did not place Ralegh under immediate arrest, although he did seize his ship and its cargo; for over a month Ralegh stayed in Plymouth with little or no supervision; it is likely that the government, or some of the more intelligent men in it, wished him to escape. It would save embarrassment and perhaps something worse, for James had got himself into serious difficulties over the affair. When Gondomar had received the news of the burning of San Thomé, he had burst in upon James with one word, uttered three times. Raising his voice each time, he shrieked, 'Piratas, piratas, piratas!' After James came out of conference with Gondomar he told his Privy Council that he would either have to hang Ralegh himself or deliver him to the King of Spain for, under the harassment of Gondomar, he had been sufficiently weak and frightened to promise in writing that Ralegh and others after a legal process 'which cannot be altogether avoided' should be sent in the *Destiny* to Spain to be hanged in the public square in Madrid unless the King of Spain decided otherwise. Gondomar triumphantly delivered that letter to Philip III. Francis Bacon was incredulous; Villiers was shocked and showed it, but Bacon suavely suggested that this, after all, was merely talk and not to be taken literally. James said that it was not talk, that he had no choice in the matter and he stormed out of the room. It was fortunate for James that Philip III had more sense than he did. The Spanish King had no desire to incur the odium of having executed an aged and ailing hero, and he declined the honour of officiating at Ralegh's death.

From this time until shortly before his death, Ralegh played the role of Hamlet; whether he was partly mad or only pretending madness, it is difficult to know. He was more than ever indecisive, moody, even hysterical; he made plans, revised and cancelled them and then planned again. While he was at Plymouth the loyal Captain King negotiated with two Huguenot captains from La Rochelle to take their old champion back to France. One night Ralegh and King rowed out toward the French barks. They were only ten minutes away; they could see the lights swaying as the barks rode at anchor when some better thought told Ralegh that this was not the way to reply to Fortune. He turned around and rowed back to harbour.

About July 25, Stukely, Bess, King, and a French apothecary who was also a quack physician set out for London with Ralegh; Stukely still had made no arrest and was pretending to be Ralegh's good friend. What he was seeking was some overt act, or better still, some confession of guilt, which would justify to the nation Ralegh's arrest and subsequent death. As they rode past Sherborne, Ralegh said, 'All this was mine, and it was taken from me unjustly.' Those words were duly reported to King James.

When the party reached Salisbury on July 27, Ralegh asked the French physician for an emetic; with his usual bad judgment and lack of caution he confided in the man that he was only pretending sickness in order to gain time to mobilize his friends, put his affairs in order, and pacify His Majesty who, as Ralegh knew, was already in Salisbury where he had come on a progress. The man who had written the history of mankind could surely write one more explanation, one more brilliant apology, which would clear everything up and satisfy the government. Ralegh now entered into another plot with Captain King. It would be best for him to go to France after all. The King, in time, would moderate his anger; not even Spain could remain outraged indefinitely over a small episode out beyond the line. So Captain King and Lady Ralegh were to continue to London where Captain King would hire a boat which was to lie off Tilbury. When cousin Stukely and Ralegh arrived, they would take a boat on the Thames and row downstream to the French ship.

After Captain King and Bess left him, Ralegh played his mad scene. By smearing some exotic medication on his skin, he caused pustules to break out on his arms and chest, sores resembling plague or leprosy; no one was quite sure what it was except that it was horrible. Then Ralegh stripped off his clothes and ran around the floor on all fours, making weird animal sounds and gnawing at the boards and rushes. Strangers were afraid to approach him; Lancelot Andrewes, the Bishop of nearby Ely cathedral, compassionately sent three different physicians to examine the madman. When no one was around, Ralegh clandestinely dined on a leg of cold mutton and wrote sections of his *Apology for the Voyage to Guiana*. Even if it was all only clever counterfeiting, there were overtones of hysteria in the deceit. When he told the French quack of his clever ruse, his laughter was wild, but when his *Apology* was completed he got well immediately and justified his strange behaviour by citing the example of King David who had feigned madness in order that he too 'might escape from his enemies'.

On Friday, August 7, Ralegh arrived at his home in London still lightly and carelessly guarded. Two days later two Frenchmen called on him. One was the French Resident in London who indicated that not only could Ralegh count on a welcome in France but the French would also assist in his escape. At that time France was attempting to forestall the Spanish marriage and a Spanish alliance; it was known that Queen Anne preferred a French bride for Prince Charles and it was also realized that

Ralegh had a good deal of influence with the Queen. Ralegh listened to the Frenchmen, thanked them but told them he would find his own way.

Captain King had hired a boat to convey Ralegh to France, but the captain of the boat had already betrayed Ralegh; so had Stukely. That Sunday night, wearing a false beard and an odd hat with a green band, Ralegh went down to the Tower dock with Stukely, Stukely's son, Captain Hart, whose ship was waiting and Captain King. Soon after the party embarked they saw another boat following along behind them. This was disturbing and so was Stukely's talk. He kept asking Captain King if he, Stukely, had not acted as an honest man. King took alarm and said he hoped Stukely would continue to do so. Ralegh then asked the rowers if they would go on even though someone came to arrest him in the King's name. The rowers replied ambiguously. Stukely began cursing and said he would himself kill the watermen if they failed to row on. But now the tide was gone and the rowers said they could not reach Gravesend before daylight. Meanwhile the following boat was closing up and Ralegh, realizing that he had been betrayed, ordered the men to row back upriver; and he put himself in Stukely's custody. When the boat docked and the party came ashore, Stukely ostentatiously arrested Ralegh in the King's name as a traitor. Ralegh now perceived that he had again been deluded and shamed, but he had also regained the demeanour of a gentleman. He replied in words that King Lear might have used in a moment of humility and insight: 'Sir Lewis, these actions will not turn out to your credit.'

The capture of Ralegh seemed to anger James. He said that Ralegh must be a coward to allow himself to be taken so easily. But now he had to kill the old eagle and justify himself before the nation. He enquired of a special commission what his options were. Edward Coke, speaking for the commission, replied that Ralegh could not be tried for any crime committed since his attainder for high treason, for he had been legally dead for fifteen years. There were, however, two courses open to the King. The first was for His Majesty to publish a narrative of Ralegh's 'late crimes and offences'. At the same time the King could summarily issue a warrant for Ralegh's execution on the old charges of high treason. Such a procedure was unquestionably legal. However, the commission was inclined toward a different course, something nearer 'to a legal procedure'. Ralegh, they thought, could be called before the entire Council of State and an assembly of certain other judges, noblemen, and men of substance who could serve as audience and witness. Before this assembly, Ralegh would be charged and then confronted with adverse witnesses (a lesson Coke had learned from the previous trial). After testimony had been heard, the Council and the Judges would advise His Majesty whether or not he might proceed 'with justice and honour' to give warrant for the execution. James read the suggestions and opposed them both. The second course would make Ralegh too popular 'as was found by experiment at the arraignment in Winchester where, by his wit, he turned the hatred of men into compassion for him'. And so the King proposed a third course. Ralegh would be called only before the Privy Council and those few additional men who had already examined him; there would be no other audience. The other recommended procedures would be followed. However, the King specifically requested that no mention be made of the French attempts to help Ralegh escape.

Before this select commission Ralegh was arraigned and charged with four 'impostures'. It was alleged that he had never known of a gold mine in Guiana and never intended to go there. His purpose had been to set war between the kings of England and Spain. He had abandoned and put in danger all of his company. And, finally, he had spoken disloyal and harsh things about his sovereign.

Ralegh's reply was brief and dignified. He believed, he said, that the King in his conscience now knew that he was innocent of any treason in the first year of his reign. He affirmed that he did believe in a mine and had spent 2,000 pounds to bring refiners and refining tools on the expedition. Despite the opinions of some witnesses, he firmly denied any attempt to abandon his men, an obviously false charge since he had not,

434

in fact, abandoned them. As for the other two charges, he simply denied them. His confidence in the King had been deceived he said, but he had not spoken ill of him. He admitted that he had thought of taking the Plate Fleet if the mine failed.

Then Sir Henry Yelverton, who was acting as Attorney, spoke.

My lords, Sir Walter Ralegh, the prisoner at the bar, was fifteen years since convicted of high treason, by him committed against the person of His Majesty and the state of this kingdom, and then received the judgment of death to be hanged, drawn and quartered. His Majesty of his abundant grace hath been pleased to show mercy upon him till now that justice calls unto him for execution. Sir Walter Ralegh hath been a statesman and a man who in regard of his parts and quality is to be pitied. He hath been as a star at which the world hath gazed; but stars may fall, nay they must fall when they trouble the sphere wherein they abide. It is, therefore, His Majesty's pleasure now to call for execution of the former judgment and I now require order for the same.

It was at least a refreshing contrast to the livid rhetoric of Coke and the pompous moralizing of the Chief Justice at the first trial.

Ralegh was then allowed to proceed with his defence. He seemed to have little interest in it; he was not fighting for his life as he had been fifteen years ago. In a weak voice he repeated the legal argument that his commission as admiral, with the power of life and death over others, had given him a new legal existence and constituted a discharge of his former judgment. His only aim, he said, had been to 'honour his sovereign and enrich his kingdom'. In pursuit of that aim he had lost his son and wasted his estate.

But his law was bad as usual. The Chief Justice explained that there could be no 'implicit pardon' for high treason. The pardon must rather be specifically given by 'words of a special nature'. Ralegh seemed almost relieved.

If your opinion be so, My Lord, I am satisfied, and so put myself upon the mercy of the King.

435

The Lord Chief Justice had prepared a few words, less graceful than the Attorney's. Sir Walter, he said, had been given a fair trial although it was long ago.

You might think it heavy if this were done in cold blood, to call you to execution, but it is not so; for new offences have stirred up His Majesty's justice.

He knows that Ralegh has been valiant and wise and believes that he still is. If so, he will have occasion to employ both virtues for he must die. 'Your faith hath heretofore been questioned, but I am resolved you are a good Christian, for your book, which is an admirable work, doth testify as much.'

Ralegh made no protest; no further defence. He asked that he might not be cut off suddenly for he still had something to say to His Majesty, and he added thoughtfully, 'to the world'. As it turned out, he was given one week of life, one week in which to compose himself, to throw away the false beard and the silly hat, to wash away the marks of leprosy and plague and to erase the indignities he had brought upon himself, to purchase some forgiveness and understanding for that fool's errand to Guiana and the stories of monsters, Amazons, and golden cities. There could be no more pleading, no more sickness. The mind must grow clear and the body strong. It must be a whole man, a man of *integritas*, who would present himself, before all England, on the scaffold.

20

The Death of Sir Walter Ralegh

James had no intention of giving Ralegh an audience before which the consummate actor could evoke memory and music. He therefore ordered the execution to take place on Lord Mayor's day, the day of London's greatest festivity. And the execution would be carried out, not in a public place, but in the relative obscurity of Westminster Palace courtyard. The shows and pageants would attract the public; surely not many, on such a day, would leave the festivities to watch a beheading. James himself would retire from London; he would do some pious thing, perhaps write a poetic version of the Lord's prayer which he would dedicate to George Villiers who had now replaced Robert Kerr in his affections.

For all his braininess James was a fool (as the French minister, Sully, had observed); he could not see the obvious: that a kingly pardon coming after Ralegh's humiliating failure in Guiana, the climax to a lifetime of failures, would soon put an end to the Ralegh legend. Give him the rags and bones of a few unheroic days, at home or in exile in France, and let advancing senility and his lifelong tendency to bore everyone with his self-justifications, put an end to it. Then when Sir Walter died he would be dead. But with Bacon nodding approval, he blundered into giving Sir Walter his final opportunity and sent him the gift of a public execution.

Sir Walter lay in the Tower of London under close guard reflecting on a lifetime of struggle between virtue and Destiny. It was, he knew, a classical struggle. Only a few years earlier, as he had been considering one of history's supreme crises, the Battle of Marathon, he had written that the Athenians now

437

found the time arrived 'wherein they were to dispute with their own virtue against fortune'. Now he had come to his Marathon and he had the same weapons as the Athenians. The word 'virtue', like many other things, was withering under the Puritan touch. The Puritans tended to equate it with chastity or the solemn observance of their joyless code. But the classical heroes had known that it meant manliness. Manliness against Destiny. Aristotle had said that the essence of virtue was rationality. Perhaps so, but there were also courage, moral and physical strength, insight, and finally fortitude and resignation if it all went bad. Those were the weapons.

The hero's one last weapon against a Fortune that overmatched him was a noble death. Such a death his fellow Englishmen admired as much as had the Greeks or Romans. Only the rules had changed slightly; Stoic fortitude was a little too simple for the England the Tudors had created. They liked wit; the word meant strength of mind as well as humorous agility. The English had inordinately admired Sir Thomas More because he had not only died bravely but he had also jested so merrily before his execution. He was manly.

And Ralegh wished also to keep in mind the Puritans who liked godliness. In the Puritan scheme, salvation was always conjectural; therefore it was a sin to be too serene and assured, but it was equally sinful to be fearful. One could never be sure whether their hidden and inscrutable Deity had elected a soul to be a Vessel of Mercy or a Vessel of Wrath. And so the death scene was crucial; it was the best indication of things to come. If there was a 'lightening', if the dying man seemed cheerful but not too cheerful, it was edifying and would encourage all to live a good life. If he departed in terror there was still a moral in his leaving. To the Puritans, it was the edification that mattered.

All ranks of Englishmen recognized and admired courage in the face of death. Mary of Scotland had redeemed what Englishmen considered a vicious life because she had died like a Queen. The Earl of Essex, on the other hand, was a great boy who had died like a calf. Those scornful words, attributed to Ralegh, sound uncomfortably like him. Well, Sir Walter knew the kind of death he must die; he would prepare his final speech carefully. He would store his quick mind with proverbs and jests, some of which might find an appropriate moment for utterance, and he had thought of a few actions he might take by which people would remember him. His approach to death was the carefully contrived design of a poet. But beyond all design, he was confident in his own pose, always greatest when danger was greatest, and hopeful that he might be given a moment of grace in which he would find the words or deeds which would live after him in the minds of his countrymen. Destiny owed him something for all those humiliations.

So the ritual began. On the morning of October 28, 1618, when Ralegh was to leave the Tower and go to the gatehouse at Westminster palace, which would serve as a prison for a day and a night until he was executed, an old servant noticed that his hair was tousled. If Sir Walter would stay a moment he would comb it. 'Let them kem it that are to have it,' Sir Walter replied. The jest was similar to one Sir Thomas More had made, as Ralegh would have known. But it was typical that he had used a Westcountry idiom, 'kem' for 'comb', for even at Court when he was the Queen's lover, whatever his other affectations, he spoke always with the Western burr that endeared him to the men from Devon and Cornwall.

Seeing tears in the old man's eyes, Ralegh spoke teasingly to him, 'Dost thou know, Peter, of any plaister that will set a man's head on again when it is off?' And his wry smile was infectious; the old servant laughed. Later he told all of his friends what Sir Walter had said.

At Westminster gatehouse that evening a few friends came to see him, among them Sir Hugh Beeston. Ralegh asked if he would come to the execution and Sir Hugh assured him that he would. Then Sir Walter said, 'I do not know what you may do for a place. For my own part, I am sure of one. You must make what shift you can.' Then both laughed heartily and Sir Hugh told the story everywhere. Within a week you could hear it in half the towns of England.

To Sir Hugh or some other visitor Ralegh gave an epigram which he had composed.

> Cowards fear to die, but Courage stout,
> Rather than live in snuff, will be put out.

The metaphor on which his epigram was constructed was that of a rush candle, which develops a long ash called a snuff. Elizabethan writing is filled with comparisons in which a snuff candle is used to describe what is faint, feeble, and on the point of extinction. The clearest meaning of his epigram is that it is better to die firmly than to live feebly. But, like most metaphors, it carries overtones of other meanings too. A snuff candle produced an unpleasant odour; it wrinkled the nose. To live in snuff was to live as a source of annoyance to others. It was better to die than to be an offence to one's countrymen. The epigram carries both meanings.

Ralegh also wrote a poetic petition to Queen Anne, who would have saved him if she could, for when her own life was in doubt once, he had given her the Balsam of Guiana. How James had resented that! She had drunk the stuff, compounded of herbs that Ralegh himself had plucked in the land of the gilded kings; her heart had been lifted; she was made well. She emotionally insisted afterwards that she owed Ralegh her life. This ageing Queen did not call from Ralegh his best poetic line, but one stanza of the petition is appropriately nostalgic.

> For what we sometime were we are no more,
> Fortune hath changed our shape, and Destiny
> Defaced the very form we had before.

Queen Anne would have understood. She was misshapen with dropsy, unloved and slowly dying. Ralegh intended a figurative meaning, but his words were literally true for the Queen.

One of the visitors to the gatehouse was Ralegh's kinsman, Francis Thynne, who was surprised to find the usually dour Ralegh in good spirits, even elated. Remembering the Puritan ideal of cheerful but not too cheerful, Thynne cautioned, 'Do not carry it with too much bravery. Your enemies will take exception if you do.'

'It is my last mirth in this world,' replied Sir Walter. 'Do not grudge it to me. When I come to the sad parting you will find me grave enough.'

They were good puns. 'Sad parting', the parting of the head from the body was Ralegh's own; the pun on 'grave' was as old as memory. Twenty years earlier Shakespeare had found it useful in *Romeo and Juliet*. 'Ask for me tomorrow,' Mercutio says after he has been thrust through by Tybalt, 'and you shall find me a grave man.'

Lady Ralegh was his last visitor that evening. Now there were no puns, no epigrams, simply the goodbyes of a man and woman who had loved one another faithfully for a long time, who had seen their fortunes fail and their love cool and were both intelligent enough to see it and sorrow for it, but who still had in common an intense loyalty and an affection that outlasts passion. Ralegh could not bear to talk of his little son, Carew, conceived in the Tower and born while his father was still a prisoner there, and the only hope now for the survival of his name. He could not trust himself to talk about that precarious future. He might lose heart.

He was worried, he told Bess, that the King's agents might forcibly prevent him from speaking before his execution; if so, he gave her instructions. One way or another his last words were to be heard. When the clock struck twelve, Lady Ralegh arose to go. She dumbly cast about for some word of comfort. They are going to let me have your body, she said at last. For the first time she saw his wry smile but the jest was tender. 'It is well, dear Bess, that thou mayst dispose of that dead which thou hadst not always the disposing of when alive.'

She smiled briefly, kissed him and left. Ralegh then spent the night writing. All that was left to him now was a few hours of darkness; when the light came it would strike the edge of an axe to which he must kneel.

Sometime in those hours, Ralegh opened his Bible and on a blank fly leaf wrote the verse that has always been associated with his death. However, he did not compose the stanza that night, except for the last two lines; he reached back into memory for that love poem he had written to Bess, probably when she was still a maid of honour. The poem had begun with a sensual celebration of physical beauty.

> Her eyes he would should be of light,
> A violet breath, and lips of jelly,
> Her hair not black, nor over bright,
> And of the softest down her belly,
> As for her inside, he'd have it
> Only of wantonness and wit.

These were cavalier and courtly sentiments. But there was always in Ralegh a counter turn of mind, an edge that turned in, and having created a peerless mistress, he couldn't help thinking of Time who would uncreate her, Time which

> being made of steel and rust,
> Turns snow and silk and milk to dust.

This metaphysical concept of Time devouring beauty and love had aroused his imagination and he had apostrophized in the final stanza, in some of the best poetry he ever wrote,

> Oh cruel Time which takes in trust
> Our youth, our joys and all we have,
> And pays us but with age and dust,
> Who in the dark and silent grave,
> When we have wandered all our ways,
> Shuts up the story of our days.

And that night, in the gatehouse, waiting for the light that would lead him into darkness, he recalled that stanza from his old love poem, changed one phrase, and added to it a couplet.

> And from which earth and grave and dust
> The Lord shall raise me up I trust.

The couplet rather spoiled the poetry, but generations of

Puritans admired it more than anything else Ralegh ever wrote. There is no reason to believe either that in writing it he was insincere, or that he was unconscious of the effect it would have after his death. He cared little, now, what men thought of his love poems, written long ago, in the days of his vanity.

Ralegh had not slept when Dr. Tounson arrived, in the grey of dawn, to offer him the Holy Eucharist according to the rites of the Church of England. Like Cousin Thynne, the doctor was disturbed to find such a cheerful prisoner, but Ralegh said that he owed God thanks that he had never feared death. It was easier, he said, to die by execution than by a burning fever.

Such Stoic resolution led Tounson into an anxious homily about the state of Ralegh's soul. He reminded the prisoner that heathen men could die bravely; it was therefore of crucial importance that his cheerfulness and assurance should spring not from mere courage but from faith in his Saviour and in his own innocence.

He answered that he was persuaded that no man that knew God and feared him could die with cheerfulness and courage, except he were assured of the love and favour of God unto him; that other men might make shows outwardly, but they felt no joy within.

This reply edified Tounson and from that moment he was one of Sir Walter's advocates.

Ralegh then received communion and expressed the hope that he would be able to persuade his auditors that he died an innocent man. This made Tounson anxious again. He felt that Ralegh might tax the justice of the realm. To soothe him, Ralegh confessed that justice had been done by the course of the law. By Dr. Tounson's leave, however, he should like to stand upon his innocence in fact.

Tounson then asked if Ralegh did not have some other guilty matter upon his conscience; he was evidently hinting at something and Ralegh asked him to be direct. Very well, said Tounson, what of your conduct at the death of the Earl of Essex? So that was it. Seventeen years ago the Earl had been executed and Tounson was still disturbed about Sir Walter's part in it. Ralegh replied courteously to the Dean and mentally resolved to add a paragraph about the Earl in his farewell speech. He and the memory of his malice towards England's darling must die together.

Sir Walter then ate a good breakfast and called for his pipe. Tobacco was offensive to King James and to many Puritans as well, but it was part of Ralegh's legend. Whenever he lighted his pipe he kindled memories of Virginia, Newfoundland, and Guiana.

It had long been a custom in England that when felons were taken to Tyburn for execution, the carts would stop at the Hospital of St. Giles where the hospitalers would bring the condemned a drink of wine. It was a humane custom that sent men to death with a warm stomach, however chill their hearts. On one occasion a hearty rogue had smacked his lips and said that a man should be allowed to tarry over such good wine. The story had gone the rounds.

Ralegh would not pass St. Giles for he would be executed in the courtyard near his prison. But some decent man, remembering the old custom, brought him a bowl of wine. Ralegh drank it and his benefactor asked if he had enjoyed it. 'I will answer you.' Sir Walter replied, 'as did the fellow who drank of St. Giles' bowl as he went to Tyburn: "It is good drink, if a man might but tarry by it." '

Sir Walter then walked toward the scaffold attended by two sheriffs and Dean Tounson. Passing through the crowd, he saw that an old man had uncovered his bald head in the raw October morning. Ralegh was wearing a cut lace nightcap beneath his velvet cap; he removed it and gave it to the man saying, 'You need this, my friend, more than I do.' And behind the gift was the wry smile, the jest lightly hidden.

Then he ascended the scaffold and the crowd had their first view of him. In his younger days he had always overdressed; bravery of apparel was the principal sign of his 'damnable pride'. He had worn his hair curled like an Italian, with pearls in his ears and shoes, emeralds and rubies sewed into his coat and diamonds flashing from the fingers of both hands. Now the effect was stark. He was dressed in a black waistcoat and breeches and was wearing a black velvet gown and cap. The only relief from the sombre black was the ash-colour of his silk stockings. He had recently suffered a second stroke; there was still some paralysis in the left side that now caused his leg to drag, the same leg that had been torn by a Spanish shell in the naval battle at Cadiz; even his slight deformity seemed heroic.

On the scaffold he turned and faced his countrymen. Seated near him on the scaffold were three peers of the realm: the earls of Arundel, Oxford, and Northampton. Out in the crowd were three unknown young commoners for whom Destiny would shortly have work: John Eliot, John Hampden, and John Pym, three of the chief architects of the Puritan revolution. They believed that they were seeing a citizen of England die by royal prerogative and without due process of law. Already the legend was abroad in the land that the real crime for which Ralegh had been originally convicted was the advocacy of the establishment of a commonwealth after Elizabeth had died. The first Stuart king, it was said, wanted the head that harboured such thoughts.

The tall, grey-haired Ralegh first explained to the crowd that he suffered from recurrent ague (it was likely malaria contracted in the South American jungles). When the fit came on, he said, he shivered involuntarily and he therefore asked his friends, if the attack recurred before he died, to attribute it to sickness rather than fear. Then he found some of the noble cadences and phrases of his speech.

I am infinitely bound to God, that he hath vouchsafed me to die in the sight of so noble an assembly, and not in the darkness, neither in that Tower, where I have suffered so much adversity, and a long sickness.

But some could not hear him. He voice had always been thin. There was some shuffling and moving about as men pressed closer and Ralegh began again. His second opening was even better.

As I said, I thank my God heartily that he hath brought me into

445

the light to die and hath not suffered me to die in the dark prison of the Tower.

Darkness and light. That was the theme of his execution. Did John Eliot feel anything at that moment, one wonders, any premonitory shudder ? For he would soon die in the darkness of that Tower which Ralegh had now escaped.

Then Ralegh began a justification of his actions. It was not now a time, he said, for him 'either to fear or flatter kings'. John Pym heard that phrase; he marked it.

I am now the subject of Death and the great God of Heaven is my sovereign, before whose tribunal seat I am shortly to appear.

In such a solemn context, he then declared his innocence of treason. He was a little long in justifying himself, but the hour of death is a bad time to break old habits. He sensed the restlessness and stopped, wryly apologizing for being tedious. He would like to borrow a little more time from Master Sheriff, however, to speak of a matter that made his heart bleed.

It was said that I was a persecutor of my Lord of Essex, and that I stood in a window over against him when he suffered, and puffed out tobacco in disdain of him. I take God to witness that my eyes shed tears for him when he died. And, as I hope to look in the face of God hereafter, my Lord of Essex did not see my face when he suffered . . . And my soul hath been many times grieved that I was not near unto him when he died because I understood that he asked for me, at his death, to be reconciled to me.

He said a few more words about Essex and was finished. Now it was time for prayer and one or two other things the prisoner had in mind to do before he died. He asked all the assembly to pray with him and for him. Many heads bowed and after a time Ralegh spoke again:

I have many, many sins for which to beseech God's pardon. Of a long time my course was a course of vanity. I have been a seafaring man, a soldier, and a courtier, and in the temptations of the least of

446

these there is enough to overthrow a good mind and a good man . . .
I die in the faith professed by the Church of England. I hope to be
saved, and to have my sins washed away, by the precious blood and
merits of our Saviour Christ.

Then he turned to the hooded headsman who knelt to him and
asked his forgiveness. Sir Walter placed both his hands on the
man's shoulders and forgave him, he said, with all his heart.
Then quite unexpectedly he continued, 'Show me thine axe.'
The headsman was confused; it was not proper to show a man
the weapon that would kill him. But Ralegh had his reasons,
and he repeated the request firmly. This time the headsman held
out the axe and Ralegh put the edge of his finger against the
blade. 'This gives me no fear,' he said. 'It is a sharp and fair
medicine to cure me of all my diseases.' There was the slight
smile again, the superb poise, the immaculate manliness.

If history could have unrolled a few of its years at that moment
what a sight it would have been. How incredible even to
imagine it. For there, within sight of the scaffold on which
Ralegh stood, another one was to be erected and on it, awaiting
the headsman, would be Charles Stuart, King James's own son,
his Baby Charles. Pym would not be there, nor Eliot or Hampden, but their wraiths would be hovering near. Cromwell would
be there, Ireton and Bradshaw, a young Puritan poet, Andrew
Marvell and, not far away, assenting fully to the destruction of
the temple of the Lord's Anointed would be John Milton. And
Marvell would write an account of Charles's death which echoed
of Ralegh's. It must have been Ralegh's business with the axe
that he had heard about and remembered in his brilliant lines
about the King's death.

> He nothing common did or mean
> Upon that memorable scene,
> But with his keener eye,
> The axe's edge did try.

The executioner, as though Shakespeare had written his part,
then took off his cloak and spread it for Sir Walter to kneel on.

And everyone suddenly remembered that this was the way Ralegh had first won favour with the Queen. Then the headsman asked Sir Walter if he didn't wish to kneel facing the east. Light and darkness. Destiny was giving him his moment.

Back to Ralegh's quick mind came a cadence he had written five or ten years earlier in his *History*, but to the crowd it seemed a wholly spontaneous reply.

The matter is not great which way we turn our faces, so our hearts stand right.

Who else in England's history could make phrases like that with his last breath? And then the crowd watched fascinated, puzzled, aware that they were spectators of some inner drama quite beyond the outward one as Ralegh, having said it was the heart that mattered, nevertheless carefully shifted his position and faced eastward. And later, when those earnest Puritans, Milton, Pym, Eliot and Cromwell came to read his *History*, chapter by chapter, they learned that Ralegh had performed, at the moment of his death, a symbolic action. They found its meaning in the first book.

We who dwell west from paradise and pray turning ourselves to the east, may remember thereby to beseech God, that as by Adam's fall we have lost the paradise on earth, so by Christ's death and passion we may be made partakers of the paradise celestial, and the kingdom of heaven.

And so the poet spoke in a dozen tongues: everything he did or said, even the articles in his pockets had voices that some ear heard, then or later.

Ralegh knelt, prayed briefly and said to the headsman, 'When I stretch forth my hands despatch me.' He then placed his head upon the block and stretched forth his hands. But this unnatural headsman could not strike. Sir Walter stretched them forth again. What had the man seen that paralysed him when the last Elizabethan gave his silent signal? Was he of the ancient faith, and did the kneeling man, his arms outspread, resemble a crucifix? Or an old eagle, wings spread, ready to rise and wheel to some unknown land?

Again Ralegh waited a moment, then spoke sharply: 'What dost thou fear? Strike man, strike.' There had been in that voice, until lately, something that most men were willing to call master, and the old authority was in it now. The axe fell, raised and fell again. The body never moved, never twitched; only the lips kept moving in prayer.

It was customary for the executioner to hold up the head. If it were some notorious traitor, he would cry out, 'Behold the traitor,' and then, 'God save the King.' The people would respond full-throated, 'God save the King.' But fifteen years earlier when George Brooke had been executed for treason, the headsman, holding up the traitorous head had cried out, 'God save the King,' and only one voice was heard to respond, that of the Sheriff whose duty it was to reply. On the present occasion the headsman said nothing. He held up Sir Walter's handsome head and there was silence. Then another Englishman found a phrase. 'We have not such another head in England,' someone cried out. And the play was finished.

Epilogue

The head was placed in a red velvet bag; the body was covered with the black velvet cloak. Both were placed in a waiting carriage and taken to Lady Ralegh. Earlier in the day she had prayed that God would hold her in her wits; but God was in his Calvinistic mood that day, inscrutable and arbitrary. And so he appeared to grant her prayer, but withheld something. Lady Ralegh lived to be eighty-two years old, to within one year of the execution of Charles Stuart. To all appearances she was rational and sane; but there was one little quirk. She refused to bury Sir Walter's head. She had it embalmed and kept it by her side, frequently inquiring of visitors if they would like to see Sir Walter. Bishop Goodman kissed those cold lips, he said, many times as a courtesy to the widow.

The severed head was to have been buried later with the body of Carew, the child the thoughts of whom had moved Ralegh so deeply the night before his execution. Carew lived to a ripe age and fathered the children that would perpetuate the name. Gossipy old John Aubrey went to school with the two boys, Walter and Tom. They were ingenious, he said, but proud and quarrelsome just like their grandfather. So something more than Ralegh's name survived in them. But his head never found its way into its intended grave; it simply vanished. No one knows where. Only the ideas that came out of it have survived.

Posterity soon began to record their feelings about Ralegh's death. Dean Tounson wrote, 'His was the most fearless death that ever was known; and the most resolute and confident, yet with reverence and conscience.' Cheerful, in other words, but not too cheerful.

John Eliot said that there was scarcely a parallel in history to the courage of 'our Ralegh'.

All preparations that are terrible were presented to his eye. Guards and officers were about him, the scaffold and the executioner, the axe, and the more cruel expectation of his enemies. And what did all this work on the resolution of Ralegh? Made it an impression of weak fear, to distract his reason? Nothing so little did that great soul suffer. His mind became the clearer, as if already it had been freed from the cloud and oppression of the body. Such was his unmoved courage and placid temper that, while it changed the affection of the enemies who had come to witness it, and turned their joy to sorrow, it filled all men else with emotion and admiration; leaving with them only this doubt, whether death were more acceptable to him or he more welcome unto death.

An anonymous writer with a classical bent said that 'his death was managed by him with so high and religious a resolution, as if a Roman had acted a Christian, or rather a Christian a Roman.'

Ralegh's courage, his manliness, contrasted so strongly with the effeminacy of James's Court that it became a kind of national treasure. It was spoken of in taverns, on the Exchange, in Court and in people's homes. There were poems, ballads, letters and tracts about it. He had intended to give England its

450

noblest death and win something back from Destiny. It was the one great design of his life that had not been flawed and broken in the performance. He had done what he set out to do.

Lady Ralegh was not a Greek heroine. She was vivacious and forthright but not subtle, and she must have spent most of her life in astonishment or dismay at her husband's activities. It is doubtful that she understood the tragic view of life, the realization that man cannot control or even understand the forces that shape his life and order his death. They are so inconceivably complex; the mesh of circumstances is so infinitely intricate and cunning. In some geologic age, so long ago no human mind can grasp it, a land mass lifted or subsided and a landscape was created that determines the moods that dominate a hero's life. Some ancestor, a thousand generations ago, transmitted a weakness in the eye or hand, the heart or brain; it lies an unquiet ghost and appears every hundred years or so, at random, to torment the flesh in which it incarnates itself. Some forgotten poet sings a song and the music of it haunts the hero's mind and moves him in mysterious ways. In some land, a man he has never met will say a word or do a deed that is not even remotely an affair of his. But that word, that deed, will send out tendrils that become tentacles; they grasp and loosen; they grow and break and seize again. They link themselves with the deeds of a thousand other unknown men and some day, when everything is just right, a trap is sprung. And then a man who has commanded armies and navies, secure in his posterity and his possessions, dangles helpless, all his supports cut at once. There are those who say that there is a Mind that understands all these remote and forgotten things, that can trace all the lines and interstices of the most complicated web that catches and kills men or sparrows. And it may be so. But would not any Mind that men could understand become sated at last with irony?

The Lord Chief Justice had once said that death brought men to repentance, and Ralegh had said it too, as eloquently as man could say it, in his *History*. But Death sometimes did more. Sometimes it took the names of men into its keeping. Hawkins and Drake were as heroic a brace of men as history could show, but they died drably, fretted out by disease and failure. Death had been kinder to others. The dying Epaminondas had called for his shield, and the symbolic courage of that act had brightened every history that recounted it. And there was Coligny, Admiral of France, deathly weak from his wounds, sick at his betrayal, listening to the assassins on the stair, calmly urging his followers to flee and save their lives. His one faithful follower, the only man who had not run, helped him out of bed in order that he might stand, though trembling from that deadly weakness, and face the battle axe and the butcher who wielded it. Most men could no longer recall the details of Coligny's life or the rights or wrongs of his murder or the excuses of Catherine de Medici. They simply remembered his courage when he died. That is what men always remembered.

'All is vanity and weariness,' had been the theme of Ralegh's *History*, and yet afterwards he had confessed that life was 'such a weariness and vanity that we shall ever complain of it and love it for all that.' He had voyaged with the Princes, oppressed the Irish and slaughtered the Italian; he had loved a princess for whom he had named a new continent and he had planted colonies there; he had met the Spaniard with honour and followed a bright dream in Guiana. He had bedded a faithful wife and begotten sons, one of whom would live after him and honour his name. War and poetry, love and honour, the mystical pursuit of darkness and the design of fighting ships, commanding fleets, educating a Prince, seeking the unattainable. In all of this the victory lay not in the result but in the effort, in the mortal joy of thrusting his manliness against the forces of that unknown Destiny. His friend Spenser had said it best.

> That noble heart that harbours virtuous thought
> And is with child of glorious great intent,
> Can never rest until it forth hath brought
> The eternal brood of glory excellent.

For reasons he would never fully understand, grace had been denied him living; but it should not be denied him dying. Death was eloquent and just. Some day all of his words, his deeds, would be measured against his death. That haunting sense of an unfulfilled destiny was gone. His life was over, but he remembered with strange clarity before he died a boy whose mind was filled with bright imaginings, and that black banner with a severed head and the motto: *Det virtus mihi finem.*

SELECT BIBLIOGRAPHY

Andrews, Kenneth R., *Elizabethan Privateering*, 1964
Anthony, Irvin, *Ralegh*, 1934
Aubrey, John, *Brief Lives*, ed. A. Clark, 2 vols., 1898
Bacon, Francis, *Works*, ed. Spedding, Ellis, Heath, 15 vols., 1861–1864
Bagwell, Richard, *Ireland under the Tudors*, 2 vols., 1885–1890
Baring-Gould, S., *A Book of Devon*, 1899
    ed., *Cornwall*, Cambridge County Geographies, 1910
Birch, Thomas, *Memoirs of the Reign of Queen Elizabeth from 1581 till Her Death*, 2 vols., 1754
    Works of Sir Walter Ralegh, 8 vols., 1829
Black, J. B., *The Reign of Elizabeth*, 1936
Boas, F. S., *Marlowe and His Circle*, 1929
Bowen, Catherine Drinker, *The Lion and the Throne*, 1956
Bradbrook, M. C., *The School of Night*, 1936
Calendar of State Papers: Colonial, Domestic, Foreign, Ireland, Spanish
Carew, Richard, *Survey of Cornwall*, 1602
Cayley, Arthur, *The Life of Sir Walter Ralegh, Knt*, 2 vols., 1806
Cecil, Algernon, *A Life of Robert Cecil*, 1915
Chapman, George, *Poetical Works*, 1875
Cobbett, William, ed., *The Parliamentary History of England . . .* 36 vols., 1806–20
Collier, J. P., ed., *Egerton Papers*, Camden Society, 1840
Corbett, Julian S. *Drake and the Tudor Navy*, I, 1898; II, 1917
    The Successors of Drake, 1900
Delmas, Louis, *The Huguenots of La Rochelle*, 1870
D'Ewes, Sir Simonds, *A Complete Journal of . . . the House of Lords and the House of Commons . . . During the Reign of Queen Elizabeth*, 1693
Dutton, L. M., *Devon*, Cambridge County Geographies, 1910
Edwards, Edward, *The Life of Sir Walter Ralegh . . . Together with His Letters*, 2 vols., 1868

454

Ehrenburg, Richard, *Capital and Finance in the Age of the Renaissance* n. d.

Falls, Cyril, *Elizabeth's Irish Wars*, 1950

Froude, J. A., *The Spanish Story of the Armada*, 1892

Gardiner, Samuel Rawson, *History of England* (1603–42), 1893

Geyl, Peter, *The Revolt of the Netherlands*, 1958

Hakluyt, Richard, *The Principal Navigations, Voyages, Traffiques and Discoveries of the English Nation*, MacLehose edition, 1904

Handover, P. M., *The Second Cecil*, 1959

Hariot, Thos., *Briefe and True Report of the New Found Land of Virginia*, 1588

Harlow, Vincent T., ed., *The Discoverie of the Large and Beautiful Empire of Guiana*, 1928
Raleigh's Last Voyage, 1932

Heath, Sidney, *South Devon and the Dorset Coast*, 1910

Hooker, John (alias Vowell), *Continuation of Holinshed's Chronicles of Ireland*

Hoskyns, W. G., *Devon*, 1954

Howell, T. B., *State Trials*, 21 vols., 1816

Hume, Martin A. S., *Sir Walter Ralegh*, 1847

Jardine, David, *Criminal Trials*, 2 vols., 1882

Jenkins, Elizabeth, *Elizabeth the Great*, 1959

Latham, Agnes M. C., *The Poems of Sir Walter Ralegh*, 1951

Lewis, G. R., *The Stannaries*, Harvard Economic Studies, 1908

Markham, C. R., *The Fighting Veres*, 1888

Mattingly, Garrett, *The Armada*, 1959

Merriman, Roger B., *The Rise of the Spanish Empire*, III, 1925

Morley, Henry, ed., *Ireland under Elizabeth and James I*, 1890

Naunton, Sir Robert, *Fragmenta Regalia*, 1870

Neale, Sir John, *Queen Elizabeth*, 1934
The Age of Catherine de Medici, 1943
The Elizabethan House of Commons, 1949
Elizabeth and Her Parliaments, I, 1953; II, 1957

Nef, John U., *Industry and Government in France and England* (1540–1640), 1940

Oman, Sir Charles, W. C., *History of the Art of War in the Sixteenth Century*, 1937

Pope-Hennessy, Sir John, *Sir Walter Ralegh in Ireland*, 1883

Quinn, D. B., *Voyages and Colonizing Enterprises of Sir Humphrey Gilbert*, 2 vols., 1940
Ralegh and the British Empire, 1949
The Roanoke Voyages, 2 vols., 1955

Read, Conyers, *Mr. Secretary Walsingham . . .*, 1925
Mr. Secretary Cecil and Queen Elizabeth, 1955

Rose-Troup, Frances, *The Western Rebellion of 1549*, 1913
Rowse, A. L., *Sir Richard Grenville*, 1937
    Tudor Cornwall, 1941
    The England of Elizabeth, 1950
    The Expansion of Elizabethan England, 1955
    The Elizabethans and America, 1959
    Ralegh and the Throckmortons, 1962
    Poems of Cornwall and America, 1967
Sharman, V. Day, *Folk Tales of Devon*, 1952
Spenser, Edmund, *Poetical Works*, ed., Selincourt, 1960
Stebbing, William, *Sir Walter Ralegh*, 1899
Strachey, Lytton, *Elizabeth and Essex*, 1928
Strathmann, E. A., *Sir Walter Ralegh: A Study in Elizabethan Scepticism*, 1951
Thompson, Gladys Scott, *Lords Lieutenants in the Sixteenth Century*, 1923
Thompson, J. W., *The Wars of Religion in France* (1559–1576), 1909
Tillyard, E. M. W., *The Elizabethan World Picture*, 1944
Townshend, Heywood, *An Exact Account of the Four Last Parliaments of Queen Elizabeth*, 1680
Versteeg, Dingman, *The Sea-Beggars*, 1901
Waldman, Milton, *Sir Walter Raleigh*, 1928
Wallace, Willard M., *Sir Walter Raleigh*, 1959
Warner, William, *Albion's England*, 1612
Webb, Henry J., *Elizabethan Military Science*, 1965
Whitcombe, Mrs. Henry Pennell, *Bygone Days in Devonshire and Cornwall*, 1874
Whitehead, A. W., *Gaspard de Coligny, Admiral of France*, 1904
Williams, Charles, *James I*, 1934
Williamson, James A., *English Colonies in Guiana and on the Amazon*, 1923
    The Age of Drake, 1938
    Hawkins of Plymouth, 1949
Wright, Louis B., *The Elizabethan's America, a collection of early reports by Englishmen on the New World*, 1965

INDEX

Adelantado of Castile, the, 264, 269, 271–2
Albert, Archduke, 251, 316, 329–30, 335, 338
Albret, 22
Alençon, Duke of, 87
Alexander the Great, 39, 80, 207, 315, 377, 387, 398
Amadas, Philip, 119, 123, 218
Amadis de Gaul, 43
Anderson, Sir Edward, 337
Andrewes, Bishop Launcelot, 432
Anjou, Duke of, see Henry III of France
Ann Boleyn (Queen of Eng.), 89, 201–2
Anne of Denmark (Queen of Eng.), 318, 319, 370, 373, 377–8, 381, 406, 409, 410, 428, 432–3, 440
Applesey, Captain, 75
Arambaru, Admiral, 195
Aremberg, Count, 324, 329, 335, 345
Arius, 155
Arthur, King, 15, 186, 187, 204, 205, 249, 379
Arundel, Earl of, 427, 455
Arundel, Humphry, 22
Ashley, Katherine Champernowne, 23–4, 47, 75
Ashton, Sir Roger, 362
Aubrey, John, 202, 325, 450

Babington, Anthony, 103, 148, 149–51, 167
Bacon, Sir Anthony, 202, 285
Bacon, Francis, 24, 26, 88, 102, 177, 261, 285, 286, 287–8, 291–3, 301, 302, 305–6, 307, 313, 322, 330, 414, 416, 431, 437
Bagenal, Sir Henry, 304
Bagot, Sir Anthony, 105
Bailey, Captain, 419–20
Barbarigo, 108
Barlow, Arthur, 119, 120–4, 129, 218
Barry, David, Lord, 67, 68, 70
Bazan, Admiral, 190, 195, 196–7
Bazan, Alvaro de, see Santa Cruz, Marquis of
Bedford, Countess of, 412
Beeston, Sir Hugh, 439, 440
Berrio, Antonio de, 218–19, 222, 223, 225, 226–7, 230, 233, 235 236, 238, 241, 245, 246–7, 405

Berry, Captain Leonard, 404
Bess of Hardwick (Elizabeth Talbot), 316
Beza, Theodore, 31
Bingham, Sir Richard, 151
Biron, Duc de, 384
Biron, Marshal, 37
Blount, Charles, Earl of Devonshire, formerly Lord Mountjoy, 305, 309, 310–11, 337, 360
Blount, Sir Christopher, 312, 313, 314, 337
Body, William, 20–1
Borough, Sir John, 210–11
Bothwell, Earl of, 318
Bowyer, Robert, 298
Boyle, Lord, 419
Bracton, Henry de, 392–3
Bradshaw, John, 447
Brett, Captain, 275
Brooke, George, 327–8, 334, 352, 364, 449
Browne, Sir Thomas, 99
Browne, William, 17
Buchanan, George, 318
Buckhurst, Lord, 186
Burghley, Lord, see Cecil, William

Cabot, Sebastian, 49
Cade, Jack, 346
Calfield, Captain, 220, 236
Callisthenes, 315, 398
Calvin, John, 32, 156
Cambises, 394–5, 396
Canterbury, Archbishop of (John Whitgift), 324
Carew, Gawen, 23
Carew, Sir George, 164, 169–70, 171, 208, 257, 262, 263, 266, 271, 305, 418, 420, 430
Carew, Sir Nicholas, 326
Carew, Sir Peter, 23, 55, 56
Carleton, Sir Dudley, 361–2, 373
Casada, Don Gonzales de, 226
Casas, Bishop Las, 232
Cassander, King, 57
Catherine of Aragon (Queen of Eng.), 202
Catherine de Medici, 42, 452
Cavendish, Thomas, 126
Cecil, Ann (later Countess of Oxford), 321
Cecil, Elizabeth, Lady, 302–3

Cecil, Sir Robert, 105, 106, 200, 207–8, 209, 211–13, 215, 218, 219–21, 224, 234–5, 261, 265, 268, 270, 291–3, 298, 301–4, 309, 310, 314–17, 320, 321–3, 324, 325, 329–30, 332, 337, 343–4, 349–50, 353, 354–5, 357, 359, 362, 366, 372, 373, 377, 380, 382, 384, 405–7, 410, 422

Cecil, Sir Thomas, 287

Cecil, William (Lord Burleigh), 25, 27, 75, 100, 101, 114, 115, 152, 166, 170, 178, 186, 211–12, 263, 265, 285–6, 300, 304, 306, 321, 353, 381

Cecil, Will (son of Robert Cecil), 303, 371

Champernowne, Arthur, 16

Champernowne, Catherine, see Ralegh, Catherine

Chapman, George, 97, 98, 99, 232, 248

Charles I (King of Eng.), 337, 382, 411, 432, 447, 449

Charles IX (King of France), 40

Charles, Prince of Sweden, 87

Charles, Archduke, 87

Chatillon, Admiral, 31

Chichester, Bishop of, 364

Churchyard, Thomas, 51, 53

Ciawani, 237–8, 239

Clare, D'Amerie, 104, 202

Clarke, Father, 326–7, 328, 330, 334, 340, 352, 364, 366

Clifford, George, see Cumberland, Earl of

Clifton, Sir John, 167

Cobham (Henry Brooke), Lord, 265, 308, 309, 311, 312–13, 314, 315, 317, 321, 323–4, 326, 327, 328–30, 332–5, 338–9, 342–60, 364–6, 371, 412

Cockram, Martin, 18, 303

Coke, Sir Edward, 285, 287, 337–9, 339, 340–4, 347–8, 352–60, 366, 380–1, 392, 433–4, 435

Coligny, Gaspard de, 27, 29, 30–2, 34–6, 38–43, 44, 45, 54, 110, 117, 118, 120, 123, 126, 148, 387, 393, 452

Columbus, Christopher, 50

Condé, Henry I (2nd Prince of), 36, 38–9, 43, 100

Condé, Louis I (1st Prince of), 27, 28, 29, 31, 43, 109

Cook, Captain, 175–6

Copley, Anthony, 327, 352, 365

Cornwall, Duke of, 294

Cortez, Hernando, 233, 234

Cosmor, Captain, 424, 425

Cottrell, Edward, 334

Courtenay, Sir Peter, 23, 331

Cranmer, Archbishop Thomas, 22

Croesus, King, 396

Cromwell, Oliver, 447, 448

Cross, Captain, 220, 235, 257

Cuitino, Don Luis, 195

Cumberland, Earl of, 210–11, 213–14, 306

Cyrus, King, 396, 397

Dare family, 173

Davies, Sir John, 59

Davis, John, 141

Demetrius (Greek captain), 398–9

Denmark, King of (Christian IV), 286, 371

De Piles, 40

Desmond, Countess of, 170, 171, 381

Desmond, Earl of, 53, 55, 69, 76

Desmond, John and James of, see Fitzgerald, James (F.) and John F.

Devonshire, Earl of, see Blount, Charles

De Voto, Bernard, 221

Digby, Sir John, 411

Dionysius, tyrant, 377

Doge of Venice, the, 89

Donne, John, 94, 267

Doria, Gian Andrea, 108

Drake, Sir Francis, 19, 23, 54, 79, 80, 84, 90, 107, 110–11, 113, 114–15, 136–8, 153, 154, 157, 160–1, 162, 165, 167, 172, 191–3, 201, 250–1, 256, 276, 278, 280, 283, 285, 300, 393, 416, 429, 451

Drake, Richard, 162

Drayton, Michael, 139

Drummond of Hawthornden, William, 88

Duncan, Geilie, 318

Durham, Bishop of, 101, 325

Dyer, pilot, 356

Edward III (King of Eng.), 16, 331, 332

Edward VI (King of Eng.), 20, 88, 111, 331, 332

Eli, 395

Eliot, Sir John, 299, 445, 446, 447, 448, 450

Elizabeth of Bohemia, 375–6

Elizabeth I (Queen of Eng.), licenses privateers, 19; accession, 23; Katherine Ashley and, 23–4; her "Shepherd of the Ocean," 24–5; Huguenots and, 27–9; Henry of Navarre and, 43; Humphrey Gilbert serves, 47–8; W. R. and, 50; Churchyard's poem for, 51; Gilbert's voyage and, 52; knights Drake, 54; Gilbert wins favour of, 57; Ireland, and

Elizabeth 1—*contd*
58, 60, 61; Pope excommunicates, 62; Ormonde and, 64; Smerwick massacre and, 67; Roche loyal to, 71; W. R.'s Irish policy and, 74, 75; impales Desmond's head, 76; Gilbert's voyage and, 79–83; W. R. her favourite, 85–6; suitors, 87–90; virginity, 88–9; W. R. and, 90–4, 97, 99, 100–103, 105–6; naval policy, 111, 113–15; America and, 118, 120, 122, 124, 128; permits Drake's raid, 136; Manteo loyal to, 141; W. R., Hawkins report to, 145; Spanish plans and, 146; Sidney's death and, 147; plots against, 148–51; defence plans, 151, 153–4; Pope supports Armada against, 155, 156; tactics against Armada, 162; promise to James, 164; W. R. and, 168–70; and Virginian relief, 175; W. R., Essex and, 178–80; W. R.'s poem and, 180–6; W. R., Essex and, 188; brings W. R. back to court, 190; W. R.'s remembrance to, 198; leases Sherborne to W. R., 199; wants W. R. in England, 200; W. R.'s marriage and, 200; orders his recall, 201, 202; humiliation, 203; love, marriage and, 204; W. R. appeals to, 207–9; treasure for, from *Madre de Dios*, 211–12; releases W. R., 212; profits from treasure, 213–14; W. R. out of favour with, 216; Virginia and, 217; gold from El Dorado and, 220; 'very famous and admirable' in Trinidad, 230–1; Guiana and, 233, 234–5, 241, 247, 248; action against Spain, 251; and servants' personal rivalries, 258; 1596 War Council, 262; mobilises Navy 264; Essex and, 265; W. R. and, 266; Fleet bases and, 267; hears from W. R. about Essex, 268; orders Spanish fleet destroyed, 270, 271; and W. R.'s absence at Finisterre, 272; 'monster of England,' 'impious Jezebel,' 279; effect on Philip, 281; W. R. and, 282, 283; succession after, 284; needs money, 285, 286, 287; no recent attempts on life of, 289; losing favour, 294; W. R.'s tin monopoly from, 295–6, 298–9; ageing, 300; power ebbing, 302; Essex, W. R. and, 304; slaps Essex's face, 305; sends him to Ireland, 306–8; Essex's return and, 309–11; rebels claim to uphold, 312–13; ailing, 315; James and, 316; 'no. 24'

in secret letters, 317; James and, 317–20; Howard and, 321; succession after, 322; favours Cobham, 323; death, 324; Durham House and, 325; new men after death of, 330; W. R.'s *Discourse* and, 343; 'time had surprised,' 346; requires security for loans, 347; libels against, 353; imprisons McCarthy, 381; always repaid loans, 382; W. R.'s views on, 384; surprised by time, 386; W. R., Guiana and, 405; era of, 415, 416; possible commonwealth after, 446; cloak-spreading by W. R. recalled, 447

Elwys, Sir Gervase, 379, 380
Ensenore, 134–5
Epaminondas, king, 397–8, 452
Essex, Lady, 201
Essex, Robert Devereux, 2nd Earl of, 86, 90, 146, 169, 171, 178–80, 186, 187, 188, 201, 202, 211, 251–60, 262, 264–6, 268, 270–3, 275–6, 278–9, 288, 292, 300–1, 304–15, 320, 330, 336, 337, 358–9, 404, 438, 443, 444, 446
Essex, Robert Devereux, 3rd Earl of, 378–9

Fernandez, Simon, 119, 126, 171, 172, 173
Fitzgerald, James, 70
Fitzgerald, James (Fitzmaurice), 52–3, 56, 62, 63
Fitzgerald, John Fitzedmund, 62, 68–9, 70, 186
Fitzwilliam, Sir William, 168, 169, 170, 214–15
Forman, Dr, 380
Francis I (King of France), 91
Frobisher, Sir Martin, 107, 114, 157, 162, 165, 200, 201, 202, 210, 300

Galileo, 96
Gascoigne, George, 47
Gaudy, Justice, 337
Genton, Viscount, 420
George, Captain, 235, 242, 247
Gideon, 395
Gifford, Captain, 219, 240
Gilbert, Adrian, 16, 50
Gilbert, Sir Humphrey, 16, 24, 45, 46, 47–57, 61, 62, 68, 72, 77–84, 109, 118, 119, 123, 125
Gilbert, Sir John, 16, 50, 245
Gilbert, Otho, 16
Gondomar, Count, 414–16, 420, 430
Goodman, Bishop, 449

Goodwin, Hugh, 246
Gorges, Arthur, 208, 266, 272, 274, 275, 277
Gorges, Sir Ferdinando, 311–12, 313
Granganimeo, 120–1
Grenville, Sir Richard (cousin of W. R.), 19, 21, 23, 24, 55, 84, 125–8, 132, 138, 151, 164–5, 168, 172, 173, 174, 191–8, 245, 283
Grenville, Sir Richard (grandfather of W. R.'s cousin), 21, 22
Greville, Fulke, 114, 147, 285
Grey, Lady Catherine, 316
Grey, Lady Jane, 331
Grey de Wilton, Arthur (14th Lord), 61, 63, 64–6, 67, 68, 69, 72, 73, 74, 75, 151, 186, 187, 309
Grey de Wilton, Thomas (15th Lord), 309, 327–8, 330, 335, 362, 363, 365–6, 371, 412
Grey de Wilton, William (13th Lord), 23
Guayanacapa, Emperor, 222
Guise, Duke of, 36, 37, 285

Haddington, Viscount, 407
Hakluyt, Richard, 45, 123-4, 129, 130, 131, 174, 217, 247
Hampden, John, 299, 445, 447
Hannibal, 399
Hanno, 399
Harcourt, Robert, 408
Harington, Sir John, 199, 336
Hariot, Thomas, 53, 90, 96, 97, 126, 129–30, 131, 134, 135, 139–42, 216, 369, 390, 391
Harrington, Lady, 428
Harris, Sergeant, 286
Hart, Captain, 433
Harvey, Sir George, 333, 334, 367, 370, 371
Hastings, Sir Francis, 292, 296
Hatton, Sir Christopher, 86, 90, 150, 186
Hawkins, Sir John, 19, 79, 107, 113–15, 119, 145, 157, 161, 162, 165, 190, 198, 200, 212, 250, 283, 300, 429, 451
Hayes, Edward, 80, 82, 83
Heale, 339, 340
Hellyons, William, 22
Heneage, Sir Thomas, 212
Henry I (King of Eng.), 104
Henry IV (King of Eng.), 310
Henry VII (King of Eng.), 388
Henry VIII (King of Eng.), 20–1, 61, 74, 107, 110, 201, 305, 331–2, 388
Henry II (King of France), 29

Henry III (King of France), 28, 40, 62, 87
Henry, Prince (of Eng.), 153, 370–1, 374, 375–7, 385, 386, 387, 393, 398, 399, 428, 452
Henry, Prince of Navarre, 29, 36, 38–9, 43, 145, 285
Herbert of Cherbury, Lord, 98
Herrick, Robert, 17
Hertford, Lord, 316
Hoby, Sir Edward, 292
Hooker, John, 70, 104
Hooker, Richard, 350, 392
Howard, Catherine (Queen of Eng.), 88, 89
Howard, Lady Frances, 378–80, 412
Howard, Lord Henry, 316–17, 320–1, 323, 330, 337, 349, 353, 354, 378, 379, 380, 381, 382, 384
Howard, Lord Thomas, 107, 190, 191–3, 198, 213, 216, 219, 221, 254, 256, 257, 258, 260, 265–6, 268–9, 276, 277, 279, 337, 378, 381
Howard of Effingham, Lord Charles, 107, 111, 113, 115, 157, 159, 160, 161–2, 163, 165, 192, 251–7, 259, 260, 305, 307, 316, 342, 355
Hughes, Robert, 369
Hunsdon, Lord, 186

Imokellie, Seneschal of, see Fitzgerald, John
Infanta of Spain, the, 315, 316, 382
Ireton, Henry, 447

James I (King of England), VI (King of Scotland), 142, 149, 163–4, 177, 309–11, 315–30, 337–9, 343, 344, 346, 351–6, 358–9, 362–6, 370–7, 379–83, 385, 388, 394–5, 405, 408, 409, 411, 414–15, 417, 420, 421, 422, 425, 427, 428–36, 444, 446, 447, 450
Jason, 395
John, Don, 108–9
John of Gaunt, 316
Jonson, Ben, 46, 88, 413
Julian the Apostate, 358
Julius Caesar, 398
Justinian I, Emperor, 392

Kepler, Johannes, 96
Kerr, Robert, 373–4, 378–9, 380, 381, 387, 412, 437
Kett, Robert, 346
Keymis, Lawrence, 145, 220, 246, 333, 343, 353–4, 403–7, 410–11, 421, 422–8

King, Captain, 426, 430, 431, 432, 433
Knollys, Sir Henry, 50-1, 52, 305

Lake, Sir Thomas, 420
Lane, Ralph, 126, 129, 130, 131-7, 142, 151, 167, 176, 238
La Noue, François de, 34, 35, 41, 43
La Renzi, 329, 335
Latimer, Bishop, 368
Leicester, Robert Dudley, Earl of, 72, 86, 87, 89-90, 146, 148, 169, 178, 180, 187, 201, 300, 306
Leigh, Captain Charles, 405
Leonard (chief), 408
Lennox, Earl of (Esme Stuart), 319, 322
Levenson, Sir Richard, 266
Lodowick, see Louis
Louis, Count of Nassau, 30, 36, 37, 38
Luther, Martin, 156

McCarthy, Florence, 381, 412
Machiavelli, 43, 306, 343
Mackworth, Captain, 65, 66
Manteo, 122, 128, 134, 141, 172, 173
Markham, Sir Griffin, 327, 335, 365
Marlowe, Christopher, 92-3, 97, 216
Martinez, Juan, 224-6, 227
Marvell, Andrew, 447
Mary I (Queen of Eng.), 23, 28, 111
Mary (Queen of Scots), 149-50, 284, 316, 318, 319, 320, 331, 332, 368, 438
Medina Sidonia, Alonzo, Count, 154-5, 157, 158, 160-1, 163, 259, 261, 264
Menatonon, 132, 133, 141
Middleton, Captain, 192
Millais, 18
Milton, John, 78, 246, 303, 390, 393, 447, 448
Mondragon, 48
Montgomery, Count, 29, 40-1
Montgomery, Gabrielle de, 29
Monson, Sir William, 192, 278
Montluc, Marshal, 41-2, 44
Montmorency, Admiral de, 417
Moray, Earl of, 148
More, Sir Thomas, 222, 438, 439
Morequito, 227, 241
Moryson, Fynes, 73
Moses, 97, 98, 216, 394, 395
Mountjoy, Lord, see Blount, Charles
Moyle, Henry, 69

Nestorius, 155

Newton, Sir Isaac, 391
Ninias, 394
Norris, Sir John, 151, 179, 186, 190, 262, 306
North, Lord, 262
Northampton, Earl of, 445
Northumberland, Earl of, 186, 321, 369, 412

Oedipus, 395
Ordas, Diego, 224
Ormonde, Earl of, 63, 64, 67-8, 69, 72-3, 75, 76, 105, 186
Osmund, Bishop of Salisbury, 103, 199, 373, 374
Ossory, Bishop, 260
Osua, Pedro de, 226
Overbury, Sir Thomas, 379-80, 381, 416
Oxford, Earl of, 103, 186, 321, 445

Parker, Captain, 426
Parma, Duke of, 146, 148, 151, 152, 157, 158, 161, 164
Parmenius, Stephen, 78-9, 121, 139
Parsons, Father, 320
Pemisapan, 130, 133, 134-6, 141, 177, 223
Pennington, Captain, 418-19
Perrot, Lady, 179
Perrot, Sir Thomas, 46, 179
Pett, Phineas, 412
Peyton, Sir John, 332-3, 334
Peyton, John, 333, 371
Philip II (King of Spain), 23, 28, 53, 62, 65, 87, 110, 114, 124, 136, 145, 146, 148, 149, 150, 151-2, 154-6, 158, 163, 165, 189, 198, 210, 219, 222, 227, 233, 250-1, 254, 260, 261, 262-3, 269, 270, 278, 279, 281, 286, 288, 295, 316, 326, 346, 362, 407
Philip III (King of Spain), 261, 330, 338, 360, 411, 414, 417, 418, 420, 430-1, 434
Philips, Sergeant, 356-7
Piedmont, Prince of, 375
Pizarro, 222, 224, 225, 233, 234
Polo, Marco, 223
Pope, the, 332; Alexander VI, 117-18, 124, 136; Clement VIII, 316; Gregory XIII, 64, 65, 77; Paul V, 332; Pius V, 62, 109, 109, 148, 169; Sixtus V, 155, 281
Pope, Alexander, 301
Popham, Sir John, 337, 339, 340, 342, 345, 348-9, 350, 351, 359, 360, 361-2, 392, 435
Portugal, King of (Henry I), 114

Powhatan, 177
Prince Palatine (Frederick V), 375, 376
Protector (Duke of Somerset), 20
Putijma, 246, 404–5, 406, 407, 408, 422
Pym, John, 299, 445, 446, 447, 448
Pyne, Henry, 214–15

Ralegh, Carew (brother of W. R.), 16, 24, 50, 52, 114
Ralegh, Carew (son of W. R.), 441, 450, 452
Ralegh, Catherine (Mother of W. R.), 16, 24
Ralegh, Damerei (1st son of W. R.), 202
Ralegh, Elizabeth, Lady (wife of W. R.) 46, 171, 200–3, 204, 207, 218, 220, 252, 266, 303, 316, 321, 326, 332, 345, 356, 361, 363, 369, 370–4, 381, 385, 409, 412, 413, 419, 421, 428, 431, 432, 441, 449, 451, 452
Ralegh family, 16, 19, 20, 55, 345, 372–4, 452
Ralegh, George (nephew of W. R.), 412, 413, 421, 426
Ralegh, Sir John de, 104, 202
Ralegh, Margaret (sister of W. R.), 16
Ralegh, Thomas (grandson of W. R.), 450
Ralegh, Sir Walter ('W.R.'), early years, 16, 18, 19, 23; Grenville's cousin, 21; relations serving Queen, 24; 'Shepherd of the Ocean,' 24; character, 24–5; year at Oxford, 26; appearance, speech, 26–7; Champernowne cousins, 29; aids Huguenots, 29–30; admires Coligny, 31; Montoncourt battle and, 32, 35–6, 38; St Jean surrender and, 40; 'Voyage of the Princes,' and, 41–2, 43; on Henry of Navarre, 43; at Oxford?, 45; Middle Temple, 45–6; piracy, duelling, 46, 47; Gilbert and, 49–51; commands Falcon, 50; Spanish ships and, 52; engages Hariot, 53; compared with Drake, 54; in Ireland, 55–7, 61–4; at Smerwick, 65, 66–7; Barry and, 67–8; Fitzgerald ambushes, 68–9; brings Roche to Munster, 70–1; dissatisfied, returns to England, 72–4; Irish policy, 74–5; Gilbert's voyage and, 77–80; wit, 81; Letters Patent transferred to, 84–5; Queen's favourite, 85; cloak legend, 86; her lover, 90; 'Shepherd of the Ocean,' 91; as poet, 91–4; mental range, interests, 94–7; 'School of Night' and, 97–9; income, 100–1; knighted, Lord Lieut. of Cornwall, 101–2; pedigree, dress, 104;

unpopular, 105; view of Queen, 106; influences naval policy, 107, 111, 113–16; Ark Royal, 115–16; American colony and, 117–24; 'Virginia' and, 124–5; sends Grenville, 125–6, 128, 129, 131, 132; colony's troubles, 136–8; wants new colony, 139, 142–3; Sarmiento and, 144–5; comp. with Essex, 146; poem on Sidney's death, 147; signs Bond of Association, 149; on War Council, 151; naval defence and, 152–4; joins fleet against Armada, 159, 162; defends Howard, 163; ordered to Ireland, 164–5; American, Irish schemes, 165–8; displeases Queen, 169–70; American colony, 171, 174–6; Queen's caprice and, 178–9; Essex and, 179; Ocean to Cynthia, 180, 182–5; Entreating of Sorrow, 182; in Faerie Queen, 185–8; privateers of, 189; at Court, 190; Truth of the Fight, 191; defends Grenville, Howard, 192–4; relates Revenge's fight, 195, 198; Sherborne leased to, 199; prepares expedition, 199–200; marriage, 200–1; recalled, imprisoned, 201; wife pregnant before marriage, 202–3; Spenser and W. R.'s marriage, 203–5; poems, 206–7; appeals over imprisonment, 207–9; The Lie, 209; ships of, under Frobisher, 210, 212; released, at Dartmouth, 212; gains little treasure, 213–14; Irish estates fail, 214–15; out of favour, 216; 'El Dorado' and, 217–21; Discovery (described), 221–49; reasons for Guiana voyage, 221–2; believes legends, 223–6; Berreo and, 226–7; in Guiana, 228; Amazons and, 229–30; in Trinidad, 230–1; after gold, 232–5; in Orinoco delta, 236–41; after silver, gold, 242–7; in England, 247–9; Cadiz expedition, results, 251–61; on 1596 War Council, 262; wrong about Spain, 263–4; prepares Navy, 265; Ferrol, 266–71; at Fayal, Angra, 272–7; in Plymouth, 279–80; in Parliament, 282–3; speech themes, 284–98; ageing Queen and, 300; Robert Cecil and, 302–4; no return to Ireland, 305, 306; fleet mobilisation and, 307; Essex and, 308–11; meets Gorges, 312; forgives Blount, 313; Essex and, 314–15; Arabella Stuart and, 316; in secret letters, 317; opposed to James, 320–1; Howard and, 321; James and, 322–3; Cobham and, 323–4;

Ralegh, Sir Walter—*contd*
meets James, loses Durham House,
325–6; *Discourse Touching War with
Spain*, 326; and plots against James,
328–9; before Privy Council, 329–30;
treason charge, 330; suicide attempt,
332; with Cobham in Tower, 333–5;
Winchester trial of, 336–7; charges
against, 338–45; replies, 345–60; guilty,
360–1; pleads for life, 362–3; poem for
wife, 364; Cobham accuses, 365; in
Tower, 366–8; Harvey and, 367–8;
herbs, medicines, experiments, 368–70;
Waad restricts, 371; Sherborne and,
372–4; treatise on James's marriage
plans, 375; *Discourse on Art of War by
Sea*, 376; influences Prince Henry, 375–
7; loses Sherborne, 378; *Prerogative of
Parliaments*, 382–3; *The Sceptic*, 384–5;
Instructions to His Sons, 385; last Guiana
voyage, 402; earlier Cadiz fight, 403–4;
earlier gold quest, 405–8; Virginia (1610),
409–10; writes to Anne, James, on
Guiana, 410–11; leaves Tower, 412;
son Walter and, 413; James and, 414–16;
seeks French aid, 416–17; last voyage,
418–20; instructions disobeyed, 422;
son killed, 425, 427; expedition fails,
428; accuses James, 428–9; mutiny
against, 429–30; returns, 430–1; *Apology*,
432; plans escape to France, 432;
betrayed, arrested, charged, 433–6; in
Tower again, 437–9; petitions Anne,
440; for execution, 441; love poem to
wife, 442; receives Communion, 443;
executed, 444–9; tributes to, 450–1;
motto, 453; *History of the World*, 30, 31,
35–6, 37, 39, 40, 43, 44, 55–6, 57, 67, 96,
105, 109, 115–16, 164, 230, 278, 315, 377,
378, 381, 385–402, 448, 451, 452
Ralegh, Walter (father of W. R.), 16, 22–3,
331,
Ralegh, Walter (grandson of W. R.), 450
Ralegh, Walter (son of W. R.), 46, 220,
332, 356, 360, 363, 372, 385, 412–14,
421, 424–5, 427, 428
Richard II (King of Eng.), 310
Robsart, Amy, 89
Roche, Lord, 70–1
Roe, Sir Thomas, 410

St Leger, Warham, 55, 168; son (Warham),
412, 421

Samson, 395
Samuel, 395
Sander, Dr Nicholas, 62, 65
Santa Cruz, Marquis of, 108, 114, 154, 158,
163, 190
Sarmiento de Gamboa, Pedro, 144–5, 159,
178, 217, 222
Savoy, Duke of, 338, 375
Saxony, Duke of, 87
Scarnafissi, Count, 417
Scipio, 399
Semiramis, 394
Sextus Empiricus, 385
Seymour, Lady Catherine, 88
Seymour, Lord Henry, 157
Seymour, Lord Thomas, 88, 89
Shakespeare, 97, 99, 104, 105, 203, 229,
246, 344, 441, 447
Sidney, Sir Henry, 47, 72
Sidney, Sir Philip, 84, 146–7, 148, 178,
187, 188, 283, 300
Skiko, 132, 135, 141
Southampton, Earl of, 307
Southwell, Sir Robert, 260
Sparrow, Francis, 245–6
Spenser, Edmund, 60–1, 62, 63, 65, 67, 147,
179, 184–7, 188, 203–5, 266, 300, 305,
452–3
Stafford, Sir Edward, 202
Stanhope, Sir John, 337
Stanley, Sir William, 169, 170
Stowell, Sir John, 167
Strozzi, Peter, 163
Stuart, Lady Arabella, 316, 338, 339, 342,
345, 348, 355, 360, 412
Stuart, Esme (Earl of Lennox), 319, 322
Stukely, Sir Lewis, 430–1, 432, 433
Suleiman, 108, 157
Sully, French minister, 437
Sussex, Duke of, 67

Tamburlane, 393
Tarleton, Richard, 105
Tavannes (French gen.), 35, 37
Tawaye, 172
Tennyson, Lord, 191
Thomas Aquinas, St, 392
Throckmorton, Arthur, 252
Throckmorton, Sir Nicholas, 201, 331–2
Thynne, Francis, 440, 443
Toparimaca, 240
Topiawari, 227–8, 234, 241–2, 244–6, 403,
408, 426; son of, 228–9, 246, 263

Tounson, Dean, 443–4, 450
Trenchard, Sir George, 99
Turner, Anne, 378, 380
Tyrone, Earl of, 73, 215, 262, 280, 292, 304, 307, 308, 310, 405

Valdes, Pedro de, 160
Vasari, 109
Vere, Sir Francis, 179, 190, 251, 252, 257, 258, 260, 262, 266, 269, 278, 306
Villiers, George, 411, 414, 416, 431, 437
Villiers, Robert, 380, 411, 414

Waad, Sir William, 336, 337, 354, 371, 379, 381
Walsingham, Frances, 188
Walsingham, Sir Francis, 72, 100, 150, 166, 186, 300
Wanchese, 122, 128, 135
Warburton, Justice, 337, 350
Warner, Walter, 97, 369
Warner, William, 98
Watson, Father, 326–7, 328, 330, 334, 340, 352, 364, 366
Wentworth, Peter, 283

Whiddon, Captain Jacob, 159, 160, 194, 217–19
White, John, 141, 172–6
Whitelocke, Captain, 369
Whitney, Captain, 419, 429
William the Conqueror, 104
William, Prince of Orange, 36, 55, 85, 100, 148
Williams, Sir Roger, 151, 165, 306
Willoughby, Sir Hugh, 48
Willoughby, Lord, 262
Winchester, Bishop of, 364
Wingfield, Captain, 65
Winter, Admiral, 65
Winwood, Sir Ralph, 411, 412, 414, 415–16, 428
Wollaston, Captain, 429
Wotton, Lord, 337
Wright, Nicholas, 70
Wyatt, Sir Thomas, 29, 331

Xerxes, 396

Yeats, William Butler, 224
Yelverton, Sir Henry, 435